THE CONVERGENCE OF PRINT, BROADCAST AND ONLINE MEDIA

SECOND EDITION

Telling the Story

THE CONVERGENCE OF PRINT, BROADCAST AND ONLINE MEDIA

THE MISSOURI GROUP

BRIAN S. BROOKS

GEORGE KENNEDY

DARYL R. MOEN

DON RANLY

School of Journalism
University of Missouri–Columbia

Bedford/St. Martin's
Boston • New York

For Bedford/St. Martin's

Developmental Editor: Joshua Levy
Senior Production Editor: Shuli Traub
Production Supervisor: Jennifer Wetzel
Marketing Manager: Richard Cadman
Art Director/Cover Designer: Lucy Krikorian
Text Design: EriBen Graphics
Copy Editor: Patricia Herbst
Photo Research: Martha Friedman
Cover Photo: Getty Images/Dennis Kitchen
Composition: Pine Tree Composition, Inc.
Printing and Binding: R. R. Donnelley & Sons Company

President: Joan E. Feinberg
Editorial Director: Denise B. Wydra
Editor in Chief: Nancy Perry
Publisher for History and Communication: Patricia Rossi
Director of Marketing: Karen R. Melton Soeltz
Director of Editing, Design, and Production: Marcia Cohen
Managing Editor: Erica T. Appel

Library of Congress Control Number: 2003107541

Manufactured in the United States of America.

9 8 7 6 5 4
f e d c b a

For information, write: Bedford/St. Martin's, 75 Arlington Street, Boston, MA 02116
(617-399-4000)

ISBN: 0-312-40906-0 (book)
      0-312-41699-7 (CD)
      0-312-41915-5 (book/CD)

Acknowledgments
Acknowledgments and copyrights appear at the back of the book on pages 385–386, which constitute an extension of the copyright page.

Preface

We wrote *Telling the Story* to provide students with a concise introduction to news reporting and writing that slights neither the craft nor the theory of journalism. We guide students with clear explanations of key principles as well as vivid real-world examples from the best work of journalists writing today. In keeping with what students will encounter in the news room—the continued convergence of media—*Telling the Story*, Second Edition, offers students more emphasis on technology and writing for multiple media than any other newswriting and reporting book.

With the increasing popularity of reporting and writing for multiple outlets, the theoretical foundations of the field are constantly being questioned. However, the fundamentals of journalism have not changed. The second edition, like the first, discusses the bedrocks of journalism, whether stressing the unchanging goals of fairness and accuracy, applying long-standing principles of ethics and law to the challenges of new media or recognizing the importance of strong writing. Students are challenged to understand the larger role of journalism in the 21st century while grappling with the day-to-day realities of reporting and writing. A new guide to the 20 most-common student writing errors emphasizes a continued focus on the practice of writing. Throughout *Telling the Story* you'll find a thorough approach to the craft of writing, and with the new appendix, the book offers even more help to make students better writers.

FEATURES

- *Offers concise yet comprehensive instruction. Telling the Story*, Second Edition, uses a streamlined approach to the field and the practice of journalism without sacrificing the nuts-and-bolts of writing and reporting or the practical advice that prepares students for careers in public relations, print, broadcast and online journalism.

- *Teaches across media.* The integration of broadcast, online and public-relations examples throughout the book makes it an up-to-date text that reflects the changing nature of journalism in both the classroom and the professional world. For example, in Chapter 8 an online article shows students how the same material can be shaped in two different ways to address the different needs of broadcast and print journalism.
- *Focuses on stories.* From obituaries to world news reports, local meetings to national press conferences, *Telling the Story* demonstrates how to recognize the "so-what" of events in order to create rich and well-crafted stories.
- *Gives insight into the profession.* Current, real-life examples—from the experience of a journalist working in a converged news room to a university's public-relations response to damaging animal-rights claims—and "On the Job" boxes spotlight today's print, broadcast, online and public-relations professionals to give students a true picture of 21st-century journalism.
- *Provides unique "Reporting with Numbers" chapter.* Unlike any competing text, *Telling the Story* provides a "Reporting with Numbers" chapter that stresses the importance of using and understanding numbers—vital skills as business news stories have come more to the forefront.
- *Offers abundant examples.* Drawn from the best work of today's journalists, powerful new examples throughout the book illustrate the skills and techniques of effective newswriting and reporting, offering superb models for students to emulate.

NEW TO THIS EDITION

- *Greater focus on media convergence.* Throughout the book students learn how to simultaneously prepare stories for print, broadcast and online media. Chapter 2, "Convergence and the Changing Media Industry," discusses in depth the role of media convergence in today's news room—from the influence of the Internet and wireless technology to the widespread effects of media-company mergers.
- *More coverage of online journalism.* The expanded Chapter 13, "Writing Online," tracks the growing influence of online journalism. New Web site screen shots illustrate the many uses and varieties of journalism on the Internet.
- *Expanded public-relations coverage.* Chapter 12, "Writing for Public Relations," includes a broader discussion of contemporary public-relations issues. From the outbreak of illnesses on cruise ships in late 2002 to spies working for PETA, exciting

new examples illustrate the challenges faced by today's public-relations practitioners.

- *More writing coverage: a most-common student errors appendix.* Because good journalists must first and foremost be good writers, the new edition includes a thoroughly class-tested list of the 20 most common student errors and practical advice on how to correct them.
- *Updated examples.* From President Bush's Sept. 12, 2002 address to the United Nations to the space shuttle Columbia tragedy, from today's converging news rooms to the ever-evolving challenges of plagiarism, *Telling the Story*, Second Edition, teaches the essentials of journalism, immersing students in current events.

ANCILLARIES

- *Workbook for* TELLING THE STORY, Second Edition. Supplementing the activities at the end of each chapter in the text, the *Workbook for* TELLING THE STORY provides students with the extra practice they need to develop and master the principles of journalism, the skills of reporting and the craft of newswriting. More than 300 class-tested assignments reinforce the essential skills students need to learn, from basic interviewing and computer-assisted reporting to writing a lead and organizing a complex story. Special attention is paid to reporting with numbers and statistics and to accessing information from electronic sources. Challenge exercises in each chapter offer more complex assignments for students to tackle.
- *Instructor's Manual to Accompany* TELLING THE STORY, Second Edition. This ancillary includes sample syllabi, chapter overviews, answers to all end-of-chapter questions in the text and answers to all the questions in the *Workbook.*
- *Crisis Coverage CD-ROM.* Created by Bob Bergland, Jeanette Browning, and his students at Missouri Western State College, this interactive journalism simulation CD-ROM presents a crime scenario in real time, using text, audio and video clips. This CD-ROM is available free to users of *Telling the Story*, Second Edition.

ACKNOWLEDGMENTS

We would like to thank our colleagues and students at Missouri who have used and critiqued the material in this book. In addition, we are grateful to the instructors who thoughtfully reviewed the text and contributed ideas to the second edition: Frank Absher, *St. Louis Community College–Forest Park*; James Aucoin, *University of South Alabama*; Michael Berlin, *Boston University*; Ted Delaney, *Roger Williams University*; Joan Deppa, *Syracuse University*; Patricia Hart, *University of Idaho*; Barbara Hipsman, *Kent State University*; Carol Lomicky, *University of Nebraska–Kearney*; Lisette Poole, *California State University, Hayward*; Larry Pryor, *University of Southern California*; Lori Ramos, *William Patterson University*; Rose Anne Robertson, *American University*; and Richard Roth, *Northwestern University*.

We would also like to thank the instructors who reviewed the text and contributed ideas to the first edition: Harry Amana, *University of North Carolina–Chapel Hill*; Sandy Barnard, *Indiana State University*; Tom Beell, *Iowa State University*; Lori Bergen, *Kansas State University*; John Erickson, *University of Iowa*; Lynne Flocke, *Syracuse University*; Peter Gade, *Oklahoma University*; Louis Liebovic, *University of Illinois–Urbana/Champaign*; Beverly Merrick, *New Mexico State University*; and Alan Neckowitz, *James Madison University*.

We would also like to thank our editors at Bedford/ St. Martin's who have guided, and sometimes prodded, us along the way. In particular, thanks are due to executive editor Patricia Rossi and developmental editor Josh Levy, whose suggestions and enthusiasm helped shape the book. In addition, we wish to thank senior project editor Shuli Traub, and production supervisor Jennifer Wetzel. And as always, we thank our wives, Anne, Robin, Nancy and Eva Joan, who have been helping us with this publishing project now for nearly 20 years.

We value your comments. You can reach any of us by e-mail by addressing it to: lastnamefirstinitial@missouri.edu.

Brian S. Brooks
George Kennedy
Daryl R. Moen
Don Ranly

Contents in Brief

Contents

PART II   REPORTING TOOLS

PART III   STORYTELLING

PART IV   COVERING AND WRITING NEWS

PART V   MEDIA WRITING

1   The Nature of News

The *Tampa (Fla.) Tribune* doesn't circulate in Sarasota, about 30 miles to the south, but its affiliated television station, WFLA, has a bureau there. So, when a spectacular murder in Sarasota led to a trial in Texas, a WFLA reporter was dispatched to San Antonio. She sent back not only daily television reports but stories for the *Tribune*. She also contributed bits of courtroom observation for **TBO.com,** the online partner of the *Tribune* and WFLA.

The same week in Sarasota, *Herald-Tribune* reporter Tom Bayles was wrapping up his year-long investigation of the state's efforts to replenish eroding beaches. Bayles was struggling to create the television story that would introduce the newspaper series. He had missed the training in television techniques the *Sarasota Herald-Tribune* provides its reporters, so he was turning for help to the staff of SNN, the newspaper's cable television station. He didn't have to go far, because the television news desk was just across the aisle from him.

There was no such struggle for Scott Powers, education reporter for the *Orlando Sentinel*. With a story in the morning paper, he was prepared for a "talk-back" on the *Sentinel*'s television partner, Channel 13. Coached by the multimedia editor, he sat down in front of a television camera mounted in the newspaper newsroom. He previewed on the TelePrompTer the questions he would be asked by the news anchor. Then he was on, explaining his story and its implications to television viewers who might not have seen the *Sentinel*.

As technology and economics drive journalism toward a multimedia future, these three news organizations about an hour's drive from one another in west-central Florida are pioneers on the frontier of convergence.

In all three newsrooms, television and online join the newspaper to share staff and information. In all three, the goal is to reach the largest possible audience with the journalism done by each staff. In all three, the plan is to take advantage of the strengths and minimize the limitations of each medium. And in all three, the learning process proceeds, as *Tampa Tribune* Managing Editor Donna Reed puts it, "one collision at a time."

News in the 21st century is not what it used to be. Neither is news-gathering. Basic elements, however, remain the same. One of those basics is journalists' definition of "news" itself. Another is the importance of accuracy and fairness. The most fundamental is the continuing central role of journalism in a democratic society.

Both the dramatic changes and the unchanging basics require that everyone who wants to be a journalist must master the skills of reporting and writing—no matter what tools you use or how your stories reach your audience.

In this chapter you will learn:

1. What news is.
2. How journalism and audiences are changing.
3. How the unchanging principles of accuracy and fairness will help you meet the challenges of permanent change.

WHAT NEWS IS

The criteria that professional journalists in print, television or online use to decide what news is can be summarized in three words:

Relevance.
Usefulness.
Interest.

Those criteria apply generally, but each journalist and each news organization uses them in a specific context that gives them particular meaning. That context is supplied by the audience.

Let's look at an example. This one comes from the morning newspaper:

Although they agree it will be complicated to implement, City Council members were unanimous last night in their intention to create a citywide curfew plan.

During a work session, the council agreed to draft an ordinance that would keep minors off the streets late at night.

Members did, however, debate how the law would be enforced and what the exact requirements would be.

First Ward Councilwoman Almeta Crayton made clear that the law should not be used to keep children from attending dances or going to the movies. It should, she said, be used to push parents to be more responsible.

"Whether we want to admit it or not, our kids are places where they have no business," Crayton said. "We need to, as parents, start to monitor where our children are going, what they're doing, why they're at these places."

The curfew could have an impact on businesses that cater to teenagers, such as Gunthers Games on Broadway. The arcade is open until midnight on weekends.

Gunthers manager Eric Weigant, who voiced concern earlier about a curfew, said he would be supportive as long as enforcement stops outside businesses' doors.

The curfew came into the spotlight in August after police had to tame unruly crowds down town on two consecutive Saturday nights. Police made 23 arrests the first weekend and 19 more a week later.

Once the ordinance is drafted, the council will hold public hearings before voting on it.

Consider that story's value to its audience. It is relevant to parents, to teenagers, to owners and patrons of downtown businesses, and to everyone concerned about conflict between rights and responsibilities. It is useful because it opens for public discussion an important issue before elected officials have made their decision. It is interesting because it is relevant and useful.

You've been looking at a story that appeared in a newspaper the morning after the city council met. On television, the evening news would include on-camera reactions from the teenagers and possibly file video from the disturbances last summer. Television is a visual medium, and it relies heavily on emotion and personality to tell its stories. Online, a quick summary of the story could have been posted as soon as council members reached agreement. Later, audio and video could be added to the text. A chat room could permit the public conversation to begin almost immediately.

The presentation would be different in each medium, but the news values that make the story important and the reporting skills required to tell it would be the same. Later chapters will help you learn those skills. For now, let's look a little more deeply at news values, the criteria journalists use to decide which stories are worth telling.

Relevance, usefulness and interest are the broad guidelines for judging the news value of any event, issue or personality. Within those broad standards, journalists look for more specific elements in each potential story. The most important are these:

> *Impact.* This is another way of measuring relevance and usefulness. How many people are affected by an event or idea? How seriously does it affect them?
>
> *Conflict.* This is a recurring theme in all storytelling, whether the stories told are journalism, literature or drama. Struggles between people, among nations or with natural forces make fascinating reading. Conflict is such a basic element of life that journalists must resist the temptation to overdramatize or oversimplify it.
>
> *Novelty.* This is another element common to journalism and other kinds of stories. People or events may be interesting and therefore newsworthy just because they are unusual or bizarre.
>
> *Prominence.* Names make news. The bigger the name, the bigger the news. Ordinary people have always been intrigued by the doings of the rich and famous.
>
> *Proximity.* Generally, people are more interested in and concerned about what happens close to home. When they read or listen to national or international news, they often want to know how it relates to their own community.
>
> *Timeliness.* News is supposed to be new. If news is to be relevant and useful, it must be timely. For example, it is more useful to report on an issue facing the city council before it is decided than afterward. Timely reporting gives people a chance to be participants in public affairs rather than mere spectators.

Important elements in a news story

Impact.
Conflict.
Novelty.
Prominence.
Proximity.
Timeliness.

Notice that this list suggests two important things about news. First, not all news is serious, life-and-death stuff. Journalism has been described as "a society's conversation with itself." The conversation that holds a society together includes talk of crime, politics and world affairs, of course; but it also includes talk of everyday life. It includes humor and gossip. All of that can be news. Second, news is more than just collections of facts. Telling the news usually means telling stories. The narrative, the humanity, the drama of storytelling is the art of journalism. To gather the facts for their stories, journalists use many of the same techniques used by sociologists, political scientists and historians. To tell their stories so that those facts can be understood, journalists often use the techniques of other storytellers, such as novelists and screenwriters.

Different news media give different weights to those criteria and require different approaches to telling stories. For example, newspapers and magazines are better than television or radio for explaining the impact of an issue or the causes of a conflict. But print can't compete with television in speed or emotional power. The differing strengths and limitations of each medium make it more likely that you'll learn about an event from television or radio and find a lengthy explanatory story in a newspaper. The newspaper lets you read the details of a budget or a box score; television shows you the worker whose job was cut or the player scoring the winning basket. The unique power of online journalism is that it brings together the visual and the verbal.

"Superficiality (on television) is not just built into the lack of time. It's that we spend a lot of time not on the phone, not in the library, but trying to show visually what we're talking about."
— **Sam Donaldson,** ABC News correspondent

THE ROLE OF JOURNALISM

The First Amendment to the United States Constitution protects the five freedoms that the nation's founders considered essential to a democracy: the freedoms of speech, religion, press, petition and assembly. In the 1830s, the French aristocrat Alexis de Tocqueville came to study the United States and wrote his classic *Democracy in America*. He was struck by the central role played by the newspapers: "We should underrate their importance if we thought they just guaranteed liberty; they maintain civilization."

Today American democracy is more than 200 years old. The freedoms of belief and expression protected by the First Amendment are still essential and still under threat. The role of journalism in maintaining civilization, which also remains essential, is also under threat from growing public skepticism about how well today's journalists fulfill that role.

In a national survey, 78 percent of the respondents agreed that the news media are biased. Asked which medium is most biased, 42 percent named television, 23 percent newspapers, 17 percent magazines and 5 percent radio. (Still, when asked which source they trust most when media offer conflicting versions of a story, 34 percent named television, 27 percent newspapers, 2 percent magazines and 8 percent radio.) More than half said that increased public discontent with the press is justified. Nearly 90 percent said sensational stories get lots of coverage just because they're exciting and not because they're important.

In that same survey, however, two-thirds said that having the press keep a close eye on politicians is a good way to prevent wrongdoing, while 80 percent approved of investigative reporting. Even though both daily newspaper circulation and television news viewing have declined, 79 percent in this survey said they watch local TV news on a typical evening, and 72 percent said they read a local newspaper during a typical day.

What citizens seem to be saying is that the work journalists do is important but isn't being done well enough. Many journalists agree. The past decade has seen the emergence of several major efforts to improve the performance of American journalism.

One of those efforts has been driven by an informal association called the Committee of Concerned Journalists and the related Project for Excellence in Journalism. The project conducts regular research on journalism and issues reports, which can be accessed on its Web site, **journalism.org.** The committee has produced a book that every student and practitioner of journalism should read. It was written by two leaders of the committee, Bill Kovach and Tom Rosenstiel. Its title is *The Elements of Journalism.*

The book argues that "the purpose of journalism is to provide people with the information they need to be free and self-governing." It proposes nine principles to achieve this purpose:

1. Journalism's first obligation is to the truth.
2. Its first loyalty is to citizens.
3. Its essence is a discipline of verification.
4. Its practitioners must maintain an independence from those they cover.
5. It must serve as an independent monitor of power.
6. It must provide a forum for public criticism and compromise.
7. It must strive to make the significant interesting and relevant.
8. It must keep the news comprehensive and proportional.
9. Its practitioners must be allowed to exercise their personal conscience.

In these principles, you can hear echoes of the Journalist's Creed, written nearly a century before by Walter Williams, founding dean of the world's first journalism school, at the University of Missouri. Williams wrote that "the public journal is a public trust. . . . that acceptance of a lesser service than the public service is betrayal of that trust."

> *The audiences of the 21st Century*
>
> - *By 2050, one-fifth of the U.S. population will be Hispanic.*
> - *By 2010, married couples will no longer make up a majority of households.*
> - *By 2025, Americans over 64 will outnumber teenagers 2-1.*
>
>   — *All from* Undercovered: The New USA, *published by New Directions for News*

"The computer is an icon for our age, but reason and imagina- tion, which yield understanding, are yet to be programmable."
— *Richard Saul Wurman*

Williams, a small-town journalist before he became an educator, would have been comfortable with a second major effort to recapture for journalism the public trust. This effort, more controversial than the Committee of Concerned Journalists, goes by several names, the best known being "civic journalism" and "public journalism." Some of its practitioners prefer to avoid labels and just think of it as journalism that seeks to strengthen democracy and citizenship.

By any name, this approach is based on two ideas: First, democracy isn't working as well as it should. Second, journalists have a responsibility to try to do something about that. Few observers of politics would argue with the first idea. The evidence ranges from low voter turnout to stalemates in Congress. Some scholars even argue that we are losing our basic sense of community. The second idea, however, runs squarely into the journalistic tradition of neutrality, of reporters' detachment from the events they cover. Jay Rosen, a scholar who is the leading theoretician of civic journalism, has come up with a set of contrasts in the beliefs of traditional and civic journalists. Here are two that illustrate the gap:

Civic journalists believe

Public life should work, and journalism has a role in making it work.

Traditional journalists believe

It would be nice if public life worked, but making it work is beyond our role and it's dangerous to think we can.

Civic journalists believe

Something basic has to change, because journalism isn't working now.

Traditional journalists believe

The traditions of journalism are fine; if anything needs to improve, it's the practice.

The journalist who is generally credited with—or blamed for—putting these principles into practice is Davis "Buzz" Merritt, then editor of *The Wichita (Kan.) Eagle*. Merritt was disgusted by the quality of journalism he saw in his paper and elsewhere during the 1988 elections. He was dismayed by the apparent lack of interest and obvious lack of involvement in civic life he saw in Wichita and around the nation. So he began a series of journalistic experiments that laid the foundation for a movement.

Beginning in 1989, journalists in Wichita—and before long in dozens of other cities ranging from Charlotte, N.C., to Bremerton, Wash.—were taking polls to learn what citizens thought the campaign issues should be instead of allowing candidates to set the terms of public debate. They were sponsoring public forums for the discussion of issues ranging from politics to race. In some cases they were even assigning or hiring staff members to help citizens attack a variety of local problems. Nonprofit organizations such as the Pew, Kettering and Knight foundations contributed money and expertise. Research showed that many civic journalism projects seemed to be changing attitudes toward public life and toward the journalistic organizations.

The critics, including top editors at *The Washington Post* and *The New York Times*, worry that civic journalists are winning goodwill at the expense of something even more important—their independence. News organizations cannot be both actors and critics, the critics argue. To them, the critic's role is the only one journalists should play. When a newspaper organizes a public discussion, instead of just reporting on a discussion organized by others, it becomes an actor in the drama it should be observing from a critical distance, the critics say. They argue that when journalists ask citizens what they want to know, instead of giving them what the journalists think they need to know, pandering replaces educating.

A decade after the movement began, a study found that at least one-fifth of American news organizations had tried to put its principles into practice. Most of those found that citizens in their communities became more engaged in public life. Most also noticed that public attitudes toward journalism improved.

These efforts to reform, or restore, journalism recognize the following vital functions of journalists in the life of a free society:

- *Journalists report the news.* The first and most obvious function, news reporting is the foundation for the rest. Reporters cover Congress and council meetings, describe accidents and disasters, show the horrors of war and the highlights of football games. This reporting takes many forms—live television, online bulletins, next-day newspaper analyses, long-form magazine narratives. No wonder journalism has been called the first rough draft of history.
- *Journalists monitor power.* Most often, Americans are concerned about the power of government. In recent years, private power has become more of a worry and more a source of news. Monitoring is required even when power is used legitimately—as governments raise taxes, for example, or businesses decide to close plants or cut health-care subsidies for employees. When the power is used illegally or immorally, another important function comes into play.
- *Journalists uncover injustice.* A television reporter learns that one brand of tires and one model of car are involved in a disproportionate number of fatal accidents. A newspaper discovers that blacks are denied mortgages at a far higher rate than whites. In those cases and thousands more, journalists bring to light dangerous or illegal abuses that might have gone otherwise unchecked.
- *Journalists tell stories that delight and amaze.* Some are the television mini-dramas of *60 Minutes*. Some are newspaper narratives that shape public policy, such as Mark Bowden's "Black Hawk Down," which ran first in *The Philadelphia Inquirer* and then became a book and a movie. Some are magazine reconstructions that set the nation talking, such as William Langewiesche's *Atlantic Monthly* account of the cleanup after the World Trade Center attack.

■ *Journalists sustain communities.* These may be small towns, cities or even virtual communities of people connected only by the Internet. By their reporting, monitoring, revealing and storytelling, journalists serve as the nervous system of the community. They convey information and argument. Their work is, in James Carey's phrase, the community's "conversation with itself."

Other scholars use other terms for this combination of functions. One is "agenda-setting," the placing of issues on the public agenda for discussion. Another is "gate-keeping," the process by which some events and ideas become news and others do not. Now that the Internet has flooded the world with information, another role is emerging, that of "navigation," guiding readers and viewers through oceans of fact, rumor and fantasy in search of solid meaning.

Richard Saul Wurman has examined this new need in his book *Information Anxiety*, another work every journalist should read. In it, Wurman says that most news could be divided into three categories: hope, absurdity and catastrophe. Journalists typically focus on absurdity and catastrophe. Audiences hunger for hope. Instead of merely pointing out problems, a journalism of hope would identify possible solutions, provide examples and tell people where to go for information or to get involved. (You'll notice a resemblance to civic journalism in Wurman's prescriptions.)

Wurman's other point relates directly to navigation. Mere information is not the most important product, he points out. Understanding is what's essential to effective communication. As journalists concentrate on telling stories that are relevant and useful, they are more likely to convey understanding. Lacking that, audiences drift, and sometimes drown, in the ever-deepening sea of information.

ACCURACY, FAIRNESS AND THE PROBLEM OF OBJECTIVITY

The goal toward which most journalists strive has seldom been expressed any better than in a phrase used by Bob Woodward, a reporter, author and editor at *The Washington Post*. Woodward was defending in court an investigative story published by the *Post*. The story, he said, was "the best obtainable version of the truth."

A grander-sounding goal would be "the truth," unmodified. But Woodward's phrase, while paying homage to the ideal, recognizes the realities of life and the limitations of journalism. After centuries of argument, philosophers and theologians have been unable to agree on what truth is. But even if there were agreement on that basic question, how likely is it that the Roman Catholic Church and the Planned

Parenthood organization would agree on the "truth" about abortion, or that a president and his challenger would agree on the "truth" about the state of the American economy?

In American daily journalism, that kind of dispute is left to be argued among the partisans on all sides, on the editorial pages and in commentaries. The reporter's usual role is simply to find and write the facts. Even this is not always so easy.

Sometimes it's hard to get the facts. The committee searching for a new university president announces that the field of candidates has been narrowed to five, but the names of the five are not released. Committee members are sworn to secrecy. What can you do to get the names? Should you try?

Sometimes it's hard to tell what the facts mean. The state Supreme Court refuses to hear a case in which legislators are questioning the constitutionality of a state spending limit. The court says only that there is no "justiciable controversy." What does that mean? Who won? Is the ruling good news or bad news, and for whom?

Sometimes it's even hard to tell what a fact is. A presidential commission, after a yearlong study, says there is no widespread hunger in America. Is the conclusion a fact? Or is the fact only that the commission said it? And how can you determine whether the commission is correct?

Daily journalism presents still more complications. Usually, as a reporter you have only a few hours, at most a few days, to try to learn as many facts as possible. Then, even in such a limited time, you may accumulate enough information for a story of 2,000 words, only to be told that there is enough space or time for 1,000 or fewer. The new media offer more space but no more time for reporting.

When you take into account all these realities and limitations, you can see that just to reach the best obtainable version of the truth is challenge enough for any journalist.

How can you tell when the goal has been reached? Seldom, if ever, is there a definitive answer. But there are two questions every responsible journalist should ask about every story before being satisfied: Is it accurate? Is it fair?

Accuracy and Fairness

Accuracy is the most important characteristic of any story, great or small, long or short. Accuracy is essential in every detail. Every name must be spelled correctly; every quote must be exactly what was said; every set of numbers must add up. And that still isn't good enough. You can get the details right and still mislead unless you are accurate with context, too. The same statement may have widely different meanings depending on the circumstances in which it was uttered and

On the Job

The Nature of News

Janet Weaver's career reflects the revolutionary changes in American journalism in the past 20 years. She graduated from journalism school in 1984 and took a job covering government at the *Irving (Texas) Daily News,* circulation 10,000. Fifteen years later, she was appointed executive editor of the *Sarasota (Fla.) Herald-Tribune,* where she presides over a newsroom that is leading the movement to convergence. Her responsibility includes not only the print news room but its affiliated Web site and a 24-hour cable news channel.

She says the greatest lesson she has learned along the way is this: "To be open to experimentation, and to the failure that sometimes accompanies it. I think journalists are incredibly resistant to change and new ideas.

Weaver sums up her career this way: "I've tried teams, I've worked in public journalism and now I manage a multimedia newsroom. Each of these efforts has challenged my assumptions about journalism, made me defend what I believe in as a journalist and determine what values I hold at the core that cannot be sacrificed no matter what."

Her advice to would-be journalists is simple: "I would tell students graduating today that they have to have that passion for news—not necessarily for newspapers or for broadcast, because the media platforms we work in will keep changing and blending over the course of their careers. Be on fire for the story, for getting it first and telling the reader or viewer. Journalists will have to be increasingly flexible about adapting to new media and new ways of getting information to the community. But that's just technology. It's the passion for the story that will lead to a satisfying and successful career in journalism."

the tone in which it was spoken. Circumstances and intent affect the meaning of actions, as well. You will never have the best obtainable version of the truth unless your version is built on accurate reporting of detail and context.

Nor can you approach the truth without being fair. Accuracy and fairness are related, but they are not the same. The relationship and the difference show clearly in this analogy from the world of sports:

The umpire in a baseball game is similar, in some ways, to a reporter. Each is supposed to be an impartial observer, calling developments as he or she sees them. (Of course, the umpire's job is to make judgments on those developments, while the reporter's is just to describe them.) Television has brought to sports the instant replay, in which a key development, say a close call at first base, can be examined again and again, often from an angle different from the umpire's view. Sometimes the replay shows an apparent outcome different from the one the umpire called. A runner who was ruled to be out may appear to have been safe instead. The difference may be due to human error by the umpire, or it may be due to the differences in angle and in viewpoint. Umpires recognize this problem. They try to deal with it by obtaining the best possible view of every play and by conferring with their colleagues on some close calls. Still, every umpire knows that an occasional mistake will be made. That is unavoidable. What can, and must, be avoided is unfairness. Umpires must be fair, and both players and fans must believe they are fair. Otherwise, umpires' judgments will not be accepted; they will not be trusted.

With news, too, there are different viewpoints from which every event or issue can be observed. Each viewpoint may yield a different interpretation of what is occurring and of what it means. There is also, in journalism as in sport, the possibility of human error, even by the most careful reporters.

Fairness requires that you as a reporter try to find every viewpoint on a story. Hardly ever will there be just one; often there are more than two. Fairness requires that you allow ample opportunity for response to anyone who is being attacked or whose integrity is being questioned in a story. Fairness requires, above all, that you make every effort to avoid following your own biases in your reporting and your writing.

Objectivity

The rules that mainstream journalists follow in attempting to arrive at the best obtainable version of the truth are commonly summarized as objectivity. Objectivity has been and still is accepted as a working credo by many, perhaps most, American journalists, students and teachers of journalism. It has been exalted by leaders of the profession as an essential, if unattainable, ideal. Its critics, by contrast, have attacked objectivity as, in the phrase of sociologist Gaye Tuchman, a "strategic ritual" that conceals a multitude of professional sins while producing superficial and often misleading coverage.

Michael Schudson, in his classic *Discovering the News*, traces the rise of objectivity to the post-World War I period, when scholars and journalists alike turned to the methods and the language of science in an attempt to make sense of a world that was being turned upside down by the influence of Freud and Marx, the emergence of new economic forces, and the erosion of traditional values. Objectivity was a reliance on observable facts, but it was also a methodology for freeing factual reporting from the biases and values of source, writer or reader. It was itself a value, an ideal.

Schudson wrote, "Journalists came to believe in objectivity, to the extent that they did, because they wanted to, needed to, were forced by ordinary human aspiration to seek escape from their own deep convictions of doubt and drift."

Objectivity, then, was a way of applying to the art of journalism the methods of science. Those methods included, along with reliance on observable fact, the employment of a variety of transparent techniques for pursuing truth. In science, transparency means that the researcher explains his or her objectives, methods, findings and limitations. In journalism, only part of that methodology has been adopted.

In *The Elements of Journalism*, Kovach and Rosenstiel worry that a kind of phony objectivity has replaced the original concept. The objectivity of science does not require neutrality or artificial balance of two sides in a dispute. However, as usually practiced today, objectivity employs both devices, sometimes instead of the kind of openness that is essential in science. True objectivity, they argue, adds scientific rigor to journalistic art. Without that, journalists and audiences alike can be misled.

Properly understood, objectivity provides the method most likely to yield the best obtainable version of the truth.

In 1947 the Hutchins Commission on freedom of the press concluded that a free society needs from journalists "a truthful, comprehensive and intelligent account of the day's events in a context which gives them meaning." The goal of this chapter is to show you how the journalists of today and tomorrow understand that need, how they are trying to meet it, and the complexity of the task. The rest of the book will help you develop the skills you'll need to take up the challenge. There are few challenges so important or so rewarding.

> *"You go into journalism because you can do good, have fun and learn."*
>
> — **Molly Ivins**,
> Reporter and columnist

Suggested Readings

Downie, Leonard Jr. and Kaiser, Robert. *The News about the News*. New York: Knopf, 2002. This is a critical, thoroughly researched examination of the contemporary practice of American journalism in all media.

Kovach, Bill and Rosenstiel, Tom. *The Elements of Journalism*. New York: Crown Publishers, 2001. This little book, a kind of applied ethics for journalists in any medium, is packed with practical advice and inspiration.

Suggested Web Sites

www.journalism.org

This is the Web site of the Project for Excellence in Journalism and the Committee of Concerned Journalists. It contains relevant research and articles on the current state of journalism.

www.people-press.org

The site of the Pew Research Center for the People and the Press includes not only surveys of public attitudes toward the press but also analysis of those attitudes.

Exercises

1. Watch the evening news on a local television station. Read the next morning's local newspaper. Then go to the Web sites of the paper and the station. First, compare the content and presentation of the news in these sources. Next, think about and discuss the strengths and weaknesses of each medium.

2. Most Americans say they get most of their news from television. Watch an evening newscast on one of the major networks. Read *The New York Times* or *USA Today* for the same day. Compare the number of stories, the topics and the details of television and newspaper coverage. How well informed are those television-dependent Americans?

3. Go to your library, and look at a recent issue of *The New York Times* and an issue from the same day 20 years ago. Describe the differences you find in subjects and sources of stories.

4. As a class project, visit or invite to class the editor of your local paper and the news director of a local television station. Study their products ahead of time, and then interview them about how they decide the value of news stories, how they assess the reliability of sources and how they try to ensure accuracy.

2 Convergence and the Changing Media Industry

The hottest buzzword in the media industry these days is **convergence,** but defining it isn't easy. In the definition of some, convergence occurs when a newspaper or television station starts publishing material on the Internet. According to others, convergence occurs when print reporters start carrying tape recorders and produce material for radio as well as the newspaper, or when advertising sales people start selling ads for radio as well as newspapers.

While those may indeed be forms of convergence, in its most complete sense convergence involves alliances of three communication forms:

- Print (usually a newspaper or magazine).
- Broadcast or cable television, and perhaps radio.
- The Internet and wireless communication devices.

Without question, that third element is essential to any serious definition of convergence. Why? Because the Internet and wireless devices such as **mobile telephones** and wireless **personal digital assistants (PDAs)** allow consumers to search for and find information they want and need whenever and from wherever they like, a possibility generally absent in traditional media. Sure, with the newspaper you can search through the stock listings for the closing share price of Merck, the pharmaceutical giant. But you cannot read about Merck's latest drugs and their chances of winning federal approval unless the newspaper's editors happen to provide that story for you. On the Internet, a simple search produces the story.

That fundamental reality has forever changed the way news organizations deal with their audiences. In the traditional media, editors serve as **gatekeepers,** deciding what information is printed or broadcast and therefore what information consumers can access. With Internet-based media, the user is in control. He or she selects from a seemingly endless variety of available material and from a seemingly endless variety of sources.

As a result, the best definition of convergence might read like this: Convergence is the practice of sharing and cross-promoting content from a variety of media, some interactive, through news room collaborations and partnerships. However one defines it, convergence is changing the face of the media landscape.

Web consultant Vin Crosbie defines three waves of online journalism:

- *The First Wave* (1982–1992), which began with ill-fated attempts by Knight Ridder Newspapers and Times Mirror to deliver text-based services to people's homes, led to proprietary online services (which in this book we call the **public information utilities**), such as America Online and CompuServe (see Chapter 4).

- *The Second Wave* (1993–2001), which began with publishers and television networks joining the proprietary services as content providers, evolved into the World Wide Web after the first commercial browser (Netscape) was introduced in 1994. Microsoft's Internet Explorer arrived the next year. The Web made it possible for almost anyone to become a publisher of information. Small, innovative sites became popular, and Internet-delivered audio became the rage. The bubble of the Second Wave burst by mid-2000 because the public refused to pay for content and owners had failed to come up with a working business model.
- *The Third Wave* (Since 2001), which arose after the end of the "dot-com boom," is characterized, Crosbie believes, by more-sophisticated owners and better-trained staffs, end users dependent on traditional news organizations for the daily global news report, and proliferating mobile platforms and news software that enables powerful forms of publishing, such as wireless push and immersive technologies. Owners, Crosbie notes, are developing more information that users are willing to pay for, and owners are developing new revenue streams in partnership with end users.

The message unmistakably conveyed in Crosbie's historical overview is this: In the current media environment, users—not publishers and editors—are in control.

THE CONVERGENCE OF MEDIA ORGANIZATIONS

Enlightened editors and publishers of this new era believe the key to success is giving readers what they want when they want it. That's precisely the attitude of those driving the most successful convergence experiments in the United States. The *Tampa Tribune*-WFLA-Tampa Bay Online convergence effort of Media General in Tampa is the most celebrated of those experiments. It also is one of the oldest, having started in 2000.

Several years after the convergence craze occurred, the converged news room in Tampa has little trouble getting either breaking or routine news onto all three platforms, says Gil Thelen, *Tampa Tribune* senior vice president and executive editor. But it wasn't easy to get to that point. Some employees quit rather than learn new ways of doing things. Others stayed, complained and ultimately complied.

"Right now we're all trying to think multimedia," Kate MacCormack, team leader for pop culture at the *Tribune*, told *Online Journalism Review*. "But I can say (that for someone trained in newspaper journalism) it's just really, really hard. . . . Every moment, every day you need to think outside the box on what could be done, but you

TBO.com is the main Web site for the *Tampa Tribune*-WFLA-Tampa Bay Online, one of the oldest examples of media convergence. The newspaper, television station and Web site joined forces in 2000.

want to take care of your world first. We're still struggling with that." Still, crossover reporting in Tampa has become increasingly common:

- A *Tribune* story about a passenger who landed a plane after the pilot became ill carried the bylines of both a *Tribune* reporter and the WFLA anchor.
- A report on dog bites ran as a two-part WFLA series, a front-page *Tribune* story and a **TBO.com** package.
- A *Tribune* story on the removal of a statue from a shopping center included a picture by the photo editor, who also shot video for WFLA.

But cultural differences in the way television and newspaper reporters have traditionally operated can cause trouble for converged operations. That became evident in Dallas when *The Dallas Morning News* and WFAA, both owned by the Belo Corp., started cooperating. How was the *Morning News'* television critic supposed to critique a television station with which the newspaper partnered? Would anything he wrote be seen as biased? Not sure, the newspaper decided that for the time being it would not do any television criticism at all.

On other fronts, things were easier. When the television station and newspaper decided to have their movie critics collaborate, both agreed that the *Morning News'* more stringent ethical standards, which called for refusing freebies from any source (see Chapter 15), would prevail. That agreement signaled a cultural shift for the television station—but arguably a positive one.

When television came along in the late 1940s and early 1950s, many of its early newscasters came from the newspaper industry. Heavyweights such as Edward R. Murrow and Walter Cronkite brought with them the demanding standards, ethical and otherwise, of the newspaper industry. But over the years, those old newspapermen died or retired, and television developed a new set of standards driven more by what was visually pleasing than by traditional news values. As convergence occurs, those disparate cultures must begin to meld.

What journalists and their editors in converged news rooms are discovering is that those cultural differences can cause problems. So can the fact that few contemporary journalists are cross-trained in the various media. Across the country, schools and departments of journalism are grappling with the difficult problem of how to provide that training, and solutions aren't always easy to find.

Cultural differences aside, convergence makes sense. Television is the unquestioned leader in providing the American public with today's news headlines. Newspapers and magazines can provide more depth. The Internet can offer even greater depth than newspapers and interactivity unmatched by either print or television. Marriages of those disparate media make sense if the news industry is to take maximum advantage of their various strengths.

So, despite the difficulties of merging separate journalistic cultures, convergence is here to stay. Now that the federal government has removed most restrictions on cross-ownership of television stations and newspapers in major markets, the number of converged news rooms is likely to increase. And even in traditional news rooms, reporters at a minimum can expect to be producing stories for both the traditional outlet and the Internet.

THE CONVERGED NEWS ROOM

Although most see media convergence as the trend of the future, it's undeniably true that to date few news rooms in the United States are truly converged. Again, the *Tampa Tribune*-WFLA-**TBO.com** operation may offer the best example.

When Media General decided to plunge head-first into conversion, it spent $40 million to create a state-of-the-art news facility to house all three news operations. The first floor houses WFLA's studios, and the second floor houses the offices of **TBO.com** and the television news room. The *Tribune* news room is a floor above, and in it are cameras where reporters can do reports for the television newscast.

But the heart of the operation is a **multimedia assignment desk** housed in the WFLA news room. WFLA assignment editors sit alongside staff members from the *Tribune* and **TBO.com.** One individual, the **multimedia editor,** has ultimate responsibility for letting each news outlet know what the others are doing. Co-location of editors from the various outlets at the assignment desk helps facilitate that interaction.

Reporters work primarily in either the television or newspaper news room, and their editors regularly ask them to produce reports for the other medium. Some original reporting occurs in the **TBO.com** news room, but producers there are more likely to concentrate on adding value to newspaper- or television-produced reports by creating links to original source material or other Internet sites.

A story told by Gayle Sierens, WFLA anchor, illustrates how the Tampa operation tries to take maximum advantage of each medium: One day Sierens got a call from a man wrongfully accused of killing his estranged wife and two daughters. After being cleared by police, the man called Sierens and wanted to tell his story—to her exclusively. Sierens wrote the broadcast story and another story for the *Tribune.* She was shocked when her editor told her that the newspaper story would be printed *before* the broadcast version was televised. In effect, she scooped herself.

Expect to hear many such stories in the years ahead. One of the greatest values of convergence is cross-promotion of print, television and online news. As the Tampa editors reasoned: If the newspaper article serves to tease Sierens' broadcast report, so much the better.

WHY CONVERGENCE?

Although converged news rooms may be the wave of the future, most news rooms today are decidedly traditional. For every Tampa-like convergence operation, there are hundreds of traditional newspaper or television news rooms. Those news rooms typically look much as they did 25 years ago except for their embedded online operations. Today, almost every television station or newspaper has a Web site.

It's also true that most traditional news operations are profitable.

It's not at all unusual for a daily newspaper to earn a profit of 20 cents or more on every dollar it brings through the door. Many television stations earn even more. So why the interest in convergence? It's quite simple, really. Most of the media-industry financial trends are headed in the wrong direction. Profits are shrinking for a variety of reasons, and media-industry managers are worried. Many see convergence as the long-term answer to their problems.

To understand today's media-industry climate, consider these facts about newspapers, published by the Newspaper Association of America, the industry's leading trade organization:

- The newspaper industry is shrinking. There were 1,468 daily newspapers in the United States at the end of 2001, compared with 1,745 as recently as 1980.
- In 1970, 78 percent of the nation's adults read a newspaper daily, but by 2001 that percentage had declined to 54. Worse, survey after survey has revealed that the biggest decline is among readers 34 and younger. That statistic sounds an ominous note for the future: As older readers die, there is no one to replace them. Research suggests that those who fail to develop the newspaper reading habit early will not acquire it later in life.

But if the newspaper industry is dying, as some argue, it is far from dead. Consider this:

- Newspapers remain one of the most profitable industries around, helped in large part by their near-monopoly situation in most cities.
- Daily newspapers continue to capture the largest share of the U.S. advertising dollar among the traditional media, edging out broadcast television 19.2 percent to 16.8 percent (see Figure 2.1). Only direct mail at 19.3 percent does better. And newspapers usually dominate the local news and advertising markets.

Newspapers' competitors have their own problems. Network television, the main competitor for both advertising dollars and audience, has experienced tough financial times. The creation of major U.S. networks such as Fox and the WB network has fragmented audiences, and the proliferation of cable television channels has divided those audiences into even smaller segments. Cable channels are worrisome indeed for network television; unlike the networks, they are ideally positioned to deliver targeted audiences to advertisers because of their focus on specific areas of information (sports, health and fitness, children, etc.). Like newspapers, network television is best able to deliver mass audiences, not the cohesive audiences that many advertisers covet. Radio does a better job of targeting specific audiences, but its impact on the media industry, as measured by its share of advertising dollars (7.7 percent), is relatively small.

Magazines, like radio and cable television, deliver target audi-

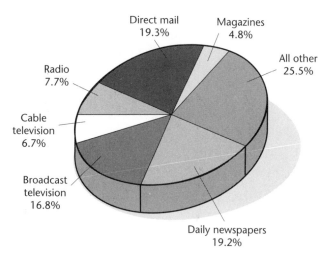

Figure 2.1
Media Share of Advertising Dollars (2001). Newspapers edge out television as the leading advertising medium in the country. (*Source:* Universal McCann, Newspaper Association of America)

ences to advertisers, but they do so at a rapidly increasing cost and together account for only 4.8 percent of U.S. advertising dollars. In the long term, like newspapers, magazines are threatened by rising production costs, and their distribution relies heavily on ever-escalating postal rates.

Many media experts conclude that the future lies in a new computer-delivered medium capable of combining the best features of television with the best of newspapers. Nicholas Negroponte, founder and director of the Media Lab at Massachusetts Institute of Technology, describes the emerging **infomedium** as a home computer system capable of searching vast online databanks and displaying its results in text, audio or video form. Thus, the primary advantages of television—color, eye appeal, immediacy and low distribution costs—can be combined with the advantages of the print media: depth, interpretation and portability. Further, users are able to interact with online material in ways that are not possible at all in traditional media. Such systems depend on high-bandwidth connections to the home, and cable television and the phone companies are rushing to provide them. All that explains why convergence is so appealing to media managers.

To produce the infomedium that Negroponte envisions, it will be necessary to have a solid footing in each of the existing media industries. That reality is challenging media companies to seek out

"Paper won't disappear (in the future), but paperless media will soak up more of our time. We will eventually become paperless the way we once became horseless. Horses are still around, but they are ridden by hobbyists, not consumers."

—Paul Saffo,
Institute for the Future

convergence opportunities, but it also means you face a challenge as you plan your media career. Not only must you prepare for a job in one of today's existing media, you also must be ready to work in the media of the future. You may work in jobs that will disappear, but you may also work in jobs that have yet to be invented. Through it all, one certainty remains: Regardless of the medium, there will continue to be a demand for news practitioners who report well, write well, edit well and communicate well visually.

THE TRADITIONAL MEDIA

As interesting as converged media may be, most jobs in the media industry today exist at more traditional media outlets—newspapers, magazines, radio and television stations—at a few online sites, and in related fields such as advertising and public relations. Let's take a look at the major players and review how things work in each medium. Along the way, we'll discuss job opportunities available to you.

Newspapers

The popular misconception that newspapers are dying contradicts reality. As measured by the U.S. government, newspapers continue to rank among the top 10 manufacturing industries in total employment. Although the industry appears to be shrinking, it is far from dead, as the existence of almost 1,500 dailies and more than 7,600 weeklies will attest.

Those newspapers appeal to diverse audiences. In the New York area alone, one finds not only the *New York Times*, the *New York Post*, the *Daily News* and *Newsday* but also the ethnic dailies, such as the *Amsterdam News*, *El Diario* and the *Jewish Daily Forward*. For various other audiences, there are the *Wall Street Journal*, the *American Banker* and *Variety*. That diversity is mirrored elsewhere on a smaller scale. Because of the industry's size, it is difficult to generalize about the internal organization of newspapers. Figure 2.2 shows the typical organization of a news room at a medium-sized daily newspaper.

Today's editors seek to improve ways of presenting the news. In the past, it was common for a reporter to finish a story before photographers or graphic designers were brought in to illustrate the piece. When that occurred, it was often too late for the visual experts to do their best work. On major stories today, teams of reporters, photographers, graphic designers and editors are assigned from the outset. As a result, the best way to present various parts of the story is determined in a team setting. The team leader is sometimes called a **maestro,**

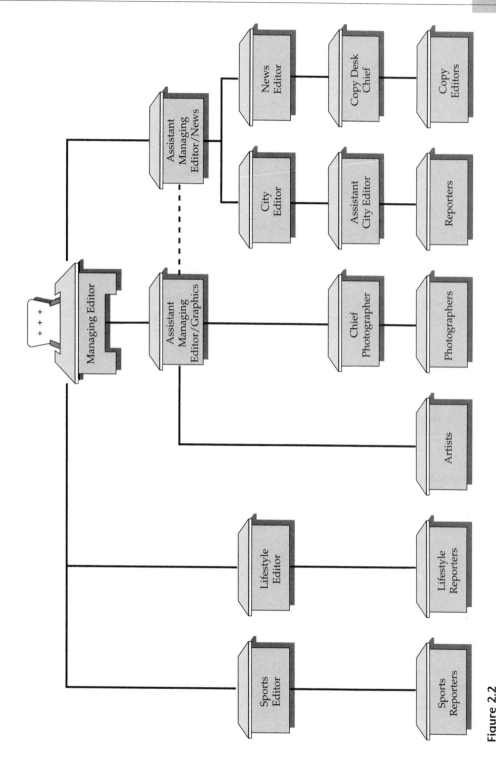

Figure 2.2
Typical News Room Organization of a Medium-Sized Daily Newspaper

someone who leads a reporting team just as a conductor leads an orchestra in the quest for the best possible result.

Some newspapers have taken the team concept beyond the realm of major stories and have reorganized their news rooms to make teams the basic organizational pattern. Typical is the *Star Tribune*, newspaper of the Twin Cities, based in Minneapolis. There, each reporter, writer, editor, photographer and graphic artist is part of a team responsible for specific coverage areas. In some ways those coverage areas are akin to the beats still found in most newspapers, but they are broader and reflect the newspaper's desire to expand types of content previously ignored or given short shrift.

Newspaper Production

Once you've landed that first job, ask for a thorough tour of the newspaper. The **editorial department** is only one of several departments that must work in close coordination if the newspaper is to be successful. If the **advertising department** fails to sell enough advertising, the news hole—the space available for news—is small, and your department's ability to provide a comprehensive news report is adversely affected. If your department misses its deadlines, the **production** and **circulation departments** could spend thousands of dollars in overtime pay, and subscribers may not receive their newspapers on time. It's important to learn how you and your department fit into the picture. To do so, you must fully understand the role of the other departments—advertising, business, circulation, production and perhaps others (see Figure 2.3). A newspaper is a product, and you must learn the role of each department in producing it.

Working with the Editor

Once the editorial package is prepared, editors polish it for publication. At first glance, the flow of **copy** through an editorial department seems simple enough (see Figure 2.4). You write your story and transfer it to the city desk queue, the electronic equivalent of an in-basket. There the **city editor** reads it and makes necessary changes. Then it is sent electronically to the **copy desk,** where it is edited again. The story is assigned a position in the newspaper, and a **copy editor** writes a headline. Finally, an editor sends the story or page electronically to a typesetting machine in the composing room. Despite the seeming simplicity of the pattern, many decisions made along the way can make the process much more complicated than it appears at first glance.

When the city editor receives your copy, that editor must read it and make initial decisions: Is information missing? Does the story need to be developed? Does it need more background? Are there enough

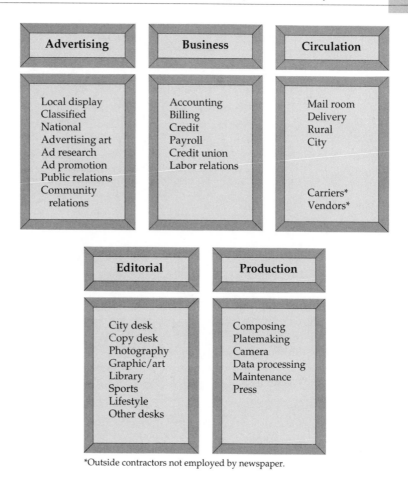

Advertising	Business	Circulation
Local display	Accounting	Mail room
Classified	Billing	Delivery
National	Credit	Rural
Advertising art	Payroll	City
Ad research	Credit union	
Ad promotion	Labor relations	
Public relations		
Community		Carriers*
relations		Vendors*

Editorial	Production
City desk	Composing
Copy desk	Platemaking
Photography	Camera
Graphic/art	Data processing
Library	Maintenance
Sports	Press
Lifestyle	
Other desks	

*Outside contractors not employed by newspaper.

Figure 2.3
Major Departments of a Typical Newspaper and Their Subsections

quotes? Are the quotes worth using? Does the **lead,** or opening, need to be polished? Have you chosen the right lead, or should another angle be emphasized? Is the story important? Is it useful, interesting or entertaining? Is there, in fact, some reason for publishing it? If it is important, should the **managing editor** and **news editor** be alerted that a potential Page One story is forthcoming? Each time a city editor reads a story for the first time, these questions and more come up. The city editor is expected to answer them quickly; there is no time for delay in the fast-paced world of daily newspapering.

After making those initial decisions, the city editor confers with you and gives direction on changes to be made. If the changes are minor ones, simply rewriting a section of the story or inserting additional information will suffice. If the changes are more substantial,

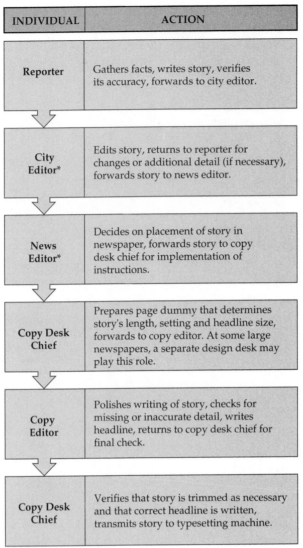

INDIVIDUAL	ACTION
Reporter	Gathers facts, writes story, verifies its accuracy, forwards to city editor.
City Editor*	Edits story, returns to reporter for changes or additional detail (if necessary), forwards story to news editor.
News Editor*	Decides on placement of story in newspaper, forwards story to copy desk chief for implementation of instructions.
Copy Desk Chief	Prepares page dummy that determines story's length, setting and headline size, forwards to copy editor. At some large newspapers, a separate design desk may play this role.
Copy Editor	Polishes writing of story, checks for missing or inaccurate detail, writes headline, returns to copy desk chief for final check.
Copy Desk Chief	Verifies that story is trimmed as necessary and that correct headline is written, transmits story to typesetting machine.

* Or assistant

Note: At any point in the process, a story may be returned to an earlier editor for clarification, amplification or rewriting.

Figure 2.4
Typical News Room Copy-Flow Pattern

involving additional interviews with sources or major rewriting, your job is more difficult.

When those changes are made, you resubmit your story to the city editor, who reads the revised version and edits it more carefully. Your work may be finished after you answer a few minor questions. Or, if the city editor is still unhappy with it, another rewrite may be ordered.

You can expect frustration in the process. Often an assistant city editor reads your story first and gives instructions on how it is to be revised. When you submit your rewrite, the city editor or another assistant may do the editing, creating the need for more changes and yet another rewrite. This can be discouraging, but such a system has its merits. Generally, a story is improved when more than one editor handles it. Each sees gaps to be filled, and a better story results.

Working with the Copy Editor

The copy editor asks many of the same questions about your story that the city editor asks. Have you selected the right lead? Does the writing need to be polished? Have you chosen the correct words? Primarily, though, the copy editor checks for misspelled words, adherence to style, grammatical errors, ambiguities and errors of fact. The copy editor reworks a phrase here or there to clarify your meaning but is expected to avoid major changes. If major changes are necessary, the copy editor calls that to the attention of the news editor. If the news editor agrees, the story is returned to the city editor, and perhaps to you, for yet another revision.

When the copy editor is satisfied with the story, work begins on the headline. The size of the headline ordered by the copy desk chief determines how many characters or letters can be used in writing it. Headline writing is an art. Those who are able to convey the meaning of a story in a limited number of words are valuable members of the staff. The quality of the copy editor's work can have a significant impact on the number of readers who will be attracted to your story. If the headline is dull and lifeless, few will be; if it sparkles, the story's exposure will be increased.

The copy editor also may write the **cutline,** or caption, that accompanies the picture. At some newspapers, however, this is done by the photographer, by the reporter or at the city desk. Large newspapers may have a photo desk to handle cutlines as well as picture cropping and sizing.

When finished, the copy editor transfers the story to the copy desk chief, who must approve the headline and may check the editing changes made by the copy editor. When the desk chief is satisfied, the story and headline are transferred to the design desk or to the composing room, where the creative effort of writers and editors is transformed into type.

The size of the newspaper may alter this copy-flow pattern substantially. At a small newspaper the jobs of news editor, copy desk chief and copy editor may be performed by one person. Some small dailies require the city editor or an assistant to perform all the tasks normally handled by the copy desk.

News room copy-flow patterns have been designed with redundancy in mind. Built into the system is the goal of having not one editor, but several, check your work. Through repeated checking, editors hope to detect more errors—in fact and in writing style—to make the finished product a better one.

In this sense editors work as gatekeepers. They determine whether your work measures up to their standards. Only when it does is the gate opened, allowing your story to take the next step in the newspaper production process.

Magazines and Corporate Communications

The magazine industry is vast, and generalizations about magazine publishers are difficult to make. Publishers range from conglomerates like AOL Time Warner, whose mass audience magazines include *Time*, *People* and *Sports Illustrated*, to companies as diverse as Pfizer and General Electric, which publish magazines written and designed for employees or customers or both. Many also are published by not-for-profit organizations like the Girl Scouts and AARP.

Most magazines, even those that are commercially published, do not target mass audiences, as *Time* does, but instead target smaller audiences with a passion for the subject matter. Those include such titles as *Popular Mechanics, Boating, PC Magazine* and *Skiing*. Even more prevalent are company magazines, such as *Walgreen World* and *Saudi Aramco World*, which usually are written and edited by corporate communications departments or public relations staffs. Another huge segment of the magazine market is the business-to-business press, magazines that seek to inform people working in a particular industry of industry trends. Smaller magazines, those published by corporations or nonprofit organizations, are often put together by tiny staffs. Editors often write the stories, design the pages and even arrange for printing by outside vendors.

Magazines are organized much like newspapers, their print cousins. Among the various departments, only the circulation department will differ much from that of newspapers. That's because the method of distribution is dramatically different. Most magazines

On the Job

Using Newswriting Skills in Corporate Communications

As a journalism student in college, Kabby Hong didn't think he wanted the daily deadline pressures demanded of newspaper writers. As a result, he majored in magazine journalism.

Nevertheless, even as a magazine major, he was required to take courses in news writing, reporting and editing before he could take courses in magazine writing and editing.

Between his junior and senior years, Hong was searching for a summer internship because his advisers had told him that nothing looked better on a journalism graduate's résumé. A couple of AT&T recruiters stopped at his school, and Hong scheduled an interview. He won the internship, liked working in corporate communications and was hired by AT&T for what he considered a good salary as soon as he graduated.

At AT&T Network Systems in Morristown, N.J., Hong is a writer for the internal newsletter and magazine.

Like thousands of his colleagues in corporate communications, Hong finds that his news courses served him well. "There is an immediacy to the issues and events that we cover even within a corporation such as AT&T that demands someone who can take complicated information and tell readers what they need to know quickly.

"Newswriting skills do not just serve the 'news rooms' of major metropolitan newspapers," Hong says. "They are essential to the success of any organization that thrives on information and the ability of its communicators to get that information out quickly, accurately and concisely."

depend heavily on the mail and on newsstand sales for distribution. Daily newspapers are distributed primarily by carriers; for most newspapers, mail service and newsstand sales are secondary.

Most of the titles and job functions in magazine and newspaper news rooms are the same. Still, a few titles are unique to the magazine industry. Major magazines are likely to have **senior editors** and **senior writers.** Senior editors usually edit a particular section of the magazine. At *Time*, for example, senior editors direct the International, Arts and other sections. Senior writers, as the name implies, are the magazine's best and most experienced writers. At *Time*, they may seldom leave the office but instead take information from numerous reporters in the field and meld their reports into a well-written, coherent story.

Some magazines also have **contributing editors.** Typically, these are columnists or reporters whose work is purchased for publication. They are not employed by the magazine, and sometimes their work will appear in several industry-related magazines each month.

Magazine Production

To those used to the fast-paced world of daily newspapers, the magazine production cycle looks terribly appealing from a distance. But looks can be deceiving. The deadline pressures that face magazine writers and editors are just as intense; they merely are spread over longer time periods. Still, magazine writers and editors have more time to produce their work, and as a result there is more pressure to produce a near-perfect product.

The tight deadlines of newspapers often result in less-than-perfect writing, typographical errors and similar gaffes. Those mistakes are not tolerated at the best magazines, where longer deadlines allow more time to strive for perfection. Additional time also allows magazine editors to expend more effort on fact-checking and polishing of writing and design.

Magazine editors also spend much more time on writing to fit. Articles often are meticulously edited to fill an exact number of typeset lines in a magazine layout. Similarly, photo captions are fine-tuned so that all lines are completely filled. Such niceties often are dismissed at newspapers, where time is more precious. The result is that most magazines have a more polished look than newspapers. That's true not only because they are printed on higher-quality paper but also because they are more meticulously edited. Unfortunately, at low-budget magazines those conditions may not exist.

Vast numbers of jobs exist for those who would work in corporate communications and public relations. The skills necessary to succeed in those jobs are the same as those needed at magazines and newspapers: the ability to write and edit well. Almost inevitably, editing a magazine will be among the jobs of the corporate communications employee.

Television and Radio

Television stations play a major role in the way the public receives its news. Increasingly, so do cable television channels like CNN, C-SPAN and CNBC. Radio, once a major player in news distribution, now is relegated to a second tier of service except for a few all-news stations in major cities and National Public Radio. Most people use radio as a news medium primarily while driving to and from work, although in major cities news-talk stations are quite popular. While stations such as WBZ in Boston and WCCO in Minneapolis do plenty of original reporting, most radio news operations rely heavily on wire services for their news.

The top news executive at a local television station typically is the **news director** or, at some group-owned stations, the vice president for news. The news director is responsible for managing news room personnel and resources and for setting news room policies. Often, the news director does not deal with details of daily news coverage. Instead, that responsibility is delegated to an **assistant news director** or **managing editor.**

The other key management role in a television news room is that of **executive producer.** The executive producer determines the overall look of the station's newscasts. This includes the use of video, graphics and animation; the length and placement of stories; whether a reporter or anchor is seen delivering the story; and how upcoming stories are "teased" going into a commercial break. Most stations also hire **show producers,** who report to the executive producer and are responsible for individual newscasts.

Producing requires an ability to see the "big picture" under the extreme pressure of broadcast deadlines. It is a high-stress, high-turnover job. Producer also is the position most in demand in local television news.

Television news, of course, requires reporters. In addition to gathering and writing the news, television reporters must know how to present it in a lively and personable fashion. To be successful in large markets or at the network level, reporters must have a distinctive style and personality. In fact, network correspondents often do little original reporting themselves, leaving the news-gathering to **field producers** or off-camera reporters.

Anchors also are critical to a successful television news operation. In important ways they represent the persona of the news broadcast. Viewers know and have strong opinions about news anchors, even

and fill-in anchor for three and a half years at WLOS-TV in Asheville, N.C. Now she's an education reporter at NewsChannel 5 in Nashville, Tenn.

"I'm having a ball. It's often said this fast-paced, hectic business that's riddled with deadlines is one that will burn out a person. It can happen to some reporters, but I'm not feeling it yet. Good pacing, I guess."

Eaton has a few words for "reporters-in-the-making":

1. If you really want to be in the news business, keep at it. Don't let "there-are-no-jobs" comments slow you down.
2. Constantly work to improve your writing.
3. It's OK to know you do good work; just don't let your head get so huge you can't make it through the news room door.
4. Remember, someone helped you get to where you are, so reach back and help others.

when they can't remember the call letters or channel of the station for which the anchors work.

Videographers play a key role in the television news room as well. TV news lives and dies by pictures. Creative videographers add to the look that often separates the top station in a market from its competitors.

In larger markets, desk assistants serve at the entry-level position in the television news room. They keep watch on material from the wire services, make routine beat calls, monitor fire and police scanners, and take in satellite feeds from networks or regional cooperatives.

Television News Production

Viewers use television news in a fundamentally different way than they do newspapers or magazines. The audience expects and demands immediacy, so local stations program several newscasts a day and put a premium on live reporting of newsworthy events.

The frequent deadlines of television news force reporters, videographers and producers to think quickly on their feet, to boil down a story to its most easily understood elements and to get on to the next assignment as quickly as possible. Television journalists often find themselves "working without a net," making split-second decisions without the benefit of editors or time for reflection.

A television report is almost always a team effort. Here, a reporter conducting an interview is accompanied by a videographer. When they finish the interview, they will edit it together into the final form.

Television reports are almost always team efforts. A reporter on assignment is accompanied by a videographer. Together, they collect the material that will form the basis of the report. When they finish collecting the material, they return to the station to edit it into the final form that will appear on the air. Or they edit their report in a mobile van capable of transmitting it back to the station by satellite or microwave. Editors and producers weave their material and that of other reporting teams into the newscasts with which we all are familiar.

By necessity, television news focuses more on process than on completeness. While radio and television journalism are capable of great depth, analysis and perspective, those qualities are more often demanded of newspapers and magazines. (For more on television news, see Chapter 11.)

ONLINE MEDIA

In the 1990s the Internet quickly earned a place as the most important new medium since television. Almost every daily newspaper, most major magazines, all the television networks and many individual stations now have significant sites on the Internet. Some Web sites carry almost all the material offered by the media's traditional services; others tease or supplement their traditional media.

Adding legitimacy to the Internet as a source for news is the presence of such major newspaper companies as the New York Times Co. and the Tribune Co. and the presence of television networks such as NBC, ABC and CNN.

Many media observers see the Internet and its news Web sites as the precursor to the infomedium of the future envisioned by MIT's Negroponte and others. Indeed, it now appears that as the Internet's bandwidth increases to permit the delivery of video, an entirely new medium is emerging.

Online Media Organization

To think of the new media as simply a new way to transmit wire service news is a mistake. Each of the new-media services maintains a news room, where at least some original material is created. Further, each buys freelance material and repackages other forms of information, such as airline schedules, restaurant reviews and stock market quotations. Most allow users to download full-color pictures and sound clips.

To be sure, online news media are so diverse and operate so differently from traditional media that it is almost impossible to create a typical organization chart. But computer users see them as ideal sources for the news they want. Now that an estimated 60 percent of

American homes have computers and that percentage is climbing monthly, journalists can no longer afford to dismiss computer-based news delivery.

For years, the Associated Press, United Press International, Reuters and other wire services have been viewed mainly as wholesalers of information to newspapers and broadcast stations. Through online services, their products are now going directly to consumers. More focused offspring such as the various Dow Jones online services and Bloomberg Business News are expanding rapidly. All of them represent new ways of delivering news online.

Online Media Production

Few newcomers are hired as reporters for the online media; instead, journalists are hired as **online editors.** That's because the strength of the new media lies not in the creation of new content but in the repackaging of content gathered for related traditional media in a form

CNN's Web site, **www.cnn.com,** takes full advantage of the capabilities of online journalism. It includes links to streaming video, a CNN television schedule, updated stock quotes, breaking news alerts and updated headlines.

that is more immediate and easier to use. That difference also helps account for how online media news rooms are organized. They are, in many ways, like one huge copy desk employing editors with multiple talents—computer skills, word skills and visual skills. Think of those editors as **multimedia journalists.**

However, this view of online media news rooms is starting to change. More and more publications are realizing that original content is needed on online sites. As a result, some original reporting is starting to appear there. Look for more such jobs to be created in the years ahead.

For the moment, though, most online media news rooms are filled with editors with titles not unlike those found at newspapers. Editors take responsibility for certain sections of the online service—news, sports, features and others. Content is gathered from both traditional and nontraditional sources. Graphic displays are designed for maximum appeal on computer screens. Immediacy is paramount.

Unlike editors at a newspaper or magazine, online media editors must have skills that more closely resemble those of the television journalist or photojournalist. It's not good enough to be a word editor for the online media; one must also have a good sense of visual design. That's because the online media, like television, depend on attractive screen presentation for impact. Journalists who work in the online media must be competent in writing, editing and design. Increasingly, they also will need audio and video skills; most of the online media now incorporate audio and video clips in their services.

Although there are relatively few reporting jobs in the online media, some companies are pioneering the concept in recognition of the fact that this new field offers many possibilities other than the repackaging of old content. As these experiments yield success, watch for others to follow. In the years ahead, there almost certainly will be many more jobs for reporters in the online media.

Like wire service journalists, online journalists are constantly on deadline. Twenty-four hours a day, users log on to get the latest news and information. Thus, producing news for the online media requires journalists who thrive on deadline pressure, who have strong computer skills, who understand both written and visual communication and who are interested in pioneering a new medium. Those who can meet these requirements should have little trouble finding jobs.

OTHER CAREER OPPORTUNITIES

Journalism training is in many ways ideal training for almost any profession. The skills of writing, editing and visual communication are in great demand worldwide. The broad applications of journalism training account for the large number of journalism graduates who find themselves in jobs quite different from those they imagined.

In this chapter, we outlined the most common routes for those with journalism training to find jobs as reporters and writers of news. But there are many others, including public relations, corporate communications, advertising, ethnic newspapers, professional periodicals, union and trade publications and practically any areas that require the skills of writing, editing or visual communication. Nationwide, the most popular majors among journalism and mass communication students are advertising and public relations. Many who receive degrees in news-editorial programs end up in other jobs, including public relations, corporate communications and new media. More than one journalism graduate has parlayed an interest in computers and journalism into a job as a newspaper systems manager. Others have found jobs training journalists to use new computer systems; vendors have learned that an understanding of how journalists work speeds the training process.

Others have gone into publications work for nonprofit organizations such as the Girl Scouts and the American Heart Association. Still others who started at newspapers have moved to television or vice versa. Because journalism and mass communications accrediting standards emphasize the importance of a broad liberal arts education, students often get the ideal mix of practical training and the ability to think. That, more than any specific skill, is the mark of a well-trained journalist.

Suggested Readings

De Wolk, Roland. *Introduction to Online Journalism: Publishing News and Information*. Boston: Allyn and Bacon, 2001. An overview of online journalism.

Dizard, Wilson Jr. *Old Media, New Media*, Third Edition. New York: Longman, 1999. A good overview of the developing new-media landscape.

Dominick, Joseph R., Sherman, Barry L. and Messere, Fritz. *Broadcasting, Cable, the Internet and Beyond: An Introduction to Modern Electronic Media*. New York: McGraw-Hill, 1999. An excellent study of television and the Internet.

Martin, Chuck. *Net Future*. New York: McGraw-Hill, 1998. An excellent overview of the competitive aspects of online media.

Negroponte, Nicholas P. *Being Digital*. New York: Vintage, 1996. A view of the changing media landscape by one of the industry's most prominent observers.

Suggested Web Sites

www.onlinenewsassociation.org

This is the site of the Association of Online Journalists, organized in 1999.

www.mediainfo.com

This site, maintained by *Editor & Publisher* magazine, provides links to many newspapers throughout North America and the world.

www.aol.com

America Online, owner of Time Warner, is the largest of the online media companies. It serves as the Internet service provider for millions around the world.

www.nab.org

The National Association of Broadcasters is the primary trade organization of the broadcast industry.

www.magazine.org

The professional organization for magazine journalists is the Magazine Publishers of America.

www.naa.org

The Newspaper Association of America, based in Reston, Va., is the newspaper industry's leading trade association.

www.spj.org

The Society of Professional Journalists is the primary membership organization for working journalists, regardless of medium.

Exercises

1. Visit either your school newspaper or the local daily or weekly newspaper. Talk with staff members about how the staff is organized. Once you understand the system, draw an organization chart of the news department.

2. Draw a copy-flow chart that shows how copy moves from reporters to the production department at the newspaper you chose for exercise 1.

3. Visit a local television station and interview the news director about how the news room is organized. Produce an organization chart that explains the operation.

4. Using the Internet, locate information on the most recent U.S. census and report the following:
   a. The population of your state.
   b. The population of your city.
   c. The range of income levels and percentages of population that fall within those income levels in your city.
   d. The demographic breakdown of your city by race.

5. Make a list of at least 10 sources of information available on the Internet that would be good resources for journalists. Explain why.

B ill Reiter was only about a year into his first job out of journalism school when he decided to interview Edith McClinton. He
knew it was important. Mrs. McClinton, 89, had lived through
the turbulent birth of the civil rights movement in Little Rock, Ark.
She had overcome racism, poverty and blindness to achieve professional success and personal dignity. He quickly discovered it wasn't
going to be easy. Here's his recollection:

> Interviewing Mrs. McClinton was difficult for a number of reasons.
> Her age alone presented a pretty daunting challenge. Some days,
> she was in fine spirits and her memory was sharp as anyone's.
> But some days we'd be talking for five or 10 minutes and then I'd lose
> her. . . .
> Another problem was my paper. The *Democrat Gazette* does not
> have an excellent reputation with the black community. Early on,
> Mrs. McClinton and her daughter Joyce (who lives with her and takes
> care of her) made it clear that they didn't trust my paper, and that
> they didn't trust me. So that's where it started.

By the time it ended eight months later, Reiter, a white 22-year-
old from Iowa, had earned the family's trust and written a seven-part,
front-page narrative telling the story of race in Arkansas through the
experiences of one courageous woman. The series ended with this
summary from Mrs. McClinton:

> "Great things can come from   freedom and pass it on to my
> freedom," she says. "I take my   children and my grandchildren."

Not every interview is that difficult, time-consuming or important. But every successful interview begins with establishing trust and
ends with a story.

Interviewing—having conversations with sources—is the key to
most stories you will write. Your ability to make people comfortable
with you spells the difference between mediocre reporting and good
reporting.

Information is the raw material of a journalist. While some of it
is gathered from records and some from observation, most of it is gathered in person-to-person conversations. The skills that go into those
conversations are the basic reporting tools of any reporter for any
medium. If you're interviewing for television, broadcast or webcast,
your goals and techniques may be different from those of a print
reporter, but the basics are the same.

BUILDING TRUST

The first requirement of any successful interview is a reasonable degree
of trust between reporter and source. Usually, as a reporter you have to
earn that trust. Here's Bill Reiter again, explaining how he broke through
the barriers of race and age to earn the trust of Edith McClinton:

**In this chapter
you will learn:**

1. **How to build trust.**
2. **How to prepare for an
   interview.**
3. **How to phrase your
   questions.**
4. **How to establish
   rapport with a source.**
5. **How to ensure
   accuracy.**
6. **How to quote directly.**

> In the beginning, I would go to Mrs. McClinton's house. Without a notebook, I'd talk to her. We often talked about her story, but more than not we talked about me, about my paper, about why she should trust her story to either of us, about her concerns.
>
> I overcame her suspicions the same way I do with most sources. First, I'm honest. I told Mrs. McClinton that I'd be fair but that the story would be personal and honest. She might not like some of the things I wrote, I told her. . . . I guaranteed only that it was honest and accurate. We had this conversation many times. . . .
>
> I never understand reporters who talk to their sources like the source is some nameless bureaucrat. So I just talked to Edith the way I talk to anyone. I got to know her. More important, she got to know me. The trust came later.
>
> By the end, Mrs. McClinton had grown to trust me. So had her daughter, I think, and this led to honesty. It's amazing what people will tell you when they trust you. . . . And the last thing I had going for me, something I think can't be faked, was empathy. I really liked this lady, respected her, and thought her story was important. I think sources, when they're around us enough, can pick up on that.

You probably won't have months to develop trust with a source. Most times, you won't need that much time. What you will need, though, are the honesty and empathy that lead strangers to be honest with you.

PREPARING FOR THE INTERVIEW

How you prepare for the interview depends in part on what kind of a story you intend to write. You may be doing a news story, a personality profile or an investigative piece. In each case, you check the newspaper library and search online databases, talk to other reporters, and, if there's enough time, read magazine articles and books.

To prepare for a news story, you pay more attention to clips about the subject of the story than to those about the personality of the individual to be interviewed. To prepare for a profile, you look for personality quirks and the subject's interests, family, friends, travels and habits. To prepare for an investigative piece, you want to know both your subject matter and the person you are interviewing. In all these stories, do not overlook other reporters and editors who know something about the person or subject. Let's look at each of these three types of stories more closely.

The News Story

One day Paul Leavitt made a routine telephone call to a law enforcement source. Leavitt, then assistant city editor for *The Des Moines (Iowa) Register,* was working on a story. He knew the source from his days as a county government and courts reporter for the *Register.*

He expected the story, and the interview, to be routine. Polk County was building a new jail. Leavitt wanted to find out about the progress on the new building. The source pleaded ignorance. He said, "Oh, Leavitt, I don't know. I haven't had time to keep up on that, what with all these meetings on the pope's visit."

Leavitt didn't say anything right away. A less astute reporter might have let the source know he was surprised. The pope in Des Moines? Are you kidding? Instead, Leavitt remembered a story he had read about an Iowan who had extended an invitation for John Paul II to stop in Iowa during his upcoming visit to the United States. At the time, Leavitt didn't think the Iowan had much of a chance. When the Vatican announced the pope's visit, people from every state were bartering for a chance to bask in the worldwide limelight.

Still, the source's slip of the tongue seemed genuine. Leavitt finally replied, "Oh, yeah, that's right. When's he coming, anyway?"

"October 4," the source said.

As the conversation progressed, Leavitt waved frantically to the *Register*'s managing editor. A major story was brewing.

"I started asking him some more questions," Leavitt recalls. "Then it dawned on him that he probably wasn't supposed to be talking about this. But it was clear from what he said that the pope was definitely coming to Iowa. He even had the hours."

Before the conversation ended, Leavitt had learned of a meeting among the Secret Service, the Vatican, the U.S. State Department and Iowa law-enforcement officials to discuss the trip. He also had learned when the pope would arrive, where he would arrive, where he would celebrate Mass and when he would leave.

As a result, the *Register* stunned its readers the next morning with a copyrighted story saying the pope would speak in Des Moines on Oct. 4. The story was printed three weeks before the Vatican released its official itinerary of the visit. Other area reporters scoffed at the story. One newspaper even printed a story poking fun at the thought of John Paul II hobnobbing in an Iowa cornfield.

Leavitt and the *Register* were vindicated. As scheduled, the pope arrived Oct. 4 — and celebrated Mass in an Iowa cornfield.

Remembering his conversation with the source, and how a routine question turned into a bona fide scoop, Leavitt said, "I don't even remember what the original question was."

Leavitt probably would not have gotten the story had he not remembered the earlier story about the invitation and known something else about interviewing: When a source unwittingly gives you a scoop, sometimes it is best to act as if you already know it. That may encourage the source to give you more information.

The Profile

A reporter who decided to write a profile of Joan Gilbert, a local free-lance writer, prepared differently. Because the reporter had used the writer as a source in an earlier story, she knew something about the writer. But she needed to know more. So she looked in *Contemporary Authors* and found biographical information. She also asked Gilbert to send her copies of some of the articles she had written. Before the reporter went to see the writer, she read several of the articles. She also interviewed the editor at one of the magazines that bought the writer's material.

The reporter was prepared. Or so she thought. She had to pass one more test. The freelance writer was an animal lover, and when the reporter arrived, she first had to make friends with a handful of dogs. Fortunately, she loved dogs. That immediately established rapport with the freelancer. The resulting story was full of lively detail:

> Joan Gilbert stretches lazily to soft sunbeams and chirping birds. She dresses casually in blue denim shorts and a plaid, short-sleeved blouse. She and her favorite work companions, five playful dogs, file out the door of her little white house to begin their day with a lazy walk in the surrounding woods. When she returns, she'll contentedly sit down at her typewriter. Such is work.
>
> Joan Gilbert is a freelance writer.

Walt Harrington specialized in in-depth profiles when he worked for the *Washington Post Magazine.* In his book, he talked about the time they take:

> Each took between one and three months to complete. All included many hours of conversation with the subjects. Most include days of tagging along as they did whatever they usually did. . . . With actress Kelly McGillis, I spent a hot August month traipsing to daily rehearsals and then back to Kelly's apartment, where she would analyze her day on stage. Most of these profiles also included numerous interviews with the subjects' family, friends, and enemies. For the George Bush and Carl Bernstein profiles, I did about eighty interviews each. Always there are also newspaper and magazine clippings, books, and documents to read.

Few journalists are afforded the luxury of three months to work on a profile, but whether you do eight or 80 interviews, the lessons are still the same: Be prepared. Be there.

The Investigative Piece

The casual atmosphere of the Joan Gilbert or Kelly McGillis interviews is not always possible for the investigative reporter. Here, the adversary relationship determines both the preparation required and the atmosphere of the interview itself. An investigative reporter is like an attorney in a courtroom. Wise attorneys know what the answers to their questions will be. So do investigative reporters. Preparation is essential.

In the early stages of the investigation, you conduct some fishing-expedition interviews: Because you don't know how much the source knows, you cast around. Start with persons on the fringes. Gather as much as you can from them. Study the records. Only after you have most of the evidence do you confront your central character. You start with a large circle and gradually draw it smaller.

Getting the interview is sometimes as big a challenge as the interview itself. Sources who believe you are working on a story that will be critical of them or their friends often try to avoid you. Steve Weinberg, author of an unauthorized biography of industrialist Armand Hammer, had to overcome the suspicion of many former Hammer associates. Their former boss had told all of them not to talk to Weinberg. Instead of calling, Weinberg approached them by mail.

"I sent letters, examples of my previous work, explained what I wanted to cover and why I was doing it without Hammer's blessing," Weinberg says.

He recommends that you use the letter, which can be an e-mail, to share some of what you know about the story that might surprise or impress the source. For instance, a remark such as "And last week, when I was checking all the land records . . . " would indicate the depth of your research.

In his letter to former Hammer assistants, Weinberg talked about how Hammer was one of the most important people in the history of business. The letter opened doors to the seven of Hammer's former executive assistants whom Weinberg contacted.

Weinberg, former director of Investigative Reporters and Editors, also offers to show the sources relevant portions of his manuscript as an accuracy check. He makes it clear in writing that he maintains control of the content.

Requesting an interview in writing can allow you to make your best case for getting it. And an offer to allow your sources to review the story assures them that you are serious about accuracy. E-mail makes both the request and the offer simpler and faster for both parties.

Broadcast Interviews

When you're interviewing someone in front of a camera, the basic rules of interviewing for print don't change. Some of your objectives and techniques, however, do. In today's news rooms, it's likely that the television partner—a broadcast or cable station working with the newspaper—will interview a print reporter about a story she or he is working on. Also, the growing importance of streaming video online pushes more print journalists into using video cameras themselves for webcast versions of their stories.

The first thing to remember is that broadcast journalism is a performance. Television journalists, at least those who appear on camera, are performers. Sure, they have to report and write; but they also have to be able to convey their stories with both words and body language to people who are watching and listening—not reading. An important part of the television reporter's performance is the interview.

Interviews for print are often conducted to develop information that can be used in further reporting. Interviews on camera usually have a different goal. That goal is the sound bite, the few seconds of words with accompanying video that convey not information as much as emotion. Print is a medium of information; television is a medium of emotion. The best interviews for television are those that reveal how a situation feels to the participants or witnesses.

Al Tompkins, the Poynter Institute's group leader for broadcast and online journalism, offers what he calls "a new set of interviewing tools" intended to produce better storytelling for television. You can find these and other tools at **www.poynter.org**. Here are some that show both differences and similarities in print and television interviewing:

- *Ask objective and subjective questions.* To gather facts, ask objective questions: "When?" "Where?" "How much?" Subjective questions, however, usually produce the best sound bites. "Why?" "Tell me more." "Can you explain?"
- *Focus on one issue at a time.* Vague, complicated questions produce vague, complicated, hard-to-follow answers. Remember that readers can reread until they understand, but viewers can't rewind an interview. Help them follow the story by taking your interviewee through it one step at a time.
- *Ask open-ended questions.* For print, you often want a simple yes or no. That kind of answer stops a television interview. Open-ended questions encourage conversation, and conversation makes a good interview.
- *Keep questions short.* Make the interviewee do the talking. Tompkins points out that short questions are more likely to produce focused responses. They also keep the viewer's attention on the person being interviewed and what she or he has to say.
- *Build to the point.* The best interviews are like the best stories. They don't give away the punch line in the first few words. Soft, easy questions encourage relaxation and trust. Then move to the heart of the issue.
- *Be honest.* As true for television as for print and online, the importance of honesty is too often overlooked by rookie reporters. You do

neither your source nor yourself a favor if you lead the source to expect an interview about softball when you have an indictment in mind. Tell the source ahead of time that you'll want to ask some tough questions. Say, and mean, that you want to get the whole story, to be fair. Then politely but firmly dig in. As Tompkins notes, honesty has the added benefit of helping you defend yourself against any later accusations of malice.

Other Preparatory Considerations

All this homework is important, but something as trifling as your appearance may determine whether you will have a successful interview. You would hardly wear cutoff shorts into a university president's suite, and you wouldn't wear a three-piece suit to talk to underground revolutionaries. Although it is your right to wear your hair however you wish and to wear whatever clothes you want, it is the source's prerogative to refuse to talk to you.

Rick Bragg, then of the *St. Petersburg (Fla.) Times*, told the editors of *Best Newspaper Writing: 1991* that his choice of clothing was important in establishing rapport with a man whose mother had died of injuries suffered 17 years earlier. Police were investigating the death as a homicide. "I think he (the son) was more than just a little put off with how brusque some of the other reporters had been," Bragg said, "and I showed up in a pair of jeans and a T-shirt because I knew where I was going, and I didn't see much point in hiding behind a Brooks Brothers suit."

Bragg chose to fit in with the environment. That environment, too, is important. You've already heard Harrington talk about spending hours with actress Kelly McGillis at work and at her apartment. Most interviews are conducted in the source's office. However, especially if the story is a profile or a feature, it usually is better to get the source away from his or her work. If you are doing a story about a rabbi's hobby of collecting butterflies, seek a setting appropriate to the topic. Suggest meeting where the rabbi keeps his collection.

In some interviews, it would be to your advantage to get the source on neutral territory. If you have some questions for the university provost or a public official, suggest meeting in a coffee shop at a quiet time. A person feels more powerful in his or her official surroundings.

It is important, too, to let the source know how much time you and whether you expect to return for further information. And don't already know how the source might react to a tape ask when you are making the appointment.

have now done the appropriate homework. You are properly have made an appointment and told the source how much

This reporter dresses to fit in with the marchers he is interviewing; he gains their confidence by being friendly and attentive.

time you need. Before you leave, you should write down a list of questions you want to ask. The best way to encourage a spontaneous conversation is to have your questions prepared. With your questions in front of you, you'll be more relaxed. Barbara Walters once told a reporter that she writes as many as 500 questions on index cards, then selects the best ones for use during the interview.

The thinking you must do to write questions will help prepare you for the interview. Having questions prepared relieves you of the need to be mentally searching for the next question as the source is answering the last one. If you are trying to think of the next question, you will not be paying close attention to what is being said, and you might miss the most important part of the interview.

Preparing the questions for an interview is hard work, even for veterans. If you are writing for your campus newspaper, Web site or television station, seek suggestions from other staff members. You will find ideas in previous stories and your newspaper's or station's electron database. If you anticipate a troublesome interview with the chancellor, you might want to seek advice from faculty members, too. What questions would they ask if they were you? Often, they have more background knowledge, or they might have heard some of the faculty talk around campus. Staff members are also valuable sources of information.

While you may ask all of your prepared questions in some interviews, in most you probably will use only some of them. Still, you will have benefited from preparing the questions in two important ways. First, even when you don't use many, the work you did thinking of the questions helped prepare you for the interview. Second, sources who see that you have a prepared list often are impressed with your seriousness.

On the basis of the information you have gathered already, you know what you want to ask. Now you must be careful about how you ask the questions.

PHRASING QUESTIONS

A young monk who asked his superior if he could smoke while he prayed was rebuked sharply. A friend advised him to rephrase the question. "Ask him if you can pray while you smoke," he said. The young monk was discovering that how questions are structured often determines the answer. Journalists face the same challenge. Reporters have missed many stories because they didn't know how to ask questions. Quantitative researchers have shown how just a slight wording change affects the results of a survey. If you want to know whether citizens favor a city plan to beautify the downtown area, you can ask the question in several ways:

- Do you favor the city council's plan to beautify the downtown area?
- The city council plans to spend $3 million beautifying the downtown area. Are you in favor of this?
- Do you think the downtown area needs physical changes?
- Which of the following actions do you favor?
   - Building a traffic loop around the downtown area.
   - Prohibiting all automobile traffic in an area bounded by Providence Road, Ash Street, College Avenue and Elm Street.
   - Having all the downtown storefronts remodeled to carry out a single theme and putting in brick streets, shrubbery and benches.
   - None of the above.

you structure the question may affect the survey results by sev-
    rcentage points. Similarly, how you ask questions in an inter-
       v affect the response.
          he phrasing of the question, many reporters signal the
            ey expect or the prejudices they hold. For instance, a

reporter who says, "Don't you think that the city council should allocate more money to the parks and recreation department?" is not only asking a question but also influencing the source or betraying a bias. A neutral phrasing would be, "Do you think the city council should allocate more money to the parks and recreation department?" Another common way of asking a leading question is this: "Are you going to vote against this amendment like the other legislators I've talked to?"

If you have watched journalists interviewing people live on television, you have seen many examples of badly phrased questions. Many times they are not questions at all. The interviewers make statements and then put the microphone in front of the source: "You had a great game, Bill"; "Winning the election must be a great feeling." The source is expected to say something. What, precisely, do you want to know?

Sometimes a reporter unwittingly blocks a response by the phrasing of the question. A reporter who was investigating possible job discrimination against women conducted several interviews before she told her city editor she didn't think the women with whom she talked were being frank with her. "When I ask them if they have ever been discriminated against, they always tell me no. But three times now during the course of the interviews, they have said things that indicate they have been. How do I get them to tell me about it?" she asks.

"Perhaps it's the way you are asking the question," the city editor replied. "When you ask someone whether they have ever been discriminated against, you are forcing them to answer yes or no. Don't be so blunt. Ask them if others with the same qualifications at work have advanced faster than they have. Ask if they are paid the same amount as men for the same work. Ask them what they think they would be doing today if they were male. Ask them if they know of any qualified women who were denied jobs."

The city editor was giving the reporter examples of both closed- and open-ended questions. Each has its specific strengths.

Open-Ended Questions

Open-ended questions allow the respondent some flexibility. Women may not respond frankly when asked whether they have ever been discriminated against. The question calls for a yes-no response. But an open-ended question, such as "What would you be doing today if you were a man?" is not so personal. It does not sound as threatening to the respondent. In response to an open-ended question, the source often reveals more than he or she realizes or intends to.

A sportswriter who was interviewing a pro scout at a college football game wanted to know whom the scout was there to see. When the scout diplomatically declined to be specific, the reporter tried another approach. He asked a series of questions:

- "What kind of qualities does a pro scout look for in an athlete?"
- "Do you think any of the players here today have those talents?"
- "Who would you put into that category?"

The reporter worked from the general to the specific until he had the information he wanted. Open-ended questions are less direct and less threatening than questions calling for yes-no or other specific responses. They are more exploratory and more flexible. However, if you want to know a person's biographical data, don't ask "Can you tell me about yourself?"

Closed-Ended Questions

Eventually the reporter needs to close in on a subject, to pin down details, to get the respondent to be specific. **Closed-ended questions** are designed to elicit specific responses.

Instead of asking the mayor, "What did you think of the conference in Washington, D.C.?" you ask, "What did you learn in the session 'Funds You May Not Know Are Available'?" Instead of asking a previous employee to appraise the chancellor-designate's managerial abilities, you ask, "How well does she listen to the people who work for her?" "Do the people who work for her have specific job duties?" "Does she explain her decisions?"

A vague question invites a vague answer. By asking a specific question, you are more likely to get a specific answer. You are also communicating to your source that you have done your homework and that you are looking for precise details.

Knowing exactly when to ask a closed-ended question or when to be less specific is not something you can plan ahead of time. The type of information you are seeking and the chemistry between the interviewer and the source are the determining factors. You must make on-the-spot decisions. The important thing is to keep rephrasing the question until the source answers it adequately. Gary Smith wrote in *Intimate Journalism*, "A lot of my reporting comes from asking a question three different ways. Sometimes the third go at it is what produces the nugget, but even if the answers aren't wonderful or the quotes usable, they can still confirm or correct my impressions."

ABLISHING RAPPORT

rtimus, former AP reporter, has interviewed hundreds of people,
g with former President Harry S. Truman while working for
town weekly at age 14. She approached the ex-president and
se me, sir, but I'm from the local paper. Could you please

"I try never to go to an interview as a hostile antagonist. I am merely a reporter asking questions, with no ax to grind. I am a person with a family, a home, an unbalanced checkbook, a weight problem and a car that goes 'thonka-thonka-thonka' when it's cold. Unless my interview subject is Ivana Trump or Meryl Streep or Richard Nixon, my life is probably, at least in one way or two ways, similar to the person of whom I'm asking the questions."

— **Tad Bartimus,**
former AP regional reporter

"Well, young lady, what would you like to know?" Truman responded.

Years later, Bartimus recalled, "For the first time in my life, I was struck dumb. What *did* I want to know? What was I supposed to ask him? How do you do this interviewing stuff, anyway?"

Bartimus knows the answers to those questions now. One piece of advice she offered her colleagues in an article for *AP World* was to share and care. Bartimus urges reporters to reveal themselves as people. "A little empathy goes a long way to defuse (the) fear and hostility that is so pervasive against the press," she says.

Rapport—the relationship between the reporter and the source—is crucial to the success of the interview. The relationship is sometimes relaxed, sometimes strained. Often it is somewhere in between. The type of relationship you try to establish with your source is determined by the kind of story you are doing. Several approaches are possible.

Interview Approaches

For most news stories and personality profiles, the reporter benefits if the subject is at ease. Often that can be accomplished by starting off with small talk. Ask about a trophy, the plants or an engraved pen.

Former U.S. tennis star John McEnroe is now a successful sports commentator. He is shown here interviewing tennis player Lleyton Hewitt of Australia.

Bring up something humorous you have found during your research. Ask about something you know the source will want to talk about. In other interviews, if you think the subject might be skeptical about your knowledge of the field, open with a question that demonstrates your knowledge.

Reporters who can show sources what they have in common also have more success getting information. When the late Janet Chusmir was a reporter for *The Miami Herald*, she was among a group of reporters who showed up expecting to witness kidnappers returning a mother's child. The kidnappers never showed up. The police slipped the mother into the back seat of a police car and edged through the crowd. As the car went by her, Chusmir tapped on the window. The mother rolled it down slightly. "I hope you find your child," Chusmir said. The woman told her to call. Chusmir did and got an exclusive story.

One of the mistakes reporters make is not being empathetic, Chusmir said. "I genuinely feel for these people. I think sources can sense that."

Rapport also depends on where you conduct the interview. Many persons, especially those unaccustomed to being interviewed, feel more comfortable in their workplace. Go to them. Talk to the business person in the office, to the athlete in the locker room, to the conductor in the concert hall. In some cases, though, you may get a better interview elsewhere if the source cannot relax at the workplace or is frequently interrupted. Reporters have talked to politicians during car rides between campaign appearances. They've gone sailing with business people and hunting with athletes. One student reporter doing a feature on a police chief spent a weekend with the chief, who was painting his home. To do a profile, which requires more than one interview, vary the location. New surroundings can make a difference.

Scott Kraft of the Associated Press once did a story on a couple who for more than two years drove the streets of Los Angeles looking for the man who had raped their 12-year-old daughter. The search was successful.

"When I knocked on their door in May, I wanted them to know that I would be careful and honest, and I wanted them to tell me everything, even though it would probably be difficult," he wrote in *Editor & Publisher.*

Kraft conducted interviews in three locations. The first was in the 'y's living room. The second was in a car as they revisited the where the family searched. The third was by phone. Kraft said her talked more candidly on the phone after her children had chool.

are times when the reporter would rather have the source s or even scared. When you are doing an investigation, you may want the key characters to feel uneasy. You may pretend you know more than you actually do. You want them to know that the material you have is substantive and serious. Seymour Hersh, a Pulitzer Prize-winning investigative reporter, uses this tactic. *Time* magazine once quoted a government official commenting on Hersh: "He wheedles, cajoles, pleads, threatens, asks a leading question, uses little tidbits as if he knew the whole story. When he finishes you feel like a wet rag."

In some cases, however, it is better even in an investigation to take a low-key approach. Let the source relax. Talk around the subject, but gradually bring the discussion to the key issues. The surprise element may work to your favor.

So may the sympathetic approach. When the source is speaking, you may nod or punctuate the source's responses with comments such as "That's interesting." Sources who think you are sympathetic are more likely to volunteer information. Researchers have found, for instance, that a simple "mm-hmmm" affects the length of the answer interviewers get.

Other Practical Considerations

Where you sit in relation to the person you are interviewing can be important. Unless you deliberately are trying to make those interviewed feel uncomfortable, do not sit directly in front of them. Permit your sources to establish eye contact if and when they wish.

Some people are even more disturbed by the way a reporter takes notes. A tape recorder ensures accuracy of quotes, but it makes many speakers self-conscious or nervous. If you have permission to use a tape recorder, place it in an inconspicuous spot and ignore it except to make sure it is working properly. Taking notes, whether by pad and pen or electronically, may interfere with your ability to digest what is being said. But not taking any notes at all is risky. Only a few reporters can leave an interview and accurately write down what was said. Certainly no one can do it and reproduce direct quotes verbatim. You should learn shorthand or develop a note-taking system of your own.

ENSURING ACCURACY

Accuracy is a major problem in all interviews. Both the question and the answer may be ambiguous. You may not understand what is said. You may record it incorrectly. You may not know the context of the remarks. Your biases may interfere with the message.

Knowing the background of your sources, having a comfortable relationship with them and keeping good notes are importa elements of accuracy. All those were missing when a journalism student, two weeks into an internship at a major daily, interviewed the public information officer for a sheriff's department about criminal activity in and around a shelter for battered women. The reporter had never met the source, whom she interviewed by phone. She took notes on her interview with the deputy and others in whatever notebook happened to be nearby. She didn't record the time, date or even the source. There were no notes showing context, just fragments of quotes, scrawled in nearly illegible handwriting.

After the story was published, the developer of the shelter sued. Questioned by attorneys, the deputy swore that the reporter misunderstood him and used some of his comments out of context. In several cases, he contended, she completed her fragmentary notes by putting her own words in his mouth. He testified that most reporters come to see him to get acquainted. Many call back to check his quotes on sensitive or complex stories. She did neither.

When the court ordered the reporter to produce and explain her notes, she had trouble reconstructing them. She had to admit on several occasions that she wasn't sure what the fragments meant.

The accuracy of your story is only as good as your notes. David Finkel, whose story on a family's TV-watching habits became a Pulitzer Prize finalist, took extra steps to be certain his material was accurate. Observing what his subject was watching, he obtained transcripts of the shows so he could quote accurately from them. If he knew transcripts would not be available, he set his tape recorder near the television to record the program.

Some possibilities for making errors or introducing bias are unavoidable, but others are not. To ensure the most accurate and complete reporting possible, you should use all the techniques available to obtain a good interview, including observing, understanding what you hear and asking follow-up questions. Let's examine these and other techniques.

"Today one has the impression that the interviewer is not listening to what you say, nor does he think it important, because he believes that the tape recorder hears everything. But he's wrong; it doesn't hear the beating of the heart, which is the most important part of the interview."
— **Gabriel García Márquez**, Colombian writer and Nobel laureate

Observing

Some reporters look but do not see. The detail they miss may be the difference between a routine story and one that is a delight to read. Your powers of observation may enable you to discover a story beyond source's words. Is the subject nervous? What kinds of questions king home? The mayor may deny that he is going to fire the chief, but if you notice the chief's personnel file sitting on an worktable, you may have reason to continue the investi-

communicate some messages nonverbally. Researchers le to correlate some gestures with meanings. For instance, ten signal unapproachability; crossed ankles often signal tension. Many nonverbal messages, however, may not be the same for all ethnic and cultural groups. Reporters should read more about the subject.

Understanding

Understanding what you see is crucial to the news-gathering process. So is understanding what you hear. It is not enough merely to record what is being said; you must also digest it. The reporter who was investigating job discrimination was listening but not understanding. Her sources were telling her about incidents of discrimination, but all she heard were their denials.

Sometimes what you don't hear may be the message. The reporter who was trying to find out if the mayor was going to fire the police chief asked several questions about the chief's performance. What struck the reporter during the interview was the mayor's lack of enthusiasm for the chief. That unintentional tip kept the reporter working on the story until he confirmed it.

Once while interviewing Joan Fontaine, the actress, a reporter mentioned that she had a daughter about the same age as Fontaine's. Fontaine asked, "Is she jealous of you?" Listening closely, the reporter correctly deduced that Fontaine was revealing a problem of jealousy in the family, and the interview took an unexpected turn.

Asking Follow-Up Questions

If you understand what the source is saying, you can ask meaningful follow-up questions. There is nothing worse than briefing your city editor or executive producer on the interview and having the editor ask you, "Well, did you ask. . . ?" Having to say no is embarrassing.

Even if you go into an interview armed with a list of questions, the most important probably will be the ones you ask in response to an answer. A reporter who was doing a story on bidding procedures was interviewing the mayor. The reporter asked how bid specifications were written. In the course of his reply, the mayor mentioned that the president of a construction firm had assured him the last bid specifications were adequate. The alert reporter picked up on the statement:

"When did you talk to him?"

"About three weeks ago," the mayor said.

"That's before the specifications were published, wasn't it?"

"Yes, we asked him to look them over for us."

"Did he find anything wrong with the way they were written?"

"Oh, he changed a few minor things. Nothing important."

"Did officials of any other construction firms see the bid specifications before they were advertised?"

"No, he was the only one."

Gradually, on the basis of one offhand comment by the mayor, the reporter was able to piece together a solid story on the questionable relationship between the city and the construction firm.

Other Techniques

Although most questions are designed to get information, some are asked as a delaying tactic. A reporter who is taking notes may fall behind. Emily Yoffe, a senior editor of *Texas Monthly*, will say, "Hold on a second—let me get that" or "Say that again." Other questions are intended to encourage a longer response. "Go on with that" or "Tell me more about that" encourages the speaker to add more detail.

Reporters should do research after an interview to ascertain specific figures when a source provides an estimate. For example, if a shop owner says he runs one of 20 pizza parlors in town, check with the city business-license office to get the exact number.

You don't have to be stalling for time to say you don't understand. Don't be embarrassed to admit you haven't grasped something. It is better to admit to one person you don't understand than to advertise your ignorance in newsprint or on the Internet in front of millions.

Another device for making the source talk on is not a question at all; it is a pause. You are signaling the source that you expect more. But the lack of a response from you is much more ambiguous than "Tell me more about that." It may indicate that you were skeptical of what was just said, that you didn't understand, that the answer was inadequate or several other possibilities. The source will be forced to react. The only problem with this, says AP special correspondent Saul Pett, "is that it invites the dull to be dull at greater length."

Many dull interviews become interesting after they end. There are two things you should always do when you finish your questions: Check key facts, figures and quotes and then put away your pen but keep your ears open. You are not breaching any ethical rule if you continue to ask questions after you have put away your pen or turned off the tape recorder. That's when some sources loosen up.

Before you leave, ask if there's anything you forgot to ask. Put the burden on the source. You are also doing your subject a favor by giving the person a chance to contribute to the direction of the interview. You may have missed some important signals during the conversation, and now the source can be more explicit about what he or she wanted ᴏ say. Sometimes this technique leads to entirely new subjects.

Quickly review your notes and check facts, especially dates, ꜱbers, quotes, spellings and titles. Besides helping you get it right, it ꜱ the source you are careful. If necessary, arrange a time when you ꜱl to check other parts of the story or clear up questions you may ꜱou are writing. Researchers have found that more than half of ꜱotations are inaccurate, even when the interview is tape ꜱhat reflects a sloppiness that is unacceptable. Make sure ꜱexception.

ꜱtter of courtesy, tell the source when the story might

Interviewing Checklist

I. Before the interview
  A. Know the subject
     1. Seek specific information
     2. Research the subject
     3. List the questions
  B. Know the person
     1. Know salient biographical information
     2. Know person's expertise regarding subject matter
  C. Set up the interview
     1. Set the time
        a. At interviewee's convenience—but suggest a time
        b. Length of time needed
        c. Possible return visits
     2. Set the place
        a. Interviewee's turf, or
        b. Neutral turf
  D. Discuss arrangements
     1. Will you bring a tape recorder?
     2. Will you bring a photographer?
     3. Will you let interviewee check accuracy of quotes?
II. During the interview
  A. When you arrive
     1. Control the seating arrangement
     2. Place tape recorder at optimum spot
     3. Warm up person briefly with small talk
     4. Set the ground rules
        a. Put everything on the record
        b. Make everything attributable
  B. The interview itself
     1. Use good interview techniques
        a. Ask open-ended questions
        b. Allow the person to think and to speak; pause
        c. Don't be threatening in voice or manner
        d. Control the flow but be flexible
     2. Take good notes
        a. Be unobtrusive
        b. Be thorough
     3. Use the tape recorder
        a. Assume it's not working
        b. Note digital counter at important parts
  C. Before you leave
     1. Ask if there's anything interviewee wants to say
     2. Check facts—spellings, dates, statistics, quotes
     3. Set time for rechecking facts, quotes
     4. Discuss when and where interview might appear
     5. Ask if interviewee wants extra copies
III. After the interview
  A. Organize your notes—immediately
  B. Craft a proper lead
  C. Write a coherent story
  D. Check accuracy with interviewee

appear. You may even offer to send along an extra copy of the article or tape of the broadcast when it's completed.

Remember that although the interview may be over, your relationship to the source is not. When you have the story written, call the source and confirm the information. Better to discover your inaccuracies before they are published than after.

WHAT TO QUOTE DIRECTLY

Crisp, succinct, meaningful quotes spice up any story. But you can overdo a good thing. You need direct quotes in your stories, and you also need to develop skill in recognizing what is worth quoting. Let's look at the basic guidelines.

Unique Material

When you can say, "Ah, I never heard that before," you can be quite sure your readers also would like to know exactly what the speaker said. Instead of quoting someone at length, look for the kernel. Sometimes it is something surprising, something neither you nor your readers would expect that person to say. For example, when Pat Williams, then general manager of the Orlando Magic, spoke about the team's bad record, he said: "We can't win at home. We can't win on the road. As general manager, I just can't figure out where else to play." When singer Dolly Parton was asked how she felt about dumb-blond jokes, she replied: "I'm not offended at all because I know I'm not a dumb blond. I also know I'm not a blond." Striking statements like these should be quoted, but there is no reason to place simple, factual material inside quotation marks.

A direct quotation should say something significant. Also, a direct quotation should not simply repeat what has been said indirectly. It should move the story forward. Here's a passage from a *USA Today* story about a proposed law that would bar health-insurance companies, employers and managed-care plans from discriminating against people because of their genetic makeup:

> Fear of insurance discrimination based on the results of genetic tests has been on the rise for years. "It stops many people cold from getting tested," says Karen Clarke, a genetic counselor at Johns Hopkins University in Baltimore.

quotation is useful, it is informative, and it moves the story

Sometimes spoken material is unique not because of individual words that are surprising or new, but because of extended dialogue the story more effectively than writers can in their

> **Use direct quotes when**
> - *Someone says something unique.*
> - *Someone says something uniquely.*
> - *Someone important says something important.*

own words. The writer of the following story made excellent use of dialogue:

Lou Provancha pushed his wire-rimmed glasses up on his nose and leaned toward the man in the wheelchair.

"What is today, Jake?" he asked.

Jake twisted slightly and stared at the floor.

"Jake," Provancha said, "Jake, look up here."

A long silence filled the tiny, cluttered room on the sixth floor of the University Medical Center.

Provancha, a licensed practical nurse at the hospital, glanced at the reporter. "Jake was in a coma a week ago," he explained. "He couldn't talk."

Provancha pointed to a wooden board propped up on the table beside him.

"Jake, what is today? What does it say here? What is this word? I've got my finger pointed right at it."

Jake squinted at the word. With a sudden effort, like a man heaving a bag of cement mix onto a truck bed, he said, "Tuesday."

Provancha grinned. It was a small victory for them both.

The Unique Expression

When looking for quotable expressions, be on the lookout for the clever, the colorful, the colloquial. For example, an elderly man talking about his organic garden said, "It's hard to tell people to watch what they eat. You eat health, you know."

A professor lecturing on graphic design said, "When you think it looks like a mistake, it is." The same professor once was explaining that elements in a design should not call attention to themselves: "You don't walk up to a beautiful painting in someone's home and say, 'That's a beautiful frame.'"

A computer trainer said to a reporter: "Teaching kids computers is like leading ducks to water. But teaching adults computers is like trying to teach chickens to swim."

Sometimes something said uniquely is a colloquialism. Colloquialisms can add color and life to your copy. For example, a person from Louisiana may say: "I was just fixing to leave when the phone rang." A person from certain parts of Pennsylvania "makes the light out" when turning off the lights. And people in and around Fort Wayne, Ind., "redd up" the dishes after a meal, meaning that they wash them and put them where they belong.

Important Quotes by Important People

If citizen Joe Smith says, "Something must be done about this teach ers' strike," you may or may not consider it worth quoting. But if th mayor says, "Something must be done about this teachers' strik many papers would print the quote. Generally reporters quote public officials or known personalities in their news stories (though not everything the famous say is worth quoting). Remember, prominence is an important property of news.

Quoting sources that readers are likely to know lends authority, credibility and interest to your story. Presumably, a meteorologist knows something about the weather, a doctor about health, a chemistry professor about chemicals. However, it is unlikely that a television star knows a great deal about cameras, even if he or she makes commercials about cameras.

QUOTING ACCURATELY

The first obligation of any reporter is to be accurate. Before there can be any discussion of whether or how to use direct quotations, you must learn to get the exact words of the source.

It's not easy.

Scribbled notes from interviews, press conferences and meetings are often difficult to decipher and interpret. A study by Adrienne Leher, a professor of linguistics at the University of Arizona, shows only 13 of 98 quotations taken from Arizona newspapers proved to be

y County, Md., police Chief Charles Moose was the public face of s investigating the Maryland and Washington, D.C., area sniper 002. His direct, assured statements lent authority to reporters' story.

verbatim when compared to recordings. Only twice, however, were the nonverbatim quotes considered "incompatible with what was intended."

A column by Bill Hosokawa of the *Rocky Mountain News* notes the following examples of changes in a quotation from former Denver Bronco quarterback John Elway:

Rocky Mountain News	"We came out of the gate slow. I said, 'Hey, come on, man, we've got to get going here. . . . You're going to be attending my funeral if you don't.'"
The Denver Post	"I just said, 'Hey, come on man. We gotta get going here. . . . We gotta put some points on the board. You're going to be attending my funeral if you don't.'"
A second *Post* story	"In case you didn't notice it, we really came out of the blocks slow. I just said, 'Hey, come on, let's get going. You're going to attend my funeral if you don't.'"

Does it matter whether Elway said they were slow coming out of the gate or out of the blocks? Perhaps not. But one thing's for sure, he said one or the other. One is correct, and the other is not.

Your passion for accuracy should compel you to get and record the exact words. Only then can you decide which words to put between quotation marks.

Verification

"When you see yourself quoted in print and you're sorry you said it, it suddenly becomes a misquotation."

— *Dr. Laurence J. Peter,*
author of Peter's Quotations
and The Peter Principle

When someone important says something important but perhaps false, just putting the material in quotes does not relieve you of responsibility for the inaccuracies. Citizens, officials and candidates for office often say things that may be partially true or altogether untrue and perhaps even libelous. Quotations, like any other information you gather, need verification.

During Sen. Joseph McCarthy's investigations into communism and espionage in the 1950s, many newspapers, in the interest of strict objectivity, day after day quoted the Wisconsin senator's charges and countercharges. Some publishers did this because they agreed with his stance and because his remarks sold newspapers. Few papers thought it was their responsibility to quote others who were pointing out the obvious errors and inconsistencies in the demagogue's remarks. Today, however, in the interest of balance, fairness and objectivity, many media sources leave out, correct or point out the errors in some quotations. This may be done in the piece itself or in an accompanying story.

If candidate Billy Joe Harkness says that his opponent Jimbo McGown is a member of the Ku Klux Klan, you should check before you print the charge. Good reporters don't stop looking and checking just because someone gives them some information. Look for yourself.

Prisoners may have an altogether different account of a riot from the one the prison officials give you. Your story will not be complete unless you talk to all sides.

Correcting Quotes

When do you, or should you, correct grammatical errors in a direct quotation? Should you expect people in news conferences or during informal interviews to speak perfect English? Journalists of an earlier generation routinely corrected the garbled syntax used in news conferences by President Dwight Eisenhower. Today, changed standards and live television have made President George W. Bush's adventures with the language common knowledge.

Although quotation marks mean you are capturing the exact language of a speaker, it is accepted practice in many news rooms to correct mistakes in grammar and to convey a person's remarks in complete sentences. None of us regularly speaks in perfect, grammatical sentences. But if we were instead writing down our remarks, presumably we would write in grammatically correct English.

Reporters and editors differ widely on when or even whether to do this. A reporter for the *Rocky Mountain News* quoted an attorney as saying, "Her and John gave each other things they needed and couldn't get anyplace else." The reporter said the quote was accurate but, on second thought, said it might have been better to correct the grammar in the written account.

Most papers have no written policy on correcting grammatical errors in direct quotations. Because so many variables are involved, these matters are handled on a case-by-case basis. Some argue you should sacrifice a bit of accuracy in the interest of promoting proper English. However, some would let public figures be embarrassed by quoting them using incorrect grammar.

Columnist James Kilpatrick asks, "When we put a statement (of a public figure) in direct quotation marks, must it be exactly what was said? My own answer is yes. On any issue of critical substance, we ought not to alter a single word." Yet, in another matter in a different column, Kilpatrick writes, "It is all very well to *tidy up a subject's syntax* (italics added) and to eliminate the ahs, ers and you-knows, but direct quotation marks are a reporter's iron-clad, honor-bound guarantee that something was actually said."

At times it may be necessary to illustrate a person's flawed use of language. In some cases, you may wish to use the word "sic" in parentheses to note the error, misuse or peculiarity of the quotation. "Sic," Latin for "thus," indicates that a statement was originally spoken or written exactly as quoted. It is particularly important to use "sic" for improper or unusual use of language when you are quoting a written source.

And if you think there is some agreement on the subject of correcting grammar in direct quotations, read what *The Associated Press Stylebook and Briefing on Media Law* (2002) says:

> Never alter quotations even to correct minor grammatical errors or word usage. Casual minor tongue slips may be removed by using ellipses but even that should be done with extreme caution. If there is a question about a quote, either don't use it or ask the speaker to clarify.

Correcting quotations is even more difficult for radio and television reporters. That's why they don't worry about it as much. Online and print writers and editors might remember that the quotation they use may have been heard by millions of people on radio or television. Changing the quote even slightly might make viewers and listeners question the credibility of print and online reports. They might also ask why print and online writers feel the need to act as press agents who wish to make their subjects look good.

That applies to celebrities of all kinds, but it might also apply to registered political candidates and elected officials. At least, some argue, news agencies should have some consistency. If a reporter quotes a farmer using incorrect grammar, then should the same be done for the mayor or for a college professor?

A letter in *The Washington Post* criticized the newspaper for quoting exactly a mother of 14 children who was annoyed at Mayor Marion Barry's advice to stop having babies. The quote read: "And your job is to open up all those houses that's boarded up." The writer then accused the *Post* of regularly stringing together quotes of the president to make him appear articulate. The writer concluded: "I don't care whether the *Post* polishes quotes or not. I simply think that everyone—black or white, rich or poor, president or welfare mother—deserves equal treatment."

That's good advice.

Suggested Readings

Biagi, Shirley. *Interviews That Work*. Belmont, Calif.: Wadsworth, 1992. A complete guide to interviewing techniques. The instruction is interspersed with interviews of journalists describing their techniques.

Burgoon, Judee K. and Saine, Thomas J. *The Unspoken Dialogue: An Introduction to Nonverbal Communication*. Boston: Houghton Mifflin, 1978. An excellent look at the subject for readers who are not acquainted with the field.

Germer, Fawn. "Are Quotes Sacred?" *American Journalism Review*, Sept. 1995, pp. 34-37. Many views of all sides of whether and when to change quotes.

Gottlieb, Martin. "Dangerous Liaisons." *Columbia Journalism Review*, July/Aug. 1989, pp. 21-35. In this excellent debate over whether interviewers betray sources, Gottlieb interviews several authors.

Harrington, Walt. *American Profiles*. Columbia, Mo.: University of Missouri Press, 1992. Fifteen excellent profiles and the author's explanation of how and why he does what he does.

Malcolm, Janet. *The Journalist and the Murderer.* New York: Knopf, 1990. Using the Joe McGinnis-Jeffrey MacDonald case, the author accuses all journalists of being "confidence men" who betray their sources.

Metzler, Ken. *The Writer's Guide to Gathering Information by Asking Questions,* Third Edition.

Boston: Allyn and Bacon, 1997. An invaluable in-depth look at problems of interviewing.

Weinberg, Steve. "Thou Shalt Not Concoct Thy Quote." *Fineline,* July/Aug. 1991, pp. 3-4. Presents reasons for allowing sources to review quotations before publication.

Suggested Web Sites

www.poynter.org

We send you to this extremely useful site repeatedly. This time, go to the "Resource Center" section, and check out the bibliography of articles, both scholarly and professional, and books on interviewing. Print, television and online are all included.

www.newslab.org

This site is an excellent source of tips on television. NewsLab works with television news rooms to find better ways of telling complex stories.

www.cjr.org

This is the site of the *Columbia Journalism Review.* Go to the "Search" function and enter "Interviewing." You'll get a list of articles you can then scan.

www.ajr.org

This is the site of the *American Journalism Review.* Follow the same procedure as for CJR, above. In both cases, you'll find a variety of references.

Exercises

1. Learn to gather background on your sources. Write a memo of up to two pages about your state's senior U.S. senator. Concentrate on those details that will allow you to focus on how the senator views the pro-life versus pro-choice issue. Indicate the sources of your information. Do an Internet search on the senator.

2. List five open-ended questions you would ask the senator.

3. List five closed-ended questions you would ask the senator.

4. Interview a student also enrolled in this reporting class. Write a two- to three-page story. Be sure to focus on one aspect of the student's life.

Ask your classmate to read the story and to mark errors of fact and perception. The instructor will read your story and the critique.

5. Using the resources suggested above and any others you can find, do a database search for articles about journalists' use of anonymous sources. Write a short report on your findings.

6. Attend a meeting, a press conference or a speech, and tape-record it. While there, write down the quotes you would use if you were writing the story for your local news source. Then listen to the tape, and check the accuracy of the quotes. What do you learn?

4 Computer-Assisted Reporting

Computers have revolutionized reporting in the United States. A good example comes from KMOL-TV in San Antonio, Texas, which documented the fact that thousands of accused criminals in Bexar County were getting off the hook because the court system could not move fast enough.

When KMOL reporters started investigating the court system, they asked officials to produce all court records by providing them electronically. What should have been a simple request to extract data from the court's computer system became a major undertaking. First the county demanded $17,000 for the data, an amount that was reduced to $2,000 after negotiations. When the court system continued to drag its feet, KMOL finally hired the programmers who extracted the required data. The cost was only $1,000, but a year had been lost by the time the data finally arrived. It took another four months to analyze the data and produce the stories, but what KMOL found was startling: Judges were dismissing thousands of criminal cases simply because they could not get the cases to court in the overloaded court system.

KMOL compared the Bexar County data to similar data in the state's other metropolitan areas and found nothing comparable. As a result, the station documented to the public the sad state of Bexar County's criminal justice system. It came as a huge surprise to many in the county.

That is merely one example of how the best reporters have embraced the considerable capability of personal computer technology. Once honed almost exclusively by investigative reporters, computer skills are now vital in all areas of the news business. Today, no reporter who hopes to succeed in the profession can afford to be without skills in searching internal and external computer databases and building his or her own databases and spreadsheets. These skills, in addition to more traditional library search skills, are among the essential tools of today's working journalist. Like the carpenter who must know how to use a hammer and saw, the journalist must know how to use words and computers.

Fine-tuning computer skills is the topic of entire books and college courses. In this chapter, however, you will be introduced to the most common computer-assisted techniques employed by reporters and editors.

> **In this chapter you will learn:**
>
> 1. The main sources of information available on computer.
> 2. How computers assist with data analysis.
> 3. The importance of more traditional sources of information.

SOURCES OF COMPUTER INFORMATION

Reporters and editors of today have a wealth of information available at their fingertips. To access it, you must have the right equipment and software, and you must be comfortable with using computers. In addi-

Primary sources of computerized information

- *The morgue.*
- *The public information utilities.*
- *The Internet.*
- *The commercial database services.*
- *Government databases.*
- *Special-interest-group databases.*
- *CD-ROMs.*
- *Self-constructed databases.*

tion to making raw data available, computers help reporters organize and analyze information.

From the news library in your local office to national databases of published newspaper, magazine and broadcast stories, the amount of information online is staggering. Primary sources of computerized information include:

- The news library maintained by your own publication or radio or television station (often called the **morgue**).
- Public information utilities (such as CompuServe, America Online and The Microsoft Network).
- The Internet.
- Commercial database services (such as Lexis/Nexis).
- Government databases (city, county, state and federal).
- Special-interest-group databases (those created by organizations with a cause).
- CD-ROMs.
- Self-constructed databases (those you compile from information you have gathered) and spreadsheets.

Let's explore the usefulness of each.

Your News Library: The Place to Start

Computer databases are a 20th-century marvel that good reporters and editors have learned to cherish. Before they were available, doing research for a story was a laborious process that involved a trip to the newspaper, magazine or television station library to sift through hundreds or even thousands of tattered, yellowed clippings and videotapes. Too often, clippings and videotapes disappeared, were misfiled or were misplaced, making such research a hit-and-miss proposition. Despite those shortcomings, the library was considered a valuable asset. Reporters were routinely admonished, "When you are assigned to a story, first check the library to see what's already been written about the subject."

You will still hear that advice in news rooms today, but many of today's news libraries are computerized, which almost ensures that an item will not disappear and will be easier to locate. Typically, you can do a check of the computerized library from your own computer, which makes it easier than ever to do good background work on a story. Your ability to search the library is limited only by your skill with search techniques.

News libraries are what computer experts call **full-text databases,** which means that all words in the database have been indexed and are searchable. Such capability gives you incredible flexibility when using what are known as **Boolean search commands** to structure searches.

Boolean operators such as AND, OR and NOT allow you to structure the search to find material most closely related to the subject being researched.

For example, if you are interested in finding articles on former South African President Nelson Mandela's visits to the United States, you might issue this command on the search line:

```
Mandela AND United ADJ States
```

The computer would then search for all articles that contain the word "Mandela" and also contain the words "United" and "States" adjacent to each other. In this example, AND and ADJ (for "adjacent to") are the Boolean operators used. Such a search would produce all articles on Mandela and the United States but would exclude any articles involving Mandela and the United Arab Emirates, despite the presence of the word "United" (it's not adjacent to the word "States").

The result of such a search in most cases would be a report from the computer telling you how many articles match your search criteria:

```
Search found 27 articles. Would you like to see them
or further narrow your search?
```

At this point, you would have the option of further limiting the search (by date, for example) or reading all 27 articles.

It is important to remember that computers don't know everything. In our sample search, an article on Mandela's visit to Miami that did not contain the words "United States" would not have been found. Therefore, it is important to understand the limitations as well as the power of computer-assisted database searching. Good reporters quickly learn to take into account such possibilities and learn to recast their searches in other ways.

There are other limitations. Many library databases do not allow you to see photos, nor can you see articles as they appeared in the newspaper or magazine. Nor do most current systems permit you to hear how a television story was used on the air. Instead, you have access only to a text-based version of what appeared. That limits your ability to learn how the story was displayed in the newspaper or magazine or how it was read on the air. If necessary, however, you can always resort to looking up the original in bound volumes or on microfilm. Most newspapers save old editions in one or both of those forms. Many radio and television stations maintain videotape libraries of old newscasts. While these older forms of storage may be less convenient to use, taking the time to do so is often worth the effort.

Some newer library computer systems overcome the traditional disadvantages of computerization by allowing you to call graphical reproductions of the printed page to the screen. You can view pho-

---

Screen or paper: Which is better?

A 1993 study by Finnish researchers is believed to be the first to compare the difficulty of reading text on a computer screen to reading that same text on paper. On average, readers read text on paper 16 to 19 percent faster than on a computer.

Surprisingly, texts read from the screen and on paper were remembered equally well across all demographic groups tested, and in some cases text on screen was remembered even better.

As screen technology continues to improve, however, the ease of reading from a computer is expected to increase, and the advantages of reading on paper are expected to diminish.

tographs, charts and maps in the same way. In television applications, more and more libraries permit storage of digital video and sound clips. As such systems proliferate, the shortcomings of present computer libraries will disappear. Despite current limitations, few veteran reporters would be willing to return to the days of tattered yellow clippings. They know that computerization has made the library a more reliable source of background information.

Thus, the best reporters of today do what good reporters have always done: Check the library first. They simply do it with computers.

The Public Information Utilities

Some might consider it strange to think of CompuServe (www.compuserve.com), America Online (www.aol.com), Prodigy (www.prodigy.com) and The Microsoft Network (www.msn.com) as useful sources of information for reporters. Don't tell that to reporters who use them.

The PIUs are access providers for the general public, but they also contain lots of content found nowhere else, including forums (or electronic bulletin boards) for discussions on topics ranging from genealogy to stamp collecting to sports. Forum participants exchange messages on every conceivable topic. Some even write computer software that facilitates the pursuit of their passion, and they frequently make that software available to others interested in the topic.

Such forums are a fertile source of information for reporters attempting to research a story. If you are assigned to do a story on genealogy and know nothing about the subject, what better way to gauge the pulse of those passionate about the subject than by tapping into their discussions? By logging on to one of the public information utilities, you can do just that.

Or, if you are seeking to interview those who participated in World War II's Battle of the Bulge, try posting a request for names on one of these services. Chances are you will be inundated with names and telephone numbers of individuals or various veterans' groups that would be delighted to help.

The popularity of such services is almost impossible to overstate. What people like about the public information utilities is that they do what radio talk shows do—give people a forum in which to exchange ideas with those who share similar interests. Writing in *Editor & Publisher*, Barry Hollander, a journalism professor at the University of Georgia, contrasts the skyrocketing popularity of talk radio with the continuing decline of newspaper circulation:

Newspapers used to be an important part of what bound communities together, a common forum for ideas and discussion. But as communities fragmented along racial and demographic lines, newspapers have done a better job of chronicling the decline than offering ways to offset the trend.

A sense of connection is needed. Newspapers, and (their) electronic editions in particular, offer one opportunity to bring people together in ways similar to talk radio.

Over the years, newspapers, magazines and radio and television stations have attempted to connect with their readers and listeners by doing people-on-the-street interviews. Interviewing people at random seldom produces good results because often those interviewed know nothing about the topic or don't care. By tapping into the forums on the public information utilities, you are assured of finding knowledgeable, conversant people to interview.

But the public information utilities are much more than a good source of people to interview. Most have news from various newspapers and wire services, and information on subjects as diverse as travel and where to attend college. Most also have the full text of an encyclopedia online. Some contain photos as well.

The oldest such service is CompuServe, which contains a large number of forums and carries the archives of several major newspapers and the current Associated Press wire. CompuServe also was the first of the PIUs to expand outside the United States. It is quite popular in Europe, especially in Germany, and has some foreign-language services.

Some television networks have chosen to form alliances with the PIUs. CBS News has allied with America Online in addition to providing a substantial Web site of its own. Other traditional media outlets have chosen to create their own public information utilities, often referred to as **community portals.** Newspapers often try to become the leading source of community information with Internet sites quite similar to the national PIUs. Television and radio stations are similarly engaged.

All of these initiatives represent efforts to expand services and to explore ways to reconnect with the public. With their huge amounts of easily accessible material, they are also useful sources of information for reporters and editors.

The Internet

When a little-known California-based cult called Heaven's Gate staged a mass suicide, newspapers and broadcast stations had no trouble finding background data on the group. The Heaven's Gate site on the Internet gave reporters a mother lode of information about the sect and its leader.

describes what attracted him to a non-traditional news job upon leaving college:

"The line between journalist and reader will blur as technology evolves. The amount of information available will be staggering. Traditional news sources will be challenged by anyone who has access to a computer, a television or even a telephone.

"To be a journalist in the new media, you must think of news as information. You must be able to present information over different media, whether it be a computer, a television, a telephone or a newspaper. But most importantly, you must not forget what you learned in your journalism classes: Present reliable, well-written information in an easy-to-read format—or the reader will go elsewhere."

Established by the *San Jose Mercury News,* **MercuryNews.com** is a substantial Internet resource for both national news and regional coverage of Northern California.

That incident illustrates what a powerful new source of information the Internet has become. It also is a publishing medium and the forerunner of the information superhighway envisioned by former Vice President Al Gore. Soon after Gore took office in 1993, it became evident that construction of the information superhighway was already under way in the form of the Internet, originally a creation of the federal government and universities in the United States. The Internet has now spread worldwide.

The Internet is not a single computer network but rather a series of interconnected networks throughout the world. That arguably makes it the world's first truly international news medium. Commercial content initially was banned, but now more than half of the Internet's users are estimated to be employees at companies throughout the world. The presence of advertising on the Internet initially sparked controversy but has gradually come to be accepted.

Evaluating Links

The Internet is a great resource for reporters, but determining the credibility of information you get there can be problematic. If the source is a respected media organization such as *The New York Times* or *The Washington Post,* chances are the information is solid. But if it is published by an organization promoting a cause, there is ample reason to be wary.

Pierre Salinger, a respected news veteran and former press secretary to President John F. Kennedy, was ridiculed when he publicly proclaimed that a document blaming the U.S. government for shooting down a TWA jetliner was authored by the French intelligence service. The document, found on the World Wide Web, was a fake.

Stan Ketterer, a journalist and journalism educator, tells reporters to evaluate information on the Web by following the same standard journalistic practices that they would use for assessing the credibility and the accuracy of any information. There are also a few evaluative tools that are unique to the Web. To provide guidance, Ketterer developed these guidelines:

- Before using information from a Web site in a story, verify it with a source. There are exceptions to this rule. They include taking information from a highly credible government site like the Census Bureau or time constraints that prevent you from contacting the source on a breaking story. An editor must clear all exceptions.
- In most cases, information taken directly from the Web and used in a story must be attributed. If you have verified the information on a home page with a source, you can use the organization in the attribution, for example, "according to the EPA" or "EPA figures show." If you cannot verify the information after trying repeatedly, attribute unverified information to the Web page, for example, "according to the Voice of America's site on the World Wide Web." Consult your editor before using unverified information.
- If you have doubts about the accuracy of the information and you cannot reach the source, get it from another source, such as a book or another contact person. When in doubt, omit the information.
- Check the extension on the site's Internet address to get clues as to the nature of the organization and the likely slant of the information. The most common extensions used in the United States are .gov (government), .edu (education), .com (commercial), .mil (military), .org (not-for-profit organization) and .net (Internet administration). Most of the government and military sites have credible and accurate information. In many cases, you can take the information directly from the site and attribute it to the organization. But consult your editor until you get to know these sites.
- The same is true for many of the sites of colleges and universities. If college and university sites have source documents, such as the Constitution, attribute the information to the source document. But beware. Personal home pages have .edu extensions, and the information is not always credible. Do not use information from a personal home page without contacting the person and without the permission of an editor.
- In almost all cases, *do not* take information directly from the home pages of commercial and not-for-profit organizations and use it without verification. Verify and attribute all information on those pages.
- Check the date when the page was last updated. The date generally appears at the top or the bottom on the first page of the site. Although a recent date

> does not ensure that the information is current, it does indicate that the organization is paying close attention to the site. If no date appears, if the site has not been updated for a while or if it was created some time ago, do not use the information unless you verify it with a source.
>
> Using the Internet as a source of information is no riskier than using books, magazines or other printed material, provided you use common sense. And remember that material on the Internet is subject to copyright laws (for guidance on that subject, see Chapter 14).

For the journalist, the Internet serves two primary purposes:

- It is an increasingly robust source of information, including federal, state and local government data, and information published by companies on almost any imaginable topic. Need information on a new drug? Chances are you can find it on the Internet, complete with more detail than you ever wanted to know. Need to know about Estonia? Plenty of Web sites are available to tell you what you need to know or to give you the latest news from Tallinn, its capital. Further, many North American newspapers, magazines and broadcast stations have a substantial Internet presence, sometimes complete with libraries of previously published stories. Some experts, in fact, now refer to the Internet as the world's largest library. That's good stuff for a reporter who needs to do a quick bit of research to provide background material or context for a news story.
- It is a publishing medium that offers new opportunities for media companies and journalists, and new jobs for journalism and mass communications graduates. In recent years, media companies large and small alike have rushed to establish a presence on the Web. Media companies also use the Internet to attract readers and viewers to their more profitable traditional products.

Just as on the public information utilities, forums for exchange of ideas and information are the Internet's most popular item. But the Internet's forums are far more comprehensive than those on the PIUs. You can find forums on topics as diverse as journalism in the Balkan countries and the French film industry.

Most cities of any size have Internet providers who sell access to the system at nominal rates, and several nationwide companies do the same. High-speed services offered by cable television and telephone companies provide access at incredible speed. This has made it easy for newspapers, magazines and broadcast stations to provide Internet access for every reporter in their news rooms. It also has made it simple for consumers to tap this valuable resource.

Some observers of the media industry believe that in the future much news and information will be consumed through an information appliance in the home capable of giving the consumer a choice of full-text, full-motion video and audio. Imagine a computer capable of providing high-quality television, and the possibilities become clear. On one device you could read the text of a presidential address or see it being delivered. On that same device, you might later watch a movie or order your groceries.

That's the information superhighway envisioned by so many, and the Internet is its forerunner. The wise journalist is in touch with what's possible today while waiting for the full potential of this powerful new medium to develop. Already it is the source of many jobs for journalists.

The Commercial Database Services

When newspapers and magazines entered the computer era in the early 1970s, publishers were quick to realize the potential value of saving and reselling previously published information. Newspapers and magazines quickly began selling access to their archives by establishing alliances with companies founded for that purpose.

On many topics, searching your own news library will not be sufficient. If U.S. Rep. Barney Frank is making his first appearance in your community and you have been assigned to cover him, your morgue probably won't help; little will have been written about him in your city. It probably will be much more useful to read recent articles published in Frank's home state of Massachusetts. By doing so, you will be armed with questions to ask about recent events of interest to him. In such situations, the national commercial databases such as Lexis/Nexis are invaluable.

Government Databases

For years, government agencies have maintained large databases of information as a means of managing the public's business. They cover almost every conceivable service that government offers, from airplane registration and maintenance records to census data to local court records. They are maintained not only by the federal and state governments but also by even the smallest of city and county agencies.

Because most of these databases were begun many years ago, they often reside on large mainframe computers or on dedicated minicomputers. Data are stored in various file formats, and it often is difficult to access the information. Independent analyses of the data once were impossible because they were controlled by government agencies. Further, few newspapers had the resources or the computers on which to do independent analyses.

The growth of commercial databases is a great asset to reporters, who easily can see what has been written about a subject in other newspapers. But there are some potential problems if you use excerpts from those stories:

- *Copyright laws must be obeyed. Take care not to use too much material without obtaining permission. The fair-use provision of copyright law is vague and confusing about how much is too much. In general, the quoted material must be a small portion of the original work.*
- *Not all articles that appeared in a newspaper can be found in a database. Wire service and market reports, death notices, box scores, social announcements and items written by freelancers often are excluded.*
- *Searching for information with Boolean commands has obvious limitations. Some sports stories, for example, never mention the sport but assume the reader will recognize the team names and make the association. As a result, if you search for all stories on soccer, there's no*

guarantee you'll find them all.

- *An account may have been published, but that doesn't mean it is accurate. History is littered with incidents of newspapers quoting each other's inaccuracies.*
- *You seldom have a good idea whether the reporter who wrote an account has any real knowledge of the subject matter. If you lift information from that reporter without such knowledge, you may introduce an inaccuracy.*
- *Databases aren't infallible. The information in them is entered by humans, who are susceptible to mistakes. Some material is even deliberately misleading. Databases occasionally are doctored in an attempt to prove a position or promote a cause.*

After the introduction of personal computers in the early 1980s, reporters began finding ways to interpret mainframe data. A breakthrough technology involved the purchase of nine-track mainframe data tapes from government agencies and subsequent analysis on personal computers equipped with nine-track drives. Newspapers using this technique started to win Pulitzer prizes, and soon the National Institute for Computer-Assisted Reporting was established at the University of Missouri to spread the word about the technique. Suddenly, reporters had the technology at their disposal to make better use of existing open-records laws at both state and federal levels. Today, more and more government agencies are putting data directly on the Internet **(www.thomas.loc.gov).**

Among the reporters taking advantage of the technology is Penny Loeb of *U.S. News and World Report.* When she worked for *Newsday* (New York), she used a computer analysis of tax and property records to reveal an astounding story: New York City owed $275 million to taxpayers as a result of overpayments on real estate, water and sewer taxes. To get that story, Loeb had to analyze millions of computer records. Doing that by hand would have consumed a lifetime, but with the assistance of a computer, Loeb accomplished the task in a matter of weeks.

Still, Loeb cautions against expecting instant stories:

> Don't just go get a computer tape and expect a great story. You need a tip that there is a problem that computerized data can confirm. Or you may have seen a problem occur repeatedly, such as sentencing discrimination. The computer can quantify the scope.

Analyses of this type usually are done with **relational database programs.** Relational database programs, unlike simpler **flat-file databases,** permit the user to compare one set of data to another. A classic example would be to compare a database of a state's licensed school-bus drivers to another database of the state's drunken-driving convictions. The result would be a list of school bus drivers guilty of such offenses.

After the introduction of this technology, investigative reporters were the first to use it. But once such databases are placed in easily accessible computer form, you can use them in your day-to-day work just as easily. For example, you might want to analyze federal records on airplane maintenance to produce a story on the safety record of a particular airline. If the records are maintained in an easily accessible format, the next time an airplane crashes it will be possible to call up the complete maintenance record of the aircraft merely by entering the plane's registration number. Such information can be extremely useful, even in a deadline situation.

Another common use of computers has been to compare bank records on home mortgages to census data. By tracking how many mortgages are issued to homeowners in predominantly black or Hispanic areas, reporters have been able to document the practice of redlining, through which banks make it difficult or impossible for minorities to obtain loans.

Again, such records are useful even after the investigation is complete. Access to driver's-license records, census data, bank records and other forms of data can be used daily to produce news stories, charts, maps and other graphic devices. Numbers can be useful in helping to tell a story. They can be particularly effective if used as the basis for charts to illustrate the impact of the numbers.

Special-Interest-Group Databases

Numerous special-interest groups have discovered the usefulness of placing information in computerized databases, and they are eager to make journalists aware of the existence of that information. Some of that material may be quite useful; indeed, it may be unobtainable from other sources. But just as journalists must be wary of press releases issued by organizations promoting a cause, they must be equally wary of information in such databases. It is important to remember that organizations of this type will promote their perspective on a topic, often without any concern for balancing the information with opposing views.

CD-ROMs as a Source of Information

During the past few years massive amounts of information stored on compact discs have become a terrific new source of reference. Encyclopedias, dictionaries, telephone directories, census data and thousands of other titles are available on CD-ROMs, which serve as an efficient and inexpensive way to store vast amounts of information. One such title is the *CIA World Fact Book*, which lists detailed information on each nation in the world. CD-ROM titles can be quick and effective references for the journalist on deadline.

Self-Constructed Databases

Reporters occasionally find that the data they want cannot be obtained from government agencies or private businesses. Despite open-records laws at the federal and state levels, public officials often find ways to

---

Building a database library

Many newspapers and magazines have begun to create large libraries of databases gleaned from public agencies. George Landau, a reporter for the St. Louis Post-Dispatch, became so intrigued by the idea that he left the newspaper to create his own consulting firm, NewsEngin Inc., to spread the idea throughout the country.

Landau continues to work with the Post-Dispatch, *which has a goal of adding a database to its collection every couple of weeks. Typical databases include records of those who have been in the state's correctional system, city and county assessors' records, campaign finance records and real estate sales information.*

"What we try to do is put up records that a reporter on deadline is going to need," Landau said.

Similar efforts are under way nationwide at papers ranging from the Sacramento Bee to the Buffalo News and the Baltimore Sun.

stall or avoid giving reporters what they want and need. Further, some things aren't available in databases.

Reporters who find themselves in that predicament sometimes resort to analyzing data after entering it by hand. When Elliot Grossman of *The Allentown (Pa.) Morning Call* tried to document abuses of parking privileges by local police officers, he sifted through thousands of paper records to prepare his story. Grossman discovered that over the years a scam had allowed hundreds of police officers to park their private cars almost anywhere simply by signing the backs of the tickets and sending them to the Allentown Parking Authority.

Some data on parking tickets were available on computer, but the Parking Authority refused to release the computer tapes necessary for a quick analysis. So Grossman, with the help of a news clerk and reporting interns, decided to do it the hard way. He set out to build his own database to document the extent of the problem.

For two weeks, Grossman and his helpers sat at laptop computers in the offices of the Parking Authority and entered data on the type of violation, location of the vehicle, date and time of violation and license-plate number. In many cases, other notations were made on the officer's badge number or the reason the officer was parked at the location. The result was a body of information that allowed Grossman to confirm his suspicions that many of the tickets were dismissed without good reason.

That's a time-consuming process, but it can be effective. If your knowledge of computer programs is limited, consult with computer experts in your news organization. They will be able to recommend an appropriate tool.

If much of what you are indexing contains textual material, you will need a **free-form database.** A popular program of that type among reporters is AskSam, which has been adopted by many of the nation's leading investigative reporters. AskSam makes it easy to construct a database of quotations, notes or similar material. Many database programs do not handle such material so easily.

If you need to create a simple list of names, addresses and telephone numbers, a flat-file database might be best. Relational database comparisons, as we have discussed, require more sophisticated programs such as Microsoft's FoxPro or Borland's Quattro Pro.

Many reporters also are turning to **spreadsheets** to help them sort through the complexity of government or corporate financial data. A business reporter might use a spreadsheet program to spot trends in the allocation of resources or changes in sources of income. After you have collected data covering several years, a spreadsheet program, which can easily create graphs from the data, makes it easy to notice trends that otherwise might go undetected.

Similarly, the government reporter might use a spreadsheet to spot changes in allocations to various city, county, state or federal departments or agencies.

New uses of computers in the coverage of news are being tried daily. Today's best reporters keep abreast of technology for that reason. For help, see the Web site of Investigative Reporters and Editors (www.ire.org).

TRADITIONAL SOURCES OF INFORMATION

As critical as the use of computers may be in modern journalism, traditional sources of information—reference books, dictionaries, encyclopedias—still play an important role in the production of the daily news product. Good reporters and editors make a habit of checking every verifiable fact. Sometimes those facts are checked in computer databases; more often they are checked in books. Many sources of information are now available in either form. Here is a list of 20 commonly used references:

- City directories. These directories, not to be confused with telephone books, can be found in most cities. They provide the same information as the telephone directory but also may provide information on the occupations of citizens and the owners or managers of businesses. Useful street indexes provide information on the names of next-door neighbors. Some are now available on CD-ROM.
- Local and area telephone directories. Used for verifying the spelling of names and addresses, these directories usually are reliable but are not infallible. Remember that people move and have similar names. Almost all telephone numbers in North America are now listed on various Internet-based services.
- Maps of the city, county, state, nation and world. Local maps usually are posted in the news room. Others may be found in atlases, on CD-ROMs or on the Internet.
- State manuals. Each state government publishes a directory that provides useful information on various government agencies. These directories sometimes list the salaries of all state employees. To date, few are online.
- *Bartlett's Familiar Quotations* (Little, Brown).
- *Congressional Directory* (U.S. Government Printing Office). Profiles of members of Congress.
- *Congressional Record* (U.S. Government Printing Office). Complete proceedings of the U.S. House and Senate.

■ *Current Biography* (Wilson). Profiles of prominent persons, published monthly.
■ *Dictionary of American Biography* (Scribner's).
■ *Facts on File* (Facts on File Inc.). Weekly compilation of news from metropolitan newspapers.
■ *Guinness Book of World Records* (Guinness Superlatives). World records listed in countless categories.
■ *National Trade and Professional Associations of the United States* (Columbia Books, Washington, D.C.).
■ *Readers' Guide to Periodical Literature* (Wilson). Index to magazine articles on a host of subjects.
■ *Statistical Abstract of the United States* (U.S. Government Printing Office). Digest of data collected and published by all federal agencies.
■ *Webster's New Biographical Dictionary* (Merriam-Webster).
■ *Webster's New World College Dictionary*, Fourth Edition (Macmillan). Primary reference dictionary recommended by both the Associated Press and United Press International.
■ *Webster's Third New International Dictionary* (Merriam-Webster). Unabridged dictionary recommended by AP and UPI.
■ *Who's Who* (Bedford/St. Martin's). World listings.
■ *Who's Who in America* (Marquis). Biennial publication.
■ *World Almanac and Book of Facts* (Newspaper Enterprise Association). Published annually.

Those useful publications, and many others like them, enable reporters to verify data and to avoid the unnecessary embarrassment caused by errors in print.

Eleven sources of story ideas

1. *Other people.*
2. *Other publications and television.*
3. *News releases.*
4. *A social services directory.*
5. *Government reports.*
6. *Stories in your local newspaper or on television.*
7. *Advertisements.*
8. *Wire copy.*
9. *Local news briefs.*
10. *The Internet.*
11. *You.*

FINDING THE STORY

Computer databases, reference books, CD-ROMs and similar resource materials not only serve as excellent sources of background material for journalists but also serve as sources of ideas for stories.

Not every story is dumped into a reporter's lap. Editors provide some ideas; readers provide others. Most ideas, though, are the result of an active imagination, a lively curiosity and a little help from friends. Journalists soon learn how stories written for other publications can be recast for their own. They get in the habit of carrying a little notebook to jot down ideas when something somebody says strikes a responsive chord.

But even for good journalists, the wellspring of ideas sometimes dries up. Bank these sources of story ideas, good for any time and any place, for the day that happens to you:

- *Other people*. As a journalist you meet many people. What are they talking about when they aren't talking business? What have they heard lately? Journalists have to listen, even when it means eaves-dropping while having a cup of coffee. What interests people? There is no better source of story ideas than the people you meet while you are off-duty. They are, after all, your readers or listeners.
- *Other publications and television*. Stories are recycled across the country. Read other newspapers, magazines, books, pamphlets, and the magazines and newsletters of businesses and organizations. Listen to radio and television programs. Not all stories will work in every community. You have to know your audience. A story about urban renewal, for example, would attract more attention in New York City than in Helena, Mont. The problems of water supply in the West could not be adapted to make a story on the East Coast. But a story about the federal government's hot-lunch program probably could be done equally well in New York, Kansas and California. When you are reading other publications for ideas, remember that you should not duplicate a story. You are looking for ideas. Think of a new angle.
- *News releases*. Some news releases from public-relations people are used, but many of them are not. Yet they can be a valuable source of story ideas. News that one company has posted increased profits may be worth one or two paragraphs; news that several companies in your community are prospering may be a front-page story. A handout stating that an employee received a 40-year pin may be worth a follow-up.
- *A social services directory*. Many cities and counties have a compos-ite listing of all agencies providing social services. Look beyond the pages. There are stories of people serving—or not serving—resi-dents. Each of those agencies and its clients is a story.
- *Government reports*. Flowing from Washington like floodwaters are pages and pages of statistics. Behind every statistic, however, is a person. And every person can be a story. The census reports, for instance, list not only the number of people in a community but also their income and education, how many cars they own, whether they rent or own a house. They tell much more, too. Find out what, and you have a treasure chest of stories.
- *Stories in your local newspaper or on television*. Many a stream has yielded gold nuggets after the first wave of miners has left. Newspapers and television stations sometimes play hit-and-run journalism. Ask yourself if the human-interest angle has been reported adequately. When your newspaper is concentrating on the election winners, maybe you can get an interesting story by talking to the losers and their supporters. After the story of the two-car accident has been written, perhaps there is a feature on the victims whose lives have been changed. And when the unemployment sta-tistics are reported in your paper, remember that behind each of

those numbers is a person without a job. News stories are not the only source of ideas. Read the records column: Can you spot a trend developing in the police report section or in the birth or divorce listings? Is the divorce rate up? Have several crimes been committed in one neighborhood?

■ *Advertisements*. In advertisements, particularly the classifieds, you may find everything from a come-on for an illegal massage parlor to an auction notice from a family losing its home. Be attentive to local radio and TV commercials, too. And look through the Yellow Pages. Your fingers might walk right up to a story.

■ *Wire copy*. Browse through the copy available from your wire services. Are there stories that can be localized? When a story describing the increase in the rate of inflation comes across the wire, you should ask how the people in your community will be affected. Or if a foundation reports that Johnny cannot read, you should talk to your local education officials. Can the Johnnys in your community read any better than the national average?

■ *Local news briefs*. Usually reports of local happenings are phoned in; sometimes they are brought in, written longhand on a piece of scratch paper. News of an upcoming family reunion may or may not be printed, but the enterprising reporter who notices in the information that five generations will attend the reunion probably has a story that will receive substantial play in the paper. A note that the Westside Neighborhood Association is planning its annual fund-raiser may result in a feature on how the neighbors plan to raise funds to upgrade recreational facilities in their area. The local news brief as a source of stories is often overlooked. A city editor once received a call from a man who said he thought the paper might be interested in a story about his daughter coming to visit. The city editor tried to brush him off. Just before the man hung up, the editor heard, "I haven't seen her in 32 years. I thought she was dead."

■ *The Internet*. Thousands and thousands of useful Web sites offer tidbits of information that can be used as the genesis of a story. Take advantage of the wealth of information at your fingertips.

■ *You*. In the final analysis, you are the one who must be alert enough to look and listen to what is going on around you. Ask yourself why, as in, "Why do people act the way they do?" Ask yourself what, as in, "What are people thinking about? What are their fears, their anxieties?" Ask yourself when, as in, "When that happened, what else was going on?" And wonder about things, as in, "I wonder if that's true in my town."

Reporters who are attuned to people rather than to institutions will find the world around them a rich source of human-interest stories. Do not tune out.

Suggested Readings

Berkman, Robert. *Find It Online: How to Uncover Expert Information on Any Subject Online or in Print.* New York: Harper, 2000. Basic information on the use of databases.

Dizard, Wilson Jr. *Old Media, New Media: Mass Communications in the Information Age,* Third Edition. New York: Longman, 1999. An interesting perspective, probably the best written yet, on the movement of society into the Information Age and the impact of that on existing media.

IRE Journal. This monthly magazine is available from Investigative Reporters and Editors, Columbia, Mo. It offers regular articles on the use of computers in the news-gathering process.

Seib, Philip M. *Going Live: Getting the News Right in a Real-Time, Online World.* Lanham, Md.: Rowman & Littlefield, 2000. A good discussion of the latest forms of journalism.

Suggested Web Sites

www.facsnet.org

An excellent collection of tools for journalists interested in finding background information for stories.

www.ire.org

Investigative Reporters and Editors is the organization that provides professional support to depth reporters, regardless of medium.

www.journaliststoolbox.com

The Journalist's Toolbox is a great source of links to all sorts of information.

www.lexis-nexis.com

This excellent database is a collection of newspaper, magazine and other resources and permits full-text searching of published articles.

www.nicar.org

The National Institute for Computer-Assisted Reporting provides databases and technical support to those engaged in data analysis.

Exercises

1. Choose any story in your local newspaper, and tell how that story could have been improved with a database search.

2. If you were interested in determining where Apple Computer Inc. is located and the name of its president, where would you look? What other sources of information might be available?

3. Write a one-page biographical sketch of each of your two U.S. senators based on information you retrieve from your library or a database.

4. Using the Internet, find the following information:
   a. The census of Rhode Island in 2000.
   b. The size of Rwanda in land area.
   c. The latest grant awards by the U.S. Department of Education.
   d. The names of universities in Norway that provide outside access via the Internet.
   e. The name of an Internet site that contains the complete works of Shakespeare.
   f. The name of an Internet site that contains federal campaign contribution data.

5. For your next class assignment, search the Internet for background material for your story. Use and properly credit such information in writing your story. Write a memo to your instructor describing your search process, the sources you used and your evaluation of the credibility of those sources.

6. Search the Internet for information on the war in Afghanistan. Find three sources you consider good and three you consider less reliable. Write a memo for your instructor that outlines your evaluation of the six sites.

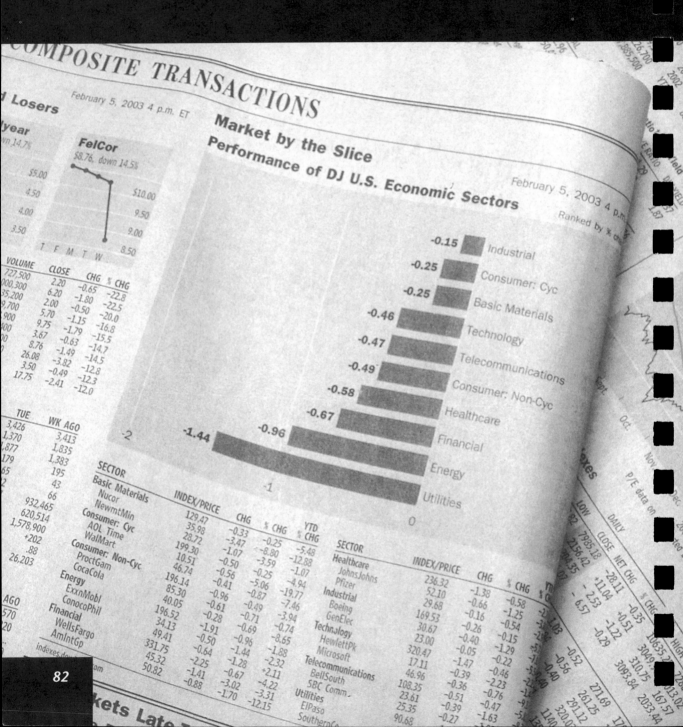

On Sept. 29, 2002, readers of *The Baltimore Sun* woke up to this news: "In Baltimore, plunging clearance rates—the number of murders in which police arrest a suspect—coupled with a 44 percent failure rate in court have repeatedly left killers on the street. In large measure, records suggest, it is these repeat offenders who have ensured Baltimore's place on the list of America's five deadliest cities for a decade."

Those and other findings emerged from a computer-assisted analysis of court files. Reporters Jim Haner, Kimberly A. C. Wilson and John B. O'Donnell also reported that "at least 83 defendants charged with homicide and later released were subsequently rearrested for new crimes—including 24 indicted in fresh murders or attempted murders.

"Over the past five years, records show, this group has been charged 683 times in such crimes as rape, carjacking, firebombing, kidnapping, armed robbery and a staggering 123 murders. A third of them were teen-agers when they were first accused of taking a life."

The findings were so significant that the Baltimore police department changed its procedures after being confronted with the statistics. Reporter John O'Donnell said the department was surprised at the results because it didn't even keep track of the disposition of its cases.

The numbers don't lie. The *Sun* reporters told the story by reciting case after case in which the police department failed to adequately investigate murders. The people in stories grab readers' attention, but the numbers make the case.

All good reporters use numbers, even those who say they never did well in math class, explains Ricardo Alonso-Zaldivar, who writes for the *Los Angeles Times*. "Almost everything you write about government involves some kind of statistic, but my stories aren't really about numbers, they're about social policy and about people," Alonso-Zaldivar says. "If you write about numbers, the story's a dead duck because no one will read it. But you can use numbers to tell a story, and that's the whole point."

PROPORTION

One of the most important courtesies journalists pay to their readers is to give **proportion** to numbers in the news—explaining things relative to the size or the magnitude of the whole. A municipal budget whose revenue is going up by $500,000 would be a windfall for a small town in New Hampshire but a minor adjustment in a metropolis like New York, Chicago or Minneapolis. Mention the total number and the increase or decrease to make your point understood.

Other figures might mean a lot or a little, depending on the context. If you know little or nothing about baseball, you might think that Babe Ruth's career batting average of .342—34.2 hits for every 100 times at bat—means that Ruth wasn't a good hitter. After all, he failed almost two out of three times at bat. When you look at the context—other players' averages—you realize that Ruth was exceptional.

Percentages and Percentage Change

Percentages are basic building blocks used to explain proportion. Batting averages explain the percentage of hits compared to the number of times at bat. The political strength of a public official is partly reflected in the percentage of the votes won at the polls. Stories about budgets, taxes, wages, retail sales, schools, health care and the environment all are explained with percentages.

To calculate a percentage, take the portion that you want to measure, divide it by the whole and then move the decimal two places to the right. Let's say you want to know what portion of the city's budget is allocated to police services. Divide the police budget by the city budget, move the decimal point two places to the right, and you get the percentage of the budget that pays for police services.

| *To calculate a* | *Step 1:* | Portion ÷ Whole = *.xxx* |
| *percentage* | *Step 2:* | Move decimal point two places to the right: *xx.x%* |

You can use percentages sometimes to verify whether newsmakers are accurately representing the facts. Frank Gallagher, a reporter at the *San Francisco Independent*, had the same quotes as every other reporter in San Francisco about how the city's Board of Supervisors President Barbara Kaufman had stripped another supervisor, Leland Yee, of his influential committee assignments. Kaufman said committee chairs were complaining about Yee's poor attendance. Yee in turn told reporters that the others were complaining because he voted against the board president's proposals too often. All the other media in San Francisco ran stories with the politicians' conflicting claims.

Gallagher took the story one step further. At the clerk's office, he checked on the supervisors' attendance records for meetings since the beginning of the year. Gallagher discovered that the unseated supervisor attended a higher percentage of meetings than many other supervisors and that Yee had an attendance record that was about the same as the record of the political appointee who replaced him (see Figure 5.1).

"This is San Francisco, so everybody pretty much figured the real reason for the committee switch was politics," Gallagher said. "But

Ranking the supes

How often they've attended committee and full board meetings so far in 1997:

Barbara Kaufman

Meetings: 45
Attended: 42

93%

Michael Yaki

Meetings: 43
Attended: 40

93%

Susan Leal

Meetings: 40
Attended: 37

93%

Tom Ammiano

Meetings: 35
Attended: 32

92%

Leland Yee

Meetings: 53
Attended: 48

91%

Gavin Newsom

Meetings: 29
Attended: 26

90%

Sue Bierman

Meetings: 44
Attended: 38

87%

Mabel Teng

Meetings: 42
Attended: 36

86%

Rev. Amos Brown

Meetings: 45
Attended: 36

80%

Jose Medina

Meetings: 55
Attended: 44

80%

Leslie Katz

Meetings: 54
Attended: 37

69%

Figure 5.1
This graphic ran with Frank Gallagher's story in the *San Francisco Independent*. Looking beyond the finger-pointing of politicians, Gallagher investigated the numbers and found Supervisor Yee had a strong attendance record.

when you put the numbers down in black and white, there's just no disputing the facts."

Precision in the use of numbers also requires that you ask the basic questions. Reporters need to be careful of percentages that might be used in misleading ways or percentages that tell just part of a story.

If someone is giving you percentages, ask on what population the figures are based. For instance, a juvenile officer told a reporter that 70 percent of the juvenile offenders do not have to return to his program. The reporter's first question should be, "What was the population used to figure the percentage?" All the juveniles in the program during the last calendar year? If so, perhaps the success rate is high because the period measured isn't long enough. And how are the juveniles who are old enough now to be certified as adults counted? How does your source account for juveniles who may have committed a crime in another jurisdiction?

His answer may be that the figure is based on a sample of the population in the program over a 10-year period: Using common statistical tables, researchers drew a sample of the names of all juveniles who were in the program over 10 years and contacted them. From those contacts, they could determine the success rate. If the figure is based on a scientific sampling like the one just described, there would also be an error rate. It would be expressed as "plus or minus x points." If x were 4, it would mean that the success rate was between 66 and 74 percent.

If you still don't think a different base can have a significant impact on the figures, try this. Say a colleague is making $40,000, and you make $30,000. The salary is the base. Your employer decides to give your colleague a 4 percent increase and to give you a 5 percent increase. Before you begin feeling too good about the honor, consider that your colleague's raise is $1,600, and your raise is $1,500. Your colleague won a bigger raise, and the salary gap between the two of you grew. You spend dollars, not percentages.

More confusion often occurs when people talk about the difference between two percentage figures. For example, say the mayor wins the election with 55 percent of the vote and has just one opponent, who receives 45 percent. The mayor won by a margin of 10 percentage points. Because the figures are based on the same whole number—in this case the total number of voters—the percentages can be compared. But if you compare the percentage of a city budget devoted to law enforcement in consecutive years, you will need to include the actual dollar amounts with the percentages because total spending probably changed from one year to the next.

Another important aspect of percentages is the concept of **percentage change.** This number explains how much something goes up or down. If a municipal budget increases by a half-million dollars in a year, you find out the percentage change by doing the following calculation: increase (or decrease) divided by the old budget. So, if the budget went from $1,785,500 to $2,285,500, you do the following calculation: $500,000 ÷ $1,785,500. The result is .28. Move the decimal point two places to the right, and the result is 28 percent.

Notice that if in the next year the budget again increases by a half-million dollars, you need to do a different calculation. Suppose the budget increases from $2,285,500 to $2,785,500. This time the equation is $500,000 ÷ $2,285,500, yielding a 21.9 percent increase from the previous year. It's a smaller percentage increase because the base year has changed.

To calculate *percentage change*	*Step 1:*	Subtract the old number from the new number: (New Number) − (Old Number) = Change
	Step 2:	Change ÷ Old Number = *.xxx*
	Step 3:	Move decimal point two places = *xx.x%* Percentage Change = *xx.x%*
	Note:	Percentage change can be a positive or a negative number.

When changes are large, sometimes it is better to translate the numbers into plain words rather than to use a percentage figure. For example, suppose the town you are covering decides to put $220,000 into buying parkland in its new budget and spent $100,000 last year. The percentage change is $120,000 ÷ $100,000, or a 120 percent increase. But it will be easier for readers and listeners to understand if you write, "The town next year will more than double the amount of money it will spend buying new parkland," and then give the actual dollar amounts.

Averages and Medians

Averages and medians are numbers that can be used to describe a general trend. For any given set of numbers, the average and the median might be quite close, or they might be quite different. Depending on what you are trying to explain, it might be important to use one instead of the other or to use both.

The **average**—also called the *arithmetic mean*—is the number you obtain when you add a list of figures and then divide the total by the number of figures in the list. The **median** is the midpoint of the list—half the figures fall above it, and half the figures fall below it.

To compute *an average*	*Step 1:*	Add the figures.
	Step 2:	Divide the total by the number of figures: Total ÷ Number of Figures
		The result is the average.

Determining Averages and Medians

Take a set of scores from a final exam in a class of 15 students. Students scored 95, 94, 92, 86, 85, 84, 75, 75, 65, 64, 63, 62, 62, 62, 62. Both the average and the median are 75.

The picture can look quite different when the figures are bunched at one end of the scale. Take an example from professional basketball. At the beginning of the 1999-2000 season, salaries for the Washington Wizards ranged from $1 million to $15 million a year. The average salary was $5.6 million, but the median was only $2.4 million. That's because four players made $4.8 million of the $61.7 million annual payroll. This is an instance where the figures are bunched at one end of the scale. Five players made $2 million or less; five players made $5 million or more. Only four players made more than the average, and seven earned less. By using the median instead of the average, you would do a more accurate job of reporting the range.

In 1999, half of the 823 players in Major League Baseball made less than $700,000 a year, and one-third of all the players made less than $300,000. You could accurately report that the average salary was $1.7 million, but you would inaccurately report the range of salaries.

To find the median	*Step 1:*	Arrange the figures in rank order.
	Step 2:	Identify the figure midway between the highest and lowest numbers. That figure is the median.
	Note:	When you have an even number of figures, the median is the average of the two middle figures.

Rates

A **rate** is a term used to make fair comparisons. One example is per capita, or per person, spending, such as for school funding ("per capita" is a Latin term that means "by heads"). Even though a big-city school budget looks incredibly large to someone in a small community, the money has to stretch over more students than it would in many suburbs. In other words, the spending per capita is a better comparison between districts with different enrollments.

| *To calculate per capita spending* | *Step 1:* | Divide the budget by the number of people: Budget ÷ Population The result is per capita spending. |

In medicine, epidemiology and crime statistics, fair comparisons come in the form of rates per 100,000 people.

At the Portland Newspapers in Maine, reporters Shoshana Hoose and Kay Lazar discovered that young people in Maine were killing themselves at an alarming rate. In early 1995 they reported in the *Maine Sunday Telegram* and the *Portland Press Herald* that from 1987 through 1993 Maine had an average suicide rate among 10- to 24-year-olds of 11.94 for every 100,000 people in that age group, compared with the national average rate of 9.48 per 100,000. Maine's rate during those years was also much higher than it had been in the previous seven years.

The actual number of young people committing suicide—219 from 1987 through 1993—might seem low in higher-population states such as New York, Texas or California. But Hoose and Lazar were able to illustrate that those deaths constituted a startling epidemic in rural counties in Maine, which has a population of just over one million people.

Three months before the newspaper's series ran in March 1995, a legislative task force had delivered its opinion on how to fight the rising tide of youth violence, including suicides. Hoose and statehouse reporter Paul Carrier showed in one story for the series how years of talk and recommendations about youth suicide had translated to almost no action. Shortly after the series ran, however, Maine Gov. Angus King appointed a new study group on youth suicide and in 1996 ordered several state agencies to take new and concerted steps to help adolescents at risk.

INTEREST AND COMPOUNDING

Interest is a financial factor in just about everyone's life. Most people have to pay it when they borrow money, and many people earn it when they deposit money at a bank. Consumers pay interest on home mortgages, car loans and credit-card balances. Individuals and businesses earn interest when they deposit money in a financial institution or make a loan. Federal regulations require the interest rates charged by or paid by most institutions to be expressed as an annual percentage rate, so that interest rates are comparable.

There are two types of interest: simple and compound. **Simple interest** is interest to be paid on the principal, the amount borrowed. It is calculated by multiplying the amount of the loan by the annual percentage rate.

Suppose a student borrows $1,000 from her grandfather at a 5 percent annual rate to help cover college expenses. She needs only a one-year loan, so the cost is figured as simple interest. To calculate simple interest, multiply the principal by the interest rate: $1,000 × .05 = $50. To find the amount the student will repay her grandfather

4A Portland Press Herald, Tuesday, March 21, 1995

DYING YOUNG: MAINE'S QUIET TRAGEDY

Suicide prevention programs are multiplying

● According to the CDC, the most successful approach is a basketful of diverse programs.

By SHOSHANA HOOSE
Staff Writer

When a sophomore at Mt. Blue High School in Farmington killed himself in February, the second suicide there in a month, the school district acted quickly.

A "crisis team" worked through the night, making plans to break the news of the death to students and to arrange counseling for anyone who needed it.

Such teams – typically made up of guidance counselors, social workers and psychologists – have formed at many Maine schools during the past decade. They can play a crucial role in helping students cope with a suicide, and preventing one death from spawning copycat attempts.

Crisis teams are among a variety of suicide prevention programs being used in Maine. Many are relatively new and untested; some have already shown their worth. According to the Centers for Disease Control and Prevention, the most successful prevention efforts use several strategies.

Here's are some of the approaches used in Maine:

Educational programs

Maine schools teach suicide prevention in health classes.

Educational programs reach everyone in the school. That's an advantage, since there's no foolproof way of knowing which kids may be at greatest risk.

A common criticism of the programs is that merely mentioning suicide will make students think about killing themselves.

That is not borne out by research. On the contrary, experts say young people should be encouraged to share their thoughts about death and suicide.

"It gives suicidal teens a chance to let out the idea ... that's been eating up their hearts and brains," write Richard E. Nelson and Judith C. Galas, in their 1994 book, "The Power to Prevent Suicide: A Guide for Teens Helping Teens."

But educational progams have been criticized for other reasons.

Dr. David Shaffer, a professor of child psychiatry and pediatrics at Columbia University, compared students who had attended such programs with those who had not. He found that none of the programs changed students' attitudes toward suicide or made them more willing to seek help.

'Peer helpers'

"Peer helper" programs are based on the idea that kids most often confide in their friends.

Peer helpers learn to take any suicide threat seriously and to notify an adult. They also can play a crucial role in reaching out to classmates who may feel isolated or depressed.

"If you just know one kid or two that you can talk to, it makes a world of difference," says Elizabeth Deering, a senior at Bonny Eagle High School in Standish. "Just to know that you're not alone."

Three-quarters of Maine high schools have peer helper programs. A growing number of middle schools are starting them, too.

Research shows that the programs are a good way to reach kids. A 1993 study found that they work better than any approach in curbing drug and alcohol abuse. That's significant: suicidal young people often have substance abuse problems.

But no research proves that peer programs help stop suicides directly.

And a big problem with Maine's peer helper programs is that they involve few young men. Four-fifths of the helpers are female, yet four-fifths of young suicides are male.

Sue Dreher, who trains peer helpers through a program run by the Lewiston–Auburn YWCA, acknowledges that many boys think "it's not cool" to participate. She says the fact that programs now are starting in younger grades may help to eliminate that stigma.

Communities elsewhere in the country have started peer support groups just for suicidal young people. The Portland Newspapers found no examples of that approach being tried in Maine.

Crisis hot lines

Maine has seven state-run "crisis programs" to help young people. All have toll-free hot lines and send crisis workers to the scene of a problem if necessary. Other hot lines are run by mental health agencies, hospitals and community groups.

Suicidal feelings in young people often are impulsive and short-lived. Hot lines can help them weather a crisis; they are one of the few resources available to young people out of school.

At least one study found that hot lines help prevent suicide among young women. But their effectiveness is less clear for young men, who are much more likely to kill themselves. Studies also show that many adolescents are not aware of hot lines in their area.

The Centers for Disease Control and Prevention recommends advertising hot lines more aggressively to young men, improving training for hot line workers and having hot lines do more follow-up work.

Assistance teams

Since the early 1990s, nearly half of Maine's public schools have started student assistance teams consisting of administrators, teachers and guidance counselors.

The teams look for kids with problems – falling grades, perhaps, or their parents' divorce. The teams then recommend help.

School Administrative District 9, in the Farmington area, goes a step further. When teachers or other school workers fear that a child may be suicidal, they notify the district's crisis team. It evaluates the child, contacts the family and, if necessary, makes a referral for help.

"We are very open to doing an initial evaluation on the child, no matter how minor the concern is," says Steven R. Brod, the crisis team coordinator. Each year, the team does about 50 suicide evaluations.

Suicide researchers are refining techniques to identify young people at risk of killing themselves, and screening programs are gaining a lot of attention nationally. But caution is in order.

Most programs that screen specifically for suicide risk are new and unproven. It can be costly to screen an entire school, and then refer high-risk students for treatment. Some might be referred even if they don't need help.

Other methods

Many educators and youth workers say the best way to prevent suicide is to build on kids' strengths rather than focusing on suicidal behavior.

"Most suicide prevention," says Coleman, the Muskie Institute researcher, "places too much emphasis on suicide, and not enough on the self-esteem of the child and the positive relationships they have with other people. ... That's what saves anyone."

This strategy encompasses a wide range of programs not usually identified with suicide prevention.

At some Maine schools, health classes teach students about stress and resolving conflicts. Programs match students with a staff member who watches out for their well-being. Volunteer projects help young people feel involved in their communities.

Gauging the impact of these activities on suicide rates is very difficult since they are, by their nature, general in scope.

Staff photo by David MacDonald

Principal Bill Marston roams the school cafeteria in front of a banner promoting the PHrends peer outreach program. That and other programs in and out of school were a reaction to a student's suicide.

A 15-year-old girl's death pushed Goffstown to act

By KAY LAZAR
Staff Writer

GOFFSTOWN, N.H. – The bullet that killed Megan Pauly pierced the soul of this quiet community.

Pauly's suicide wasn't the first in Goffstown. Between May 1991 and Oct. 10, 1993, when the 15-year-old died, four other teen-agers killed themselves.

But Pauly's death was different. She left a note saying that she had been bullied by friends and that she was afraid to go back to school.

Suddenly, community confusion, anger and fear rained on Goffstown High School. The town could have crawled into a cocoon and waited for the frenzy to pass. It did not.

In the 16 months since Megan Pauly's suicide, Goffstown has pieced together an impressive array of programs aimed at teenagers, programs that are more time-intensive than costly.

It is a good example of a community tackling the issue of suicides, even though it did so only after the problem had become painfully clear.

"Megan's death brought a quick focus to the need to accelerate programs that we already had in the planning stage," says Bill Marston, Goffstown High's principal.

Many of the new programs speak directly to the two main concerns identified by a community task force after Pauly's suicide. Those concerns centered on the lack of positive after-school activities and the perceived lack of people for troubled teens to turn to.

In response, Goffstown has:

- Added a new drug and alcohol counselor at the high school and a fourth guidance counselor, at an additional yearly cost of $70,000.
- Started a high school teen counseling group called PHrends, with 23 students who are trained to listen, confidentially, to their peers' problems and assist them.
- Intensified reporting to town police of any fights or even verbal threats at the middle and high schools to see, in the words of Goffstown Police Lt. Mike French, "if a pattern of behavior is developing and deal with it before it gets to be a problem."

After 39 years as a principal – 14 of them in Goffstown – Marston says the Pauly suicide was a haunting wake-up call.

He remembers that just two days before her suicide, the freckle-faced redhead was in Marston's office, calmly assuring him that the seemingly minor tiff she had with three girlfriends was resolved.

"I'm still saying, 'What did I miss?'" Marston says. "Now I'm much more tuned-in to making sure we don't overlook anything." And part of that gnawing lesson has been woven into new training for teachers and staff.

Marton's advice: "Get your crisis intervention plans in place before a tragedy."

Yet the most powerful weapon in Goffstown's anti-suicide arsenal extends beyond school walls.

Called The Partnership, it's a comprehensive linking of community businesses, civic organizations and the high school. The aim is to introduce students to career and volunteer paths they might pursue after school hours.

Twice during the last year, students have been matched with business owners during a day-long, on-site "Shadowing Program" to learn about job opportunities.

The bulk of The Partnership's programs are scheduled to start later this month. Among them is an effort to help high school students learn about volunteer opportunities at the local nursing home, garden club and other organizations.

Goffstown hasn't had any more youth suicides since Pauly died.

Many Goffstown High students feel that town and school officials should be applauded for their accomplishments.

"We have all of these wonderful programs now, though it was possible before," says Matt Hunter, a 17-year-old senior who is the first student representative to the school board. "A little good comes out of everything bad."

Mike Ryan, a lawyer who works with juvenile offenders and who has spearheaded The Partnership plan, knows he's got a lot of hard work ahead of him.

Finding creative ways to capture teen attention – particularly kids on the fringe, the non-joiners, the ones more likely to feel suicidal – hasn't been easy.

And because of limited funds and volunteers already tapped to the brink, The Partnership has yet to come up with programs for 20- to 24-year-olds, an age group that's 36 percent more likely to commit suicide than high school kids.

Staff photo by David MacDonald

Sally Durgan of AmeriCorps chairs a meeting of The Partnership at Goffstown High School. The Partnership helps knit the school and town together in helping at-risk teens.

At 774-TALK, teens talk down other teens

● About 10 percent of last year's calls to the hot line were classified 'depressed/suicidal.'

By KAY LAZAR
Staff Writer

It was the most draining phone call Derek Absher ever had. The young woman on the other end of the line told him she was going to kill herself. She had a plan.

For 45 minutes, Absher, 16, stayed on the line with the teen-ager – listening, talking and finally convincing her to ask a friend to stay with her until more help could be found.

"It was exhausting," Absher said, recalling that early December call. "It took every idea in my head to feel I helped her."

Welcome to 774-TALK, the only crisis intervention hot line in Maine staffed by teens, for teens. Its goal: to provide a confidential service for young adults who need someone to listen when they are confused, depressed or suicidal.

There is plenty of debate about whether hot lines can stanch the rising tide of suicides among young people. Social workers and those staffing the lines are quick to relate instances of suicidal callers checking back to say, "Thanks, you talked me out of it."

But scientific evidence of such success is hard to come by. In fact, the national Centers for Disease Control said in a 1992 report on youth suicide prevention that "all we can say – and scientifically defend – is that (hot lines) may or may not prevent youth suicide."

As the experts debate, the phones at 774-TALK keep ringing.

Staffing the line are 27 teen volunteers, all of whom have received three weeks of training on crisis intervention.

The bulk of the work involves talking callers through problems. Frequently callers complain they can't communicate their angst to their parents. The volunteers are trained to suggest that callers confide in a trusted adult – a coach, teacher, neighbor or other relative the teen might not have considered.

The Portland-based hot line is run by Ingraham, one of Portland's best-known private, nonprofit social services organizations.

Teen line 12 years old

Ingraham has operated a 24-hour adult crisis hotline, 774-HELP, for 25 years. The TALK line was launched 12 years ago, when the number of kids on the brink started exploding, and Ingraham realized it needed a separate service that spoke directly to young adults. Recently, the teen line has been tied into a statewide, toll-free number: 1-800-870-9991.

"Kids are really thirsting for information," said Pamela McNally, Ingraham's hot line coordinator.

Cloaked in anonymity, teenagers often ask questions and confide problems and fears they wouldn't share with a best friend.

"I have a lot of close friends," said Tina Parsons, 15, a TALK volunteer. "But on the TALK line, people are so much more open."

What do they say?

Some are about to get kicked out of their homes and are looking for a place to live. "That's more of a problem than I ever realized," Parsons said.

Nearly a third of the calls last year concerned sexuality, according to the agency's statistics.

There are drug-related calls. "I've had 10- and 11-year-olds call," Parsons said. "At first it stuns you, like what is this 10-year-old doing with this issue?"

And there are teen-agers, already parents themselves, who are unable to handle the stress.

The line received 811 calls last year – 100 more than the year before. Roughly 10 percent of the calls last year were classified "depressed/suicidal," according to McNally, who reviews the notes volunteers are instructed to take during every phone call.

That 10 percent is an increase over 1993, when 8 percent of the calls were logged as "depressed/suicidal."

McNally said that before 1992, the agency didn't keep such detailed breakdowns on calls, so there's no way to measure whether suicide calls have gone up over the hotline's 12-year history. But McNally senses they have.

"In recent years," she said, "things have gotten incredibly more serious on the hot line."

McNally said that at least one adult is always in the office for teen volunteers to turn to if they sense the caller is slipping away from them. Only as a "last resort" are calls traced and police dispatched to intervene, McNally said. In the three years she has coordinated the teen line, that has not happened.

Staff photo by John Patriquin

Derek Absher, 16, talks to a caller on the Ingraham teen crisis intervention line.

Confidentiality a must

It's tough to get a handle on exactly who is calling the line because of it's strict adherence to confidentiality. Unless the callers offer the information, volunteers don't press to find out ages or locations. McNally said she suspects that most calls come from Cumberland County.

She also suspects the line would get a lot more calls from the generally services-poor northern part of the state if teens there were more aware of TALK's toll-free line.

Another hurdle is the TALK line's limited hours: Monday through Thursday from 2:30 p.m. to 8 p.m., and Friday from 2:30 p.m. to 5 p.m. No weekends, no late evening hours. McNally acknowledges that's like asking kids to fit a crisis into business hours. But another reality takes precedence: it's tough to get teens to volunteer on weekends and evenings.

During hours when TALK line is unstaffed, there's a recording directing callers to dial Ingraham's 24-hour adult line: 774-HELP.

TALK volunteers are instructed to encourage kids to keep in touch, and especially to call back if things still aren't working out.

And what of the young woman who dialed 774-TALK and reached Derek Absher in early December? He hasn't heard from her.

This much he knows: "When I hung up with her, I felt like she was safer than when she had called. But there's no absolute surety that you know they are."

HOT LINES

The following state-funded crisis programs serve people 18 or younger who are suicidal, mentally ill or have other severe emotional needs. All programs operate round-the-clock hot lines:

Shoreline Mental Health Center (serves Sagadahoc and parts of Lincoln and Cumberland counties), 1-800-834-4673.

Mid-Coast Mental Health Center (serves Waldo, Knox and parts of Lincoln county), 1-800-540-2072.

Tri-County Mental Health Center (serves Androscoggin, Franklin and Oxford counties), 1-800-499-9141.

Sweetser Children's Services (serves Cumberland and York counties), 1-800-660-8500.

Here's a partial list of other crisis hot lines:

Ingraham, a Portland-based social service organization, 774-TALK.

Southern Maine Medical Center Hotline, 282-6136 or 1-800-660-8500.

Portsmouth Pavilion, 1-800-221-9666.

These stories from the *Portland Press Herald* were part of a series that brought attention to Maine's high suicide rate among 10- to 24-year olds and led to government action to address the problem.

at the end of a year, add the principal to the interest. The student will owe $1,050.

> *To calculate simple interest and total amount owed*
>
> **Step 1:** Express the interest rate as a decimal by moving the decimal point two places to the left.
>
> **Step 2:** Multiply the principal by the interest rate:
> Principal × Interest Rate
> The result is the amount of simple interest owed.
>
> **Step 3:** Add the principal to the interest owed:
> Principal + Interest
> The result is the total amount owed.
>
> **Note:** The same result can be obtained another way. Multiply the principal by 1 plus the interest rate expressed as a decimal:
> Principal × (1 + .xx) = Total Amount Owed

If the loan is made over a period longer than a year, the borrower pays compound interest. **Compound interest** is interest paid on the total of the principal and the interest that already has accrued.

Suppose the student borrows $1,000 at an annual percentage rate of 5 percent and pays her grandfather back four years later, after graduation. She owes 5 percent annual interest for each year of the loan. But because she has the loan for four years, each year she owes not only simple interest on the principal but also interest on the interest that accrues each year.

At the end of year 1, she owes $1,050. To see how much she will owe at the end of year 2, she has to calculate 5 percent interest on $1,050: $1,050 × .05 = $52.50.

Here is the formula for calculating the interest for all four years:

$$\$1,000 \times (1.05) \times (1.05) \times (1.05) \times (1.05)$$
$$\text{or:} \quad \$1,000 \times (1.05)^4$$

At the end of four years, the student owes $1,215.51.

> *To calculate compound interest*
>
> **Step 1:** Add 1 plus the interest rate expressed as a decimal:
> 1 + .xx = 1.xx
>
> **Step 2:** Using a calculator, multiply
> Principal × (1.xx)^n
> (The superscript n represents the number of years of the loan.)
> The result equals the total amount owed.

A host of computer programs offer consumers interest formulas and payment plans. Since most consumers pay off student loans, car loans, mortgages and credit-card debt over a period of time, and because interest is compounded more often than once a year, calculations usually are far more complicated than the example. Many financial Web sites offer such programs. For instance, select "Financial Calculators" in the Money section on *USA Today*'s Web site **usatoday.com.**

Student loans taken out through federal programs administered by banks, credit unions and universities are a prime example of more complicated transactions. Suppose a student has a $5,000 guaranteed student loan with an interest rate of 8 percent per year. After finishing school, the student has 10 years to pay, and each year she pays 8 percent interest on the amount of the original principal that is left unpaid. If the student makes the minimum payment of $65 on time each month for the 10-year life of the loan, she will pay the bank a total of $7,800. She pays $2,800 in interest on top of the original principal of $5,000.

Consumers get the benefits of compounding when they put money in interest-bearing accounts because their interest compounds. The same effect takes place when people make good investments in the stock market, where earnings are compounded when they are reinvested.

INFLATION

Inflation is an increase in the cost of living as time goes by. Because prices rise over time, wages and budgets, too, have to increase to keep up with inflation. A worker who received a 2 percent pay increase each year would have had the same buying power each year if the yearly rate of inflation rose at 2 percent. Because of inflation, reporters must use a few simple computations to make fair comparisons between dollar amounts from different years.

Here is how inflation affects the accuracy of a story, in this case, about teachers' salaries.

If teachers whose starting salary in 1975 was $12,000 a year were making $40,000 a year in 2002, you could stir up readers by pointing out that teacher salaries have skyrocketed so much that they have nearly tripled in the last 27 years. However, if you adjust the $12,000 for inflation, the $12,000 in 2002 dollars would be $39,120—far from skyrocketing.

Numbers that are adjusted for inflation are called **constant,** or real, **dollars.** Numbers that are not adjusted for inflation are called **nominal,** or current, **dollars.**

The most common tool that is used to adjust for inflation is the **Consumer Price Index,** which is reported each month by the U.S. Bureau of Labor Statistics of the U.S. Department of Labor. You can

Some guidelines for reporting numbers

- Cite sources for all statistics.
- Use numbers judiciously for maximum impact.
- Long lists of figures are difficult to read in paragraph form. Put them in charts and graphs when appropriate.
- Graphs sometimes include estimates. If you use figures from a graph, make sure they are precise.
- Round off large numbers in most cases. For example: $1.5 million rather than $1,489,789.
- Always double-check your math and any statistics a source gives you.
- Be especially careful with handwritten numbers. It is easy to drop or transpose figures in your notes. Write neatly; when you read your notes, you'll want to be able to tell a "1" from a "7."
- If you don't understand the figures, get an explanation.

get current CPI numbers online at **www.bls.gov.** To calculate inflation rapidly, turn to **www.newsengin.com/neFreeTools.nsf/CPIcalc.**

To adjust for inflation	*Step 1:*	Find the CPI for the year you wish to adjust figures *to,* and the CPI for the year you wish to adjust *from.*
	Step 2:	Divide the CPI of the base year (the year you are adjusting *to*) by the CPI of the year in question:

CPI of Base Year ÷ CPI of Year in Question
The result is a multiplier.

Step 3: Take the multiplier from Step 2 and multiply it by the figure you are adjusting:
Multiplier × Figure to Be Adjusted
The result is the amount adjusted for inflation.

Here is the calculation for adjusting 1975 teacher salaries for inflation to 2002:

$$\frac{2002\ CPI}{1975\ CPI} = \frac{175.4}{53.8} = 3.26$$

$3.26 \times \$12,000 = \$39,120$
$= 1975$ teacher salaries in 2002 dollars

TAXES

Taxes are a subject just about every reporter has to cover. And all reporters pay taxes, as do the owners of the companies they work for.

Governments collect taxes in a variety of ways, but the three major sources of revenue are sales taxes, income taxes and property taxes.

Sales Taxes

State, county and municipal governments can levy sales taxes on various goods and services. Sales taxes—also known as excise taxes—are the simplest to figure out.

To figure a sales tax, multiply the price of an item by the sales tax rate. Add the result to the original price to obtain the total cost.

Take the example of a student buying an $1,800 computer before beginning school at the University of Florida. If he shops in his home state of Iowa, where the sales tax is 5 percent, he will pay a tax of $90, and the computer will cost him $1,890. If he buys the computer after arriving in Florida, where the sales tax is 6 percent, he will pay a tax of $108, and the computer will cost him $1,908.

Math You Can Count On

Many journalists joke about their mathematical ineptitude. They suggest that fear of math is why they went into the profession. But even for those who are genuinely afraid of statistics, there is no avoiding numbers in journalism. Numbers are at the heart of reporting government, business, sports and investigative issues, and they can surface in areas as diverse as obituaries, food, religion and entertainment.

Journalists who fear numbers had better learn to overcome it. That might mean learning some math. Before using figures in your writing, be sure you understand what they mean.

Say you want to describe the volume of a child's screaming. Would you say the child belted out "a 25-decibel roar"? (No—25 decibels is barely above a whisper.) Do you know how many centimeters are in a foot? (The answer is 30.5 centimeters.) Do you know how far it is from home plate to the pitcher's mound? (The distance is 60 feet 6 inches.) It is vital to check reference books when such questions arise.

Even the most respected journalists can run afoul of numbers. When reporting a Supreme Court case in 1987, *The New York Times* and other media outlets reported that defendants charged in Georgia with killing whites were four times as likely to receive death sentences as were defendants charged with killing blacks. However, reporters—and the Supreme Court itself—confused "probability" and "odds."

Probability represents the likelihood something will happen. For example, the probability of getting heads when flipping a coin is ½ (one of two possible outcomes) or .5. *Odds* represent the likelihood that one thing will happen rather than another. The odds of getting heads—figured as the likelihood of getting heads vs. the likelihood of getting tails—are .5 ÷ .5 ("even money," in betting terms) or 1.

The Georgia study concluded that the odds of a death sentence when a white person was killed were 4.3 times greater than the odds when a black person was killed. That doesn't mean the same thing as "four times as likely."

The lessons from that example are that "probability" and "odds" are not synonymous and that math errors can creep into reporting even when your source is the Supreme Court.

Income Taxes

The government taxes a percentage of your income to support such services as building roads, running schools, registering people to vote and encouraging businesses to grow. Income taxes are paid to the federal government, to most state governments and to some municipalities.

Calculating income taxes can be tricky because a lot of factors affect the amount of income that is subject to the tax. For that reason, the only way to figure a person's income tax is to consult the actual numbers and follow tables published by the Internal Revenue Service (**www.irs.gov**) or the state department of taxation.

Governments use tax incentives to encourage people to undertake certain types of economic activities, such as buying a home, saving for retirement and investing in business ventures. By giving individuals and businesses tax deductions, the government reduces the amount of income that is taxable.

A tax deduction is worth the tax rate times the amount of the tax deduction. That's why tax deductions are worth more to people with higher incomes. Take the example of two families who own homes. Both pay $2,500 in interest on their home mortgage in a year, the cost of which is deductible for people who itemize deductions. The lower-income family is in the lowest federal income tax bracket, in which the tax rate is 15 percent, so they save $375 on their tax bill: $2,500 × .15 = $375. The higher-income family is in the federal income tax bracket with a tax rate of 28 percent, so they save $700 on their tax bill: $2,500 × .28 or $700.

We all pay the same amount of tax on the first dollars we make. A family with an adjusted gross income of $35,000 pays roughly the same tax rate on the first $20,000 in adjusted gross income as a family with a $20,000 income. But the wealthier family pays a higher rate on the next $15,000.

Property Taxes

Property taxes are the domain of city and county governments. When people talk about property taxes, they are usually talking about taxes on the value of houses, buildings and land. In some places, people also are taxed each year on the value of their cars, boats and other personal property.

The two key factors affecting property taxes are the assessed value and the millage rate. The **assessed value** is the amount that a government appraiser determines a piece of property is worth. The **millage rate**—it literally means the rate per thousand (dollars)—is the tax rate determined by the government. You figure the property taxes by multiplying the assessed value by the millage rate. For example, owners of a house valued at $100,000 and taxed at a millage rate of 2.25 would pay 100 × 2.25, or $225 in taxes.

To calculate a property tax	Step 1:	Find the assessed value and divide it by 1,000.
	Step 2:	Multiply the result from Step 1 by the millage rate.
		The result is the amount of property tax.

Counties and cities hire professional appraisers to assess the values of land and buildings in their jurisdiction, and typically their assessments have been far lower than the actual market value of the property. Because of abuses and public confusion, most states in recent years have ordered revaluations to bring assessments into line with market values, and they have adjusted millage rates accordingly, though assessments can vary widely from appraiser to appraiser. Appraisals are based on complicated formulas that take into account the size, location and condition of the property. Still, the government may say your house is worth $60,000, but you know you could sell it for $80,000.

MAKING SENSE OF BUDGETS

The budget is the blueprint that guides the operation of any organization, and a reporter must learn to read a budget just as a carpenter must learn to read an architect's blueprint. In either case, doing so isn't as difficult as it appears at first glance.

Computers allow reporters to perform budget analyses that were once only in the power of an institution's budget director. In many cases, you'll be able to get the budget (and other financial information as well) for your city or school district on computer disk or find it posted online. You can use the information to create a spreadsheet and interpret the data on your own. However, even with the computer, first you need to know the basics of budgeting.

Every budget, whether it's your personal budget or the budget of the U.S. government, has two basic parts—revenues (income) and expenditures (outgo). Commercial enterprises earn their income primarily from sales; not-for-profit organizations depend heavily on contributions from public funding and private donors. Government revenues come from sources like taxes, fees and service charges, and payments from other agencies (such as state aid to schools). The budget usually shows, in dollar figures and percentages, the sources of the organization's money. Expenditures go for such things as staff salaries, purchase of supplies, payment of utility bills, construction and maintenance of facilities, and insurance. Expenditures usually are listed either by line or by program. The difference is this: A **line-item budget** shows a separate line for each expenditure, such as "Salary of police chief—$50,000." A **program budget** provides less detail but shows more clearly what each activity of the agency costs—for example, "Burglary prevention program—$250,000."

Now let's see what kinds of stories budgets may yield and where to look for those stories. Take a minute to scan the following table, a summary page from the annual budget of a small city. You can apply the skills of reading a city's annual budget to similar accounting documents on other beats—for example, annual reports of businesses and not-for-profit organizations.

The most important budget stories usually deal with changes, trends and comparisons. Budget figures change every year. As costs increase, so do budgets. But look in our sample budget, in the

On the Job

Working with Numbers

Before graduating from the University of Maryland's master's program, Sarah Cohen worked as an economist in the federal government, producing some of the statistics that journalists report on each month. Early in that job, she had to be reminded how to compute a percentage change, but she learned fast.

Cohen is database editor for *The Washington Post*. She sometimes works weeks to find or compute the number that tells the story best and most accurately.

Before joining the *Post,* she worked as training director for Investigative Reporters and Editors. There, she met many reporters who were terrified of the numbers.

At a recent seminar of city editors, she heard the managers' side of dealing with numbers-phobia on deadline. Reporters who proudly say "I don't do numbers" or "I have a problem with numbers" are sometimes viewed by editors in the same way that reporters would be if they said "I don't do names—it's too scary to get the spelling right."

"Many reporters had to overcome a natural reluctance to knock on neighbors' doors or call a grieving family. Otherwise they could never be reporters. They have to overcome their fear of numbers to understand the increasingly sophisticated stories expected of us," Cohen says.

She believes the most difficult habit to overcome is the notebook-dumping syndrome.

"We're willing to throw out quotes or anecdotes we've collected. But somehow the carefully selected quote or elegantly crafted lead is sometimes followed by three paragraphs of incomprehensible numbers."

Cohen is the author of *Numbers in the Newsroom: Using Math and Statistics in News,* published by Investigative Reporters and Editors.

The Summary Page of a Typical City Budget

Purpose

The General Fund is used to finance and account for a large portion of the current operation expenditures and capital outlays of city government. The General Fund is one of the largest and most important of the city's funds because most governmental programs (Police, Fire, Public Works, Parks and Recreation, and so on) are generally financed wholly or partially from it. The General Fund has a greater number and variety of revenue sources than any other fund, and its resources normally finance a wider range of activities.

Appropriations

	Actual Fiscal Year 2000	Budget Fiscal Year 2001	Revised Fiscal Year 2002	Adopted Fiscal Year 2003
Personnel services	$9,500,353	$11,306,619	$11,245,394	$12,212,336
Materials and supplies	1,490,573	1,787,220	1,794,362	1,986,551
Training and schools	93,942	150,517	170,475	219,455
Utilities	606,125	649,606	652,094	722,785
Services	1,618,525	1,865,283	1,933,300	2,254,983
Insurance and miscellaneous	1,792,366	1,556,911	1,783,700	1,614,265
Total operating	15,101,884	17,316,156	17,579,325	19,010,375
Capital additions	561,145	1,123,543	875,238	460,143
Total operating and capital	15,663,029	18,439,699	18,454,563	19,470,518
Contingency	——	200,000	200,000	100,000
Total	$15,663,029	$18,639,699	$18,654,563	$19,570,518

Department Expenditures

	Actual Fiscal Year 2000	Budget Fiscal Year 2001	Revised Fiscal Year 2002	Adopted Fiscal Year 2003
City Council	$75,144	$105,207	$90,457	$84,235
City Clerk	61,281	70,778	74,444	91,867
City Manager	155,992	181,219	179,125	192,900
Municipal Court	164,631	196,389	175,019	181,462
Personnel	143,366	197,844	186,247	203,020
Law Department	198,296	266,819	248,170	288,550
Planning & Community Development	295,509	377,126	360,272	405,870

(continued)

The Summary Page of a Typical City Budget (continued)

Department Expenditures

	Actual Fiscal Year 2000	Budget Fiscal Year 2001	Revised Fiscal Year 2002	Adopted Fiscal Year 2003
Finance Department	893,344	940,450	983,342	1,212,234
Fire Department	2,837,744	3,421,112	3,257,356	3,694,333
Police Department	3,300,472	4,007,593	4,139,085	4,375,336
Health	1,033,188	1,179,243	1,157,607	1,293,362
Community Services	50,882	74,952	74,758	78,673
Energy Management	——	——	54,925	66,191
Public Works	2,838,605	3,374,152	3,381,044	3,509,979
Parks and Recreation	1,218,221	1,367,143	1,400,334	1,337,682
Communications & Info. Services	532,153	730,129	742,835	715,324
City General	1,864,200	1,949,543	1,949,543	1,739,500
Total Department Expenditures	15,663,028	18,439,699	18,454,563	19,470,518
Contingency	——	200,000	200,000	100,000
Total	$15,663,028	$18,639,699	$18,654,563	$19,570,518

"Department Expenditures" section, at the line for the Parks and Recreation Department. There's a decrease between Fiscal Year (FY) 2002 and 2003. Why? The summary page doesn't tell you, so you would have to look at the detail pages. There, you would discover that the drop results from a proposal by the city staff to halt funding of a summer employment program for teenagers. That's a story.

Another change that may be newsworthy is the increase in the Police Department budget. You'd better find out the reasons for that, too. In this case, the detail pages of the budget would show that most of the increase is going to pay for an administrative reorganization that is adding new positions at the top of the department. The patrol division is actually being reduced. Another story.

Look again at that Police Department line. Follow it back to FY 2001 and you'll see that the increase between 2001–02 was about $800,000. In two years, the budget for police increased by nearly one-third. That's an interesting trend. The same pattern holds true for the Fire Department as well. Some more checking is in order. With copies of previous budgets, you can see how far back the growth trend runs. You can also get from the departments the statistics on crimes and fires. Are the budget makers responding to a demonstrated need for more protection, or is something else at work behind the scenes?

More generally, you can trace patterns in the growth of city services and city taxes, and you can compare those with changes in population. Are the rates of change comparable? Is population growth outstripping growth in services? Are residents paying more per capita for city services than they were paying five or 10 years ago? More good story possibilities.

Another kind of comparison can be useful to your readers, too. How does your city government compare in cost and services with the governments of comparable cities? A few phone calls can add perspective to budget figures. Some professional organizations have recommended levels of service, such as number of police or firefighters per 1,000 inhabitants, which can help you help your readers assess how well they're being governed.

The same guidelines can be applied to the analysis of any budget. The numbers will be different, as will the department names, but the structures will be much the same. Whether you're covering the school board or the statehouse, look for changes, trends and comparisons.

Another document that is vital to understanding the finances of local government is the annual financial report. The financial report may be a few pages long, or it may be a book. In any case, its purpose is relatively simple. As its name suggests, the report is an explanation of the organization's financial status at the end of a *fiscal* year, which often is not the same as the end of the *calendar* year. Here you will find an accounting of all the income the organization received during the year from taxes, fees, state and federal grants, and other sources. You'll also find status reports on all the organization's operating funds, such as its capital improvement fund, its debt-service fund and its general fund.

Making sense of a financial report, like understanding a budget, isn't as hard as it may look. For one thing, the financial officer usually includes a narrative that highlights the most important points, at least from his or her viewpoint. But you should dig beyond the narrative and examine the numbers for yourself. The single most important section of the report is the statement of revenues, expenditures and changes in fund balance, which provides important measures of the organization's financial health. Depending on the comprehensiveness of the statement, you may have to refer to the budget document as well. You can check:

- Revenues actually received compared with budgeted revenues.
- Actual spending compared with budgeted spending.
- Actual spending compared with actual revenue.
- Changes in fund balances available for spending in years to come.

Look, for example, at the table on pp. 100–103. This combined statement gives a picture of the city's financial health. Notice first that the general fund was overspent by $2 million. Why? Was there a large

All Governmental Fund Types and Expandable Trust Funds
for the Year Ended September 30, 2003

	Governmental Fund Types		
	General Fund	Special Revenue Funds	Debt Service Funds
REVENUES			
General property taxes	$663,932	$530,713	$192,104
Sales tax	3,967,138	3,367,510	——
Other local taxes	3,138,904	228,718	——
Licenses and permits	253,287	5,146	——
Fines	378,207	——	——
Fees and service charges	244,356	——	——
Special assessments authorized	——	——	——
Intragovernmental	4,139,690	——	——
Revenue from other governmental units	796,292	1,164,482	——
Building rentals	——	——	——
Interest	1,314,130	196,612	6,228
Miscellaneous	53,548	——	——
TOTAL REVENUES	14,949,484	5,493,181	198,332
EXPENDITURES			
Current:			
Policy development and administration	2,328,546	291,493	——
Public safety	8,403,851	——	——
Transportation	2,387,534	——	——
Health and environment	1,617,146	——	——
Personal development	1,915,376	622,065	——
Public buildings	——	——	——
Miscellaneous non-programmed activities:			
Interest expense	273,195	——	——
Other	34,975	——	——
Capital outlay	——	——	——
Debt service:			
Redemption of serial bonds	——	——	175,000
Interest	——	——	278,488
Fiscal agent fees	——	——	758
TOTAL EXPENDITURES	16,960,623	913,558	454,246
EXCESS (DEFICIENCY) OF REVENUES OVER EXPENDITURES	(2,011,139)	4,579,623	(255,914)

	Governmental Fund Types		Fiduciary Fund Type	Total (memorandum only)	
	Capital Projects Fund	Special Assessment Funds	Expendable Trust Funds	2003	2002
	$ ——	$ ——	$ ——	$1,386,749	$1,961,851
	——	——	——	7,334,648	4,967,691
	——	——	——	3,367,622	2,923,775
	——	——	——	258,433	247,608
	——	——	——	378,207	346,224
	——	——	1,129,784	1,374,140	328,185
	——	490,159	——	490,159	359,862
	——	——	——	4,139,690	3,911,418
	154,919	——	901,815	3,017,508	3,087,431
	——	——	172,766	172,766	175,479
	23,282	——	88,428	1,628,680	1,869,874
	29,226	——	——	82,774	97,593
	207,427	490,159	2,292,793	23,631,376	20,276,991
	——	——	3,338	2,623,377	2,285,509
	——	——	——	8,403,851	6,998,232
	——	——	——	2,387,534	1,996,520
	——	——	1,080,811	2,697,957	1,652,809
	——	——	——	2,537,441	2,084,648
	——	——	371,942	371,942	336,204
	——	——	——	273,195	486,031
	——	——	——	34,975	4,296
	1,287,520	2,357,784	——	3,645,304	1,990,648
	——	——	——	175,000	155,000
	——	——	——	278,488	32,435
	——	——	——	758	285
	1,287,520	2,357,784	1,456,091	23,429,822	18,022,617
	(1,080,093)	(1,867,625)	836,702	201,554	2,254,374

(continued)

	Governmental Fund Types		
	General Fund	Special Revenue Funds	Debt Service Funds
OTHER FINANCING SOURCES (USES):			
Proceeds of general obligation bonds	—	—	—
Operating transfers from other funds	3,011,358	62,974	266,711
Operating transfers to other funds	(1,292,723)	(3,348,303)	—
TOTAL OTHER FINANCING SOURCES (USES)	1,718,635	(3,285,329)	266,711
EXCESS (DEFICIENCY) OF REVENUES AND OTHER FINANCING SOURCES OVER EXPENDITURES AND OTHER FINANCING USES	(292,504)	1,294,294	10,797
FUND BALANCES BEGINNING OF YEAR	4,195,912	3,004,533	43,645
Equity transfer to Recreation Services Fund	—	—	—
Contribution to Water & Electric Utility Fund	—	—	—
Contribution to Sanitary Sewer Utility Fund	—	—	—
Contribution to Regional Airport Fund	(200,000)	—	—
Contribution to Public Transportation Fund	—	—	—
Contribution to Parking Facilities Fund	—	—	—
Contribution to Recreation Services Fund	—	(152,000)	—
FUND BALANCES, END OF YEAR	$3,703,408	$4,146,827	$54,442

one-time expenditure, or couldn't the city live within its means? The general fund is the largest of all the budget categories, so overspending there is critical. Note, too, that when you go to the bottom of the 2003 Total column, the city has a small surplus of $201,554. Note also that spending rose more than $5.4 million, or 30 percent.

That is a significant increase. All these facts will lead you to good stories.

	Governmental Fund Types		Fiduciary Fund Type	Total (memorandum only)	
	Capital Projects Fund	Special Assessment Funds	Expendable Trust Funds	2003	2002
	5,681,633	1,134,261	——	6,815,894	——
	415,038	469,865	——	4,225,946	3,466,261
	——	(99,667)	(527,506)	(5,268,199)	(4,401,847)
	6,096,671	1,504,459	(527,506)	5,773,641	(935,586)
	5,016,578	(363,166)	309,196	5,975,195	1,318,788
	628,856	781,248	514,378	9,168,572	8,489,184
	——	——	(1,532)	(1,532)	(292,958)
	——	——	——	——	(30,395)
	——	——	——	——	(71,367)
	——	——	——	(200,000)	(160,191)
	——	——	——	——	(4,000)
	——	——	——	——	(15,489)
	——	——	——	(152,000)	(65,000)
	$5,645,434	$418,082	$822,042	$14,790,235	$9,168,572

Other clues may lead to other stories. Better look closely. As in the previous examples, they'll require more reporting and more explanation than reporters can pull from the numbers by themselves. Document in hand, head for the budget office. The guidelines offered here should help you shape your questions and understand the answers. With financial statements, as with budgets, look for changes, trends and comparisons. And always look hard at those numbers in parentheses.

MAKING SENSE OF NUMBERS FROM POLLS

Every day, new poll results come out that illustrate what people think about various topics in the news. And just about every day, journalists confuse readers when they try to interpret the results.

The most important thing to keep in mind about polls and surveys is that they are based on samples of a population. Every survey has a margin of error. That's because a survey reflects the responses of a small number of people within a population, so the results must be presented with the understanding that the scientific sampling method is not a perfect predictor for the entire population.

Suppose your news organization buys polling services and discovers that Candidate Smith has support from 58 percent of the people surveyed, Candidate Jones has support from 32 percent, and 10 percent are undecided. The polling service indicates that the margin of error of the poll is plus or minus 5 percent. The margin between the candidates is well above the margin of error, so you can write that Smith is leading in the poll.

But what happens if Smith has 50 percent support and Jones has 45 percent? The margin between the candidates is only as large as the margin of error, so you must report that the race is too close to call. If the margin between the candidates were less than 10 percent (two times the margin of error), you would only report that one candidate "appears to be leading."

The size of the margin of error is derived with mathematical formulas based on the size of a sample. It will always be readily available with reputable poll results.

In news story after news story, reporters forget the second lesson of reporting on polls: Subgroups within a sample are subject to a larger margin of error because fewer people are in the subgroup. Fewer respondents means less accuracy. If you want to write about how many women support Candidate Smith, you have to find out the appropriate margin of error, probably about 8 or 9 percent. That means if Candidate Smith shows 50 percent support among women surveyed, and Candidate Jones shows 38 percent, the survey results only reflect a slight lead because the margin of error is high. Being honest about figures that are that unreliable can be difficult, but it is the only way to keep your reporting accurate and fair.

Requirements for Sound Polling

The Associated Press Managing Editors Association prepared a checklist of the information you should have and should share with your audience about any poll on which you are reporting. Several of those points require some explanation.

Information about a poll to share with your audience

- *The identity of the sponsor of the survey.*
- *The exact wording of the questions asked.*
- *A definition of the population sampled.*
- *The sample size and, when the survey design makes it relevant, the response rate.*
- *Some indication of the allowance that should be made for sampling error.*
- *Which results are based on only part of the sample (for example, probable voters, those who have heard of the candidate or other subdivisions).*
- *When the interviews were collected.*
- *How the interviews were collected—in person, in homes, by phone, by mail, on street corners or wherever.*

Potential problems with polls

- *The people interviewed must be selected in a truly random fashion if you want to generalize from their responses to the whole population.*
- *The closer the results, the harder it is to say anything definitive.*
- *Beware of polls that claim to measure opinion on sensitive, complicated issues.*

Identity of sponsor. The identity of the survey's sponsor is important to you and your readers because it gives some clues to possible bias.

Exact wording of questions. The exact wording of the questions is important because the answer received often depends at least in part on how the question was asked.

Population. In polling, **population** means the total number of people in the group being studied. For an opinion survey, the population might be all registered voters in the state, black males under 25 or female cigarette smokers. The word "sampled" refers to the procedure in which a small number—or **sample**—of persons is picked at random so as to be representative of the population as a whole.

Sample size and response rate. The sample size is important because— all other things being equal—the larger the sample, the more reliable the survey results should be.

Margin of error. The sampling error or margin of error of any survey is the allowance that must be made for the possibility that the opinion expressed by the sample may not be exactly the same as the opinion of the whole population. Generally, the larger the sample, the smaller is the sampling error.

Which results are based on part of the sample. The existence of sampling error helps explain why it is important to know which results may be based on only part of the sample. The smaller that part, the greater is the margin of error.

When interviews were collected. When the interviews were collected may be of critical importance in interpreting the poll, especially during campaigns when the candidates themselves and other events may cause preferences to change significantly within a few days.

How interviews were collected. When the poll is your newspaper's, the obligation remains to let your readers know how it was taken. It is also incumbent on the paper to reveal how reliable the poll is.

The Need for Caution in Interpreting Polls

Whether you are helping to conduct a survey or reporting on someone else's, be on guard for the following potential problems:

The people interviewed must be selected in a scientific random fashion. If they are not, you have no assurance that the sample is representative. The people-in-the-street interview is practically worthless as an indicator of public opinion. Also invalid are such "polls" as the questionnaires interest groups mail to their members, whether the group is Planned Parenthood or the National Rifle Association.

The closer the results, the harder it is to say anything definitive. If the difference is 51-49 and the margin of error is ± 4 points, you can only report that the outcome is too close to call.

Beware of polls that claim to measure opinion on sensitive, complicated issues. Many questions of morality, or social issues such as race relations, do not lend themselves to simple answers. Opinions on such matters can be measured, but only by highly skilled researchers using carefully designed questions.

MIXING NUMBERS AND WORDS

Whatever the story and whatever the subject, numbers can most likely be used to clarify issues for readers and viewers. All too often, however, numbers are used in ways that muddy the water. Many journalists have some trepidation about working with numbers and often create confusion unwittingly when they work with the volatile mixture of numbers and words.

In *Mathsemantics: Making Numbers Talk Sense*, Edward MacNeal asserts that reporters and editors need to be far more careful in applying numbers in the news by questioning the accuracy and meaning of the numbers they gather and report.

For example, consider the following lead: "Each year 65,000 bicyclists go to the emergency room with injuries. Of those, 70–80 percent die because they weren't wearing helmets." Mathematically, that means that more than 45,000 bicyclists, and perhaps as many as 52,000, are dying each year, or between about 125 and 140 each day. It's much more likely that the figures meant something else entirely—that 70 to 80 percent of the bicyclists who died of their injuries would have been spared had they been wearing helmets. With the figures given, we still don't know how many bicyclists died.

Journalists can also encourage misunderstandings by describing large increases in percentage terms. For example, a news story reported that Nigerian drivers were quitting the roads because gas prices had increased "more than 300 percent." The headline said, "Tripling of gasoline prices empties roads in Nigeria." They can't both be true. A 300 percent increase would actually be a quadrupling of prices.

Another trouble spot for reporters is the calculation of how much more powerful or expensive something has become. For example, a class that grows from 20 students to 100 students is five times as big as it was, but it has four times more students than it had before.

The lesson to be learned from these examples is not to avoid numbers, but rather to use great care to ensure accuracy. Picking the right numbers to use and using them wisely will help your news stories have the biggest impact.

Suggested Readings

Campbell, Donald and Stanley, Julian. *Experimental and Quasi-Experimental Designs for Research.* Skokie, Ill.: Rand McNally, 1966. A classic guide to field experimentation that is also useful in providing a better understanding of scientific research.

Cohen, Sarah. *Numbers in the Newsroom: Using Math and Statistics in News.* Columbia, Mo.: Investigative Reporters and Editors, 2001. This book teaches you how to select the right numbers, just as you learn to select the right quotes, anecdotes or images.

Crossen, Cynthia. *Tainted Truth: The Manipulation of Fact in America.* New York: Simon & Schuster, 1994. An illuminating account of several instances in which public relations executives manipulated press coverage by twisting the numbers.

Cuzzort, R. P. and Vrettos, James S. *The Elementary Forms of Statistical Reason.* New York: St. Martin's Press, 1996. A basic guide for nonmathematicians in the humanities and social sciences who must work with statistics.

Demers, David Pearce and Nichols, Suzanne. *Precision Journalism: A Practical Guide.* Newbury Park, Calif.: Sage Publications, 1987. A primer for students and journalists, simply written and complete with examples.

MacNeal, Edward. *Mathsemantics: Making Numbers Talk Sense.* New York: Penguin USA, 1995. An entertaining and elucidating look into the semantics of numbers.

Meyer, Philip. *Precision Journalism*, Second Edition. Bloomington: Indiana University Press, 1993. A detailed introduction to surveying, conducting field experiments and using statistics to analyze the results by a reporter who pioneered the use of these methods in journalism. The theoretical justification of the techniques is included as well.

Paulos, John Allen. *A Mathematician Reads the Newspaper.* New York: Basic Books, 1995. The book, structured like the morning paper, investigates the mathematical angles of stories in the news and offers novel perspectives, questions and ideas.

Seltzer, Richard A. *Mistakes That Social Scientists Make.* New York: St. Martin's Press, 1996. A useful book about the kinds of errors often made by social scientists during their research.

Suggested Web Sites

www.math.temple.edu/~paulos

You've read his book, *Innumeracy: Mathematical Illiteracy and Its Consequences.* Get more writings from the master of numbers. Paulos is a professor at Temple University.

www.newsengin.com

The Newsengin site will do several computations for you, ranging in difficulty from figuring simple percentages to converting money for the impact of inflation. Also provided is a percentage calculator. As they say, you don't have to tell anyone you had to use it.

minneapolisfed.org/Research/data/us/calc/

The Federal Reserve Bank of Minneapolis maintains a great Web site for all calculations needed for calculating inflation. It also has a clear and simple explanation of how inflation is calculated and how to use the Consumer Price Index.

www.xe.net/ucc

This site will convert all currencies for you.

www.usatoday.com/money/calculator.htm

This site offers 12 calculators, including home mortgages and credit cards.

www.people-press.org

The Pew Research Center offers its own credible polls on politics and public issues. They offer all the data you need to accurately assess the polls.

Exercises

1. Find out from your campus financial aid office how much the graduating class has borrowed in Stafford Loans, the largest category of student loans. Calculate how much debt the average graduate will have in Stafford Loans. Then calculate how much debt the average indebted graduate will have. (The results will probably be quite different.) Find out what the total amount of payments owed will be for the average graduate with loans.

2. Find out how much your college charged for tuition in 1950, 1960, 1970, 1980 and 1990, and how much it charges today. Adjust those numbers for inflation so they can be compared to this year. Write a story about the cost of going to college.

3. Find a story in the newspaper that uses a lot of numbers. Rewrite the story to use the numbers for better effect.

4. Look up numbers in *The Chronicle of Higher Education* that show the incidence of different sorts of crimes on college campuses. Write a story about crime on your campus after comparing rates of crime on different campuses.

5. Get a copy of your city's or town's current budget, and come up with 10 questions a reporter should ask about the changes, patterns and trends the budget suggests.

6. Find a poll reported in a newspaper. Determine how many of the items that the Associated Press Managing Editors Association recommends appear in the story.

6   The Inverted Pyramid

William Caldwell, winner of a Pulitzer Prize in 1971, remembers the best lead he ever heard. He tells the story in an Associated Press Managing Editors "Writing" report:

One summer afternoon in 1922, I was on my way home from school and my daily stint of work as editor of the village weekly, unhonored and unpaid. Like my father and two uncles, I was a newspaperman.

My little brother came running to meet me at the foot of our street. He was white and crying. A telegram had come to my mother. "Pa drowned this morning in Lake George," he gasped, and I am ashamed to be remembering my inward response to that.

Before I could begin to sense such elements as sorrow, despair, horror, loneliness, anger—before all the desolation of an abandoned kid would well up in me, I found myself observing that the sentence my brother had just uttered was the perfect lead. Noun, verb, predicate, period, and who-what-when-where to boot.

Caldwell's brother had blurted out the essential information, just as journalists attempt to do in a more deliberate fashion. A story with this type of opening is called the **inverted pyramid** because it inverts, or reverses, the traditional story form. Rather than presenting the outcome or most important information at the end, the inverted pyramid places the main events at the beginning of the story. This form allows busy readers and listeners to get the news quickly. One of the oldest of journalism's story forms, it is still widely used.

Specialized news delivered to customers' desktop computers relies on the inverted pyramid. So do newspapers. Despite many editors' emphasis on encouraging new writing forms, 69 percent of the stories in U.S. newspapers use the inverted pyramid **(http://readership .org/content/editorial/feature-style/main.htm).** So do radio, television stations and newsletters. Business executives often use the inverted pyramid in company memos so their bosses don't have to read to the end to find the main point.

Frequently misdiagnosed as dying, the inverted pyramid has more lives than a cat—perhaps because the more people try to speed up the dissemination of information, the more valuable the inverted pyramid becomes. In the inverted pyramid, information is arranged from most important to least important. The king in Alice in Wonderland would never succeed in the electronic news service business. When asked where to start a story, he replied, "Begin at the beginning and go on till you come to the end; then stop." Reporters, however, often begin a story at its end. Subscribers to Dow Jones News Retrieval, Reuters and Bloomberg, for instance, react instantly to news about the financial markets to get an edge. They don't want narration; they want the news.

So do many newspaper readers, who, on average, spend 15 to 25 minutes a day reading the paper. If a reporter were to write an account of a car accident by starting when the driver left the house, many readers would never read far enough to learn that the driver was killed. Instead, such a story starts with its climax:

> Two people died Thursday when a backhoe fell off a truck's flatbed and sliced the top off an oncoming vehicle near Fairchild Air Force Base.

The inverted pyramid was fairly common by the 20th century. Before then, reporters were less direct. In 1869, the *New York Herald* sent Henry Morton Stanley to Africa to find the famous explorer-missionary David Livingstone. Stanley's famous account of the meeting began:

> Only two months gone, and what a change in my feelings! But two months ago, what a peevish, fretful soul was mine! What a hopeless prospect presented itself before your correspondent!

After several similar sentences, the writer reports, "And the only answer to it all is (that) Livingstone, the hero traveler, is alongside of me."

Stanley reported the most important information so casually that today's subscriber probably would not have learned that Livingstone had been found. Today's reporter would probably begin the story like this:

> David Livingstone, the missionary-explorer missing for six years, has been found working in an African village on the shores of Lake Tanganyika.

"Because a story is important, it doesn't follow that it must be long."

— *Stanley Walker,*
City Editor

The inverted pyramid saves readers time and editors space. It saves time by allowing readers to get the most important part of the story first—the climax of the event, the theme of a speech, the key finding in an investigation. It saves space by allowing editors to shorten stories by whacking from the bottom. If an editor had cut Stanley's story from the bottom, we would not have had the now-famous lines that end the story:

> "Dr. Livingstone, I presume?"
> And he says, "Yes."

Most journalism history books attribute the introduction of the inverted pyramid to the use of the telegraph during the Civil War. Forced to pay by the word, newspapers supposedly instructed their correspondents to put the most important information at the top.

Researchers at the University of Southern California have found that the inverted pyramid was used even earlier **(www.elon.edu/ dcopeland/mhm/volume1.htm)**. Whatever its origins, the inverted pyramid lead is presented as simply and clearly as possible. It sets the tone. It advertises what is coming in the rest of the story, and it conveys the most important information in the story.

The lead sits atop paragraphs arranged in descending order of importance. These paragraphs explain and provide evidence to support the lead. Print editors can quickly shorten the story because the paragraphs at the bottom are the least important. The need to produce multiple newspaper editions with the same story running different lengths in each one makes it important that stories can be shortened quickly. The inverted pyramid serves that need well. The format also serves web editors. Web consultants John Morkes and Jakob Nielsen found in a study that web users appreciate the utility of the inverted pyramid. One of their test subjects said, "I was able to find the main point quickly, from the first line. I like that." Another commented, "It got my attention right away. This is a good site. Boom. It gets to the point" **(www.useit.com/papers/webwriting/writing.html)**.

The inverted pyramid does have some shortcomings. Although it delivers the most important news first, it does not encourage people to read the entire story. Stories stop; they don't end. There is no suspense. In a Poynter Media Institute study published in the book *Eyes on the News*, researchers reported that of the 25 percent of readers who started a story, half of them dropped out midway through the story. Interest in an inverted pyramid story diminishes as the story progresses. But the way people use the inverted pyramid attests to its value as a quick means of information delivery. Readers can leave whenever their needs are met, not when the writer finishes the story. In an age when time is golden, the inverted pyramid still offers value.

The day when the inverted pyramid is relegated to journalism history has not yet arrived and probably never will. Nearly 70 percent of the stories in today's newspapers and almost 100 percent of the stories on news services for target audiences such as the financial community are written in the inverted pyramid form. The trend is changing—as it should be—but it's changing slowly. Some of the new media will require other forms. For instance, tailored stories for news-on-demand services that will reach a general audience need not use the inverted pyramid. Still, as long as newspaper, electronic and broadcast journalists continue to emphasize the quick, direct, simple approach to communications, the inverted pyramid and modifications of it will have a role.

Every journalist should master the inverted pyramid. Those who do will have mastered the art of making news judgments. The inverted pyramid requires you to identify and rank the most newsworthy elements in each story. That is important work. No matter what kind of stories you write—whether obituaries, accidents, speeches, press conferences, fires or meetings—you will be required to use the skills you learn here.

HOW TO WRITE LEADS

To write a **lead**—a simple, clear statement constituting the first paragraph or two of a story—you must first recognize what goes into one. As you read in Chapter 1, you begin by determining the story's *relevance, usefulness* and *interest* to readers. One way to measure those standards is to ask "So what?" or "Who cares?" So what if there's a car accident downtown? If it's one of hundreds of accidents a month, it may not be news. Any holdup in a community of 5,000 may be news because the "so-what" is that holdups are uncommon and residents probably know the person who was held up. Newspapers and broadcast stations in a metropolitan area may choose not to report a holdup because holdups are so common. But if a holdup appears to be part of a pattern or if someone is killed, the story becomes more significant. One holdup may not be news, but a holdup that authorities believe is one of many committed by the same person may be news. The "so-what" is that if the police catch this robber, they stop a crime spree.

To determine the "so-what," you have to answer six basic questions: who, what, where, when, why and how. The information from every event you witness and every story you hear can be reduced to answers to those six questions. If they add up to a significant "so-what," you have a story.

The six basic questions

1. *Who?*
2. *What?*
3. *Where?*
4. *When?*
5. *Why?*
6. *How?*

Consider this example of a sleepy television viewer who awakes to a fire in his house and frantically calls the Fire Department. The conversation at headquarters would likely have gone like this:

> "Fire Department."
> "FIRE!" a voice at the other end yells.
> "Where?" the dispatcher asks.
> "At 1705 West Haven Street."

When fire is licking at their heels, even non-journalists know the lead. How the fire started is not important to the dispatcher; that a house is burning—and where that house is located—is.

The journalist must go through essentially the same process to determine the lead. Whereas the caller served himself and the fire department, reporters must serve their readers. What is most important to them?

After the fire is over, there is much information a reporter must gather. Among the questions a reporter would routinely ask are these:

- When did it start?
- When was it reported?
- Who reported it?
- How was it reported?
- How long did it take the fire department to respond?
- How long did it take to extinguish the fire?
- How many fires have been attributed to careless smokers this year?
- How does that compare to figures in previous years?
- Were there any injuries or deaths?
- What was the damage?
- Who owned the house?
- Did the occupant or owner have insurance on the house?
- Will charges be filed against the smoker?
- Was there anything unusual about this case?
- Who cares?

With this information in hand, you can begin to write the story.

Writing the Lead

Start looking over your notes.

> *Who?* The owner, a smoker, Henry Smith, 29. The age is important. Along with other personal information, such as address and occupation, it differentiates him from other Henry Smiths in the readership area.
>
> *What?* Fire caused damage estimated by the fire chief at $2,500.
>
> *Where?* 1705 W. Haven St.
>
> *When?* The call was received at 10:55 p.m., Tuesday. Firefighters from Station 19 arrived at the scene at 11:04. The fire was extinguished at 11:30.
>
> *Why?* The fire was started by carelessness on the part of Smith, according to Fire Chief Bill Malone.
>
> *How?* Smith said he fell asleep in bed while he was smoking a cigarette.

"Writing is easy; all you do is sit staring at a blank sheet of paper until the drops of blood form on your fore-head."

—*Gene Fowler,*
Author

If you had asked other questions, you might have learned more from the fire department: This was the eighth fire this year caused by smoking in bed. All last year there were four such fires. Smith said he had insurance. The fire chief said no charges will be filed against Smith. It was the first fire at this house. Smith was not injured.

Have you figured out the "so-what"?

Assume your city editor suggests that you hold the story to about four paragraphs. Your first step is to rank the information in descending order of importance. There are lots of fires in this town, but eight this year have been caused by smoking in bed. Perhaps that's the most important thing about this story. You begin to type:

```
A fire started by a careless smoker caused an esti-
mated $2,500 in damage to a home.
```

Only 16 words. You should try to hold every lead to fewer than 25 words unless you use more than one sentence. Maybe it's too brief, though. Have you left anything out? Maybe you should include "when," the time element—to give the story a sense of immediacy. You rewrite:

```
A Tuesday night fire started by a careless smoker
caused an estimated $2,500 in damage to a home at 1705
W. Haven St.
```

The reader would also want to know "where." Is the fire near my house? Is it someone I know? Besides, you still have only 23 words.

Just then the city editor walks by and glances over your shoulder. "Who said it was a careless smoker?" the editor asks. "Stay out of the story."

You realize that you committed a basic error in newswriting: You allowed an unattributed opinion to slip into the story. You have two choices. You can attribute the "careless smoker" information to the fire chief in the lead, or you can rewrite. You choose to rewrite by using the chief's exact words. You also realize that your sentence emphasizes the damage instead of the cause. You write:

```
Fire that caused an estimated $2,500 in damage to a
home at 1705 W. Haven St. Tuesday was caused by smok-
ing in bed, Fire Chief Bill Malone said.
```

Now 28 words have answered the questions "what" (a fire), "where" (1705 W. Haven St.), "when" (Tuesday) and "how" (smoking in bed). And the information is attributed. But you have not answered "who" and "why." You continue, still ranking the information in descending order of importance. Compare this fire story with the approach in Figure 6.1.

```
The owner of the home, Henry Smith, 29, said he fell
asleep in bed while smoking a cigarette. When he awoke
about 30 minutes later, smoke filled the room.
    Firefighters arrived nine minutes after receiving the
call. It took them about 26 minutes to extinguish the
fire, which was confined to the bedroom of the one-story
house.
```

A four-vehicle accident on eastbound I-70 near Stadium Boulevard ended in two deaths on Sunday.

Barbara Jones, 41, of St. Louis died at the scene of the accident, and Juanita Doolan, 73, of St. Joseph died at University Hospital, according to a release from Springfield police. Two other people, William Doolan, 73, of St. Joseph and Theodore Amelung, 43, of Manchester, Mo., were injured in the accident.

Both lanes of traffic were closed on the eastbound side and limited to one lane on the westbound side as rescue workers cleared the scene.

Authorities said a westbound late-model Ford Taurus driven by Lan Wang of Springfield was traveling in the right lane, developed a tire problem and swerved into the passing lane. A Toyota pickup truck in the passing lane, driven by Jones , was forced over the grassy median along with the Taurus. The two vehicles entered eastbound traffic where the truck struck an Oldsmobile Delta 88, driven by Juanita Doolan, head on.

Wang and the one passenger in his car, Kenneth Kuo, 58, of Springfield, were not injured.

John Paul, a semi-tractor trailer driver on his way to Tennessee, said he had to swerve to miss the accident.

"I saw the red truck come across the median and hit the blue car," Paul said. "I just pulled over on the median and called 911."

Jones, who was wearing a seat belt, died at the scene, Officer Stan Williams said. Amelung, a passenger who had been in the truck, was out of the vehicle when authorities arrived, but it was unknown whether he was thrown from the truck or was pulled out by someone else, Williams said.

No charges have been filed, but the investigation continues.

What
Where
When
Provides details

Impact

How

Eyewitness

What's next

Figure 6.1
Note how this story, typical of the inverted pyramid structure, delivers the most important news in the lead and provides less essential details toward the end.

```
        According to Chief Malone, careless smokers have caused
    eight fires this year.
        Smith, who was not injured, said the house was insured.
```

You take the story to the city editor, who reads through the copy quickly. As you watch, she changes the lead to emphasize the "so-what." The lead now reads:

```
    A smoker who fell asleep in bed ignited a fire that
    caused minor damage to his home on W. Haven Street
```

```
Tuesday, Fire Chief Bill Malone said. It was the city's
eighth fire caused by smokers, twice as many as occurred
all last year.
```

The lead is 44 words, but it is broken into two sentences, which make it more readable. The importance of the "so-what" changes the direction of the story. The fire was minor; there were no injuries. However, the increase in the number of fires smokers caused may force the fire department to start a public-safety campaign against careless smoking. The city editor continues:

```
The owner of the home, Henry Smith, 29, of 1705
W. Haven St., said he fell asleep in bed while smoking
a cigarette. When he awoke about 30 minutes later,
smoke filled the room.
```

Then the city editor tells you to check the telephone book and the city directory. And you discover a serious problem. Both list the man who lives at 1705 W. Haven St. as Henry Smyth: S-m-y-t-h. City directories, like telephone books or any other sources, can be wrong. But at least they can alert you to possible errors. Confirm by going to original sources, in this case, Mr. Smyth himself.

Never put a name in a story without checking the spelling, even when the source tells you his name is "Smith."

You can learn several lessons from this experience:

Too many numbers bog down a lead. Focus on the impact of the figures in the lead, and provide details later in the story.

■ *Always* check names.
■ Keep the lead short, usually fewer than 25 words, unless you use two sentences.
■ Attribute opinion. (Smoking in bed is a fact. That it is careless is an opinion.)
■ Find out the "who," "what," "where," "when," "why" and "how." However, if any of these elements have no bearing on the story, they might not have to be included.
■ Write a sentence or paragraph telling readers what the news means to them.
■ Report information basic to the story even if it is routine. Not everything you learn is important enough to be reported, but you'll never know unless you gather the information.

Alternate Leads

In the lead reporting the fire, the "what" (fire) is of secondary importance to the "how" (how the fire started). A slightly different set of facts would affect the news value of the elements and, consequently, your lead. For instance, if Smyth turned out to be a convicted arsonist, you probably would emphasize that bizarre twist to the story:

```
A convicted arsonist awoke Tuesday to find that his
bedroom was filled with smoke. He escaped and later said
that he had fallen asleep while smoking.
    Henry Smyth, 29, who served a three-year term for . . .
```

That lead emphasizes the news value of novelty. If Smyth were the mayor, you would emphasize prominence:

```
Mayor Henry Smyth escaped injury Tuesday when he
awoke to find his bedroom filled with smoke. Smyth
said he had fallen asleep while smoking in bed.
```

The preceding examples also illustrate the "so-what" factor in news. A $2,500 fire is not news to many people in a large community where there are dozens of fires daily. Even if you crafted a tightly written story about it, your editor probably would not want to print or broadcast it. In a small community the story would have more impact because a larger proportion of the community is likely to know the victim and because there are fewer fires.

The "so-what" grows more important as you add other information. If the fire occurred during a fire-safety campaign, the "so-what" would be an example of the need for fire safety in a community where awareness of the problem had already been heightened. If the fire involved a convicted arsonist or the mayor, the "so-what" would be even stronger. Oddity or well-known people increase the value of a story. If someone was injured or the damage was $250,000 instead of $2,500, the "so-what" might even push the story into the metropolitan press. After you answer all six of the basic questions, remember to ask yourself what the answers mean to the reader. The answer is your "so-what" factor.

No journalist relies on formulas to write inverted pyramid leads, but you may find it useful, especially in the beginning, to learn some typical types of leads. The labels in the following sections are arbitrary, but the approaches are not.

Regardless of which of these leads you use, you as a journalist are trying to emphasize the relevance of the news to the reader. One good way to highlight the relevance is to speak directly to the reader by using "you." This informal second-person lead allows the writer to tell readers why they should care. For instance:

```
You will make more money buying Savings Bonds starting
tomorrow.
    The Treasury boosted the semiannual interest rate on
Series EE Savings Bonds to 5.92 percent from 4.7 percent
effective Tuesday.
```

"Selecting the quotes isn't so hard; it's presenting them that causes the trouble. And the worst place to present them is at the beginning. Quote leads deserve their terrible reputation. Yet they still appear regularly in both print and broadcast journalism.

We can make three generalizations about quote leads. They're easy, lazy, and lousy. They have no context. The readers don't know who's speaking, why, or why it matters. Without context, even the best quotations are wasted."

—**Paula LaRocque,**
Assistant Managing Editor,
The Dallas Morning News

Types of leads that can help you write once you decide what is most important

- Immediate-identification leads.
- Delayed-identification leads.
- Summary leads.
- Multiple-element leads.
- Leads with flair.

Readers want to know what's in it for them. The traditional approach is less direct:

```
The Treasury boosted Savings Bonds interest Tuesday
   to the highest rate in three years.
```

Like any kind of lead, the "you" lead can be overdone. You don't need to write "You have another choice in the student president's race." Just tell readers who filed their candidacy.

Immediate-Identification Leads

In the **immediate-identification lead,** one of the most important facts is the "who," or the prominence of the key actor. Reporters often use this approach when someone important or someone whose name is widely recognized is making news. Consider the following example:

CRAWFORD, Texas (AP)— President Bush said Thursday he will unveil an economic-stimulus package next week, promising a plan that will benefit all Americans and rejecting criticism that his policies are tailored to help the wealthy.

The president's name is in the lead because many people will recognize it. When writing for your campus newspaper or your local newspaper, you would use names in the lead that are known, not necessarily nationally but locally. The name of your student body president, the chancellor, the city's mayor or an entertainer who has a local following would logically appear in the lead. None of them would be used in a newspaper 50 miles away.

In any accident, the "who" may be important because it is someone well known by name or position. If so, the name should be in the lead.

In small communities the "who" in an accident may always be in the lead. In larger communities names are not as recognizable. As a rule, if a name is well-known, it should appear in the lead.

Delayed-Identification Leads

As Andy Warhol said, people have their 15 minutes of fame, yet that fame can be fleeting. While Terry Anderson of the AP was held captive from 1985-92 by the Islamic Jihad in Lebanon, even casual consumers of the news recognized his name. But a few years later when a court ruled that Anderson was entitled to damages, a **delayed-identification lead** was appropriate.

WASHINGTON—A former AP newsman was awarded $341 million from Iran on March 24 by a federal judge who said his treatment during his nearly seven years of captivity in Beirut was "savage and cruel by any civilized standards."

U.S. District Judge Thomas Penfield Jackson ordered Iran to pay $24.5 million to Terry Anderson, $10 million to his wife, Madeleine Bassil, and $6.7 million to their daughter, Sulome. The judge also ordered the Iranian Ministry of Information and Security to pay the three $300 million in punitive damages.

Usually a reporter uses a delayed-identification lead because the person, persons or organization involved has little name recognition among the readers. Thus, in fairly large cities an accident is usually reported like this:

MADISON, Wis.—A 39-year-old carpenter was killed today in a two-car collision two blocks from his home.

Dead is William Domonske of 205 W. Oak St. Injured in the accident and taken to Mercy Hospital were Mary Craig, 21, of 204 Maple Ave., and Rebecca Roets, 12, of 207 Maple Ave.

However, in a smaller community, names almost always make news. If Domonske lived in a city of 10,000, his name probably would be in the lead.

By the same token, most people know that IRS stands for "Internal Revenue Service." But many don't know that AARP stands for "American Association of Retired Persons." An Associated Press reporter used a delayed-identification lead in a story about AARP:

The nation's largest senior citizens organization paid $135 million to settle a dispute with the IRS over the income it earns from royalties.

However, the settlement leaves open the question of whether future income earned by the American Association of Retired Persons will be taxed, said the group's spokesman, Peter Ashkenaz.

In the wake of the destruction of the World Trade Center, Americans were attuned to all news about terrorists. When police arrested Robert Reid on charges that he had planned to bring an airliner down by detonating a bomb hidden in his shoe, his name was common currency among news consumers. But nearly a year later when a story appeared about him, the writer decided that a delayed-identification lead would be appropriate because many readers and listeners would have forgotten his name.

The man who pleaded guilty to trying to blow up an airplane with a shoe bomb cannot have a radio in his prison cell, a federal judge ruled Thursday.

Prosecutors argued that Robert Reid, 29, a self-proclaimed member of al-Qaida who has pledged support to Osama bin Laden, could use information gained from radio

broadcasts about al-Qaida to send coded messages to other al-Qaida followers outside prison.

A name that would appear in the lead in one city would appear in the second paragraph in another. The mayor of Birmingham, Ala., would be identified by title and name in Birmingham and by title only in Bridgewater, Conn.

Some titles are bulky: "Chairman of the Federal Communications Commission" assures you of clutter even before you add the name. "United Nations ambassador" takes away many options from the writer. When dealing with these types of positions, writers often choose to use the title and delay introducing the name until the second or third paragraph. When the title is better known than the name, writers usually use that title and delay the name until the second paragraph.

Summary Leads

Reporters dealing with several important elements may choose to sum up what happened in a **summary lead** rather than to highlight a specific action. It is one of the few times that a general statement is preferable to specific action.

When Congress passed a bill providing family members with emergencies the right to unpaid leaves from work, the writer had to make a choice: Focus on the main provision or write a summary lead. The writer chose the latter:

> A bill requiring employers to give workers up to three months unpaid leave in family emergencies won Senate approval Thursday evening.

Several other provisions in the bill are explained later in the story: The unpaid leave can be for medical reasons or to care for a new child, and employers would have to continue health-insurance benefits and restore employees to their previous jobs or equivalent positions.

You can also show readers the "so-what" with the "you" lead:

> The Senate voted Thursday to allow you to take up to three months unpaid leave in family emergencies without losing your health benefits.

Likewise, if a city council rewrites the city ordinances, unless one of the changes is of overriding importance, most reporters will use a summary lead:

> MOLINE, Ill.—The City Council replaced the city's 75-year-old municipal code with a revised version Tuesday night.

"Because the inverted pyramid has become a natural reflex in both my reporting and writing, I had enough time to go back and tell readers about foursomes who finished their rounds rather than seek shelter and panicked members who tried to save their Great Big Berthas from a fiery locker room," she said.

St. Clair, a staff writer at the *Daily Herald* in the Chicago suburbs, believes the inverted pyramid suffers from an unfair stereotype. "Editors and professors regularly call the writing style uninspired or elementary, but it doesn't have to be. Using the inverted pyramid does not release reporters from the responsibilities of good writing. Pacing, word choice, description, anecdotes—all have a place in the inverted pyramid," she said.

The inverted pyramid forces you to ask "What's important here? What's the story really about?" As St. Clair notes, "Once it becomes second nature, the inverted pyramid teaches you how to focus on a story whether it's a 60-inch feature or a 9-inch car crash story."

Summary leads don't only appear in reports of board meetings. A Spokane, Wash., reporter used a summary lead to report a neighborhood dispute:

An Idaho farmer's fence apparently was cut last week. It set off a chain of events Friday night that landed three people in the hospital, killed a cow and totaled a vehicle in the eastern Spokane Valley.

The basic question the reporter must answer is whether the whole of the action is more important than any of its parts. If the answer is yes, a summary lead is in order.

Multiple-Element Leads

In some stories, limiting the lead to one theme would be too restrictive. In such cases the reporter can choose a **multiple-element lead** to work more information into the first paragraph. But you should write the lead within the confines of a clear, simple sentence or sentences. Consider this example:

PORTLAND, Wash.—The City Council Tuesday ordered three department heads fired, established an administrative review board and said it would begin to monitor the work habits of administrators.

Notice that not only the actions but also the structure of the verb phrases within the sentence are parallel. Parallel structure also characterizes the following news extract, which presents a visual picture of the scene of a tragedy:

BAY CITY, Mich.—A flash fire that swept through a landmark downtown hotel Saturday killed at least 12 persons, injured 60 more and forced scores of residents to leap from windows and the roof in near-zero cold.

In the last example, we are told where the fire happened, what happened and how many were killed and injured.

Some multiple-element leads actually consist of two paragraphs. This occurs when the reporter decides that several elements need prominent display. For example:

The Board of Education Tuesday voted to lower the tax rate 12 cents per $100 valuation. Members then approved a budget $150,000 less than last year's and instructed the superintendent to decrease the staff by 25 people.

The board also approved a set of student conduct rules, which include a provision that students with three or more unexcused absences a year will be suspended for a week.

> *"Language is a very difficult thing to put into words."*
> —**Voltaire,** *Philosopher*

This story, too, could emphasize the "so-what" while retaining the multiple elements:

> The Board of Education lowered your real estate taxes Tuesday. Members also approved a budget $150,000 less than last year's and instructed the superintendent to decrease the staff by 25 people.

Simpler leads are preferable. But a multiple-element lead is one of the reporter's options. Use it sparingly.

Many newspapers are using graphic devices to take the place of multiple-element leads in some cases. Summary boxes can be used to list other actions. Because the box appears under the headline in type larger than text, it serves as a graphic summary for the reader who is scanning the page. The box frees the writer from trying to jam too many details into the first few paragraphs (see Figure 6.2).

Another approach is to break the coverage of a single event into a main story and a shorter story or stories, called **sidebars.** This approach offers the advantage of presenting the information in shorter, more palatable bites. It also allows the writer to elevate more actions into lead positions.

Both these methods of presentation have advantages over the more complicated multiple-element lead.

> *"The lead should be a promise of great things to come, and the promise should be fulfilled."*
> —**Stanley Walker,** *City Editor*

Leads with Flair

Although the inverted pyramid is designed to tell readers the news first and fast, not all stories begin with the most important statement. When the news value you want to emphasize is novelty, often the lead is unusual.

When a group of suspected drug dealers was arrested at a wedding, the Associated Press focused on the novelty:

> NARRAGANSETT, R.I. (AP)—The wedding guests included drug suspects, the social coordinator was a narcotics agent, the justice of the peace was a police chief, and 52 officers were party crashers.
>
> For the unsuspecting bride and groom, the ceremony Friday night was truly unforgettable—a sting operation set up by state and local police that led to 30 arrests.

Other council action
In other action, the council:
✓Voted to repave Broadway Ave.
✓Rejected a new sign ordinance.
✓Hired four school crossing guards.
✓Expanded bus hours.

Figure 6.2
A summary box can take the place of a multiple-element lead.

Not exactly your traditional wedding or your traditional lead. Yet the essential information is contained within the first two paragraphs. A less imaginative writer would have written something like this:

> Thirty suspected drug dealers, including a couple about to be married, were arrested at a wedding Friday night.

That approach is like slapping a generic label on a Mercedes-Benz. The inverted pyramid approach is not so rigid that it doesn't permit fun and flair.

What is the difference between the two-paragraph multiple-element lead on the board of education and the two-step lead on the wedding story? In the first, the reporter was dealing with several significant actions. In the second, the reporter was dealing with only one, so she used the first paragraph to set up the surprise in the second.

Writing for the Web

In Chapter 13, you will learn details about writing news for the Web. You will find that most Web news sites rely on the inverted pyramid to present information quickly. For example, when surgeons in Wheeling, W.Va., took a leave of absence to protest malpractice costs, **CNN.com** ran this lead:

> WHEELING, West Virginia (CNN)—Four West Virginia hospitals are transferring emergency room cases or canceling procedures as at least 39 surgeons stayed off the job for a second day Thursday to protest rising medical malpractice insurance costs.

That's 33 words. **MSNBC.com** ran the Associated Press dispatch, which consists of three sentences, one 31 words, one 13 and one eight words:

> CHARLESTON, W.Va., Jan. 1—Almost all surgeries were canceled at four Northern Panhandle hospitals Wednesday as more than two dozen surgeons started a job action in a protest against the high cost of malpractice insurance. At least one patient had to be transferred 90 miles to another hospital. In Pennsylvania, a similar work stoppage was averted.

Although the two sites emphasized different angles, both used the traditional inverted pyramid.

Some news sites, however, create summaries of a story rather than present just the most important information. They display a lead, then require readers to click to the rest of the story or scroll deeper into the site, often past an advertisement. A summary serves as information and as an invitation to continue reading.

For instance, **MSNBC.com** ran this 90-word summary:

U.S. Secretary of State Colin Powell lambasted Baghdad on Monday, citing a series of unanswered questions about Iraq's weapons raised by a report of U.N. inspectors earlier in the day. Powell said consultations would be needed before the United States would launch military action, but said that there was "not much more time" for Iraq to comply. The inspectors reported to the U.N. Security Council that Iraq had cooperated with inspectors, but Baghdad has not demonstrated a "genuine acceptance" of the need to disarm itself of weapons of mass destruction.

By contrast, look at AP's more typical lead on the story:

The Bush administration dismissed Iraq's response to U.N. disarmament demands as inadequate Monday, arguing that nothing in the inspection report shows Baghdad has done enough to avert war. "They are not cooperating unconditionally," John Negroponte, the U.S. ambassador to the United Nations, said in New York.

AP's lead is long—46 words—by traditional standards. It concentrates on one aspect, the administration's rejection of Iraq's response. MSNBC's summary includes the administration's response, offers additional details from Powell and includes what the inspectors reported to the United Nations. The mini-summary is the most notable departure from standard inverted pyramid leads in Web news sites.

Another notable difference in writing the inverted pyramid story for the Web arises because of readers' ability to link to additional information. By including links, the writer can leave out some of the background and context that ordinarily might be in the story. The Web also allows the writer to package everything from maps to vocabulary to complete texts in the links. Readers choose the depth they prefer.

STORY ORGANIZATION

Like the theater marquee, the lead is an attention-getter. Sometimes the movie doesn't fulfill the promises of the marquee; sometimes the story doesn't fulfill the promises of the lead. In either case the customer is dissatisfied.

The inverted pyramid is designed to help reporters put information in logical order. It forces the reporter to rank, in order of importance, the information to be presented.

Just as there is a checklist for writing the lead, there is also a checklist for assembling the rest of the inverted pyramid. Included on that checklist are the following items:

■ Introduce additional important information you were not able to include in the lead.

- If possible, indicate the significance or "so-what" factor.
- Elaborate on the information presented in the lead.
- Continue introducing new information in the order in which you have ranked it by importance.
- Develop the ideas in the same order in which you have introduced them.
- Generally, use only one new idea in each paragraph.

Now let's see how the pros do it. The following examples are full stories using the inverted pyramid structure.

One-Subject Stories

Most newspaper stories concentrate on a single subject. The following articles, from the Associated Press and the Wheeling, W.Va., *News-Register,* are both about the surgeons who took leaves of absence to protest the cost of malpractice insurance. The AP story is for a national audience; the *News-Register* story is for a local audience. The different audiences explain the differences in story organization and emphasis.

CHARLESTON, W.Va. (AP)—Four West Virginia hospitals cut staff hours and transferred more patients Thursday because of a surgeons' walkout to protest malpractice costs.

State officials planned to announce an emergency program Thursday afternoon to ensure medical service to patients in the state's northern panhandle.

In February 2003, doctors, nurses and hospital staff organized walkouts to protest medical malpractice costs.

More than two dozen ortho-pedic, general and heart surgeons in the area began 30-day leaves of absence Wednesday or planned to begin leaves in the next few days to protest medical malpractice costs.

They want the state to make it harder to file malpractice lawsuits, which they say would eventually lower their insurance premiums. They also want the state to seek help from insurance companies and other third parties to pay a larger share of their costs.

The state's emergency program will involve ambulance transfer and patient referral procedures, State Insurance and Retirement Services Director Tom Susman said.

"We know there's concern among area residents, and our top priority is to ensure the citizens of the northern panhandle get the medical care they need," Susman said.

Four patients, including two heart patients, were moved Thursday, raising the number in the two-day protest to seven.

The four affected hospitals also began reducing shifts of operating room nurses and other surgical support staff.

"It's definitely generating worries within our staff, both about their own financial needs and about the health of the community," said Howard Gamble, spokesman for Ohio Valley Medical Center in Wheeling.

A surgeon taking part in a job action said doctors' pleas for help have been ignored by state officials.

"We have had many meetings with state legislators and past governors. We have asked for help in the past. It seems as if it has fallen on deaf ears," Dr. Greg Saracco said on CBS' "Early Show." "Physicians no longer want to come to work. Physicians are afraid to accept liability."

State Insurance and Retirement Services Director Tom Susman has said Gov. Bob Wise will offer details of a new malpractice insurance plan in his State of the State address next week.

Last-minute talks with state officials failed to stop the protest. A similar walkout in Pennsylvania was averted when Gov.-elect Ed Rendell promised to work for a solution.

At least 18 of 19 surgeons at Wheeling Hospital are beginning 30-day leaves of absence, and 11 others have asked for leaves from Weirton Medical Center. Ohio Valley Medical Center in Wheeling and Reynolds Memorial Hospital in Glen Dale said surgeons there were taking leaves, but it was unclear how many.

All four hospitals are keeping emergency rooms open. But, with the exception of plastic surgeons, they have almost no emergency surgeons available, which will require most patients to be transferred to hospitals in Ohio, Pennsylvania and Morgantown.

Dr. Donald Hofreuter, Wheeling Hospital's chief executive officer, said he understands the doctors' frustration, but he also is concerned about patient care.

One Wheeling Hospital patient needing emergency surgery Wednesday morning was transferred 88 miles to Ruby Memorial Hospital in Morgantown, and two heart patients were transferred to Pennsylvania hospitals, Hofreuter said.

On Thursday, Weirton Medical Center transferred two patients to a hospital in

Steubenville, Ohio. Wheeling Hospital transferred two heart patients to Pittsburgh-area hospitals. The four required non-emergency surgery.

Wheeling Hospital temporarily reinstated one of its surgeons who had taken a leave of absence so the surgeon could help a patient who couldn't be transferred, Hofreuter said. He declined to give details.

The *News-Register* writers are able to assume local knowledge about local names of people and hospitals. They focus on the impact to the local hospitals, and, by extension, the impact on the community, two angles not of interest across the rest of the country.

Tom Diana and Kristen Burrier
News-Register

The first day of the year marked the first day of leaves of absence for at least 30 days by most surgeons at Ohio Valley Medical Center and Wheeling Hospital. Meanwhile, ten Weirton Medical Center surgeons joined them in a walkout Wednesday.

The leaves of absence are in response to what the doctors view as a crisis in the cost of medical malpractice insurance premiums, which have dramatically increased in the last several years. After pushing for liability insurance and tort reform for the past two years, they are hoping their action puts enough political pressure on the West Virginia State Legislature and Gov. Bob Wise's administration to enact meaningful reform very soon. The legislative session will commence Jan. 8.

Dr. Donald Hofreuter, administrator and chief executive officer of Wheeling Hospital, said 18 out of 19 surgeons in the fields of general, orthopedic and cardiovascular surgery have submitted letters requesting at least a 30-day leave of absence.

"The one that's not involved is an employee of the hospital and he is an orthopedic surgeon," Hofreuter said.

Howard Gamble, spokesman for OVMC, said 13 surgeons have asked for leaves of absence.

"Only surgeons have asked for leaves of absence," he said.

According to Weirton Medical Center Senior Administrator John Frankovitch, as of Wednesday, Weirton Medical Center's orthopedic and urology departments are without staff.

"The walkout did occur (Wednesday)," Frankovitch said. "We did not have to transfer any patients. As of (Wednesday) we have no coverage for orthopedic surgery and urology."

According to Frankovitch, WMC has received 11 formal leave of absence requests from surgeons in four departments, but Dr. Jayapal Reddy, a general surgeon, rescinded his request Tuesday.

Hofreuter said when a surgeon is on a leave of absence, he relinquishes his privileges to practice medicine at the hospital. He said that some of the surgeons requested 30-day leaves of absence with the option of extending them further.

"That 30 days is the shortest time a physician can request a leave of absence (by law)," he said.

Hofreuter said since the walk-outs there has been one person in need of emergency surgical treatment who came to the hospital after midnight (Wednesday morning). This person was transferred to Ruby Memorial Hospital in Morgantown via Tri-State Ambulance, which is a wholly owned subsidary of Wheeling Hospital.

Hofreuter said if a person were transported to the emergency unit of Wheeling Hospital and needed immediate surgery, a surgeon on a leave of absence could be contacted to come in and be granted an emergency lifting of their leave of absence status.

On the possibility of someone dying as a result of a lack of surgical care because of the leaves of absence by surgeons at Wheeling Hospital Hofreuter said, "Not on my watch."

Frankovitch said patients requiring the services of orthopedic or urologic surgeons in an emergency will have to be transferred to other area hospitals. He also said many surgeries come to WMC through primary care physician referrals that will have to be referred to other area hospitals.

"We have relationships with a variety of Pittsburgh hospitals," Frankovitch said. "And we are working to make sure that our relationships with other facilities we have are so that patients can be transferred. A lot of those patients come directly from the primary care. So what we're doing is making sure our primary care physicians have information. If they need to get a physician, or specialist, or surgeon they have a list of our referral sources.

"From the ER perspective, the most problematic are general surgery and orthopedics."

One solution that has been proposed for the problem by the

Wise Administration is to make a combined OVMC/Wheeling Hospital Trauma Level II center. Tom Susman, director of Insurance and Retirement Services for the state, said such an emergency center would have the required medical personnel, including a neurosurgeon, so that emergency patients would not have to be life-flighted out of the area. Currently, the Wheeling area does not have a neurosurgeon available.

Susman said that by having a state-designated Trauma Level II center, it would offer the surgeons working there an opportunity to have a portion of their medical malpractice insurance coverage with the state, known as BRIM I.

BRIM I insurance rates, reserved for trauma physicians and other state physicians and employees, offers lower rates than BRIM II rates, which cover most other doctors in the state. Susman said that BRIM I rates are about one-third lower than BRIM II rates.

However, trauma physicians are only covered by BRIM I rates in the proportion of their practice that is spent at a trauma center. Furthermore, even BRIM I rates are expected to rise by 23 percent on July 1, Susman said.

"It's (BRIM I) an artificially low rate and it's in the process of being increased," he said.

Gamble said providing lower malpractice insurance premiums for trauma physicians would not help others who do not provide medical service at a trauma center.

"Many of the physicians do not provide service to the trauma centers," Gamble said. "We don't see that plan as a solution."

Although surgeons are involved in the leaves of absence,

Gamble said other physicians support their cause. "There are other physician specialties that are in the same position and are behind them."

Gamble also mentioned the hospital itself needs insurance premium relief. He said the parent company of OVMC and East Ohio Regional Hospital pays $10,000 per day for its insurance under BRIM for medical facilities. That cost, he said, is expected to rise this year.

Susman believes the proposal to make a combined Trauma Level II center would provide benefits to more than the physicians.

"What's nice about Wheeling being Level II is it's good for the community," Susman said.

He also said that the political leaders of the state have been working on a solution to the problem that they hope to implement as soon as possible

after the legislature meets on Jan. 8.

"We have to do something that's a broad-based fix for the whole state," Susman said. "We're trying to determine how to structure that. We're going to be working within the administration to see what our resources are. With or without the walkout we know we have to fix this thing in this (legislative) session."

However, Susman noted the leaves of absence have not helped the situation.

"It's taking our time from working on the solution (by having) to address the walkout," he said.

Gamble doesn't believe it's good policy to wait until the Jan. 8 legislative session. He believes it should happen "before the state legislature meets because seven days without certain surgical coverage could be catastrophic."

Multiple-Element Stories

Earlier in this chapter, we discussed multiple-element leads. They occur most often when you are reporting on councils, boards, commissions, legislatures and even the U.S. Supreme Court. These bodies act on numerous subjects in one sitting. Frequently, their actions are unrelated, and more than one action is often important enough to merit attention in the lead. You have three options:

Options for multiple-element stories

- *More than one story.*
- *A summary box.*
- *A multiple-element lead and story.*

You can write more than one story. That choice, of course, depends on permission from your editor. There may not be enough space.
You can write a summary box. The box would be displayed along with the story. In it you would list the major actions taken by the council or decisions issued by the court.
You can write a multiple-element lead and story. Let's go back to the one we used earlier when discussing leads:

The Board of Education Tuesday night voted to lower the tax rate 12 cents per $100 valuation. Members then approved a budget $150,000 less than last year's and instructed the superintendent to decrease the staff by 25 people.

The board also approved a set of student conduct rules, which include a provision that students with three or more unexcused absences a year will be suspended for a week.

There are four newsworthy actions in those two paragraphs: establishing a tax rate, approving a budget, cutting staff and adopting conduct rules. In this and all stories that deal with several important elements, the writer highlights the most important. Sometimes there are several that can be equated, as in the school board example. But most of the time, one action stands out above the rest. When it does, it is important to summarize other actions after the lead. For instance, if you and your editor judged that establishing the tax rate was more important than anything else that happened at the school board meeting, you would approach it like this:

Lead	The Board of Education Tuesday night voted to lower the tax rate 12 cents per $100 valuation.
Support for lead	The new rate is $1.18 per $100 valuation. That means that if your property is assessed at $30,000, your school tax will be $354 next year.
Summary of other action	The board also approved a budget action that is $150,000 less than last year's, instructed the superintendent to cut the staff by 25 and approved a set of rules governing student conduct.

Notice that the lead is followed by a paragraph that supports and enlarges upon the information in it before the summary paragraph appears. Whether you need a support paragraph before summarizing other action depends on how complete you are able to make the lead.

In all multiple-element stories, the first two or three paragraphs determine the order of the rest of the story. To maintain coherence in your story, you must then provide the details of the actions in the order in which you introduced them.

Suggested Readings

Brooks, Brian S., Pinson, James L. and Wilson, Jean Gaddy. *Working with Words*, Fourth Edition. New York: Bedford/St. Martin's, 2000. A must reference book for any journalist. Excellent coverage of grammar and word usage and a strong chapter on "isms."

Gillman, Timothy. "The Problem of Long Leads in News and Sports Stories." *Newspaper Research Journal*, Fall 1994, pp. 29-39.

Walker, Stanley. *City Editor.* New York: Frederick A. Stokes Co., 1934. Out of print, the book may be difficult to find, but it's worth the search. Walker was city editor of the *New York Herald Tribune*. His tips about writing news remain valid.

Suggested Web Sites

www.elon.edu/dcopeland/mhm/volume1.htm

Marcus Errico and others from the University of Southern California posit that the traditional history of the evolution of the inverted pyramid is more myth than fact.

www.journalism.org/resources/research/reports/
framing/default.asp

The Committee of Concerned Journalists is conducting an in-depth study of news framing to determine whether what is important has changed. The results track changes in the use of the inverted pyramid.

www.wsu.edu:8080/~brians/errors/index.html

Paul Brians, a professor of English at Washington State University, will answer your questions about the English language.

www.readership.org/content/editorial/feature-style/main.htm

The Readership Institute, which studies ways to improve newspapers, reports on reader reactions to various writing styles.

www.inms.umn.edu/elements/

This site helps practitioners to develop new storytelling forms for the Web.

Exercises

1. Identify the "who," "what," "where," "when," "why" and "how," if they are present, in the following:

    The United Jewish Appeal is sponsoring its first-ever walk-a-thon this morning in Springfield to raise money for The Soup Kitchen, a place where the hungry can eat free.

2. Here are four versions of the same lead. Which of the four leads answers more of the six questions basic to all stories? Which questions does it answer?
   a. What began 12 years ago with a federal staff investigation and led to hearings and a court fight culminates today with a Federal Trade Commission rule to prevent funeral home rip-offs.
   b. The nation's funeral home directors are required to offer detailed cost statements starting today, a service they say they are now ready to provide despite nearly a dozen years of debate over the idea.
   c. A new disclosure law going into effect today will make it easier for us to determine the cost of a funeral.
   d. Twelve years after first being proposed, a federal regulation goes into effect Monday to require funeral homes to provide an itemized list of services and materials they offer, along with the cost of each item, before a person agrees to any arrangements.

3. Rewrite two of the leads in exercise 2 as "you" leads. Which are better, the third-person or second-person leads, and why?

4. From the following facts, write a lead.
   Who: a nuclear weapon with a yield equivalent to 150,000 tons of TNT.
   What: detonated.
   Where: 40 miles from a meeting of pacifists and 2,000 feet beneath the surface of Pahute Mesa in the Nevada desert.
   When: Tuesday.
   Why: to test the weapon.
   How: not applicable.

   Other information: Department of Energy officials are the source; 450 physicians and peace activists were gathered to protest continued nuclear testing by the United States.

5. From the following facts, write the first paragraph of a news article.
   Who: eight people killed, 16 injured, an unknown number trapped inside.
   What: Explosion demolished a plastics factory. Fire followed the explosion.
   Where: Kinston, N.C.
   When: approximately 9 a.m. Wednesday
   How: Fire followed the explosion.
   Why: not applicable

6. From the following facts, write the first two paragraphs of a news article.
   Who: 40 passengers.

What: evacuated from a Northwest Airlines jet, Flight 428.
Where: at the LaCrosse, Wis., Municipal Airport.
When: Monday following a flight from Minneapolis to LaCrosse.
Why: A landing tower employee spotted smoke near the wheels.
How: not applicable.

Other information: There was no fire or injuries; the smoke was caused by hydraulic fluids leaking onto hot landing brakes, according to Bob Gibbons, a Northwest spokesman.

7. Describe picture and information-graphic possibilities for the story in exercise 6.

8. From the following information, write the first two paragraphs of a news story:
Who: about 1,000 high school students.

What: protest that turned into a rock- and bottle-throwing melee. 10 people were arrested, and nearly 30 were injured.
Where: outside Montwood High School in your community.
When: Thursday.
Why: Students were protesting changes in class schedules.
How: Students walked out of class in protest, then began attacking security personnel with rocks and glass bottles.

9. Using a database that includes several newspapers, find at least two versions of the same story. Analyze the similarities and differences between them; then decide which of the two is preferable and why.

Beyond the Inverted Pyramid

Barney Calame, the deputy managing editor of *The Wall Street Journal*, was chatting with a group of journalists. Talking about the number of his family members who had lived long lives, Calame offered an example:

> "My grandmother, who had one leg, lost the other when she tried to flee the nursing home in a wheelchair when she was 96."
> He stopped. Everyone looked at him expectantly.
> "Well?" said one listener.
> "Well what?" Calame asked.
> "How did your grandmother lose her other leg? Why was she fleeing the nursing home?"
> "Grandmother decided that she didn't like living in the nursing home," Calame responded. "She took off in her wheelchair, tipped going over the curb and spilled onto the street. She developed an infection in her injured leg and later had to have it amputated."

Calame was telling stories to friends. When we tell stories, we start at the beginning, or at least close enough to the beginning so the story makes sense. The approach allows the speaker to build to the climax.

Using the inverted pyramid, we get to the point as quickly as possible. That approach saves readers' and listeners' time, but it's not the way to tell stories. If we want to engage our readers intellectually and emotionally, if we want to inform and entertain, we must use writing techniques that promise great things to come and then fulfill that promise. To that end, we should use the techniques of narration: scene re-creation, dialogue, foreshadowing and anecdotes. With these devices, we reward readers.

Although narrative techniques can and should be used in all kinds of writing, narration thrives in structures other than the inverted pyramid. Some story structures are hybrids of the inverted pyramid and chronology structures. Others are adaptations of chronology. These structures are even suitable for breaking news stories if you are able to gather enough information to re-create scenes jammed with pertinent detail, if you are able to confirm the chronology and if you are able to capture the dialogue. These structures also support investigative reports, profiles, oddities and issue stories—all genres that allow you more time to gather and write.

If time, detail and space are available, use the techniques of narration and structures other than the inverted pyramid. Whether you are writing about a car accident, the Boy Scouts, the health-care system, corruption in government or the 8-year-old running the corner lemonade stand, writing the story will be easier if you know how to use some of the alternative techniques and story forms.

THE TECHNIQUES OF NARRATION

Exposition is the ordering of facts. **Narration** is the telling of a story. When we arrange facts from most to least important, we call the resulting structure the *inverted pyramid*. When we use scenes, anecdotes and dialogue in chronology to build to a climax, we call the structure narrative.

Narrative writing appears in all media these days—newspapers, magazines, on the Web and on television. Wherever it appears, storytellers don't speak in monotone. They add inflection to maintain listeners' interest. To avoid telling stories in monotone, writers re-create scenes with detail and dialogue, foreshadow the good stuff to come, and tempt readers to continue reading by offering them treats in the form of anecdotes.

In exposition, the writer clearly stands between the reader and the information; the people in the story whisper to the writer, who turns and speaks to the reader. In narration, the storyteller moves aside and allows the reader to watch the action unfold.

> *Move your story along by*
>
> - *Re-creating vivid scenes.*
> - *Letting the characters speak to each other through dialogue.*
> - *Foreshadowing important events.*
> - *Relating memorable anecdotes.*

Vivid Scenes

Gene Roberts, former managing editor of *The New York Times*, tells about his first job at a daily newspaper. His publisher, who was blind, had the newspaper read to him each morning. One day, the publisher called Roberts into his office and complained, "Roberts, I can't see your stories. Make me see."

We should all try to make readers see, smell, feel, taste and hear. One way to do that is to re-create scenes. First, you have to be there. You need to capture the sights, sounds and smells that are pertinent.

A student reporter at South Dakota State University was there to capture this opening:

> Don Sheber's leathery, cracked hands have been sculpted by decades of wresting a living from the earth.
>
> But this year, despite work that often stretches late into the evening, the moisture-starved soil has yielded little for Sheber and his family.
>
> Sheber's hands tugged at the control levers on his John Deere combine last week as rotating blades harvested the thin stands of wheat that have grown to less than a foot high. . . .

> *Good writing shows*
>
> 1. *Gather information with all your senses. Gather smells, sounds, sights. Touch and taste.*
> 2. *Don't tell readers that your subject is funny; show her pulling a prank on a friend. Don't tell readers that the speaker was angry; show him pounding the lectern so hard he broke a finger.*
> 3. *Telling is story in outline; showing fills in the spaces between the lines.*

The writer stepped aside and allowed the reader to visit Sheber on the farm. We can see and feel his hands. We can touch the John Deere, the small stands of wheat.

To re-create such scenes, you must use all your senses to gather information, and your notebook should reflect that reporting. Along with the results of interviews, your notebook should bulge with details of sight and smell, sound and touch. Gather details indiscriminately. Later, you can discard those that are not germane. When you are there, you can re-create the scene as if you were writing a play, even on deadline.

Read this scene from part of an award-winning story by Bartholomew Sullivan (**www.asne.org/kiosk/writingawards/1999/sullivan .html#Aug22**):

In their closing arguments Friday, Special Asst. Atty. Gen. Lee Martin and Helfrich urged jurors to look at the consistent evidence of guilt, not the moral character of the former Klansmen who testified against the former Imperial Wizard. . . .

Martin asked jurors to consider the testimony of Cathy Lucy, the former wife of Klansman Burris Dunn of Jackson, who recalled Bowers arriving at her house with headlines of Dahmer's death from the daily newspaper and "jubilant" at what his "boys" had done to the Dahmer family.

Helfrich banged an index finger on the rail of the jury box as he recalled Thursday's testimony in which a string of Bowers's Jones County friends testified that he was a solid businessman, a Christian—"a gentleman." One of the witnesses was Nix, who called Bowers a "real, real nice man."

"They talk of gentlemen," Helfrich whispered. Then, shouting, he said: "These people don't have a gentle bone in their bodies. They were nightriders and henchmen.

"They attacked a sleeping family and destroyed all they owned."

Reading that scene puts you in the courtroom.

Contrast a traditional report using the inverted pyramid with a narrative report in the next two examples:

JERICHO, N.Y. (AP)—The joy of Dana Quigley's first professional victory was quickly tempered with the news of his father's death.

Quigley made a 2½-foot par putt on the third playoff hole to defeat Jay Sigel and win the $1 million Senior PGA Tour Northville Classic on Sunday.

After the presentation ceremony, Quigley received a phone call from his brother, Paul, informing him that 82-year-old Wallace Quigley had succumbed to cancer only hours earlier. . . .

Now look at *The New York Times'* narrative treatment of the same event:

Dana Quigley was celebrating as joyously as any winner of a golf tournament has, and deservedly so, after working his whole life toward this moment.

Quigley had just pulled off a dramatic playoff victory in the Northville Long Island Classic at the Meadow Brook Club. But after throwing his hat into the crowd, hugging his wife and receiving the trophy, his triumphant walk to the clubhouse was interrupted as he was handed a cellular phone.

Quigley took the call and then collapsed alone on the grass in tears while well-meaning fans continued to shout their congratulations.

On the other end, his brother Paul was calling from a hospital in Providence, R.I., with the news that their father, Wallace, had died during the afternoon at the age of 82. He had had cancer for 10 years.

"Oh man, I didn't do it soon enough," Quigley said, sobbing, as he stepped into the interview room. He paused and added under his breath as he struggled for words, "God, this one was for him."

The first version uses exposition. Readers learn the facts. The second version uses the techniques of narration. The writer weaves the facts into the scene. Readers watch and listen to events as they unfold rather than listening to the journalist-narrator tell them what is happening.

Dialogue

Dialogue allows the narrator to recede and the characters to take center stage. When you use quotations, you—the writer—are telling the reader what the source said. The reader is listening to you relate the quotation instead of listening to the source speak. When you use dialogue, the writer disappears and the reader listens directly to the characters speaking. Compare these examples:

During the public hearing, Henry Lathrop accused the council of wasting taxpayers' money. "If you don't stop voting for all this spending, I am going to circulate a recall petition and get you all kicked off the council," he said.

Mayor Margorie Gold told Lathrop he was free to do as he wished. "As for us," she said, "we will vote in the best interests of the city."

That is the traditional way of presenting quotes. The reporter is telling readers what was said instead of taking readers to the council chambers and letting them listen. This is how it would sound handled as dialogue:

When Henry Lathrop spoke to the City Council during the public hearing, he pounded on the podium. "You folks are wasting taxpayers' money. If you don't stop voting for all this spending, I am going to circulate a recall petition and get you all kicked off the council."

Mayor Margorie Gold slammed her gavel on her desk.

"Mr. Lathrop," she said as she tried to control the anger in her voice. She looked at him directly. "You are free to do as you wish. As for us, we will vote in the best interests of the city."

Lathrop and Gold were speaking to each other. The second version captures the exchange without the intercession of the writer.

When you do not witness the conversation, you have to ask enough questions to get the dialogue: "What did you say to your husband? What was his response? Then what happened? Where were you when that happened? Then what did you do?" Repeat the same questions to other participants until you are satisfied you know what happened.

Dialogue is a conversation between two or more people, none of whom normally is the reporter. This is dialogue between Cindy Martling, a rehabilitation nurse, and Mary Jo, the patient's wife, after Martling scolded the patient for feeling sorry for himself:

She wandered around a bit, then saw Mary Jo standing in the hallway. The two women went to each other and embraced. "I'm sorry," Martling said through more tears. "I didn't mean to lose control. I hope I didn't offend you."

"What you did was wonderful," Mary Jo said. "He needed to hear that. Dan is going to work through it, and we're all going to be OK."

Dialogue is a key element in re-creating scenes. A good reporter permits the characters to talk to each other.

Foreshadowing

Foreshadowing is the technique of advertising what's coming. Moviemakers tease you with the scenes they think will encourage you to buy a ticket. Broadcast journalists foreshadow to keep you from leaving during a commercial: "Coming up, there's a burglar prowling your neighborhood." Every lead foreshadows the story. The leads that not only tell but promise more good stuff to come are the most successful.

Tom Koetting, then of *The Wichita Eagle*, spent nine months observing the recovery of a doctor who had nearly lost his life in a farm accident. He produced a story of about 100,000 words. The simple lead promised great things to come: "Daniel Calliendo Jr. had not expected to meet death this calmly."

A student at Florida A&M University used the same technique to invite readers to continue the story:

A North Carolina family thought the worst was behind them when they were robbed Saturday morning at a gas station just off Interstate 95.
The worst was yet to come.

"The worst was yet to come." That's another way of saying, "Read on; it gets even better." Here is a longer opening that is packed with promises of great things to come. It also was written by a college student, this one from the University of Missouri.

Good writing uses figures of speech

1. *Similes help explain the unknown by comparing it to the known: "Her legs, so rubbery they wobbled like jelly, shook and then surrendered."*
2. *Metaphors equate one thing with another: "Michael is a lion with a gazelle's legs."*
3. *Allusions add value: "Nat King Cole was the Ricky Martin of his time."*
4. *Personification allows you to breathe life into inanimate objects: "The houses have eyes."*

Deena Borman's relationship with her roommate, Teresa, during her freshman year in college had shattered long before the wine bottle.

Weeks had gone by with Teresa drawing further and further away from Deena. Finally, after repeatedly hearing Teresa talk about suicide, Deena says, "I kept telling her how silly she was to want to die."

That made Teresa angry, so she threw a full wine bottle at Deena. It shattered against the wall and broke open the simmering conflict between them. That was when Deena tried to find out what had gone wrong with Teresa's life, and that was when Teresa told Deena that she wanted to do something to get rid of her.

And that was when Deena began to be scared of her own roommate.

The writer is promising a great story. What is wrong with Teresa? Does Teresa really try to hurt Deena? Does Deena really have something to be scared about? There is a promise of great things to come. Would you keep reading?

Anecdotes

The ultimate treats, **anecdotes,** are stories embedded in stories. They can be happy or sad, funny or serious. Whatever their tone, they should illustrate a point. You are likely to remember the anecdotes longer than anything else in the story. You probably remember the stories that your professors tell regardless of whether you remember the rest of the lecture. Long after you've forgotten this chapter, you'll probably remember the Barney Calame anecdote and some of the other examples. Facts inform. Anecdotes inform and entertain.

As befits something so valuable, anecdotes are hard to obtain. You can't get them by asking your source, "Got any good anecdotes?" But you can get them by asking your source for examples so you can re-create the story.

That's what Kelly Whiteside of *USA Today* did after Michelle Snow of the Tennessee Lady Vols stole the ball, thundered the length of the court and dunked the ball two-handed during a game. Players on her team jumped and screamed; even the opposing team and its fans cheered. Five days later, Whiteside wanted to know what happened in the locker room at halftime after this historic event in women's basketball. It was only the third time in NCAA history that a woman had dunked during a game.

Afterward, the Lady Vols waited for coach Pat Summitt to come into the locker room. They wondered how she would react. After all, Summitt, the John Wooden of the women's game, is a purist who always said that dunking was overrated. At halftime, the locker room door creaked open, and Summitt walked in. Her piercing blue eyes were focused intensely, and a serious look was frozen on her face. Summitt turned toward Snow.

"Nice high-post steal there, Snow," Summitt said. And everyone in the locker room dissolved in laughter as Summitt gave Snow a high-five.

If Whiteside had handled the story in typical expository fashion, she would have quoted Snow or other sources within the locker room:

Snow said she and her teammates wondered if Coach Pat Summitt approved of the dunk. "We were all sitting quietly in the locker room at halftime," Snow said. . . .

Instead, Whiteside called Snow and asked her several specific questions, such as, "What did you do when you got in the locker room?" "What did Pat Summitt say?" "She needed to be my eyes and ears," Whiteside said.

Whiteside also needed to talk to others to get more detail and to corroborate the information. Summitt told her that she came into the locker room with a serious look on her face and that she had given Snow a high-five, two details Snow hadn't volunteered. Whiteside talked to Debby Jennings, the Sports Information Director, who also was in the locker room. "Each person added something," Whiteside said. As a result, she was able to reconstruct the scene rather than merely report what happened.

You should phrase your questions in specific ways to get stories: When someone tells you that another person is a practical joker, you want to ask, "Can you give me an example of that?" Some of the best anecdotal examples come from phrasing questions in the superlative: "What's the funniest thing that ever happened to you while you were standing in front of an audience?" "What's the worst case you've ever seen come into this emergency room?" "Everyone tells me Rodney is always the first one they call when they need help on a project. Has he ever helped you?" "Can you give me an example?"

All of these elements—scene re-creation, dialogue, foreshadowing and anecdotes—are the ingredients of narration. Most stories move from exposition to narration several times. Now let's look at the structures in which you can use these techniques.

HOW TO MODIFY THE INVERTED PYRAMID

The structures of stories change with the types of information you are reporting. For service journalism stories, you'll be writing everything from lists to inverted pyramid stories. For narrative stories, you'll concentrate on characters and action.

Six ways to avoid sexism

- *Use gender-free terms, such as "flight attendant" and "firefighters."*
- *Participate in the movement to avoid feminine endings: "comedian," "hero," "poet."*
- *Make the subject plural: "Reporters must keep their minds open."*
- *Rewrite to eliminate unnecessary allusions to gender: "A reporter must not prejudge."*
- *Replace a sexist pronoun with an article: "A teacher must know what the students' interests are."*
- *Use the second person: "You must know what your students' interests are."*

Service Journalism

In Chapter 1, you read that one of the criteria of news is usefulness. Many, if not most, of the magazines you find on the racks appeal to readers by presenting information they might find useful. More than that, they attempt to present this useful information in the most usable way. This approach to presenting information has been called **service journalism.** Often, you see it labeled "News you can use." Even television news stations boast of "news that works for you." Also, the best Web sites are those that provide usable information.

Newspapers, too, are doing more service journalism. Some sections, such as travel, food and entertainment, use many service journalism techniques. Front-page news stories also often contain elements of service journalism, such as a box listing a sequence of events or directing readers to a map, telephone numbers or e-mail addresses. Even in this textbook, you see examples of service journalism in the pullout elements that list the learning objectives for each chapter or highlight important points.

The techniques of service journalism require that you think about content and presentation even as you are reporting. Ask yourself, "What does the reader need to act on this information?" The answer might range from an address to a phone or fax number to instructions on how to fix a lawnmower or make a loaf of bread. It might include directions on how to travel to a festival or where and when to buy tickets. As these examples illustrate, you move from simply talking about something to providing the information the reader needs to act on your story.

Much of the basic service journalism information can be presented as sidebars or lists or boxed material. Figure 7.1 presents more information about service journalism in common service journalism presentation style.

The News Narrative Structure

In Chapter 6, you saw examples of inverted pyramid stories that didn't have the news in the first paragraph. But as soon as the writer set the hook, the news lead appeared, and the writer arranged the rest of the story in the traditional descending order of importance. Further modification offers writers more choices. For instance, when Jane Meinhardt of the *St. Petersburg Times* wrote about an unusual burglary ring, she started with a non-news lead, went to news and then went back to chronology. Let's see how it works:

Setting the scene   PALM HARBOR—They carried knapsacks and bags to tote loot. They had a screwdriver to pry open doors and windows. They used latex gloves.

---

*Good writing
is coherent*

1. *Logical thinking produces logical story structures. If you don't know where you are going, readers won't know either. Construct an outline before you write a story.*
2. *Choose the proper sentence structure to show the relationship among ideas. Compound sentences equate ideas. Complex sentences show cause and effect or sequence.*
3. *Carefully construct transitions between paragraphs. Transitions are like road signs; they tell readers where you are going.*

They acted like professional criminals, but officials say they were teen-age burglars coached and directed by a Palm Harbor woman whose son and daughter were part of her gang.

Traditional lead information

Pinellas County Sheriff's deputies arrested Rovana Sipe, two of her children and two other teens Wednesday after a series of home burglaries.

"She was the driver," said Sheriff's Sgt. Greg Tita. "She pointed out the houses. She's the one who said 'Do these.'"

Support lead

Sipe, 38, of 2333 State Road 584, was charged with two counts of being a principal in burglary. She was held Thursday in lieu of $20,000 bail.

Her daughter, Jackie Shifflet, 16, was charged with grand theft. Her son, Ryan Shifflet, 15, was charged with two counts of burglary.

Charles Ruhe, 17, of 1600 Ensley Ave., in Safety Harbor, and Charles Taylor, 16, of 348 Jeru Blvd. in Tarpon Springs, also were held on four counts of burglary each.

"They were very well-prepared to do burglaries, especially with the guidance they were given," Tita said. "We recovered thousands of dollars of stolen items. Anything that could be carried out, was."

Back to chronology

The burglary ring unraveled Tuesday, Tita said. A Palm Harbor woman saw a large, yellow car driven by a woman drop off three boys, he said. The three went to the back of her house.

They put on gloves and started to pry open a window with a screwdriver, she said. When she tapped on a window, they ran.

She called 911. As she waited for deputies, other neighbors saw the boys walk through a nearby neighborhood carrying bags.

Deputies chased the boys and caught two. The third got into a large yellow car driven by a woman.

The bags contained jewelry, a shotgun and other items deputies say were taken from another house in the neighborhood. Tita said the boys, later identified as Taylor and Ruhe, told detectives about other burglaries in Dunedin and Clearwater and who else was involved.

At Sipe's house, detectives found stolen VCRs, televisions, camcorders and other valuables. They arrested the other two teens and Sipe.

"We're very familiar with this family and its criminal history," Tita said. "We have found stolen property at the house in the past and made juvenile arrests."

This is news, but it is presented as a story rather than as facts arranged in order of most-to-least important. The traditional lead isn't in the first paragraph, but it's not too deep in the story, either. And when the writer returns to the chronology, she uses a transition that

Service Journalism

In today's microwave world, in-a-hurry readers want practical information presented in the most efficient and effective way.

Bill Watterson once drew a comic strip of Calvin that shows Calvin reading the label on the package of a microwave dinner. In his classic outraged face, Calvin screams his protest: "Six minutes to microwave this?? Who's got that kind of time?!"

Perhaps the primary rule of writing today is: Did you give the message in such a way as to take the reader the least amount of time? Readers will pay attention to what you say only if you show them respect. Today you show respect by paying heed to people's lack of time.

After all, time is more than money. Time is life. You waste my time; you waste my life.

Readers are most likely to give you time if you offer them something useful. Yes, they'll read for relaxation and entertainment, but many don't turn to you for that.

Remember, **the opposite of useful is useless.**

But more than that, you must present useful information in the most usable way. You must present it in such a way that people will clip it out and stick it on the refrigerator — or bulletin board, or place it in a retrievable file. Some have called it refrigerator journalism.

What this means is that you must think not just of a message of words on paper. You must think of how these words will appear on the page. You must become concerned about presentation.

• •

Basics   Service journalism is:

• **Useful.** You must inform readers, yes. But if you find ways to demonstrate how the reader can use the information, you will be more successful. You've heard of WIIFM. What's in it for me? "You" and "your" are the most used words in advertising. See how often you can get "you" in the first sentence of your copy. Using "you" will force you to consider the reader.

• **Usable.** Here's a rule. Whenever you can make a list, make a list. Lists get more attention, better comprehension and more retention. Five ways to save money. Do this; don't do that. Advantages, disadvantages. (Don't think you have to write sentences.) "Tips" is a magical word.

• **Used.** Service journalism is action journalism. You are successful only if people use the information. People stop paying attention to information they never use. You should be able to prove to advertisers and others that your readers do what you tell them to do. That means, you must devise ways to get readers to respond. To get readers involved and doing things, you must promise them something. Offer a prize; give them something free. Give a T-shirt for the best suggestion or to the first five to respond. People will kill for a T-shirt or a coffee mug.

• *Refrigerator Journalism* •

10 tips to serve today's readers

1. **Save them time.**

2. **Help them make more money, save money, get something free.**

3. **Address different levels of news interest.**

4. **Address niche audiences more effectively.**

5. **Become more personally useful.**

6. **Become more immediately usable.**

7. **Become more accessible.** Give readers your name, phone number, fax number, e-mail address.

8. **Become more user-friendly.** Learn to layer the news, use cross-references, put things in the same place, color-code when you can, tell readers where to find things, use page numbers on contents blurbs — even on covers, use glossaries, show them where to find more information.

9. **Become more visual and graphic.** Use charts, infograms, pictograms because they are more effective and efficient.

10. **Become more engaging and interactive.** Use contests, quizzes, crosswords, games — make your readers do things. They remember better if they do something, if they are active rather than passive. Give awards to those who send answers in to you. Give a coffee mug to the reader with the best tip of the month. Readers who are more involved in your publication are more likely to resubscribe.

Figure 7.1
Employing the common presentation devices of service journalism—such as boxes and sidebars—this example shows how to highlight information so that readers can find and use it easily.

Print is a hot, intense medium. Refrigerator journalism cools off a hot medium and invites access and participation.

Other devices of service journalism

1. Use blurbs. After a title and before the article begins, write a summary/contents/benefit blurb. David Ogilvy says no one will read the small type without knowing the benefit upfront. Use the same benefit blurb in a table of contents or menu or briefs column. Every publication needs such a column. The best word in a benefit blurb is "how." How to, how you, how I, how Jane Doe did something. Be personal. Use people in your messages.

Also, use internal blurbs, little summaries, pullquotes, tips to tease and coax readers on to the page.

2. Use subheads. When you write, outline your piece to make it more coherent. Put the main points of the outline into the copy. Perhaps a better word than subhead is "entry point." Let readers enter the copy where they find something interesting.

3. Have a question-and-answer column. A Q&A format allows readers to save time by skipping over things they already know or are not interested in.

4. Repeat things in different ways for different people. Don't be afraid to say something in a box or a graphic that you have said elsewhere. Reinforcing a message and involving more of the senses aid retention.

> *"Never be above a gimmick."*
> —Dave Orman, ARCO

5. Think more visually. Stop using pictures and graphics that do not contain information. Make them useful. When you can, put information in a graphic that speaks to the subject matter it contains. Don't be afraid of gimmicks or of being too obvious. Remember, being effective and efficient is the only thing that matters.

Cliff Edom, founder of photojournalism, taught thousands of students and professionals not just how to take pictures, but to take pictures that tell or show the news. He called it photojournalism.

We used to write articles and then look for graphics or photos to enhance the message. Now, we put the information in the graphic (where it will get more attention and have more impact), and write a story to enhance the graphic. It's called "graphic journalism."

The power of the box

When you can, put some information in a box. Boxes or sidebars, like lists, get more attention, cause better comprehension and aid retention.

1. A reference box. For more information, see, read, call.

2. A note box. Take notes from your articles as if you were studying for an exam. Give them to your readers to complement, reinforce, supplement your message.

3. A glossary box. If you wonder whether all of your readers will understand all of your terms, put those terms in a glossary box. Find a way to indicate which words are defined by putting them in color or in a different typeface or underlining them. Also, teach readers how to pronounce difficult words. They will remember them better.

4. A bio box. When you are writing about a person and need to say something about where the person lived, went to school, and worked, put this information in a separate box so that your main story is not interrupted by these facts. If you have more than one person in the story, bio boxes are even more useful.

In a nutshell

4 goals of the service journalist:

1. **Attention**
2. **Comprehension**
3. **Retention**
4. **Action**

PR Tip

Newspapers, magazines and newsletters such as "pr reporter" are doing more and more service journalism. "News you can use" or "tips & tactics" has become a familiar head. Both newspapers and magazines are becoming more visual. Yet, most news releases sent out by PR professionals look the same as they did five and 50 years ago. Why not try refrigerator journalism techniques in your next news release?

signals a story to come: "The burglary ring unraveled Tuesday, Tita said." The transition has echoes of "Let me tell you how it happened." Journalists shouldn't be afraid to experiment with different story forms.

THE FOCUS STRUCTURE

For centuries, writers have told stories by focusing on one individual or group that represents a bigger population. This approach allows the writer to make large institutions, complex issues and seven-digit numbers meaningful (see Figure 7.2). Not many of us can understand—let alone explain—the marketing system for wheat, but we could if we followed a bushel of wheat from the time it was planted until a consumer picked up a loaf of bread in the supermarket.

The Wall Street Journal knew that not many readers would be attracted to a story about the interaction of two or more pesticides. That's why one reporter told the story of an individual to tell a story of pesticide poisoning:

> Thomas Latimer used to be a vigorous, athletic man, a successful petroleum engineer with a bright future.
> Then he mowed the lawn.

Want to read on?

Even though former Soviet dictator Joseph Stalin was hardly talking about literary approaches, he summed up the impact of focusing on a part of the whole when he said, "Ten million deaths are a statistic; one death is a tragedy." Think about your reaction when you

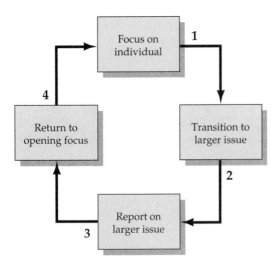

Figure 7.2
Steps in Applying the Focus Structure

heard that the seven astronauts on the space shuttle Columbia were killed. You were undoubtedly more affected if you knew one of them or even if you knew a member of one of their families. If you were able to write a story of any tragedy by focusing on a couple of the victims, you would have a better chance of emotionally involving your readers. Issues such as health care, budget deficits and sexual harassment don't have much emotional appeal. You make them relevant if you discuss the issue by focusing on someone affected by it.

One college writer examining atypical hyperplasia found a specific person through whom she could tell the story:

> Karen Elliott, 44, remembers the phone call from Dr. Jonathen Roberts, a general surgeon, as if it had happened yesterday. Dr. Roberts' nurse called one afternoon two years ago and told Karen to hold the line. She froze. She had just had a biopsy on her right breast because of a new lump. It's never good news when the doctor calls at home. Dr. Roberts cut to the chase.
>
> "You have atypical hyperplasia," he said.
>
> Being a nurse, Karen knew exactly what he meant. No number of breast self-exams could have detected this. Atypical hyperplasia is a lifelong condition characterized by abnormal cells. Affecting only 4 percent of the female population, it puts Karen and others at an increased risk for breast cancer. With her family history of the disease, her risk of breast cancer jumps sky-high.
>
> What Karen didn't know was that her pleasant life in New Bloomfield would become a roller coaster of ups and downs for the next two years, a ride that nearly destroyed her. Her husband of 19 years, Bob, and their two children, Bethany, 6, and Jordan, 8, could only watch as she struggled with the decision of whether to voluntarily have her breasts removed because Karen, and only Karen, could make that choice.

Karen is concrete; atypical hyperplasia is abstract. If the writer is skillful enough, readers will develop empathy for Karen and will read the story to see what choice she made.

Reporters working on local stories have just as many opportunities to apply the focus structure as those writing national and international stories. For example, instead of keeping score on the United Way fund drive, focus on the people who will benefit—or fail to benefit—from the campaign. If the streets in your city are bad, write about the problem from the point of view of a driver. The focus structure offers the writer a powerful method of reducing institutions, statistics and cosmic issues to a level readers can relate to and understand.

Organizing the Story

You've completed your reporting. You have all the information about the issue. You've found a person through whom you can tell your story. You know you are going to open with a scene or an anecdote or some

---

Good writing is concrete

1. Use "highway," not "infrastructure." Use "arena," not "facility." Use "reading group," not "learning pod."
2. Be specific. "Big" or "loud" or "ugly" mean something only in comparison to something else.
3. Good writing begins with good reporting. Move from generalities, such as "The business is downsizing," to concrete details, such as "The business is laying off 150 employees."

The set-up consists of

- The transition to the theme paragraph.
- The theme paragraph.
- Foreshadowing.
- The "so-what."
- The "to-be-sure."

other approach that will say to the reader, "I've got an interesting story to tell." Now you must finish the set-up to the story. The **set-up** consists of five elements: the transition to the theme paragraph, the theme paragraph, foreshadowing, the "so-what" and the "to-be-sure." Let's look at each of these.

Add the Transition and the Theme Paragraph

When you open with a scene or an anecdote, you must construct a transition that explicitly makes the connection to the theme paragraph, also commonly called the **nut paragraph.** "Explicitly" is the key word. If you fail to help readers understand the point of the opening, however interesting it is, you risk losing them. The transition in this example is in italics:

> Anita Poore hit the rough pavement of the parking lot with a thud. She had never felt such intense, stabbing pain and could barely lift her heavy head. When she reached for the car door, a police officer stared at her and asked her husband, "Is she drunk?" A wave of nausea swept over her, and she vomited.
>
> "That's it. Get her out of here!" the officer demanded.
>
> Poore was not drunk. She avoided jail, but she faces a life sentence of pain. Now 25, she has suffered migraine headaches since she was in seventh grade.
>
> *Not that it is much comfort, but she's not alone.* Health officials estimate that Americans miss 157 million workdays a year because of migraines and spend more than $2 million a year on over-the-counter painkillers for migraine, tension and cluster headaches. Researchers haven't found a cure, but they have found methods to lessen the pain.

The transition explicitly places Anita Poore among those who miss work, buy painkillers and are still waiting for a cure. What follows is the theme.

Earlier in this chapter, you were introduced to wheat farmer Don Sheber. Here is how the writer connected Sheber to the theme paragraph (italics added):

> In a normal year, Sheber's 600 acres of farmland in Kay County should be thick with nearly waist-high wheat stalks, and by harvest's end, his grain bins should be stuffed with 20,000 bushels of golden grain.
>
> *But this is not a normal year.* As Sheber finished his harvest early this week, he counted only 6,500 bushels from his shriveled crop, less than one-third his normal yield.

When you have involved the reader and successfully written the explicit transition to the theme paragraph, you are ready to build the rest of the set-up.

me see," editor
Henry Belk told his
reporters. "You
aren't making me
see." Belk was blind.
Even spending a
half-hour with the
subject of a quick-
hit profile is better
than just conducting
a phone interview.

4. *Think scenes.* Use
dialogue and
descriptions to
make readers feel as
if they're watching
the action unfold as
it happens. Move
your camera shots—
from panning the
crowd to close-ups.

5. *Follow the crowd.*
Then turn and go
the opposite direc-
tion. When Presi-
dent Kennedy was
assassinated, the
reporters flocked to
the rotunda. Jimmy
Breslin went to
Arlington National
Cemetery and
talked to the man
digging the presi-
dent's plot.

6. *Take ownership of a
story.* Roy Peter
Clark of the Poynter
Institute uses music
to show that differ-
ent artists can sing
the same song with
quite different
results. No matter
what the assign-
ment—even if it's
that hardy peren-
nial, the day-after-
Thanksgiving shop-

(continued)

Add Foreshadowing

Foreshadowing can be done in a single line ("The killing started early and ended late"), or it can be developed as part of several paragraphs. The goal is to assure readers they will be rewarded if they continue reading. This is what Susan Kinzie of *The (Raleigh) News & Observer* promised her readers in the opening to one in a series of stories about three generations of a family investigating whether they shared a DNA link to cancer:

> Linda Brenner-David pushed up the sleeve of her sweater and looked away as the needle pierced her vein. Blood flowed into the vial, which the technician labeled and packed carefully into the foam of a white-and-red box. That blood sample would be sent to a laboratory in Utah to tell Linda whether she, like her youngest sister, Marcy Brenner, had a genetic mutation that put her at higher risk for breast and ovarian cancer, whether she faced the threat of a disease that had almost killed her sister and may have killed her mother. Or whether she, like her other sister, Judi Coyne, had escaped the family legacy.
>
> If Linda tested positive, that would set off another round of questions for her family. It could mean her 30-year-old daughter, Christine Morgan, had a higher risk of cancer, could mean her son did, could mean her 18-month-old grandson did, too. It could influence Christine's choices about having more children.

Kinzie tells readers that if they want to learn the results of the tests and how the women reacted to the news, they will have to read this story.

Add the "So-What"

The "so-what" tells readers explicitly why they should care. Don Sheber's harvest dropped by two-thirds. So what? Anita Poore almost got arrested for having a migraine headache. Interesting, but so what? Reporters and editors know the "so-what," or they wouldn't spend time on the story. Too often, however, they fail to tell it to readers.

Thomas Latimer was poisoned when he mowed his lawn. Latimer's story is interesting, but it's much more important when you are told why you should care. The parentheses identify the "so-what":

> The makers of the pesticide, diazinon, and of Tagamet firmly deny that their products had anything to do with Mr. Latimer's condition. The pesticide maker says he doesn't even believe he was exposed to its product. And in fact, Mr. Latimer lost a lawsuit he filed against the companies. (Even so, the case intrigues scientists and regulators because it illustrates the need for better understanding of the complex interactions between such everyday chemicals as pesticides and prescription drugs.
>
> Neither the Food and Drug Administration nor the Environ-

mental Protection Agency conducts routine tests for such interactions. Indeed, the EPA doesn't even evaluate the synergy of two or more pesticides commonly used together. "We have not developed ways to test any of

that," says an EPA spokesman. "We don't know how to do it." And a new congressional report says the FDA lacks both the resources and the enforcement powers to protect Americans from all kinds of poisons.)

The "so-what" is the impact—the relevance—to people who have no warning that two or more pesticides may interact to poison them. In other cases, the "so-what" may be included in the theme statement.

Let's look at the migraine story again:

(1) Not that it is much comfort, but she's not alone. (2) Health officials estimate that Americans miss 157 million workdays a year because of migraines and spend more than

$2 million a year on over-the-counter pain-killers for migraine, tension and cluster headaches. (3) Researchers haven't found a cure, but they have found methods to lessen the pain.

The first sentence is the transition; the second is the "so-what"; the third is the theme, which includes foreshadowing. The "so-what" establishes the dimensions of the problem. When you define the "so-what," you are establishing the story's impact.

Add the "To-Be-Sure"

To maintain an evenhanded approach, writers must acknowledge that there are two or more sides to the story. We've read in the pesticide story that the makers of the drugs and pesticides "firmly deny that their products had anything to do with Mr. Latimer's condition." We see the technique again in an article about the impact of gambling on Tunica, Miss.

Writer Jenny Deam opens with a scene in the mayor's store. The mayor says gambling is the best thing that ever happened to the town. At the front counter, a woman is asking for the $85 back she paid on furniture last week. She lost her grocery money gambling. What comes next is a combination theme and "to-be-sure" statement (italics added):

And so is the paradox of this tiny Mississippi Delta county, now that the casinos have come to call.

On the one hand, unemployment in a place the Rev. Jesse Jackson once called "America's Ethiopia" has dropped from nearly 24 percent to a low last

fall of 5 percent. Anyone who wants a job has one with the casinos. There are more jobs than people to fill them. In a county of about 8,100 people, the number of food stamp recipients fell from 4,218 before the casinos to 2,907 now.

(Continued)

ping spree story—make it your own.
7. *Use your voice.* The best stories have the feeling of a personal column. It's not that the reporter is telling you what he or she thinks, but you have the feeling as a reader that a real person is talking to you.
8. *Look for humor opportunities.* This is the most underused tool in our writing kit. Readers love humor almost as much as they love real stories.
9. *Take risks.* I once wrote a one-sentence, one-paragraph weather story that (much to my amazement) has been reprinted in two books. It's not just a matter of trying to be clever. It's a matter of doing anything to get read.
10. *Remember Tammy Gaudette.* Tammy is a housewife in Iowa who was invited to appear on a panel of newspaper readers. She was asked what she read. "Oh, I don't like the news," she said. "I like the interesting stories."

But there is another side. New problems never before seen.

Since the first casino opened in 1992, the number of DUI arrests has skyrocketed by 400 percent. U.S. Highway 61 leading to Memphis is constantly jammed. On a busy weekend as many as 28,000 cars head toward the nine casinos now open.

The criminal court system is just as overloaded. In 1992, there were 1,500 cases filed. A year later, 2,400. As of last month there had already been 6,800 cases filed for this year.

"Well," says the mayor, "It's just like anything else in life: You got to take the evil with the good."

Now that the story has been defined, the writer is ready to examine all sides of the issue.

And now that you have constructed the set-up, you are ready to enter the body of the story.

Writing the Body

Think of readers as people antsy to do something else. To maintain their interest, offer them frequent examples to support your main points. In narration, you use anecdotes, scenes and dialogue to move the story line. You mix exposition—the facts—with narration, the story line.

Every few paragraphs, Tina Smithers offered readers another story to keep them reading about atypical hyperplasia. Here's one of them:

Karen was walking downstairs to get the beach ball out of the summer box for Bethany's Hawaiian swim party at Kindercare. Suddenly, Karen fainted and fell down the stairs. She knew she had broken something.

Coming to, she blindly made her way upstairs and lay on the bed.

"The cat was staring me in the eyes," she mumbled as Bob, fresh from the shower, grabbed ice and a pillow.

Karen noticed Bethany crying in the doorway. At this point, Karen realized she had been shouting, "Call 9-1-1! Call

9-1-1!" She didn't want her daughter to see her lose control. She quieted down and told Bethany to come to her bed.

"It's okay, honey. Mommy broke her arm, but they'll be over soon to fix it."

In the ambulance, one of the paramedics tried to cut off her yellow Tommy Hilfiger sweater.

"It's brand new," Karen shouted. "Can't you pull it off?"

They gave one small yank, and Karen immediately changed her mind. Every bump along the way was agonizing. Karen pleaded for more morphine. Her wrist, it turned out, was broken in 20 places.

That anecdote helps show how the stress of dealing with atypical hyperplasia had weakened Karen.

Think of your story as an interstate highway. The highway is your story's infrastructure. In one story, the infrastructure might be chronology. In another, it might be movement from one location to another. At times, you need to exit the highway to introduce other examples and ideas. The exits should be smooth—easy off, easy on.

Writing the Ending

Stories should end, not just stop. One good technique, called a **tie-back,** is one of the significant differences between the inverted pyramid and the focus structure. The inverted pyramid story diminishes in importance and interest as the story proceeds, so it can be cut from the end. The focus structure, in contrast, has an ending, so if the story has to be shortened, the writer or editor will have to delete something other than the ending.

Earlier in this chapter, Linda Brenner-David was introduced, who was being tested to see if she had a genetic disposition toward cancer. Eventually we learn that Linda tested positive. The story ends with a scene that echoes the opening when Linda was being tested. The Brenners are asking the next question: What about Christine, Linda's daughter?

Down the hall at Duke, as she waited to get her blood drawn, Christine looked nervous and out of place, so young and healthy in a room full of old, sick people. "Now I'm in a whole 'nother box," she said. "Now it's 'what do we do for me?'" Thinking out loud in scraps of phrases, she wondered, too, what it would mean for her family.

A technician called her name, and she sat down in a small room surrounded by blinking machines and medical equipment. A sudden noise at her side made her jump. She rolled up the sleeve of her magenta turtleneck, made a fist and waited as a tube slowly filled with dark blood.

She took the white-and-red box back to Shelly, who put it in a FedEx envelope addressed to a lab in Utah.

Even the ending, which is a tie-back, is a tease to the next story in the series.

Anecdotes, dialogue, scenes and good quotes all can end the story. What you must avoid is ending the last section of the story instead of wrapping up the story line.

Good writing is precise

1. *Know the meaning of your words. Don't use "uninterested" when you mean "disinterested" or "allude" when you mean "refer."*
2. *Avoid biased language. Doctors aren't always "he," nor are nurses always "she." Elderly women are not "blue-haired." Ascribe actions to individuals, not to races.*
3. *Be specific. "City Council members favor . . ." is less specific than "Some City Council members . . ." unless you have polled all the members. Better yet: "Five City Council members. . ." Use the conditional verbs when discussing proposals: "The bill would make it illegal . . ." (not "will make").*

Suggested Readings

Brooks, Terri. *Words' Worth: A Handbook on Writing and Selling Nonfiction.* New York: St. Martin's Press, 1989. Full of detailed advice and examples.

Franklin, Jon. *Writing for Story: Craft Secrets of Dramatic Nonfiction by a Two-Time Pulitzer Prize Winner.* New York: Plume, 1994. If you want to write nonfiction narration, this book is must reading.

Harrington, Walt H. *Intimate Journalism.* Thousand Oaks, Calif.: Sage Publications, 1997. Harrington, a newspaper writer and book author, offers insights into the how and why of telling stories of common people. He includes several of his own stories and those of others, with commentary on reporting and writing techniques.

Scanlon, Christopher, ed. *Best Newspaper Writing: 1999.* St. Petersburg, Fla.: Poynter Institute, 1999. Each year the winning entries in the American Society of Newspaper Editors writing contest are published in a book, which also contains interviews with the writers.

Sims, Norman, ed. *The Literary Journalists.* New York: Ballantine Books, 1984. With an introductory essay defining literary journalism, this book offers reprints from the best of the bunch.

Zinsser, William. *On Writing Well*, Fourth Edition. New York: HarperPerennial, 1994. An entertaining narrative on the art of writing.

Suggested Web Sites

www.mcclatchy.com/about/featured_works/

This site contains links to winners in the McClatchy newspaper group writing competition.

www.asne.org

The American Society of Newspaper Editors conducts a prestigious writing contest every year. Winners are posted on the Web. At the site, select "Kiosk" to go to the winners.

www2.sptimes.com/Angels_Demons/default.html

For excellent examples of narrative writing, read Thomas French's follow-up story about the murder of three members of the Rogers family. The site also includes other serial narratives.

www.projo.com/words/main.htm

The Providence Journal maintains an excellent Web site full of writing and reporting tips from its staff members and the stories they do.

www.poynter.org

Select "Writing/Editing" to find scores of stories on writing and reporting.

www.inkstain.net/narrative

Entitled "The Narrative Newspaper," the site posts narrative stories. A great source of inspiration.

Exercises

1. Write four to eight paragraphs about how you and your classmates learned to be reporters. Pick a scene from one of your classes and re-create it. Provide the transition into the body of the story and then stop.

2. Interview a student in your reporting class. Ask questions that elicit anecdotes. Write an anecdote about the person.

3. Using a chronology, write approximately eight paragraphs of a story about some aspect of your experience in the reporting class.

4. Choose a personal experience that is worth telling in a first-person story. Write two to three pages using chronology in the first person.

5. In newspapers or magazines find examples of service journalism and analyze them. Find an example of a story that would have benefited from service journalism techniques. Tell what you would have done to make the information more usable.

6. Analyze focus structure stories found on the front page of either *The Wall Street Journal* or *USA Today.* How many elements of the set-up can you identify? Find all the anecdotes. Identify any dialogue.

7. Write the first two pages of an event in your life. Try to include as many narrative techniques as you can: scenes, dialogue, foreshadowing and the "so-what" statement.

8 Speeches, News Conferences and Meetings

The president of the United States knows that taking his case to the public is a critical component of the job. When President Bush spoke to the United Nations on Sept. 12, 2002, a year and a day after the worst-ever terrorist attack on U.S. soil, his job approval rating immediately rose from 66 to 70 percent.

As an astute politician, Bush knew that winning the battle of public opinion is essential in a democracy. Most governors, mayors and school board members understand that, too, which is why speeches, news conferences and meetings are the staples of the news industry across the media. Your first assignment as a beginning reporter is almost certain to involve one of those three basic story types. Your editor or news director will use those assignments to determine quickly how well prepared you are for a career as a journalist.

Such stories are often routine, occasionally of great importance. Because many of them involve elected or appointed officials, communities often elect and re-elect their leaders on the basis of their performance at these events. Communities are rallied to causes and nations to wars by speeches, news conferences and meetings.

Some argue that John F. Kennedy's display of intelligence and wit at news conferences got him elected and earned him respect as president. During Bill Clinton's troubles with the Whitewater real estate deal, a *USA Today*/CNN/Gallup poll showed that the president's news conference raised his approval rating by 11 percentage points. Ronald Reagan felt at home in front of cameras, and although he disliked news conferences, his televised speeches helped boost his image tremendously. And Bush, though arguably not as comfortable in front of cameras as some of his predecessors, also knows how to use public addresses to gain popular support.

On the local level, every politician knows that his or her performance will be evaluated by the public in the light of media reports of meetings where major decisions are made that affect everyone in the community. It's important not to make the mistake of handling such stories with indifference. To the people of your community, and to the subject of every story, that story is the most important item in the newspaper or broadcast report of the day. Even the most routine speeches, news conferences and meetings require careful reporting and writing.

YOUR PREPARATION

Good reporters know that preparation makes covering a story much easier. A savvy broadcast reporter unfamiliar with an assigned topic often will review videotape of previous stories on the subject. If that's not possible, a check of online information—from the local newspaper to national news Web sites to other online sources—may provide good background. A good starting point for a print reporter is the **morgue**—the newspaper or magazine library. There, you'll find all your publication has previously written about a subject. If you are assigned to cover a meeting or attend a press conference, a morgue check is likely to provide you with ample background. If it doesn't, a check in a national database such as Nexis/Lexis should help. So might one of the many reference books you'll find in the office. As we discussed in Chapter 4, most media libraries are computerized, so you'll probably be able to do most of the checking from your own computer.

Let's examine how to prepare for each of the basic story types.

Preparing for the Speech Story

Failure to get enough background on the speaker and on the speech almost guarantees failure to write a useful speech story. Not every speech you are assigned to cover will demand a lot of research. Many speakers and speeches will be dry and routine. The person giving the speech will be someone you know or someone you have covered before. At other times you may be given an assignment on short notice and may be forced to find background information after hearing the speech. Whatever the case, never take the speaker or the topic for granted.

The first step in your research is to identify the speaker correctly. Middle initials are important; sometimes even they are not enough. Sometimes checking the address is not enough. One reporter wrote about the wrong person because he did not know that a father and son shared the same name at the same address.

USA Today had to print a clarification when it reported that television celebrity Larry King had made a $1,000 donation to the Clinton campaign. The donor was Larry L. King, author and playwright.

A hospital in Boston was threatened with a lawsuit after telling relatives that Robert J. Oliver had died. His fiancée was surprised a few days later when Robert J. called her. It was Robert W. Oliver who had died. Robert W. was not listed in the phone book; Robert J. was.

Be sure you have the right person. Then, before doing research on the speaker, contact the group sponsoring the speech and ask for the topic. You might find you need to do some reading to prepare you to understand the subject. If you are lucky, you may get an advance copy of the speech.

If the speech is important enough, you might want to contact the speaker ahead of time for a brief interview. If he or she is from out of town, you might plan for a meeting at the airport. You might also

Think technical thoughts

Preparing to cover speeches, news conferences and meetings presents many technical questions for the television journalist. Here are three things to keep in mind:

- Think visuals. *What will your backdrop be? Will there be signs, photos, samples, logos or flipcharts to help tell the story?*
- Think sound. *Will there be one microphone or a multi-box for you to insert your mike, or will you be free to set up your own microphone?*
- Think light. *Will the event take place outdoors or in a well-lit room, or must you bring your own lighting? How far is the camera throw (the distance from the event to your camera)? Will there be a camera platform or a set space, or will you be free to set up your camera anywhere?*

arrange ahead of time to interview the speaker after the speech. You may have some questions and some points to clarify.

For the broadcast reporter, a one-on-one interview with the speaker is important. Few things are more boring than lengthy video clips of a speech. You can avoid that problem by highlighting the key points of the speech in your report and perhaps interspersing a few choice quotes from the speech itself.

Not every speech will demand significant research, but even the most routine speech assignment requires some preparation. It may seem obvious, for instance, that the reason Gene Martin, director of the local library, is addressing the state Writer's Guild is to tell members how to use the library to write better stories. Not so. Gene Martin also is a successful "true confessions" writer who has been published dozens of times. He may be addressing the guild to tell members how he does it.

Sooner or later you may be called on to cover speeches of major political candidates, perhaps even of the president of the United States. For this task, too, you need background—lots of it. Being a journalist requires you to read the news and to know what is going on. You must keep up with current events.

Preparing for the News Conference Story

Preparing for a news conference is similar to preparing to cover a speech. You must know the background of the person giving the news conference, and you must learn why the news conference is being held.

If the news is really important, the broadcast reporter may merely introduce the subject and broadcast the news conference live. When snipers began shooting people at random in the Washington, D.C., area, Charles Moose, Montgomery County, Md., police chief, became a national celebrity for several weeks. His handling of the investigation—and news conferences—was widely admired.

Often the person holding the news conference has an announcement or an opening statement. Unless that statement is leaked to the media, you will not know its content ahead of time. But you can do some educated guessing. Check out rumors. Call the person's associates, friends or secretary. The more prepared you are, the better chance you have of coming away with a coherent, readable story.

Every reporter at a news conference has a line of questions to pursue. Your editor may want certain information, and other editors may want something else. You will not have time to think out your questions once you are there: The job of recording the responses to other reporters' questions will keep you too busy.

Former Beatle Paul McCartney and his wife Heather Mills giving a news conference before their wedding.

It may be impossible to arrange an interview before or after the news conference. If the person holding the news conference wanted to grant individual reporters interviews, he or she probably would not have called the news conference. But you can give it a try. You never know, and you may end up with some exclusive information.

Preparing for the Meeting Story

You never know exactly what to expect at a meeting, either, unless an agenda is made available in advance. That's sometimes the case for meetings of city councils and zoning commissions. But if no agenda is available, you still must do your best to prepare for the meeting. Who are the people holding the meeting? What kind of an organization is it? Who are the key figures? What are the main issues to be discussed? Again, a database or your organization's morgue should be your first stop.

Contact some of the key figures to learn what the meeting is about. If you know the main subject to be discussed, you will be able to study and investigate the issues before arriving. Knowing what to expect and being familiar with the issues will make covering the meeting much easier.

To achieve total coverage of content and event, you must remember to

- *Get the content correct. Tape recorders can be helpful, but always take good notes. Quote people exactly and in context.*
- *Note the background, personal characteristics and mannerisms of the main participants.*
- *Cover the event. Look around the edges — at the audience (size, reactions) and sometimes at what is happening outside the building.*
- *Get there early, position yourself and hang around afterward.*

A reporter with a regular **beat**—an assigned area of responsibility—usually covers the scheduled meetings of more important organizations and of groups such as the city council, the school board or the county board. (Beat reporting is discussed in detail in Chapter 10.) A beat reporter has ongoing familiarity with the organization and with the issues involved. Often, the meetings of important organizations are preceded by an **advance**—a report outlining the subjects and issues to be dealt with in the upcoming meeting.

Broadcast reporters often don't cover beats and are, in the best sense of the phrase, general-assignment reporters. Meetings of city councils are not regular fare for broadcasters because video of a meeting can be exceedingly dull. As a result, broadcast reporters face some serious challenges in deciding how to portray the importance of what's coming out of the meeting.

The key is finding video to accompany the piece. If the city council is debating how to improve snow removal, for example, video footage of city trucks doing just that can add immeasurably to the story. Because television is a visual medium, broadcast reporters have to be creative in finding ways to illustrate important but visually limited stories.

If you know snow removal will be a primary topic, someone back at the station can be searching for snow-removal footage while you're covering the meeting. Without good background work to determine the main theme of the meeting, such preparation would be impossible.

COVERING THE STORY

An often-told story is that of a newspaper reporter who prepared well for a speech assignment, contacted the speaker, got an advance copy of the speech, wrote the story and spent the evening in a bar. He didn't know until after the speech story was handed in that the speech had been canceled.

And then there's the yarn about the young reporter who was assigned to cover a meeting and came back to tell the city editor there was no story.

"Why not?" the city editor asked.

"Because the meeting was canceled."

"Why was that?"

"Well," replied the reporter, "when the meeting started, some of the board members got in this big argument. Finally, three of them walked out. The president then canceled the meeting because there was no quorum."

The reporter had been sent to cover a meeting. But the canceled meeting and the circumstances surrounding its cancellation probably were of more interest to readers than the meeting itself would have been.

Preparing to cover events is only the beginning. Knowing what to do when you get there is the next step. Remember this: Covering the content of a speech, news conference or meeting often is only half of the job—and sometimes the less important half. You must cover the entire event—the time, place, circumstances, number of people involved and possible consequences of what was said or of the actions taken.

If you are a print or online reporter, you may find a tape recorder useful. Tape recorders often scare reporters, but they need not. As with anything else, you must practice using a tape recorder. Use it again and again to become completely familiar with its idiosyncracies.

The most frequent complaint about tape recorders is that listening to the entire recording just to find a certain quote that you want to check takes too long. But you may avoid this problem if you have a tape recorder with a digital counter. At any point in a speech or a meeting when something of importance is said, note the number on the counter. Finding it later will be no problem.

Even when you tape-record an event, you must take notes exactly as if you were not tape-recording. Malfunctions can occur, even with the best machines, at the most inopportune times. So, with or without a tape recorder, you must become a proficient note taker. Many veteran reporters wish they had taken a shorthand or speed-writing course early in their careers. You may find it useful to buy a speed-writing manual and become used to certain symbols. Every reporter sooner or later adopts or creates some shortcuts in note taking. You will have to do the same. Learn to abbreviate whenever you can (*wh* for "which," *th* for "that," *bk* for "book," *st* for "street," *bldg* for "building," etc.). Make up signs (*w/* for "with," *w/o* for "without," *acc/* for "according to").

You may be one of those fortunate people with a fantastic memory. Some reporters develop an incredible knack for re-creating whole conversations with complete accuracy without taking a note. But you may be one of those who takes reams of notes. If you are, take them as neatly as you can. Many of us cannot read our own handwriting at times—a nuisance, particularly when a proper name is involved.

Taking notes is most crucial when you wish to record direct quotes. As you learned in Chapter 3, putting someone's words in quotation marks means only one thing: You are quoting the person word for word, exactly as the person spoke. Almost all stories demand that you be able to record direct quotes. Your stories will be lifeless and lack credibility without them. A speech story, for example, should contain many direct quotes.

Using the tape recorder

Be familiar with the machine. *Practice using it. Make sure you understand its peculiarities. Check its sound capabilities.*

Set it where you can see it's working. *If it has a digital counter, note the number when you hear a quote you want.*

Take notes as if it might not be working. *After all, it might not be.*

You need to develop your own shortcuts in note taking. Clear note taking is essential— but the notes need be clear only to you. That means you must develop a consistent habit, or you won't remember what your shortcuts mean when you get to writing the story.

It is important to remember that quoting the speaker at length or printing a speech in its entirety is recording, not reporting. The overall content of the speech may or may not be news. Sometimes context is missing. Sometimes the news may be what a speaker left unsaid. You must decide what is newsworthy, and to do that you must be well-prepared and knowledgeable about the subject you are covering.

A key to reporting any event is talking with as many sources as possible and checking as many written sources as possible. It's much better to leave out material you have collected than to leave questions unanswered. Without a doubt, the biggest single failure of inexperienced reporters is leaving gaps in a story. Your editor will ask the unanswered questions and force you to find answers. If you're smart, you'll do so before you are asked. Thorough reporting is the key.

In the process of gathering material, don't be a passive observer. You can vastly improve many a story by describing a person or place. Such reporting can help bring a story to life.

The television reporter has the luxury of recording the whole event on videotape. The challenge, then, is deciding which clips to use from the speech or meeting itself and how best to tell the story. Usually that involves a stand-up report by the reporter combined with clips of the speaker or speakers. In many ways, the broadcast reporter's challenge is much greater than one facing the newspaper reporter; the broadcast reporter must report the same story in far fewer words.

WRITING THE STORY

As we discussed in Chapter 6, one of the most important parts of writing the story for any medium is the lead. Without a good lead, the reader or viewer won't be hooked, and the story will have been wasted. But crafting the lead is merely the beginning. In this section, we'll discuss some peculiarities about each type of story we cover in this chapter.

Writing the Speech Story

Although you may not be called upon to cover a speech by the president of the United States, you can learn a lot about how to write a speech story from the way the pros handle an important address. Let's take a look at how Fox News wrote the story of President Bush's Sept. 12, 2002, address at the United Nations:

WASHINGTON — The United Nations must set out to protect the world from the likes of Saddam Hussein, President

President George W. Bush addresses the U.N. General Assembly on Sept. 12, 2002, about the need to invade and disarm Iraq.

Bush told the international body Thursday morning.

Bush cited Iraq as an example of a rogue regime that poses an immediate threat in its willingness to act against other nations or assist terrorist groups.

"In one place and one regime, we find all these dangers in their most lethal and aggressive forms, exactly the kind of aggressive threat the United Nations was born to confront," Bush told the General Assembly. "Saddam

Hussein's regime is a grave and gathering danger. To suggest otherwise is to hope against the evidence. Saddam Hussein has made the case against himself."

After appeasing the U.N. by announcing that the U.S. would return to the United Nations Educational, Scientific and Cultural Organization, Bush told the international body that Iraq must comply with U.N. sanctions or be punished accordingly.

"We will work with the U.N. Security Council for the necessary resolutions, but the purposes of the United States should not be doubted. The Security Council resolutions will be enforced. The just demands of peace and security must be met or action will be unavoidable and a regime that has lost its legitimacy will also lose its power."

"Events can turn in one of two ways," Bush said.

Armed with a point-by-point list of Saddam Hussein's transgressions included in a White House paper entitled "A Decade of Defiance and Deception of the United Nations," the president detailed how Saddam has continued to develop weapons of mass destruction, engaged in egregious human-rights violations, participated in international terrorism, sought to evade economic sanctions and kept Kuwaiti property that should have been returned after the 1991 Gulf War.

Bush said Saddam has engaged in systematic human-rights violations, including the "arbitrary arrest and imprisonment, summary execution and torture by beating and burning, electric shock, starvation, mutilation and rape" of tens of thousands of Iraqis.

"(Saddam) has fired ballistic missiles at Iran and Saudi Arabia, Bahrain and Israel. He has gassed many Iranians and 40 Kurdish villages.

"From 1991-1995 the Iraqi regime said it had no biological or chemical weapons," Bush said. After a science team defected, Iraq admitted that it had enough anthrax to load it onto SCUD missiles and in other dispersal mechanisms.

"United Nations inspections also reviewed that Iraq likely maintains stockpiles of VX, mustard and other chemical agents, and that the regime is rebuilding and expanding facilities capable of producing chemical weapons," Bush said.

"Open societies do not threaten the world with mass murder," he added.

After the president's speech, Iraq's U.N. ambassador accused Bush of speaking out of revenge and political ambition. . . .

That's a fairly typical approach to writing a speech story for print or online publication. The lead summarizes the main theme of the speech, and the reader is given enough information to understand the gist of the story. By necessity, a speech story should be full of rich direct quotes, and the first one usually is inserted high in the story. In this case, it comes in the third paragraph. Rarely does the lead itself contain a quote because it's rare to find a direct quote that adequately summarizes the speech in a sentence or two.

Because a speech story must contain lots of quotes, a tape recorder is a good thing to have. Good note taking also is essential.

For the broadcast reporter, the key is writing a good introduction, then carefully selecting excerpts of the speech itself from the video-tape recording. The print reporter selects the choicest quotes and sprinkles them throughout the story, and the broadcast reporter does the same on videotape.

Writing the News Conference Story

Writing the news conference story may be a bit more challenging than writing the speech story. Because you will come to the conference with different questions in mind than your fellow reporters, you may come away with a different story. At the very least, your lead may be different from the leads of other reporters.

A news conference often covers a gamut of topics. It sometimes begins with a statement from the person who called the conference.

For example, when the mayor of Springfield holds a news conference to announce her candidacy for a second term, you can be sure she will begin with a statement to that effect. Although her candidacy might be news to some people, you may want to ask her questions about the location of a new landfill that the city is rumored to be planning. Most citizens will admit the need for landfills, but their location is always controversial. And then there's that tip you heard about the possibility of the city manager resigning to take a job in a large city.

Other reporters will come with other questions. Will there be further cuts in the city budget? Will the cuts mean that some city employees will lose their jobs? What happened to the plans to expand the city jail?

After you come away from a news conference that covered many topics, you have the job of organizing the material in some logical, coherent order. Usually you will treat the most newsworthy subject first and deal with the other subjects in the order of their importance. Rarely would you report on them in the chronological order in which they were discussed.

Suppose you decided the location of the landfill was the most important item of the news conference—especially if the mayor revealed the location for the first time. You might begin your story this way:

```
The city will construct its new landfill near the
intersection of State Route 53 and Route E, four miles
north of Springfield, Mayor Juanita Williams said
today.
```

On the Job

Speeches, News Conferences and Meetings

After receiving a master's degree in journalism, Barry Murov worked as an associate editor of a Washington, D.C., newsletter, where he covered federal job programs. Then after working for the *St. Louis Business Journal* for six years, first as a reporter, then as managing editor, Murov became editor of *St. Louis* magazine. Now he's employed by Fleishman-Hillard Inc., an international public-relations firm.

Murov has written and edited dozens of stories covering speeches, meetings and news conferences. Here are some tips he has for you:

"Always ask for a copy of the speech ahead of time," Murov

says. "Even when you are lucky enough to get a copy, don't assume that the speaker will stick to the text."

As a consultant for Fortune 500 corporations, Murov knows that "many executives tend to tinker with their speeches, even making significant changes, up until the final minute."

He recommends that you follow along in the text to note where the actual presentation differs. "You don't want your story to include a statement from the text that the speaker deleted. Also, you may find the real news nugget buried in the speech."

Don't leave a meeting or news conference immediately. "Go up to the spokesperson or the leader of the meeting and ask a question that hasn't been covered during the actual event.

"That can benefit in two ways: One, you will have something extra for your readers. Two, it helps you build a relationship with the spokesperson that may pay off in the future."

"After nearly a year of discussion and the best advice we could obtain, we are certain the Route E location is best for all concerned," Williams said at a news conference.

The mayor admitted there would be continued opposition to the site by citizens living in the general area, especially those in the Valley High Trailer Court. "No location will please everyone," Williams said.

Williams called the news conference to make the expected announcement of her candidacy for a second term.

Now you have to find a way to treat the other topics of the conference. You may want to list them first with a series of bullets in this way:

In other matters, Williams said:

- City Manager Diane Lusby will not be resigning to take another post.
- Budget constraints will not permit any new construction on the city jail this year.
- Budget cuts will not cost any city employees their jobs. However, positions vacated by retiring personnel will not be filled.

After this list, you will either come back to your lead, giving more background and citing citizens or other city officials on the subject, or go on to treat, one at a time, the matters you listed. Pay particular attention to making proper transitions from paragraph to paragraph so that your story is coherent: "On other subjects, the mayor said . . . ," "The mayor defended her position on . . . ," "Again she stressed. . . ."

If one of the subjects is of special interest, you may want to write a **sidebar,** a shorter piece to go with your main story. For this story, you may want to do a sidebar on the mayor's candidacy, her record, her possible opponents and so on.

With a longer or more complicated story, you may want to make a summary list of all the main topics covered and place them in a box or sidebar.

News conference stories can be tough for broadcast reporters because it's impossible to mention all items discussed at the conference in a two-minute television segment. Almost inevitably, a broadcast reporter must select the single most important topic and highlight that. As a result, the typical broadcast report of a news conference will not touch on all the topics listed in the newspaper report. A broadcast reporter at the news conference mentioned above probably would highlight the landfill story and skip most of the other items, perhaps mentioning only that the city manager is not resigning.

Writing the Meeting Story

Meetings are especially challenging for broadcast reporters. A discussion about setting tax rates for the coming year makes for boring television footage. But such news is important, and good broadcast reporters find a way to make it interesting.

That often means finding a subject who is or will be affected by the change in that tax rate. If the city council is cutting support to the fine arts, for example, an interview with the head of the local arts council may be in order. Finding creative ways to include video is the key to a good broadcast report.

Readers and viewers expect reporters to take their place at a meeting. Let's look at a simple meeting story—in this case a meeting of a local school board:

The decision of three national corporations to protest a formula used to compute their property taxes is causing more than $264,000 to be withheld from the Walnut School District's operating budget for the 2004-05 school year.

Superintendent Max Schmidt said at Monday's school board meeting that International Business Machines Corp., ACR Corp. and Xerox are protesting that the method used in computing their 2001 property taxes was no longer valid. Nine California counties are involved in similar disputes.

The taxes, totaling $264,688, are being held in escrow by the county until the matter is resolved. Some or all of the money eventually may be returned to the district, but the administration cannot determine when or how much.

"If we take a quarter million dollars out of our program at this time, it could have a devastating effect," Schmidt said. "Once you've built that money into your budget and you lost it, you've lost a major source of income."

Mike Harper, the county prosecuting attorney, and Larry Woods, the school district attorney, advised board members to take a "wait-and-see attitude," Schmidt said. He said that one alternative would be to challenge the corporations in court. A final decision will be made later.

The board also delayed action on repayment of $80,000 to IBM in a separate tax dispute. The corporation claims the district owes it for overpaid 2000 property taxes. The county commission has ruled the claim is legitimate and must be repaid.

A possible source of additional income, however, could be House Bill 1002, Schmidt said. If passed, this appropriations bill would provide an additional $46 million for state education, approximately $250,000 of which could go to the Walnut School District.

The issue of the meeting was money problems—a subject that concerns every taxpayer. The writer jumped right into the subject in the lead and then in the second paragraph gave us the "who," "when" and "where." The reporter then dealt with specifics, naming names and citing figures, and quoted the key person at the meeting. In the last two paragraphs the writer dealt with other matters discussed in the meeting.

A broadcast reporter might tackle the same story by interviewing a teacher faced with larger class sizes. Again, knowing what's on the agenda and doing advance work to find such a teacher requires thought and planning.

But the issues discussed at a meeting are not your only concerns in covering a meeting story. Remember, too, to cover the event. Who was there? Who represented the public? Did anyone have reactions after the meeting was over?

Reporter Jennifer Galloway of the *Columbia Missourian* began her meeting story in this way:

Even though they are footing the bill, only one of Boone County's residents cared enough to attend a Tuesday night hearing on the county's budget for next year.

With an audience of one citizen plus two reporters, County Auditor June Pitchford presented her official report on the $21 million budget to the Boone County Commission in a silent City Council chambers.

Even when covering routine, seemingly boring events, you are allowed to use your imagination. In addition to getting all the facts, your job is also to be interesting, to get people to read the story. Remember, one of the criteria of news is that it be unusual. Another is that it be interesting.

Remember, too, never to lead a story with something like this:

The City Council met Tuesday. . . .

What the council did is the news, not the fact that it met. When covering a meeting, your job is to tell what happened. And in the process, you are expected to write well. Even events as common as town meetings call for good writing to hook your readers or viewers and keep them coming back for more.

Suggested Readings

Biography and Genealogy Master Index. Detroit: Gale Research Co., 1981 to present. A compilation of a large number of biographical directories with names of people whose biographies have been written. Indicates which date and volume of those reference books to consult for the actual biography.

Biography Index. New York: H. W. Wilson Co., 1946 to present. Helps you locate biographical articles that have appeared in 2,000 periodicals and journals, as well as in biographical books and chapters from collective biographies.

Carter, T. Barton, Franklin, Marc A. and Wright, Jay B. *The First Amendment and the Fourth Estate.* Water-bury, N.Y.: Foundation Press, 1994. A good explanation of the law of the press.

Teeter, Dwight L. Jr. and LeDuc, Don R. *Law of Mass Communication.* Waterbury, N.Y.: Foundation Press, 1998. An excellent compilation of law as it affects the working reporter.

Weinberg, Steve, et al. *The Investigative Reporter's Handbook,* Fourth Edition. New York: Bedford/St. Martin's, 2002. A guide to using government documents to find sources of information.

Suggested Web Sites

www.asne.org

The American Society of Newspaper Editors publishes a magazine called *American Editor* that often contains useful stories to help reporters write better. Some of those stories can be found at ASNE's Web site.

www.apme.com

Associated Press Managing Editors is an organization that publishes useful advice to working editors.

www.vlib.org

The World Wide Web Virtual Library helps reporters find online links to organizations useful in providing background information.

Exercises

1. Journalist Bill Moyers is coming to town to speak on the current U.S. president's relationship with the press. Prepare to cover the speech. Record the steps you will take to prepare for the speech and the information you have gathered on Moyers.

2. You learn that actor Robert Redford is holding a news conference before speaking to a local group about environmental issues. You also learn that Redford is personally and actively involved in these issues. Using appropriate databanks, gather and record background information on Redford.

3. Find out when the Faculty Council or similar faculty representative group is having its next meeting. Record the steps you take to prepare for the meeting and the information you gather as you prepare. Then cover the meeting and write the story.

4. The following speech by President Bush on June 25, 2002, focused on Israel and a Palestinian state. Write a speech story that concentrates on the content of Bush's speech.

Israel and a Palestinian State

For too long, the citizens of the Middle East have lived in the midst of death and fear. The hatred of a few holds the hopes of many hostage. The forces of extremism and terror are attempting to kill progress and peace by killing the innocent. And this casts a dark shadow over an entire region. For the sake of all humanity, things must change in the Middle East.

It is untenable for Israeli citizens to live in terror. It is untenable for Palestinians to live in squalor and occupation. And the current situation offers no prospect that life will improve. Israeli citizens will continue to be victimized by terrorists, and so Israel will continue to defend herself.

In the situation the Palestinian people will grow more and more miserable. My vision is two states, living side by side in peace and security. There is simply no way to achieve that peace until all parties fight terror. Yet, at this critical moment, if all parties will break with the past and set out on a new path, we can overcome the darkness with the light of hope. Peace requires a new and different Palestinian leadership, so that a Palestinian state can be born.

I call on the Palestinian people to elect new leaders, leaders not compromised by terror. I call upon them to build a practicing democracy, based on tolerance and liberty. If the Palestinian people actively pursue these goals, America and the world will actively support their efforts. If the Palestinian people meet these goals, they will be able to reach agreement with Israel and Egypt and Jordan on security and other arrangements for independence. And when the Palestinian people have new leaders, new institutions and new security arrangements with their neighbors, the United States of America will support the creation of a Palestinian state whose borders and certain aspects of its sovereignty will be provisional until resolved as part of a final settlement in the Middle East.

In the work ahead, we all have responsibilities. The Palestinian people are gifted and capable, and I am confident they can achieve a new birth for their nation. A Palestinian state will never be created by terror—it will be built through reform. And reform must be more than cosmetic change, or veiled attempt to preserve the status quo. True reform will require entirely new political and economic institutions, based on democracy, market economics and action against terrorism.

Today, the elected Palestinian legislature has no authority, and power is concentrated in the hands of an unaccountable few. A Palestinian state can only serve its citizens with a new constitution which separates the powers of government. The Palestinian parliament should have the full authority of a legislative body. Local officials and government ministers need authority of their own and the independence to govern effectively.

The United States, along with the European Union and Arab states, will work with Palestinian leaders to create a new constitutional framework and a working democracy for the Palestinian people. And the United States, along with others in the international community, will help the Palestinians organize and monitor fair, multi-party local elections by the end of the year, with national elections to follow.

Today, the Palestinian people live in economic stagnation, made worse by official corruption. A Palestinian state will require a vibrant economy, where honest enterprise is encouraged by honest government. The United States, the international donor community and the World Bank stand ready to work with Palestinians on a major project of economic reform and development. The United States, the EU, the World Bank, the International Monetary Fund are willing to oversee reforms in Palestinian finances, encouraging transparency and independent auditing.

And the United States, along with our partners in the developed world, will increase our humanitarian assistance to relieve Palestinian suffering. Today, the Palestinian people lack effective courts of law and have no means to defend and vindicate their rights. A Palestinian state will require a system of reliable justice to punish those who prey on the innocent. The United States and members of the international community stand ready to work with Palestinian leaders to establish finance—establish finance and monitor a truly independent judiciary.

Today, Palestinian authorities are encouraging, not opposing, terrorism. This is unacceptable. And the United States will not support the establishment of a Palestinian state until its leaders engage in a sustained fight against the terrorists and dismantle their infrastructure. This will require an externally supervised effort to rebuild and reform the Palestinian security services. The security system must have clear lines of authority and accountability and a unified chain of command.

America is pursuing this reform along with key regional states. The world is prepared to help, yet ultimately these steps toward statehood depend on the Palestinian people and their leaders. If they energetically take the path of reform, the rewards can come quickly. If Palestinians embrace democracy, confront corruption and firmly reject terror, they can count on American support for the creation of a provisional state of Palestine.

With a dedicated effort, this state could rise rapidly, as it comes to terms with Israel, Egypt and Jordan on practical issues, such as security. The final borders, the capital and other aspects of this state's sovereignty will be negotiated between the parties, as part of a final settlement. Arab states have offered their help in this process, and their help is needed.

I've said in the past that nations are either with us or against us in the war on terror. To be counted on the side of peace, nations must act. Every leader actually committed to peace will end incitement to violence in official media and publicly denounce homicide bombings. Every nation actually committed to peace will stop the flow of money, equipment and recruits to terrorist groups seeking the destruction of Israel—including Hamas, Islamic Jihad, and Hezbollah. Every nation actually committed to peace must block the shipment of Iranian supplies to these groups and oppose regimes that promote terror, like Iraq. And Syria must choose the right side in the war on terror by closing terrorist camps and expelling terrorist organizations.

Leaders who want to be included in the peace process must show by their deeds an undivided support for peace. And as we move toward a peaceful solution, Arab states will be expected to build closer ties of diplomacy and commerce with Israel, leading to full normalization of relations between Israel and the entire Arab world.

Israel also has a large stake in the success of a democratic Palestine. Permanent occupation threatens Israel's identity and democracy. A stable, peaceful Palestinian state is necessary to achieve the security that Israel longs for. So I challenge Israel to take concrete steps to support the emergence of a viable, credible Palestinian state.

As we make progress towards security, Israeli forces need to withdraw fully to positions they held prior to September 28, 2000. And consistent with the recommendations of the Mitchell Committee, Israeli settlement activity in the occupied territories must stop.

The Palestinian economy must be allowed to develop. As violence subsides, freedom of movement should be restored, permitting innocent Palestinians to resume work and normal life. Palestinian legislators and officials, humanitarian and international workers, must be allowed to go about the business of building a better future. And Israel should release frozen Palestinian revenues into honest, accountable hands.

I've asked Secretary Powell to work intensively with Middle Eastern and international leaders to realize the vision of a Palestinian state, focusing them on a comprehensive plan to support Palestinian reform and institution-building.

Ultimately, Israelis and Palestinians must address the core issues that divide them if there is to be a real peace, resolving all claims and ending the conflict between them. This means that the Israeli occupation that began in 1967 will be ended through a settlement negotiated between the parties, based on U.N. resolutions 242 and 338, with Israeli withdrawal to secure and recognize borders.

We must also resolve questions concerning Jerusalem, the plight and future of Palestinian refugees, and a final peace between Israel and Lebanon, and Israel and a Syria that supports peace and fights terror.

All who are familiar with the history of the Middle East realize that there may be setbacks in this process. Trained and determined killers, as we have seen, want to stop it. Yet the Egyptian and Jordanian peace treaties with Israel remind us that with determined and responsible leadership progress can come quickly.

As new Palestinian institutions and new leaders emerge, demonstrating real performance on security and reform, I expect Israel to respond and work toward a final status agreement. With intensive effort by all, this agreement could be reached within three years from now. And I and my country will actively lead toward that goal.

I can understand the deep anger and anguish of the Israeli people. You've lived too long with fear and funerals, having to avoid markets and public transportation, and forced to put armed guards in kindergarten classrooms. The Palestinian Authority has rejected your offer at hand and trafficked with terrorists. You have a right to a normal life; you have a right to security; and I deeply believe that you need a reformed, responsible Palestinian partner to achieve that security.

I can understand the deep anger and despair of the Palestinian people. For decades you've been treated as pawns in the Middle East conflict. Your interests have been held hostage to a comprehensive peace agreement that never seems to come as your lives get worse year by year. You deserve democracy and the rule of law. You deserve an open society and a thriving economy. You deserve a life of hope for your children. An end to occupation and a peaceful democratic Palestinian state may seem distant, but America and our partners throughout the world stand ready to help, help you make them possible as soon as possible.

If liberty can blossom in the rocky soil of the West Bank and Gaza, it will inspire millions of men and women around the globe who are equally weary of poverty and oppression, equally entitled to the benefits of democratic government.

I have a hope for the people of Muslim countries. Your commitments to morality, and learn-ing and tolerance led to great historical achievements. And those values are alive in the Islamic world today. You have a rich culture, and you share the aspirations of men and women in every culture. Prosperity and freedom and dignity are not just American hopes, or Western hopes. They are universal, human hopes. And even in the violence and turmoil of the Middle East, America believes those hopes have the power to transform lives and nations.

This moment is both an opportunity and a test for all parties in the Middle East: an opportunity to lay the foundations for future peace; a test to show who is serious about peace and who is not. The choice here is stark and simple. The Bible says, "I have set before you life and death; therefore, choose life." The time has arrived for everyone in this conflict to choose peace, and hope, and life.

Thank you very much.

5. Prepare for, cover and write a
   a. Speech story.
   b. News conference story.
   c. Meeting story.

Then compare your stories to those appearing in the local paper.

9 Other Types of Basic Stories

Speeches, news conferences and meetings are the most common types of stories that first-time reporters cover, but other story forms also are common. Among them are obituaries; crime, accident and fire stories; and court reports. All of these story forms are likely to be assigned to beginning reporters. They are the staples of modern journalism, whether broadcast, print or online.

When the World Trade Center and the Pentagon were attacked on Sept. 11, 2001, hundreds of reporters, both print and broadcast, were pressed into service to cover the disasters. They all employed lessons learned while covering small accidents and fires on their first jobs.

Consider this report by *Boston Globe* writer Fred Kaplan:

NEW YORK—It was a billowing hell, an ashen war scene, as thousands fled the World Trade Center yesterday, sending the nation's largest city into a shudder of fear and uncomprehending mourning.

Thousands were able to escape the buildings between the explosions, but countless others—50,000 work there daily—were trapped within, hurt or dead. Dozens of people leaped from up high, some charred by fire, as horrified rescue workers looked on.

"Oh, those poor people! Oh, those poor people, Oh, my God," a woman wailed as she fled.

More than 10,000 police, fire and rescue workers struggled to clear the entire lower half of Manhattan as subways jammed, highways clogged and panicked pedestrians frantically called loved ones, fights breaking out over pay phones.

Manhattan became an isolated island; bridges and tunnels into the city were sealed off. The enormous municipality's resources were immediately taxed, with disruptions in power and phone service. The day's mayoral primary was canceled.

F-16 fighter planes flew over the scene. FBI and CIA vans pulled up to the base of the towers.

A woman in a red dress, running north from the World Trade Center minutes after the second blast, wailed, "Oh my God, this city's in chaos!"

The first blast went off about 8:45 a.m. as a jet hit the top portion of one of the World Trade Center towers. But the building stayed firm, allowing for escapes.

One witness, Keith Butterfield, was working at a Xerox office building across from the World Trade Center and sensed that the city was under attack, right after the first blast.

"We thought it was a bomb. Last week, there was a bomb-threat scare. We thought this was it," Butterfield said.

"Then we saw the fuselage of a plane, and body parts falling from the sky. There were body parts in front of us strewn all over the street." . . .

A basic story? Certainly not. But at the same time, it is a story crafted by someone well-grounded in the basics.

Information for such a report is gathered in many ways: through observation, by talking with public officials and by interviewing witnesses and, if possible, victims.

No one reporter covers an event of that magnitude. In both print and broadcast, reports from multiple reporters are fed to someone back at the office who sifts through massive amounts of information in an attempt to help the public make sense of what happened. On television, that's done on the fly by producers and anchors. At newspapers, writers meld reports from multiple reporters into a cohesive whole. On the front line, however, are reporters employing lessons learned long ago while covering fires or accidents on their first jobs.

Nothing really prepares a reporter to cover something of the magnitude of the World Trade Center collapse, so drawing upon coverage of earlier accidents, fires and disasters is about the best one can do. Similarly, nothing really prepares a reporter for the first time he or she encounters death on the job—a woman mangled in an automobile wreck or a child burned to death in an apartment fire. Some lessons are learned the hard way, but newspaper editors and broadcast news directors agree on one thing: Good reporters know how to handle basic story types. Knowing how to handle basic stories is the best training for almost anything you will encounter on the job, including a task as daunting as covering the World Trade Center disaster.

One of those basic story types is the obituary, a staple of newspapers but also important to broadcasters. Most people's names appear in local newspapers only when they are born and when they die. When the latter occurs, newspapers try to take note. Although metropolitan papers often charge for obits, small- and medium-sized papers still pay respects to local residents who die. Often, such stories are more than mere recitation of facts. They are stories about a person's life, and to family and friends they are extremely important. Such stories usually find their way into scrapbooks or family Bibles. Newspapers and broadcast stations record major events in the life of a community, and these often involve reporting on crime, accidents, fires and court proceedings. And although television doesn't run a story on each person who dies in a community, the death of prominent individuals certainly gets play on the broadcast report. As a result, it's likely that as a beginning reporter—print, online or broadcast—you will have a chance to cover such events. This chapter is designed to help prepare you to do so.

YOUR PREPARATION

When writing an obit or an account of a crime, an accident, a fire or a court proceeding, begin as you do any other story—with a check in a database or your publication's library. There you'll find background on the subject of an obit. Or you will learn whether a similar crime has occurred before, whether accidents are common at the location of the latest one, whether similar fires have occurred suspiciously often or whether a person charged with a crime has been in trouble before.

Preparing for the Obituary

Sources for obits

- *Mortuary forms.*
- *The newspaper.*
- *The newspaper's library.*
- *Interviews with family and friends of the deceased.*

The newspaper library is the starting point for background research on someone who died. In all probability, your editor will have learned of the death from a death report issued by a local mortuary. Typically, mortuaries issue forms that contain all the basics you will need to write the story: the name of the deceased, his or her occupation, the names of relatives, the time and place of the funeral, and the burial site (see Figure 9.1). The purpose of your search in the library is to find background material on the deceased to make the obituary more compelling to readers.

Some large newspapers use formula writing to produce obituaries, but more and more newspapers are treating these stories as real news worthy of extra reporting. A call to a close friend of the deceased, for example, might produce a more interesting story if you learn that he was an Olympic gold medalist in 1936. The library might reveal that achievement. A friend is almost certain to do so.

Broadcast and online reporters often have access to files on prominent individuals. They also usually have online access to a nearby newspaper library. Again, that's a good place to start when writing an obituary.

Preparing for the Crime Story

Meetings, news conferences, speeches and court proceedings usually are scheduled, so on most occasions there should be ample time beforehand for you to do background research on the individual or topic to be covered. Many obituaries call for a first stop in your publication's library. Crime reporting may be different. If the police radio reports a murder in your area, you may be dispatched to the scene as the story is breaking. At that point, no one will know who is involved or what happened. There will be no time to check the library, and you will have to do your initial reporting at the scene.

Most information about crimes comes from three sources:

- Police officials and their reports.
- The victim or victims.
- The witness or witnesses.

The circumstances of the crime may determine which of these sources is most important, which should be checked first or whether they

NAME OF FUNERAL HOME: _____

PHONE: _____

PERSON TO CONTACT: _____

NAME OF DECEASED: _____

ADDRESS: _____

_____

OCCUPATION: _____

_____

AGE: _____

CAUSE OF DEATH: _____

_____

DATE AND PLACE OF DEATH: _____

_____

TIME AND PLACE OF FUNERAL SERVICES: _____

_____

CONDUCTED BY: _____

BURIAL: _____

TIME AND PLACE FOR VISITATION: _____

_____

BIOGRAPHICAL INFORMATION: _____

_____

_____

_____

_____

SURVIVORS: _____

_____

_____

_____

Figure 9.1
A mortuary form provides basic information. However, the information is not always accurate or complete, so check it against other sources.

should be checked at all. If the victim is available, as a reporter you should make every effort to get an interview. If the victim and witnesses are unavailable, the police and their report become primary sources.

When your editor assigns you to a crime story is important. If you are dispatched to the scene of the crime as it happens or soon afterward, you will probably interview the victim and witnesses first. The police report will have to wait; most likely, it isn't even ready. But if you are assigned to write about a crime that occurred the night before, the police report is the starting point.

A police officer investigating a crime covers much of the same ground as you. The officer is interested in who was involved, what happened, when, where, why and how. Those details are needed to complete the official report of the incident, and you need them for your story.

When you write about crime, the police report always should be checked. It is often the source of basic information:

- A description of what happened.
- The location of the incident.
- The name, age and address of the victim.
- The name, age and address of the suspect, if any.
- The offense police believe the suspect has committed.
- The extent of injuries, if any.
- The names, ages and addresses of the witnesses.

The reporter who arrives at the scene of a crime as it takes place or immediately afterward has the advantage of being able to gather much of that information firsthand. When timely coverage is impossible, however, the police report allows the reporter to catch up quickly. The names of those with knowledge of the incident usually appear on the report, and the reporter uses that information to learn the story (see Figure 9.2).

Print and online reporters sometimes write crime stories from the police report alone. For routine stories, some editors view such reporting as sufficient. Good newspapers, however, demand more because police reports frequently are inaccurate. Most experienced reporters have read reports in which the names of those involved are misspelled, ages are wrongly stated and other basic information is inaccurate. Sometimes such errors are a result of sloppy reporting by the investigating officer or mistakes in transcribing notes into a formal report. Occasionally, an officer may lie in an attempt to cover up shortcomings in an investigation or misconduct at the scene of a crime. Whatever the reason, good reporters do their own reporting and do not depend solely on a police officer's account. Remember that good editors frown on single-source stories of any kind, basic or not. Your

BURGLARY

1 OFFENSE: Burglary
2 CASE #: 32701
3 OCCURRED AT (ADDRESS): 308 Maple St.
4 DATE/TIME OCCURRED: 0100 - 0800
5 DATE/TIME REPORTED: 0830
6 DATE/TIME REPORT WRITTEN: 0945 - 11 March

	RAC	SEX	DOB	ADDRESS	HOME PHONE	BUS PHONE
7 PERSON REPORTING: Linda L. Mellotti	W	F	9-11-45	308 Maple St.	372-1124	372-9988
8 OWNER OF BUILDING: VICTIM						
9 WITNESS: NONE						
10 VICTIM (FIRM OR INDIVIDUAL)						

11 RESIDENCE ☒ NONRESIDENCE ☐
12 FORCE ☒ NO FORCE ☐
13 DAY ☐ NIGHT ☒ UNKNOWN ☐
14 TYPE OF BUSINESS:
15 POINT OF ENTRY: Back door
16 HOW WAS ENTRY GAINED: Glass broken to unlock door
17 TYPE OF LOCK OR STRUCTURE DEFEATED: Type A
18 DAMAGE CAUSED BY ENTRY: Broken window glass
19 WHO SECURED BLDG: Occupant
TIME/DATE:

STOLEN PROP	20 QUAN	21 TYPE	22 BRAND	23 SERIAL #	24 PHYSICAL DESCRIPTION	25 VALUE	26 DATE ENTERED	BY	27 DATE CLEARED	BY
A	1	Console	GE	Unknown	TV set	$300				

28 SUSPECT NAME	RAC	SEX	DOB	ADDRESS	HOME PHONE	BUS PHONE
NONE						

HT | WT. | EYES | HAIR | BUILD | FACIAL HAIR | HAT | COAT | SHIRT | TROUSERS | SHOES

UNUSUAL IDENTIFIERS | MARKS SCARS & TATTOOS | PHOTO OBTAINED

SUSPECT VEHICLE COLOR | YEAR | MAKE | MODEL | STYLE | VIN | LIC YR | LIC STATE | LIC TYPE | LIC NUMBER

29 INVESTIGATING OFFICER | DEPT | 30 APPROVED BY | 31 EVIDENCE COLLECTED BY | 32 PHOTOGRAPHY BY | 33 REASSIGNED TO | BY

34 NARRATIVE:
Victim works night shift at Milan Hospital. Residence entered while she was working. TV set only item known missing.

WORK SHEET

Figure 9.2
This burglary report is typical of the reports available to reporters at most police stations.

job is to do solid reporting, and you are expected to consult multiple sources.

Broadcast reporters do extensive on-the-scene coverage of crime, which has become a common element on local newscasts. Live reporting from crime scenes is likely to be a key component of a beginning reporter's job because on-the-scene reporting is the only way to get good video for the story.

Robert Snyder, a former history professor at Princeton University, studied U.S. crime reporting while he was a research fellow at the Gannett Center for Media Studies in New York. What he found alarmed him. Crime stories, he discovered, still rely heavily on one police source. That, Snyder insists, is a dangerous and seemingly irresponsible practice. One of journalism's first principles is that a story's credibility rests on the number of sources used.

On crime stories, the background check in your publication's library often is done after you return to the office. Once you have the names of those involved, you can see whether the library reveals relevant material about them. Was the suspect arrested before? Was the store robbed before? The library might help provide the answers to those kinds of questions.

Preparing for Accident and Fire Stories

If you are assigned to cover an accident or fire, you can expect some of the same problems you'd encounter if covering a crime. Much depends on whether the police or fire report is available before or after you are assigned to the story.

If the accident or fire took place overnight, the report prepared by officials is the place to start. It will give you most of the basic information you need. It also will lead you to other sources.

If you are sent to the scene of an accident or fire, your job is to collect much of that information yourself. As with crimes, you will need basic information:

- A description of what happened.
- The location and time of the incident.
- The name, age, address and condition of the victim or victims.
- The extent of injuries, if any.
- The names, ages and addresses of the witnesses.

Preparing for the Court Story

Most court stories you are likely to cover will be follow-ups to earlier stories. If a murder suspect is appearing for a preliminary hearing, details of the crime probably were reported earlier. A library check may give you ample background information as you prepare for your visit to the courtroom. In the absence of that, a chat with the district attorney, the police chief or one of their assistants might provide ample background for writing the story.

Court stories are increasingly popular on television because most jurisdictions now allow cameras in the courtroom. There is plenty of opportunity for coverage in key local cases. In federal jurisdictions—which still prohibit cameras—print, online and broadcast reporters often rely on artists' sketches of courtroom scenes to provide visuals.

Court stories often are difficult for beginners to write because it is difficult to understand the complex process used in prosecuting criminals. In addition to criminal court cases, there are civil court proceedings—lawsuits that charge an individual or company with harming another. The legal system can be quite confusing. Here's our best advice on how to approach court stories: Ask plenty of questions of the judge and attorneys before or after the court proceeding or during recesses. It's much better to admit your lack of knowledge than to make a serious error because you didn't understand what was happening.

WRITING THE STORY

Learning to organize accounts of these types of events is essential. It helps to have a model, and the stories that follow are designed to assist you.

Writing the Obituary

An obituary is a news story. You should apply the same standards to crafting a lead and building the body of an obituary as you would do for other stories. You begin by answering the questions you would answer in any news story: who (Michael Kelly, 57, of 1234 West St.), what (died), where (at Regional Hospital), when (Tuesday night), why (heart attack) and how (suffered while jogging). With this information, you are ready to start the story.

Creating a Lead

The fact that Kelly died of a heart attack suffered while jogging may be the lead, but the reporter does not know this until the rest of the information essential to every obituary is gathered. You also must know:

- Time and place of the funeral.
- Time and burial place.

Five safeguards for obit writers

1. Confirm spellings of names.
2. Check the addresses. If a telephone book or city directory lists a different address, contact the mortuary about the discrepancy.
3. Check the birth date against the age, noting whether the person's birthday was before or after the date of death.
4. Verify with the mortuary or family any obituary phoned or faxed to the newspaper.
5. Check your newspaper's library for stories about the deceased, but be sure you don't pull stories about someone else with the same name.

- Visitation time (if any).
- Survivors.
- Date and place of birth.
- Achievements.
- Occupation.
- Memberships.

Any of those items can yield the nugget that will appear in the lead. But if none of them yields notable information, the obituary probably will start like this:

> Michael Kelly, 57, of 1234 West St. died Tuesday night at Regional Hospital.

Later in the news cycle, another standard approach could be used:

> Funeral services for Michael Kelly, 57, of 1234 West St. will be at 2 p.m. Thursday at St. Catherine's Roman Catholic Church.

Good reporters, however, often mention a distinguishing characteristic of a person's life. It may be volunteer service, an unusual or important job, service in public office or even just having a name of historical significance. Whatever distinguishes a person can be the lead of the obituary. These leads demonstrate the technique:

> Byran MacGregor, a TV and radio journalist whose pro-U.S. recording "The Americans" got wide airplay in the 1970s, died Tuesday of pneumonia. He was 46.
>
> Jeanne Calment of France, the world's oldest person, died Tuesday at age 122.

> Luther Allison, whose passionate, original vocals and searing guitar playing made him one of the leading bluesmen and an influence on rock 'n' roll, died Monday. He was 57.

Writing approaches can be as varied for obituaries as for any other news story. The following story emphasizes the personal reactions of individuals who knew the deceased:

> Few persons knew her name, but nearly everyone knew her face.
>
> For 43 years, Mary Jones, the city's cheerful cashier, made paying your utility bills a little easier.
>
> Tuesday morning after she failed to report to work, two fellow employees found her dead in her home at 432 East St., where she apparently suffered a heart attack. She was 66.
>
> By Tuesday afternoon, employees had placed a simple sign on the counter where Miss Jones had worked.
>
> "We regret to inform you that your favorite cashier, Mary

Jones, died this morning. We all miss her."

"She had a smile and a quip for everybody who came in here," said June Foster, a book-keeper in the office.

"She even made people who were mad about their bills go away laughing."

Building the Story

Most of the obituary information is provided by the mortuary on a standard form (see Figure 9.1). When the obituary is written straight from the form, this is usually what results:

Michael Kelly, 57, of 1234 West St., died Tuesday night at Regional Hospital.

Kelly collapsed while jogging and died apparently of a heart attack.

Services will be at 2 p.m. Thursday at St. Catherine's Roman Catholic Church. The Rev. Sherman Mitchell will officiate. Burial will be at Glendale Memorial Gardens in Springfield.

Friends may visit at the Fenton Funeral Chapel from 7 to 9 p.m. Wednesday.

Born Dec. 20, 1935, in Boston to Nathan and Sarah Kelly, Kelly was a member of St. Catherine's Roman Catholic Church and a U.S. Navy veteran of the Korean War. He had been an independent insurance agent for the last 25 years.

He married Pauline Virginia Hatfield in Boston on May 5, 1954.

Survivors include his wife; a son, Kevin of Charlotte, N.C.; and a daughter, Mary, who is a student at the University of North Carolina at Chapel Hill.

Also surviving are a brother, John of Milwaukee, Wis., and a sister, Margaret Carter of Asheville, N.C.

The Kelly obituary is a dry biography, not a story of Michael Kelly's life. There is no hint of his impact on his friends, family or community. Here is an example of a better story built on good reporting:

Ila Watson Portwood died Sunday at the Candlelight Care Center of complications stemming from a stroke she suffered about two weeks earlier. She was 89.

She was born on Aug. 30, 1908, in Boone County. She graduated from Howard-Payne School in Howard County and attended the University of Michigan.

She was the former owner and operator of the Gem Drug Co. She and her late husband, Carl, started as employees in 1929 and bought the business in 1956. They retired in 1975 and sold the company to Harold Earnest.

"She was a total lady," Earnest said. "I've never seen her mistreat anyone. Just the sweetest lady anyone can meet."

need to know some banking history.

"You want to know if he or she survived the Crash of '29. Did the people who worked with him or her jump out of the building? What did that person do to get where he or she is now? Did the person sell apples on street corners? Was he or she part of the WPA program?

"A reporter from Mars couldn't write a good obit. Here's why. You have to have a frame of reference to start with. That way you will find other avenues that will lead you to other interesting places. You have to know a bit about the Crash of '29 to talk to other people about it."

Colon brings a broad frame of reference to his work. He reported for the *Herald* for three years, then was an editor at Voice of America for two years. He earned his master's degree, taught journalism and directed a program to train professional journalists in management techniques with a multicultural perspective. He returned to the *Herald* in 1993.

Mrs. Portwood volunteered from 1974 to 1980 at the Cancer Research Center's Women's Cancer Control Program and was named volunteer of the year in 1977.

"She was a people person," said Rosetta Miller, program coordinator. "Her caring personalized her commitment to the staff and patients. . . ."

Portwood was an ordinary person whose life affected others. An obituary should celebrate such a life rather than merely note the death.

Because much of the information in any obituary comes directly from the family, it generally is accurate. But you still should check the spelling of all names and addresses and the deceased's age against the birth date. You should never print an obituary based on information obtained by phone from someone purporting to be a funeral home representative. Too many newspapers have been the victims of hoaxes. Always call the funeral home to confirm the death.

Choosing Your Words

Avoid much of the language found on mortuary forms and in obituaries prepared by morticians. The phrasing often is more fitting for a eulogy than for a newspaper story.

Because of the sensitivity of the subject matter, euphemisms have crept into the vocabulary of obituary writers. "Loved ones," "passed away," "our dearly beloved brother and father," "the departed" and "remains" may be fine for eulogies, but such terms are out of place in a news story.

Watch your language, too, when you report the cause and circumstances of a death. Unless the doctor is at fault, a person usually dies not "as a result of an operation" but "following" or "after" one. Also, a person dies "unexpectedly" but not "suddenly" (all deaths are sudden). A person dies "of" cancer, not "from" it. Note, too, that a person dies "apparently of a heart attack" but not of "an apparent heart attack." And a person dies of injuries "suffered," not "received."

Be careful with religious terms. Catholics "celebrate" Mass. Jews worship in "synagogues," which are sometimes referred to as "temples." An Episcopal priest who heads a parish is a "rector," not a "pastor." Followers of Islam are called "Muslims." Consult your wire service stylebook when you have a question.

The stylebook prescribes usage in other instances, too. A man is survived by his wife, not his widow, and a woman is survived by her husband, not her widower. Do you use courtesy titles such as Mr. and Mrs.? Many newspapers do in obits. Do you mention divorced spouses, deceased spouses or live-in companions? Do you identify pallbearers? Do you say that the family requests memorial contributions instead of flowers? You will need to consult your local stylebook often when you are writing an obit.

Cause of Death

If the person who dies is not a public figure and the family does not wish to divulge the cause of death, some newspapers and television stations will comply, though such a decision is questionable news judgment. The reader or viewer wants to know what caused the death. A reporter should call the mortuary, the family, the attending physician and the appropriate medical officer. Only if none of these sources will talk should the newspaper leave out the cause of death. Some newspapers, such as the *Des Moines (Iowa) Register*, *Cincinnati Enquirer* and *Detroit News*, require obituaries to include the cause of death, as do many television stations.

If the death is caused by cancer or a heart attack or is the result of an accident, most families do not object to including the cause in the obituary. But if the cause is, for example, cirrhosis of the liver brought on by heavy drinking, many families do object, and many papers do not insist on printing the cause.

If the deceased was a public figure or a young person, most newspapers and broadcast stations insist on the cause of death.

If the death is the result of suicide or foul play, reporters can obtain the information from the police or the medical examiner. Some newspapers and broadcast stations mention suicide as the cause of death in the obituary, others print it in a separate news story, and still others ignore it altogether. This is one way to report it:

> Services for Gary O'Neal, 34, a local carpenters' union officer, will be at 9 a.m. Thursday in the First Baptist Church. Coroner Mike Pardee ruled that Mr. O'Neal died Tuesday of a self-inflicted gunshot wound.

Embarrassing Information

Another newspaper policy affecting obituaries concerns embarrassing information. When the *St. Louis Post-Dispatch* reported in an obituary that the deceased had been disbarred and had been a key witness in a bribe scandal involving a well-known politician 13 years earlier, several callers complained. The paper's Reader's Advocate defended the decision to include that history in the obituary.

When author W. Somerset Maugham died, *The New York Times* reported that he was a homosexual even though the subject generally

Obituary policy options

- *Run an obituary that ignores any embarrassing information and, if necessary, leave out the cause of death. If circumstances surrounding the death warrant a news story, run it separate from the obituary.*
- *Insist on including embarrassing details and the cause of death in all obituaries.*
- *Insist on including embarrassing details and the cause of death in the obituaries of public figures only.*
- *Put a limit on how far back in the person's life to use derogatory information such as a conviction.*
- *Print everything newsworthy that is learned about public figures but not about private figures.*
- *Print everything thought newsworthy about both public and private figures.*
- *Decide each case as it comes up.*

"People are a lot more open than they were, but I think that they're still not open enough when it comes to AIDS. It's been my experience that nobody will admit it unless they are in the arts. If somebody in business dies of AIDS, we may never know about it."

—Irvin Horowitz,
Obituary writer,
The New York Times

had not been discussed in public. When public figures die, newspapers sometimes make the first public mention of drinking problems in their obituaries. Acquired immune deficiency syndrome (AIDS) is one of the more recent causes of death to challenge editors. The death of actor Rock Hudson in 1985 brought AIDS to the attention of many who had never heard of the disease before. Because it was a stigmatized disease, many newspapers agonized over whether to say that Hudson had AIDS. However, as other public figures died of AIDS, it became almost routine to report the cause of death. Unfortunately, because society still regards AIDS negatively, some spokespeople go out of their way to mention the cause of death so people don't think AIDS was the cause. Yet history shows that the more AIDS or any other disease is reported as a cause of death, the more accepted it becomes.

The crucial factor in determining the extent to which you should report details of an individual's private life is whether the deceased was a public or private person. A public figure is someone who has been in the public eye. A participant in civic or social activities, a person who spoke out at public meetings or through the mass media, a performer, an author, a speaker—these all may be public figures. Public officials, individuals who have been elected or appointed to public office, are generally treated like public figures.

Whether the subject is a public figure or private citizen, the decisions newspapers and broadcast stations must make when dealing with the obituary are sensitive and complicated. It is the reporter's obligation to be aware of the newspaper or station policy. In the absence of a clear policy statement, the reporter should consult an editor.

Writing the Crime Story

There is no magic formula for writing crime news. Solid reporting techniques pay off just as they do in other types of reporting. Then it is a matter of writing the story as the facts demand. Sometimes the events of a crime are most effectively told in chronological order, particularly when the story is complex. More often, a traditional inverted pyramid style is best. The amount of time the reporter has to file the story also influences the approach. Let's take a look at how the newspaper accounts of two crimes were developed and why different writing styles seemed appropriate for each.

The Chronologically Ordered Story

Gathering facts from the many sources available and sorting through conflicting information can be time-consuming tasks. Sometimes the reporter may have to write the story before all the facts are gathered.

The result is a bare-bones account written to meet a deadline. Such circumstances often lead to poor crime stories. When there is time to learn the full story, readers or viewers get a complete account of what occurred:

James Phipps and Anthony Lilly, a pair of 17-year-olds from Kansas City, Kan., were heading west on Interstate 70 at 7:30 a.m. Friday, returning from a trip to Arkansas.

Within the next hour and a half, Phipps had used a sawed-off shotgun stolen in Arkansas to take Lilly hostage, and, after holding that shotgun to Lilly's head, was shot and killed by a Highway Patrol captain on the edge of a rugged wooded area south of Springfield.

As the episode ended, local officials had only begun to piece together a bizarre tragedy that involved a high-speed chase, airplane and helicopter surveillance, a march through a wooded ravine and the evacuation of several frightened citizens from their country homes.

As police reconstructed the incident, Phipps and Lilly decided to stop for gas at the Millersburg exit east of Springfield at about 7:30 a.m. With them in the van was Robert Paul Hudson Jr., a San Francisco-bound hitchhiker.

Hudson was not present at the shooting. He had fled Lilly's van at the Millersburg exit after he suspected trouble.

The trouble began when Lilly and Phipps openly plotted to steal some gasoline at Millersburg, Hudson told police. He said the pair had agreed to display the shotgun if trouble arose with station attendants.

Hudson said he persuaded Phipps to drop him off before they stopped for gas. He then caught a ride to Springfield and told his driver of the robbery plans he had overheard. After dropping Hudson off near the Providence Road exit, the driver called Springfield police, who picked up Hudson.

Meanwhile, Phipps and Lilly put $5.90 worth of gas in the van and drove off without paying. The station attendant notified authorities.

As he approached Springfield, Phipps turned onto U.S. 63 South, where he was spotted by Highway Patrol troopers Tom Halford and Greg Overfelt. They began a high-speed chase, which ended on a dead-end gravel road near Pierpont.

During the chase, which included a U-turn near Ashland, Phipps bumped the Highway Patrol car twice, forcing Halford to run into the highway's median.

Upon reaching the dead end, the suspects abandoned the van and ran into a nearby barn. At that point, Phipps, who Highway Patrol officers said was wanted in Kansas for escaping from a detention center, turned the shotgun on Lilly.

When Halford and Overfelt tried to talk with Phipps from outside the barn, they were met with obscenities. Phipps threatened to "blow (Lilly's) head off," and vowed not to be captured alive.

Phipps then left the barn and walked into a wooded area, pressing the gun against Lilly's head. Halford and Overfelt followed at a safe distance but were close enough to speak with Phipps.

wracked by a high offi-
cer death rate and
embarrassed by a sen-
sational, racially divisive
trial of a black man
acquitted of shooting
to death a white police
officer in what he said
was self-defense.

Once, as coroners
removed a charred
body from a San Diego
trash bin, Grimaldi was
on the scene. He later
was the first to report
that the death prob-
ably was the work of a
serial killer. He wrote
about police corrup-
tion, mentioning the
chief's use of city-
owned video equip-
ment to tape a TV
show on bass fishing.

"There's no better
way to learn how to
report and write
than covering crime,"
Grimaldi says. "It is the
quickest way to ex-
plore any community.
There's humor and
pathos, politics and
social issues. Every
rookie reporter should
spend some time cov-
ering crime."

From the *Tribune*,
Grimaldi went to *The
Orange County (Calif.)
Register* in 1989 as a
general-assignment
reporter.

In 1994, Grimaldi
was named the *Reg-
ister*'s bureau chief in
Washington.

While other officers from the Highway Patrol, the Lincoln County Sheriff's Department and Springfield police arrived at the scene, residents in the area were warned to evacuate their homes. A Highway Patrol plane and helicopter flew low over the woods, following the suspects and the troopers through the woods.

The four walked through a deep and densely wooded ra-vine. Upon seeing a partially constructed house in a nearby clearing, Phipps demanded of officers waiting in the clearing that his van be driven around to the house, at which time he would release his hostage. Halford said, "They disappeared up over the ridge. I heard some shouting (Phipps' demands), and then I heard the shot."

After entering the clearing from the woods, Phipps appar-ently had been briefly confused by the officers on either side of him and had lowered his gun for a moment.

That was long enough for Highway Patrol Capt. N.E. Tinnin to shoot Phipps in the abdomen with a high-powered rifle. It was about 8:45 a.m. Phipps was taken to Boone County Hospital, where he soon died.

The story is as complete as possible under the circumstances. The reporter who wrote it decided to describe the chain of events in chronological order both because of the complexity of the story and because the drama of the actual events is most vividly communicated in a chronological story form.

The story is also made effective by its wealth of detail, including the names of the troopers involved, details of the chase and more. To piece together this account, the reporter had to talk with many wit-nesses. The hard work paid off, however, in the form of an informative, readable story.

Notice how the third paragraph sets the scene and provides a transition into the chronological account. Such attention to the details of good writing helps the reader understand the story with a minimum of effort.

The Sidebar Story

If a number of people witnessed or were affected by a crime, the main story may be supplemented by a sidebar story that deals with the personal impact of the crime. The writer of the preceding chronological account decided to write a separate story on nearby residents, who had little to add to the main story but became part of the situation nonetheless:

In the grass at the edge of a woods near Pierpont Friday afternoon, the only remaining signs of James Phipps were a six-inch circle of blood, a doctor's syringe, a blood-stained button and the imprints in the mud where Phipps fell after he was shot by a Highway Patrol officer.

Elsewhere in the area, it was a quiet, sunny, spring day in a countryside dotted by farms and houses. But inside some of those houses, dwellers still were shaken by the morning's events that had forced a police order for them to evacuate their homes.

Mrs. James G. Thorne lives on Cheavens Road across the clearing from where Phipps was shot. Mrs. Thorne had not heard the evacuation notice, so when she saw area officers crouching with guns at the end of her driveway, she decided to investigate.

"I was the surprise they weren't expecting," she told a Highway Patrol officer Friday afternoon. "I walked out just before the excitement."

When the officers saw Mrs. Thorne "they were obviously very upset and shouted for me to get out of here," she said. "I was here alone and asked them how I was supposed to leave. All they said was, 'Just get out of here!'"

Down the road, Clarence Stallman had been warned of the situation by officers and noticed the circling airplane and helicopter. "I said, 'Are they headed this way soon?' and they said, 'They're here,'" said Stallman.

After Stallman notified his neighbors, he picked up Mrs. Thorne at her home and left the area just before the shooting.

On the next street over, Ronald Nichols had no intention of running.

"I didn't know what was happening," Nichols said. "The wife was scared to death and didn't know what to do. I grabbed my gun and looked for them."

Another neighbor, Mrs. Charles Emmons, first was alerted by the sound of the surveillance plane. "The plane was flying so low I thought it was going to come into the house," she said. "I was frightened. This is something you think will never happen to you."

Then Mrs. Emmons flashed a relieved smile. "It's been quite a morning," she said.

The Inverted Pyramid Account

The techniques of writing in chronological order and separating the accounts of witnesses from the main story worked well in the preceding case. More often, however, crime stories are written in the classic inverted pyramid style because of time and space considerations:

A masked robber took $1,056 from a clerk at Gibson's Liquor Store Friday night, then eluded police in a chase through nearby alleys.

The clerk, Robert Simpson, 42, of 206 Fourth St., said a man wearing a red ski mask entered the store at about 7:35 p.m. The man displayed a pistol and demanded that Simpson empty the contents of the cash register into a brown grocery bag.

Simpson obeyed but managed to trigger a silent alarm button under the counter.

The robber ordered Simpson into a storage room in the rear of the building at 411 Fourth St.

Officer J.O. Holton, responding to the alarm, arrived at the store as the suspect left the building and fled south on foot.

Holton chased the man south on Fourth Street until he turned west into an alley near the cor-

Annual crime statistics are a common source of stories. Reporters must take care when reporting them, however, if they involve small numbers. It is dramatic to say, "Murders increased by 200 percent in 2003," but it is misleading if the increase was from one murder to three.

To provide a more accurate picture, reporters can perform the equivalent of adding apples and oranges. "Unlike" items can be added, subtracted, multiplied and divided, if they are grouped in a category that makes them "like" items.

For example, you can group murders, rapes, assaults and armed robberies in the category of "violent crimes." That way, you can add murders to rapes to assaults to armed robberies. This can be useful if an individual category such as murder isn't large enough to provide much insight (as in many small towns). However, the larger category must be logical and meaningful.

ner of Olson Street. Holton said he followed the suspect for about four blocks until he lost sight of him.

Simpson said receipts showed that $1,056 was missing from the cash register. He described the robber as about 5 feet 11 inches with a bandage on his right thumb. He was wearing blue jeans and a black leather coat.

Police have no suspects.

Such an account is adequate and can be written directly from the police report (see Figure 9.2). That, of course, would be a single-source story, so a good reporter would supplement the official version by taking the time to interview the clerk and police officer.

Writing Accident and Fire Stories

When you are assigned to cover an accident or a fire, you will gather many of the facts and all of the color at the scene. Being there will give you a clearer picture of what happened, and you will be able to write a better story. For a broadcast reporter, being there is essential to getting the necessary video to tell the story.

Too many reporters cover accidents and fires as passive observers. Of course, you must observe. But you also must actively solicit information from people at the scene. Many of them, including those directly involved, you may never be able to find again.

The Scene of an Accident

When you are dispatched to the scene of an accident, move as quickly as possible to collect this information:

- The names, ages, addresses and conditions of the victims.
- Accounts of witnesses or police reconstructions of what happened.
- When the accident occurred.
- Where it occurred.
- Why or how it happened or who was at fault, as determined by officials in charge of the investigation.

If that list sounds familiar, it should. You could simplify it to read "who, what, when, where and why." As in any news story, that information is essential. You must gather it as quickly as possible after being assigned to the story.

If the accident has just taken place, a visit to the scene is essential. Just as important is knowing what to do when you get there. These suggestions will help:

- *Question the person in charge of the investigation.* This individual will attempt to gather much of the same information you want. If you are able to establish a good relationship with the investigator, you

Visiting the scene of an accident, such as this train derailment in Alabama, is essential to gathering crucial information and writing an effective story.

What to do at the scene of an accident

- *Question the person in charge of the investigation.*
- *Try to find and interview witnesses.*
- *Try to find friends or relatives of the victims.*
- *If possible, interview the victims.*
- *Talk with others at the scene.*
- *Be sensitive to victims and their families.*

may be able to secure much of the information you need from this one source, though single-source stories are usually inadequate.

Remember that the spellings of names, addresses and similar facts must be verified later. Police officers and other public officials often make errors in recording the names of victims. To avoid such errors, call relatives of the victims, or consult the city directory or other sources to check your information.

- *Try to find and interview witnesses.* Police and other investigators may lead you directly to them. The most accurate account of what happened usually comes from witnesses, and the investigators will try to find them. You should, too. A good way to do that is to watch the investigators. Listen in as they interview a witness, or corner the witness after they are finished. If there is time, of course, try to find your own witnesses.
- *Try to find friends or relatives of the victims.* These sources are helpful in piecing together information about the victims. Through them you often get tips about even better stories.
- *If possible, interview the victims.* Survivors of an accident may be badly shaken, but if they are able to talk, they can provide firsthand details that an official report never could. Make every attempt to interview those involved.
- *Talk with others at the scene.* If someone has died at the scene of the accident, an ambulance paramedic or the medical examiner may be able to give you some indication of what caused the death. At least you can learn where the bodies or the injured will be taken; later the mortician or hospital officials may be able to provide information.
- *Be sensitive to victims and their families.* You have a job to do, and you must do it. That does not mean, however, that you can be insensitive to those involved in an accident.

Of course, your deadline will have a major impact on the amount of information you are able to gather. If you must meet a deadline soon after arriving at the scene, you probably will be forced to stick to the basics of who, what, when, where, why and how. Thus it is important to gather that information first. Then, if you have time, you can concentrate on more detailed and vivid information to make the story highly readable.

The following account of a tractor-trailer accident was produced in a race against the clock by the staff of an afternoon newspaper:

A truck driver was killed and a woman was injured this morning when a tractor-trailer believed to be hauling gasoline overturned and exploded on Interstate 70, turning the highway into a conflagration.

Both lanes of I-70 were backed up for miles after an eastbound car glanced off a pickup truck, hurdled the concrete median and collided with a tanker truck heading west.

The explosion was immediate, witnesses said. Residents along Texas Avenue reported the initial fireball reached the north side of the street, which is about

300 yards from the scene of the accident. A wooded area was scorched, but no houses were damaged.

Police evacuated the 600 block of Texas Avenue for fear that the fire would spread, but residents were returning to their homes at 12:35 p.m., about an hour after the collision. Authorities also unsuccessfully attempted to hold back the onlookers who gravitated to a nearby shopping center parking lot to view the blaze.

Police did not identify the driver of the truck, which was owned by a Tulsa, Okla., firm named Transport Delivery Co.

"Apparently it was gasoline," said Steve Paulsell, chief of the County Fire Protection District. "That's what it smelled like." Other officials reported the truck may have been hauling fuel oil or diesel fuel.

For an afternoon newspaper with an early afternoon deadline, such a story presents major problems, particularly when it occurs, as this one did, at about 11:30 a.m. Four reporters were dispatched to the scene; all of them called in information to a writer back at the office. There was little time to interview eyewitnesses. Because of the pressing deadline, the reporters were forced to gather most of their information from fire and police officials at the scene.

Writers for the morning newspaper or daily Web site, by comparison, had plenty of time to gather rich detail to tell the story in human terms. Much of the breaking news value was diminished by the next day because of intense coverage by afternoon newspapers, radio and television stations and updated Web sites. It was time to tell the story of a hero:

Witnesses credited an off-duty fireman with saving a woman's life Monday following a spectacular four-vehicle collision on Interstate 70 just east of its intersection with Business Loop 70.

The driver of a gasoline truck involved in the fiery crash was not so lucky. Bill Borgmeyer, 62, of Jefferson City died in the cab of his rig, which jackknifed, overturned and exploded in flames when he swerved in a futile attempt to avoid hitting a car driven by Leta Hanes, 33, of Nelson, Mo.

Hanes, who was thrown from her auto by the impact, was lying unconscious within 10 feet of the blazing fuel when firefighter Richard Walden arrived at the crash scene.

"I knew what was going on," Walden recalled, "and I knew I had to get her away from there." Despite the intense heat, Walden dragged the woman to safety.

"She had some scrapes, a cut on her knee and was beat around a little bit," Walden said. "Other than that, she was fine."

Hanes was taken to Boone Hospital Center, where she was reported in satisfactory condition Monday night.

Smoke billowing from the accident scene reportedly was visible 30 miles away. Westbound interstate traffic was backed up as far as five miles. Several city streets became snarled for several hours when traffic was diverted to Business Loop 70. The eastbound lane of I-70 was reopened about 2 p.m.; the westbound lane was not reopened until 3 p.m. . . .

The richness of detail in the second account and the eyewitness descriptions of what happened make the story more interesting.

The Scene of a Fire

Accidents and fires present similar problems for the reporter, but at a fire of any size you can expect more confusion than at the scene of an accident. One major difference, then, is that the officer in charge at a fire will be busier. At the scene of an accident the damage has been done and the authorities usually are free to concentrate on their investigation. At a fire the officer in charge is busy directing firefighters and probably will be unable to talk with you. The investigation will not even begin until the fire is extinguished. In many cases the cause of the fire will not be known for hours, days or weeks. In fact, it may never be known. Seldom is that the case in an accident, except perhaps for air accidents.

Fire scenes generally provide plenty of good opportunities for newspaper and online photographers and television videographers. Reporters help their visual counterparts gather information to accompany the images.

Hazards at the scene of a disaster, such as this fire resulting from a Los Angeles-area earthquake, can make a reporter's job difficult and dangerous.

One potential problem is that you may not have access to the immediate area of the fire. Barriers often are erected to keep the public—and representatives of the news media—from coming too close to a burning structure. The obvious reason is safety, but such barriers may hamper your reporting. You may not be able to come close enough to firefighters to learn about the problems they are having or to obtain the quotes you need to improve your story.

These problems usually make covering a fire more difficult than covering an accident. Despite the difficulties, you cover a fire in much the same way, interviewing officials and witnesses at the scene. You also should try to interview the property owner. Moreover, because the official investigation will not have begun, you must conduct your own.

When covering any fire, you must learn:

- The location of the fire.
- The names, ages and addresses of those killed, injured or missing.
- The name of the building's owner or, in the case of a grass fire or forest fire, the name of the landowner.
- The value of the building and its contents or the value of the land.
- Whether the building and contents were insured for fire damage. (Open land seldom is.)
- The time the fire started, who reported it, and how many firefighters and pieces of equipment were called to the scene.
- What caused the fire, if known.

As in any story, the basics are who, what, when, where, why and how. But the nature of the fire will raise other questions. Of primary importance is whether life is endangered. If it is not, the amount of property damage becomes the major emphasis of the story. Was arson involved? Was the building insured for its full value? Was there an earlier fire in the building? Did the building comply with the fire codes? Were any rare or extremely valuable objects inside? Were there explosives inside that complicated fighting the fire and posed an even greater threat than the fire itself?

Your job is to answer those questions for the readers or viewers. You will be able to obtain some of that information later, from the official fire reports if they are ready before your story deadline (see Figure 9.3). But most of the answers will come from interviews that you conduct at the scene with the best available sources. Finding your sources may not be easy, but you can begin by looking for the highest-ranking fire official. Large fire departments may have a press officer whose job is to deal with you and other reporters.

Another important source in covering fire stories is the fire marshal, whose job is to determine the cause of the fire and, if arson is involved, to bring charges against the arsonist. You should make every effort to talk with the fire marshal at the scene, if he or she is available.

DATE	TIME	ADDRESS

FD-500

PAGE   OF   CASUALTY REPORT

CHANGE 2 ☐
(74)
DELETE 3 ☐

INCIDENT NO.   EXP
8 0 9 0 5 1 3
1 2 3   7 8 9

NAME
S A N D O Z A   M A N U E L   R
LAST, FIRST MIDDLE   33 34 35 36

AGE Time of Injury MONTH DAY YEAR
3 2   0 9 4 5   0 2   0 8   9 6
                 39 40   45

HOME ADDRESS
307 Banning Ave., Apt. 3

TELEPHONE
555-9088

46 SEX	47 CASUALTY TYPE	48 SEVERITY	49 AFFILIATION
1 ☒ Male	1 ☒ Fire Casualty	1 ☒ Injury	1 ☐ Fire Service
2 ☐ Female	2 ☐ Action Casualty	2 ☐ Death	2 ☐ Other Emergency Personnel
	3 ☐ EMS Casualty		3 ☒ Civilian

FAMILIARITY WITH STRUCTURE	LOCATION AT IGNITION	CONDITION BEFORE INJURY
Occupant 50	Unknown 51	Unknown 52

CONDITION PREVENTING ESCAPE	ACTIVITY AT TIME OF INJURY	CAUSE OF INJURY
N/A 53	Leaving building 54	Falling debris 55

NATURE OF INJURY	PART OF BODY INJURED	DISPOSITION
Broken leg 56	Leg 57	Hospitalized 58

REMARKS:
Occupant was leaving burning structure when burning eave fell and struck his leg.

By #31   Ambulance to General   Hospital

NAME
LAST, FIRST MIDDLE   33 34 35 36

AGE Time of Injury MONTH DAY YEAR
                 39 40   45

HOME ADDRESS

TELEPHONE

46 SEX	47 CASUALTY TYPE	48 SEVERITY	49 AFFILIATION
1 ☐ Male	1 ☐ Fire Casualty	1 ☐ Injury	1 ☐ Fire Service
2 ☐ Female	2 ☐ Action Casualty	2 ☐ Death	2 ☐ Other Emergency Personnel
	3 ☐ EMS Casualty		3 ☐ Civilian

FAMILIARITY WITH STRUCTURE	LOCATION AT IGNITION	CONDITION BEFORE INJURY
50	51	52

CONDITION PREVENTING ESCAPE	ACTIVITY AT TIME OF INJURY	CAUSE OF INJURY
53	54	55

NATURE OF INJURY	PART OF BODY INJURED	DISPOSITION
56	57	58

REMARKS:

By   Ambulance to   Hospital

Nelson Riley
Supervisor*
*Injury reports for fire personnel,
Immediate supervisor to sign here.

SIGNATURE of person completing form/DATE
John R. Sanders.

Printed in U.S.A.

Figure 9.3
This casualty report is typical of the reports available to reporters at most fire stations.

In most cases, though, the marshal will be the primary source of a second-day story.

As in covering any **spot news** — a story in which news is breaking quickly — deadlines will determine how much you can do at the scene of a fire. If your deadline is hours away, you can concentrate on the event and individuals connected with it. You will have time to find the little boy whose puppy was killed in the fire or interview the first firefighter who entered the building. But if you have only minutes until your deadline, you may have to press the fire official in charge for information. You may have to coax from that person every tidbit, even making a nuisance of yourself, to gather the information you need. Through it all, you can expect confusion. There is little order to be found in the chaos of a fire.

Writing the Court Story

Throughout a complicated court procedure, a reporter has opportunities to write or broadcast several stories. The extent to which the reporter does so, of course, depends on the importance of the case and the amount of local interest in it. In a major case the filing of every motion may prompt a story; in other cases only the verdict may be important. As in any type of reporting, news value is the determining factor.

Also, as in any form of reporting, accuracy is important. Perhaps no other area of writing requires as much caution as the reporting of crime and court news. The potential for libel is great.

Avoiding Libelous Statements

Libel is damage to a person's reputation caused by a written statement that makes the person an object of hatred, contempt or ridicule, or that injures his or her business or occupational pursuits (see Chapter 14). Reporters must be extremely careful about what they write. One of the greatest dangers is the possibility of writing that someone is charged with a crime more serious than is the case.

After checking clippings in the newspaper library, for example, one reporter wrote:

> The rape trial of John L. Duncan, 25, of 3925 Oak St. has been set for Dec. 10 in Jefferson County Circuit Court.
>
> Duncan is charged in connection with the June 6 rape of a Melton High School girl near Fletcher Park.

Duncan had been charged with rape following his arrest, but the prosecutor later determined the evidence was insufficient to win a rape conviction. The charge had been reduced to assault, and the newspaper had to print a correction.

Any story involving arrests should raise caution flags. You must have a sound working knowledge of libel law and what you can and cannot write about an incident. The reporter who writes the following, for example, is asking for trouble:

> John R. Milton, 35, of 206 East St. was arrested Monday on a charge of assaulting a police officer.

Only a prosecutor, not a police officer, may file charges. In many cases, a police officer arrests a person with the intent of asking the prosecutor to file a certain charge, but the prosecutor who examines the evidence finds that it warrants a lesser charge. For that reason, most newspaper editors prefer to print the name of an arrested person only after a charge has been filed. Unfortunately, when deadline constraints make that impossible, many newspapers publish the names of arrested individuals before charges are filed.

A decision to publish a name in such circumstances requires extreme caution. If an individual were arrested in connection with a rape and the newspaper printed that information but later learned that the prosecutor had filed a charge of assault, a libel suit could result. Many states, however, give journalists a **qualified privilege** to write fair and accurate news stories based on police reports.

Once the charge is filed, the lead should be written like this:

> John R. Milton, 35, of 206 East St. was charged Monday with assaulting a police officer. Prosecutor Steve Rodriguez said. . . .

By wording the lead this way, the reporter shows not only that Milton was arrested but also that the prosecutor charged him with a crime.

Reporters who cover court news must know how to avoid many such pitfalls. They are not trained as attorneys, and it takes time to develop a sound working knowledge of legal proceedings. The only recourse is to ask as many questions as necessary when a point of law is not clear. It is far better to display ignorance of the law openly than to commit a serious error that harms the reputation of the accused and opens the newspaper to costly libel litigation.

However, it is also important to know that anything said in open court is fair game for reporters. If, in an opening statement, a prosecutor says the defendant is "nothing but scum, a smut peddler bent on polluting the mind of every child in the city," then by all means report the remark in context in your story. But if a spectator makes that same statement in the hallway during a recess, you probably would not report it. Courts do not extend the qualified privilege to report court proceedings beyond the context of the official proceeding.

Continuing Coverage of the Prosecution

With the preceding points in mind, let's trace a criminal case from the time of arrest through the trial to show how a newspaper might report each step. Here is a typical first story:

An unemployed carpenter was arrested today and charged with the Aug. 6 murder of Springfield resident Anne Compton.

Lester L. Rivers, 32, of 209 E. Dillow Lane was charged with first-degree murder, Prosecuting Attorney Mel Singleton said.

Chief of Detectives E.L. Hall said Rivers was arrested on a warrant after a three-month investigation by a team of three detectives. He declined to comment on what led investigators to Rivers.

Compton's body was found in the Peabody River by two fishermen on the morning of Aug. 7. She had been beaten to death with a blunt instrument, according to Dr. Ronald R. Miller, the county medical examiner.

This straightforward account of the arrest was filed on deadline. Later the reporter would interview neighbors about Rivers' personality and write an improved story for other editions. This bare-bones story, however, provides a glimpse of several key points in covering arrest stories. Notice that the reporter carefully chose the words "arrested . . . and charged with" rather than "arrested for," a phrase that may carry a connotation of guilt.

Another important element of all crime and court coverage is the **tie-back,** a sentence or sentences that relate a story to events covered in a previous story—in this case, the report of the crime itself. It is important to state clearly—and near the beginning of the story—which crime is involved and to provide enough information about it so that the reader recognizes it. Clarification of the crime is important even in major stories with ready identification in the community. This story does that by recounting when and where Compton's body was found and by whom. It also tells that she died after being hit with a blunt instrument.

The following morning the suspect was taken to Magistrate Court for his initial court appearance. Here is part of the story that resulted:

Lester L. Rivers appeared in Magistrate Court today charged with first-degree murder in connection with the Aug. 6 beating death of Springfield resident Anne Compton.

Judge Howard D. Robbins scheduled a preliminary hearing for Nov. 10 and set bail at $10,000. Robbins assigned Public Defender Ogden Ball to represent Rivers, 32, of 209 E. Dillow Lane.

Rivers said nothing during the 10-minute session as the judge informed him of his right to remain silent and his right to an attorney. Ball asked Robbins to set the bail at a "reasonable amount for a man who is unemployed." Rivers is a carpenter who was fired from his last job in June. Despite the seriousness of the charge, it is essential that Rivers be free to help prepare his defense, Ball said.

Police have said nothing about a possible connection between Rivers and Compton, whose body was found in the Peabody River by two fishermen on the morning of Aug. 7. She had been beaten to death.

> "To make inroads into the mind-set that 'if the press reported it, it must be true' is the lawyer's most challenging task."
>
> —*Robert Shapiro,*
> *Attorney*

The reporter clearly outlined the exact charge and reported on key points of the brief hearing. Again, the link to the crime is important, to inform the reader about which murder is involved.

Next came the preliminary hearing, where the first evidence linking the defendant to the crime was revealed:

Lester L. Rivers will be tried in Jefferson County Circuit Court for the Aug. 6 murder of Springfield resident Anne Compton.

Magistrate Judge Howard D. Robbins ruled today that there is probable cause to believe that a crime was committed and probable cause that Rivers did it. Rivers was bound over for trial in Circuit Court.

Rivers, 32, of 209 E. Dillow Lane is being held in Jefferson County Jail. He has been unable to post bail of $10,000.

At today's preliminary hearing, Medical Examiner Ronald R. Miller testified that a tire tool recovered from Rivers' car at the time of his arrest "could have been used in the beating death of Miss Compton." Her body was found floating in the Peabody River Aug. 7.

James L. Mullaney, a lab technician for the FBI crime laboratory in Washington, D.C., testified that "traces of blood on the tire tool matched Miss Compton's blood type."

In reporting such testimony, the reporter was careful to use direct quotes and not to overstate the facts. The medical examiner testified that the tire tool could have been used in the murder. If he had said it was used, a stronger lead would have been needed.

Defense attorneys usually use such hearings to learn about the evidence against their clients and do not present any witnesses. This apparently was the motive here, because neither the police nor the prosecutor had made a public statement on evidence in the case. They probably were being careful not to release prejudicial information that could be grounds for a new trial.

The prosecutor then filed an *information*, as state law required. The defendant was arraigned in Circuit Court, and the result was a routine story that began as follows:

Circuit Judge John L. Lee refused today to reduce the bail of Lester L. Rivers, who is charged with first-degree murder in the Aug. 6 death of Springfield resident Anne Compton. Rivers pleaded not guilty. Repeating a request he made earlier in Magistrate Court, Public Defender Ogden Ball urged that Rivers' bail be reduced from $10,000 so he could be freed to assist in preparing his defense.

The not-guilty plea was expected, so the reporter concentrated on a more interesting aspect of the hearing—the renewed request for reduced bail.

Finally, after a series of motions was reported routinely, the trial began:

Jury selection began today in the first-degree murder trial of Lester L. Rivers, who is charged with the Aug. 6 beating death of Springfield resident Anne Compton.

Public Defender Ogden Ball, Rivers' attorney, and Prosecuting Attorney Mel Singleton both expect jury selection to be complete by 5 p.m.

The selection process started after court convened at 10 a.m. The only incident occurred just before the lunch break as Singleton was questioning prospective juror Jerome B. Tinker, 33, of 408 Woodland Terrace.

"I went to school with that guy," said Tinker, pointing to Rivers, who was seated in the courtroom. "He wouldn't hurt nobody."

Singleton immediately asked that Tinker be removed from the jury panel, and Circuit Judge John L. Lee agreed.

Rivers smiled as Tinker made his statement, but otherwise sat quietly, occasionally conferring with Ball.

The testimony is about to begin, so the reporter sets the stage here, describing the courtroom scene. Jury selection often is routine and becomes newsworthy only in important or interesting cases.

Trial coverage can be tedious, but when the case is an interesting one, the stories are easy to write. The reporter picks the most interesting testimony for leads as the trial progresses:

A service station owner testified today that Lester L. Rivers offered a ride to Springfield resident Anne Compton less than an hour before she was beaten to death Aug. 6.

Ralph R. Eagle, the station owner, was a witness at the first-degree murder trial of Rivers in Jefferson County Circuit Court.

"I told her I'd call a cab," Eagle testified, "but Rivers offered her a ride to her boyfriend's house." Compton had gone to the service station after her car broke down nearby. Under cross-examination, Public Defender Ogden Ball, Rivers' attorney, questioned whether Rivers was the man who offered the ride.

"If it wasn't him, it was his twin brother," Eagle said.

"Then you're not really sure it was Mr. Rivers, are you?" Ball asked.

"I sure am," Eagle replied.

"You think you're sure, Mr. Eagle, but you really didn't get a good look at him, did you?"

"I sold him some gas and got a good look at him when I took the money."

"But it was night, wasn't it, Mr. Eagle?" Ball asked.

"That place doesn't have the best lighting in the world, but I saw him all right."

The reporter focused on the key testimony of the trial by capturing it in the words of the participants. Good note-taking ability becomes important here, because trial coverage is greatly enhanced with direct quotation of key exchanges. Long exchanges may necessitate the use of the question-and-answer format:

Ball: In fact, a lot of the lights above those gas pumps are out, aren't they, Mr. Eagle?

Eagle: Yes, but I stood right by him.

Q. I have no doubt you thought you saw Mr. Rivers, but there's always the possibility it could have been someone else. Isn't that true?

A. No, it looked just like him.

Q. It appeared to be him, but it may not have been because you really couldn't see him that well, could you?

A. Well, it was kind of dark out there.

Finally, there is the verdict story, which usually is one of the easiest to write:

Lester L. Rivers was found guilty of first-degree murder today in the Aug. 6 beating death of Springfield resident Anne Compton.

Rivers stood motionless in Jefferson County Circuit Court as the jury foreman returned the verdict. Judge John L. Lee set sentencing for Dec. 10.

Rivers, 32, of 209 E. Dillow Lane could be sentenced to death in the electric chair or life imprisonment in the State Penitentiary.

Public Defender Ogden Ball, Rivers' attorney, said he will appeal.

After the verdict was announced, Mr. and Mrs. Lilborn O. Compton, the victim's parents, were escorted from the courtroom by friends. Both refused to talk with reporters.

Many other types of stories could have been written about such a trial. Lengthy jury deliberations, for example, might prompt stories about the anxiety of the defendant and attorneys and their speculations about the cause of the delay.

Covering court news requires care and good reporting. As in any kind of reporting, you must be well-prepared. If you understand the language of the courts and how they are organized, your job is simplified.

The Free-Press/Fair-Trial Controversy

Covering the courts is not a simple task. If done poorly, it inevitably leads to criticism of the press, as evidenced by the 1954 murder trial of Dr. Samuel Sheppard in Cleveland. Sheppard was accused of murdering his wife. News coverage in the Cleveland newspapers, which included front-page editorials, was intense. In 1966, the Supreme Court said the trial judge had not fulfilled his duty to protect the jury from the news coverage that saturated the community and to control disruptive influences in the courtroom.

That case more than any other ignited what is known as the **free-press/fair-trial controversy.** It is a controversy that continues. On numerous occasions, Judge Lance Ito, the judge in the O. J. Simpson

When cameras are banned from the courtroom, reporters often rely on artists' sketches to provide a visual element for their stories. This is a sketch of Oklahoma City bombing suspects Timothy McVeigh and Terry Nichols seated with their attorneys.

case, threatened to end television coverage of court proceedings to protect Simpson's rights during his criminal trial. Lawyers charged that the media ignored the Sixth Amendment right of the accused to an impartial jury, and the media countered with charges that lawyers ignored the First Amendment.

Editors realize that coverage of a crime can make it difficult to empanel an impartial jury, but they argue that courts have available many remedies other than restricting the flow of information. In the Sheppard case, for example, the Supreme Court justices said a **change of venue,** which moves the trial to a location where publicity is not as intense, could have been ordered. Other remedies suggested by the court in such cases are to continue (delay) the trial, to grant a new trial or to head off possible outside influences during the trial by sequestering the jury. Editors also argue that acquittals have been won in some of the most publicized cases in recent years.

Despite the remedies the Supreme Court offered in the Sheppard case, trial judges continued to be concerned about empaneling impartial juries. Judges issued hundreds of gag orders in the wake of the Sheppard case. Finally, in 1976, in the landmark case of Nebraska Press Association vs. Stuart, the Supreme Court ruled that a gag order is an unconstitutional prior restraint that violates the First Amendment to the Constitution. The justices did not go so far as to rule that all gag orders are invalid. But in each case, the trial judge has to prove that an order restraining publication would protect the rights of the accused and that there are no other alternatives that would be less damaging to First Amendment rights.

Suggested Readings

Buchanan, Edna. *Never Let Them See You Cry*. New York: Random House, 1992. An excellent description of covering crime in Miami.

Buchanan, Edna. *The Corpse Had a Familiar Face*. New York: Random House, 1987. The first of two books by one of America's best crime reporters.

Dalton, Laura. "Remembrance of Things Past." *Gannetteer* (Gannett Publishing Co.), Dec. 1993, pp. 10-11. Describes how various Gannett newspaper reporters handle obituaries.

Hart, Jack and Johnson, Janis. "A Clash between the Public's Right to Know and a Family's Need for Privacy." *The Quill*, May 1979, pp. 19-24. An account of the backlash against a newspaper that printed a syndicated story of how the daughter of a locally prominent family had died a big-city prostitute.

Hipple, John and Wells, Richard. "Media Can Reduce Risks in Suicide Stories." *Editor & Publisher*, Oct. 14, 1989, p. 72. A counselor who specializes in treating suicidal young people and a journalist combine to offer suggestions on handling stories involving suicide.

Randolph, Eleanor. "AIDS and Obituaries." *Chicago Tribune*, Sept. 24, 1989. A round-up of how various newspapers handle AIDS as a cause of death.

Singer, Eleanor and Endreny, Phyllis M. *Reporting on Risk: How the Mass Media Portray Accidents, Diseases, Disasters and Other Hazards*. New York: Russell Sage Foundation, 1993. A critical look at media reporting of accidents and disasters.

Weinberg, Steve, et al. *The Investigative Reporter's Handbook*, Fourth Edition. New York: Bedford/ St. Martin's, 2002. A guide to using government documents to find sources of information.

Suggested Web Sites

www.ap.org

Excellent examples of how to write obituaries and crime, accident, fire, and court stories can be found on the Associated Press Web site.

www.nna.org

Small newspapers are served by the National Newspaper Association. Its members are more likely than metro papers to write obituaries as news stories.

www.google.com

Google is a good search engine that will help you find examples of the types of stories covered in this chapter.

www.nsc.org

The National Safety Council Web site offers accident statistics, information on safety and links to other sites.

Exercises

1. Which elements are missing from the following obituary information?
   a. John Peterson died Saturday at Springfield Hospital. Funeral services will be at 1:30 p.m. Tuesday. Friends may call at the Restwell Funeral Home, 2560 Walnut St., from 6 to 9 p.m. Monday. The Rev. William Thomas will officiate at services in the First Baptist Church. Burial will be at City Cemetery.

b. Richard G. Tindall, Springfield, a retired U.S. Army brigadier general, died at his daughter's home in Summit, N.J. Graveside services will be at 2 p.m. July 3 at Arlington National Cemetery in Arlington, Va.

2. Write a lead for an obituary from the following information:

   Martha Sattiewhite, born July 2, 1974, to Don and Mattie Sattiewhite, in Springfield. Martha was killed in a car accident June 30, 2003. Funeral services will be July 2. She was president of her Springfield High School senior class and of the sophomore class at the University of Oklahoma.

3. An obituary notice comes from a local mortuary. It contains the basic information, but under achievements it lists only "former member of Lion's Club." Your city editor tells you to find out more about the deceased. Whom would you call and why?

4. If George Thomas, private citizen, committed suicide while alone in his home, would you include the cause of death in his obituary? Why or why not?

5. A few newspapers write obituaries of notable people in advance because the time between the death and publication can be short. Some papers even interview the subject. Write a two-page advance obituary of one of the following: Benjamin Chavis Muhammad, Henry Cisneros, Abe Rosenthal or Madonna. At the end, list your sources.

6. Find an accident story in a local newspaper. List all the obvious sources the reporter used in obtaining information for the story. List additional sources you would have checked.

7. Talk with a firefighter in your local fire department about the department's media policy at fire scenes. Based on what you learn, write instructions for your fellow reporters on what to expect at fires in your city or town.

8. Make a list of at least 10 federal agencies that may be of help in reporting accident, fire and disaster stories. Also list the telephone numbers of the agency offices nearest to you.

9. Cover a session of your local municipal court. Write a story based on the most interesting case of the day.

10. Find a court story in a local newspaper. Determine what sources the reporter used in the story, and tell how the story could have been improved.

10 Beat Reporting

In Chapter 1, you met some journalists whose work has changed in news rooms where television, print and online have converged. Now let's travel from the sunbelt to the snowbelt to see the impact of convergence on one of the most important roles of reporters—beat reporting. The *Democrat and Chronicle* in Rochester, N.Y., is owned by one of America's biggest media chains, Gannett. Jane Sutter is the managing editor. She directs the news coverage.

"Our convergence commitment has definitely changed reporters' work," she says. "Now, reporters are expected to file a few paragraphs from the scene of a press conference, fire, accident, etc., or write those up as soon as they come back to the office. We know that we get our greatest number of online readers early in the morning, at lunchtime, and between 4-5 p.m., so it's very important that we update the Web site continuously throughout the day." Reporters are equipped with cell phones, and photographers have laptop computers to permit posting of pictures shot digitally.

The *D&C* also has a partnership with the Rochester ABC affiliate. Newspaper reporters are regularly interviewed on Channel 13. ("And they do dress up," Sutter says.) For the 11 p.m. news program the paper even provides exclusive summaries of stories that will appear in the next morning's paper. The station gets stories its broadcast competitors don't have, and the newspaper gets wider exposure for its work.

Convergence also changes the learning of student journalists. Liz Davis was looking for a new challenge in her advanced reporting course. So she decided to cover city government for the online edition of her school's newspaper. She quickly discovered that—in addition to covering council meetings and writing about zoning issues—her work now included gathering agendas, maps and other documents for posting online. She started carrying a digital camera for the extra photographs the online edition could use in its unlimited space. And her tape recorder became more than a backup to note taking. Online journalism adds sound to print.

Graduate student Ingrid Young developed a new beat for her master's project. She covered music, from bluegrass to ragtime to classical: She covered it with words, with photography and—for her online audience—with recordings of the music itself.

New technology is bringing new opportunities, as well as new challenges, to beat reporting—the core of daily journalism. And not only the technology is changing. You saw in Chapter 1 how the definition of news itself is broadening. That change broadens the range of **beats.** They now often include, along with such standard beats as local government, police, business and sports, cultural beats such as Ingrid Young's and others that reflect the interests and activities of a changing America. Some beat reporters now cover shopping malls. Some cover commuting. Some cover spiritual life. Some cover the Internet.

In this chapter you will learn:

1. Basic principles for covering any beat.
2. How to apply those principles to some of the most common beats.

Increasingly, beat reporters tell their audiences not only what is happening but how to get involved. Stories include the telephone numbers and e-mail addresses along with the names of decision makers. Much of the most useful reporting is done in advance of public meetings, with the goal of enabling citizens to become participants instead of passive onlookers. Readers are regularly invited to comment, question, even criticize coverage, and to speak up on public issues via e-mail or by entering computer chat rooms. Reporters post online original documents and additional photography and audio that won't or can't be published on newsprint

With all these changes, though, beat reporters remain the eyes and ears of their communities. They are surrogates for their readers, keeping track of government, education, police, business and other powerful institutions that shape readers' lives.

This chapter focuses on reporting for print and online. That's because beat reporting is less common in local television. Small staffs, heavy demands and wide areas of coverage require most television reporters to work on general assignment.

The principles of good reporting apply to the coverage of any beat. The same principles also apply to specialized publications, including those aimed at particular ethnic groups, industries or professions. A reporter for *Women's Wear Daily* may cover designers. A reporter for *Diario las Americas* in Miami may cover Cuban exile politics. But each is doing the same job—discovering and writing news that's relevant and useful to the publication's readers.

Many news organizations are responding to audience interests by creating teams of reporters to cover interrelated topics. One such team may write about issues of home and family life. Another may cover the arts and popular culture. Another team may focus on the problems and opportunities of urban living. Other teams or individual reporters may be responsible for such relevant but nontraditional topics as commuting, day care and aging, or the village centers of modern America, the malls.

Editors and audiences expect reporters on these new beats, like those in more traditional assignments, to provide information and understanding that will help readers improve the quality of their lives. That's important work. It's rewarding work. But it's not easy.

The successful beat reporter is

- *Prepared.*
- *Alert.*
- *Persistent.*
- *There.*
- *Wary.*

PRINCIPLES FOR REPORTERS ON A BEAT

Whether the beat you cover is the public library or the Pentagon, the county courthouse or the White House, the principles of covering it are the same. If you want to succeed as a reporter on that beat, you must be prepared, alert, persistent, there and wary.

That checklist will help you win the trust of your sources, keep up with important developments on your beat, and avoid the trap of writing for your sources instead of your readers. Let's take a closer look at what each of those rules means in practice.

Be Prepared

Where should preparation begin? For you, it has already begun. To work effectively, any journalist needs a basic understanding of the workings of society and its various governments. You need to know at least the rudiments of psychology, economics and history. That is why the best education for a journalist is a broad-based one, providing exposure to the widest possible sampling of human knowledge. But that exposure will not be enough when you face an important source on your first beat. You will need more specific information, which you can acquire by familiarizing yourself with written accounts or records or by talking to sources.

Reading for Background

In preparing to cover a beat, any beat, your first stop should be the newspaper library (see Chapter 4). Many newspaper libraries have computer access not only to material that has appeared in that newspaper but also to worldwide networks of information on nearly any topic. You can often access the contents of major newspapers, magazines, research publications and other reference libraries without regard to physical distance. Use the **Internet** as a tool to acquire background information and to understand the context of local events and issues. For example, if you're new to the medical beat or the science beat, you might begin with the Web site of the Association of Health Care Journalists **(www.ahcj.umn.edu)** or the National Association of Science Writers **(nasw.org).**

In your local research, make notes of what appear to be continuing issues, questions left dangling in previous stories or ideas for stories to come. Go back several years in your preparation. History may not repeat itself, but a knowledge of it helps you assess the significance of current events and provides clues to what you can expect in the future.

The library is only the start of your preparation. You must become familiar with the laws governing the institution you cover. If a governmental organization is your beat, find the state statutes or the city charter that created the agencies you will be covering. Learn the powers, duties and limitations of each official. You may be surprised to discover that someone is failing to do all that the law requires. Someone else may be doing more than the law allows.

Look at your state's open-meetings and open-record laws, too. Every state has such laws, though they vary widely in scope and effectiveness. Knowing what information is open to the public by law can be a valuable tool for a reporter dealing with officials who may find it more convenient to govern privately.

Talking to Sources

Now you're ready to start talking to people. Your first interviews should be conducted in the news room with your predecessor on the beat, your city editor and any veterans who can shed light on the kinds of things that rarely appear in statute books or newspaper stories. Who have been good sources in the past? Who will lie to you? Who drinks to excess? Who seems to be living extravagantly? Whose friends are big land developers? Who wants to run for statewide or national office? Who has been hired, fired or promoted? Who has moved to a competing company? Remember that you are hearing gossip, filtered through the biases of those relating it. Be a little skeptical.

Some understanding of the workings of your own news room won't hurt, either. Was your predecessor on the beat promoted, or transferred because he or she was unsatisfactory? Will an introduction from your predecessor help you or hurt you with your sources? And what are your city editor's expectations? Is your assignment to report practically every activity of government, or will you have time to do some investigative work and analysis? Trying to live up to your boss's expectations is easier if you know in advance what they are.

Only after gaining as much background as possible are you ready to face the people you will be covering. A quick handshake and a superficial question or two may be all you have time for in the first encounter, but within a week you should arrange for sit-down conversations with your most important sources. These are get-acquainted sessions. You are trying to get to know the sources, but don't forget that they need to know you, too, if they are going to respect and trust you.

You may have noticed that the preparation for covering a beat is similar to the preparation for an interview or for a single-story assignment (see Chapter 3). The important difference is that preparing for a beat is more detailed and requires more time and work. Instead of just preparing for a short-term task, you are laying the foundation for an important part of your career. A beat assignment nearly always lasts at least six months and often two years or more. That understanding helps shape your first round of meetings with sources.

A story may emerge from those first interviews, but their purpose is much broader. You are trying to establish a relationship, trying to convert strangers into helpful partners in news-gathering. To do that, you should demonstrate an interest in the sources as people as well as officials. Ask about their families, their interests, their philosophy, their goals. Make clear with your questions that you are interested rather than ignorant. (Don't ask if the source is married. You should already know that. Say, "I understand your daughter is in law school. Is she going into politics, too?" Similarly, don't ask if your source has any hobbies. Find that out beforehand. Say, "So you collect pornographic comic books. Sure takes your mind off the budget, doesn't it?")

And be prepared to give something of yourself. If you both like to fish, or you both went to Vassar, or you both have children about the same age, seize on those ties. All of us feel comfortable with people who have something in common with us. This is the time, too, to let your sources know that you know something about their work and that you're interested in it.

Solid preparation will help you avoid asking stupid questions. More important, it will help you make sure you ask the right questions. And because you have taken the trouble to get to know your sources, you are more likely to come away with responsive answers to the questions you ask.

Be Alert

On his way to lunch, Nik Deogun, then a young reporter for the *Atlanta Business Chronicle*, drove at least once a week past the old Sears building, a huge derelict purchased by the city in what the mayor proclaimed "the deal of the century." Deogun began to wonder how renovation was proceeding. Then, as he worked on another story, he heard gossip that the project was running over budget. He began to devote a few spare minutes here and there to re-examining the city's great deal. His story for the *Chronicle* began:

> After only three years, the city of Atlanta is considering refinancing what it called at the time the "deal of the century."

The $10 million set aside for renovation was about $4 million too little, he reported. The great deal had become a huge bust. A reporter's curiosity paid off for the public.

Important stories are seldom labeled as such. In many cases the people involved may not realize the significance of what they are doing. Probably more often they realize it but hope nobody else will. The motivation for secrecy may be dishonesty, the desire to protect an image, or a conviction that the public will misunderstand.

If your beat is a government agency, you will find that many public officials and public employees think they know more about what is good for the public than the public does. The theory of democratic government is that an informed citizenry can make decisions or elect representatives to make those decisions in its own best interests. If you are the reporter assigned to city hall, the school board or the courthouse, you carry a heavy responsibility for helping your readers put that theory into practice. To discharge that responsibility, you must probe beneath the surface of events in search of the "whys" and "hows" that lead to understanding.

When you are presented with a news release or hear an announcement or cover a vote, ask yourself these questions before passing the event off in a few paragraphs:

- *Who will benefit from this, and who will be hurt?* If the tentative answer to the first part suggests private interests, or the answer to the second part is the public, some digging is in order.
- *How important is this?* An event that is likely to affect many people for good or ill usually deserves more explanation than one affecting only a handful.
- *Who is for this, and who is against it?* When you know the answers to these questions, the answers to the first two questions usually become clearer.
- *How much will this activity cost, and who will pay?* An architect's design for renovating downtown may look less attractive when the price tag is attached. The chamber of commerce's drive to lure new industry may require taxpayers to pay for new roads, sewers, fire protection, even schools and other services for an increased population.

Once you have asked the questions and gotten answers, the story may turn out to be about no more than it appeared to be on the surface. But if you don't ask them, you—and your readers—may find out too late that more was there than met the eye. The answers allow you to judge that most important element of news value—impact.

Be Persistent

Persistence means two things to a reporter on a beat. First, it means that when you ask a question, you cannot give up until you get an answer. Second, it means that you must keep track of slow-developing projects or problems.

Insisting on a Responsive Answer

One of the most common faults of beginning reporters is that they give up too easily. They settle for answers that are unresponsive to their questions, or they return to the news room not sure they understand what they were told. In either case the result is an incomplete, confusing story.

"Why is it that our fourth-graders score below average on these reading tests?" you ask the school superintendent.

To evaluate a story, ask yourself

- *Who will benefit from this, and who will be hurt?*
- *How important is this?*
- *Who is for this, and who is against this?*
- *How much will this activity cost, and who will pay?*

Skilled reporters are persistent interviewers and insist on responsive answers. Make sure your questions are answered satisfactorily.

He may reply, "Let me first conceptualize the parameters of the socioeconomic context for you."

The real answer probably is, "I only wish I knew."

Your job is to cut through the jargon and the evasions in search of substance. Often that is not an easy task. Many experts, or people who want to be regarded as experts, are so caught up in the technical language of their special field that they find it almost impossible to communicate clearly. Many others seek refuge in gobbledygook or resort to evasion when they don't know an answer or find the answer embarrassing. Educators and lawyers are particularly adept at such tactics.

Listen politely for a few minutes while the school superintendent conceptualizes his parameters. Then, when he finishes or pauses for breath, lead him back toward where you want to go. One way is to say, "It sounds to me as if you're saying . . . ," and then rephrase in plain English what he told you. At those times when you are in the dark — and that may be often — confess your puzzlement and ask for a translation. And keep coming back to the point: "But how does all that affect reading scores?" "How can the problem be solved?" "What are you doing about it?"

The techniques you have learned for preparing for interviews and conducting them will help you. Your preparation for the beat will help, too. Probably most helpful, though, are the questions you keep asking yourself rather than your source: "Does that make sense to me?" "Can I make it make sense to my readers?" Don't quit until the answer is yes. You should not be obnoxious, but you do have to be persistent.

Following Up Slow Developments

Persistence is also required when you are following the course of slow-developing events. Gardeners do not sit and watch a seed germinate. Their eyes would glaze over long before any change was apparent. Gardeners do, however, check every few days, looking for the green shoots that indicate the process is taking place as it should. If the shoots are late, they dig in to investigate.

Beat reporting works much the same way. A downtown redevelopment plan, say, or a revision in a school's curriculum is announced. The story covers the plans and the hoped-for benefits. The seed is planted. If it is planted on your beat, make a note to yourself to check on it in a week or two. And a week or two after that. And a month after that. Start a file of reminders so you won't forget. Such a file often is called a **tickler** because it serves to tickle your memory.

Like seeds, important projects of government or business take time to develop. Often what happens during the long, out-of-public-view development is more important than the announcements at the occasional news conferences or the promises of the promotional brochures. Compromises are made. Public money is spent. The public interest may be served, or it may not.

Sometimes the story is that nothing is happening. At other times the story may be that the wrong things are happening. Even if nothing improper is taking place, the persistent reporter will give readers an occasional update. At stake, after all, is the public's money and welfare.

Be There

In beat reporting there is no substitute for personal contact. Trying to cover a beat by telephone or e-mail won't work. The only way to do it is to be there—every day, if possible. Joking with the secretaries, talking politics with council members and lawyers, worrying over the budget or trading gossip with the professional staff—you must make yourself a part of the community you are covering.

The payoff for this kind of cultivation? Meet Susan Drumheller, a young but experienced beat reporter for *The (Spokane, Wash.) Spokesman-Review*. In just a few years, she has learned the secret of mastering a beat:

When I covered City Hall, I got to know the people there really well. They knew my face. They gave me tips. I treated them fair.

The fun stories had to do with the elected or prominent officials who would do stupid things. One of my favorites was the elementary school principal who illegally passed a school bus with its stop-arm down as he rushed to work. The bus driver only recognized him because his daughter was in the car, and she usually rode that bus. That came from a tip. . . .

Not only does a beat reporter have to have a reputation among the people he or she covers as being fair, but you also need a reputation for pursuing controversial and hard stories.

Remember that the sources who are most important to you probably are in great demand by others, too. They have jobs to do. Maneuver to get as much of their time as you need, but don't demand too much. Do your homework first. Don't expect a school superintendent to explain basic concepts of education. You can learn that information from an aide or from reading. What you need to learn from the superintendent is how he or she intends to apply those concepts, or why they seem to be inapplicable here. Find out what a "Class I felony" is before asking the police chief why they are increasing. You will get the time you need more readily if busy sources know their time will not be wasted.

There are other simple techniques you can use to build and maintain good relationships with the people on your beat. Here are some of them:

- *Do a favor when you can.* As a reporter you spend much of your time asking other people to do favors for you—giving you their time, sharing information they need not share, looking up records and figures. If a source wants a favor in return, don't refuse unless granting the favor would be unethical. The favors asked usually are small things, such as getting a daughter's engagement picture in the paper or procuring a print of a picture taken with the governor to decorate the official's wall.
- *Don't shun good news.* One ill-founded but common complaint is that news media report nothing but bad news. Admittedly, there is usually no story when people are doing what they are supposed to do. Sometimes there should be, if they do their duty uncommonly well or have done it for a very long time or do it under the burden of some handicap.
- *Protect your sources.* Many people in government—politicians and bureaucrats alike—are willing to tell a reporter things they are not willing to have their names attached to in print or otherwise. The same is true of people in private business, who may fear reprisals from their employer, co-workers or competitors. Sometimes such would-be anonymous sources are trying to use you to enhance their own positions. You have to protect yourself and your readers against that possibility. Confer with an editor if you have doubts. Most papers are properly wary of relying on unnamed sources. Sometimes, though, requests for anonymity are valid, necessary to protect

On the Job

Where the Action Is

Lewis Diuguid is vice president for community relations of *The Kansas City Star,* but he hasn't forgotten the lessons he learned nearly 20 years ago, covering a suburban beat fresh out of journalism school:

Reporters should strive to build drama into their copy, think about how people looked, sounded and even smelled when they were doing their reporting. Of course, that means that reporters will have to go out to meet with people for stories instead of trying to handcuff the news by telephone.

The best beat reporters get personal with their sources. Newsmakers place great stock in getting to know the people who write about them. If they feel comfortable with a reporter they will gossip, talk and tell more. Getting personal doesn't involve anything close to pillow talk or sacrificing your liver to drinking at all hours for better stories.

But it does require that reporters share information about themselves with sources. What do you like to do in your spare time? What are your hobbies? Do you have a family? What are your kids' names? Share pictures that you have of them. Reporters do not have to do this the first day they get on a beat, but it is important to gradually warm up to sources so that they will share more with you.

Journalism has to be something a person would do for free. The check is for putting up with hassles associated with getting stories into the paper.

Journalists of color should never shy away from covering stories involving minorities, especially when their backgrounds and education give them in-depth knowledge of issues related to those communities. White readers are just as happy to see stories about minorities as minorities are. Because of the push for diversity in industry, whites are looking for ways to better understand our multicultural world.

the source's career. Once you have agreed to protect a source, you must do it. Don't tell anyone but your editor. An inability to keep your mouth shut can cost you more than a source. It can cost you your reputation. (The protection of sources has legal as well as ethical implications. So-called **shield laws** in some states offer journalists limited exemptions from legal requirements to disclose sources—see Chapter 14. But there are no blanket exemptions.)

▪ *Above all, be accurate.* Inaccurate reporting leads first to loss of respect from sources, then to loss of the sources themselves and finally to loss of the job. If you are a good, tough reporter, not all your contacts on your beat will love you. But if you are an accurate reporter, they will respect you.

The best way to ensure accuracy is to check and double-check. Many of the stories you will write are likely to be complicated. You will be expected to digest budgets, master plans, legal opinions and complicated discussions, and to translate these into language your readers can understand. When in doubt, ask somebody.

If you are unclear about the city manager's explanation of the budget before the council, arrange a meeting afterward and go over it. If a company's brief in a legal case has you confused, call the lawyer who wrote it. If the new master land-use plan strikes you as vague, consult with the planner. If you are writing a story on a subject you feel tentative about, arrange to read it back to the sources when it is complete. Not all experts relish being asked to translate their jargon into English, so in some cases you will have to insist, politely. The best persuader is the assurance that it is far better for your sources to take a few minutes to explain now than to see themselves misrepresented in print.

Remember, beat reporting is a lot like gardening. Both require you to be in the field every day, cultivating. And in both, the amount of the harvest is directly proportional to the amount of labor invested.

Be Wary

The point of all this effort—the preparation, perceptiveness, persistence and personal contact—is to keep your readers informed. That is an obvious statement, but it needs to be made because every reporter on a beat is under pressures that can obscure the readers' importance. You must be wary of this problem.

You will have little to do with 99.9 percent of your readers. They will not write you notes when you have done a story they like or call you when they dislike what you have written. They will not offer to buy you a cup of coffee or lunch, or stop you in the hall to urge you to see things their way. But your sources will.

If you write that city council members are thinking about raising the property tax rate, you probably will hear complaints from council members about premature disclosure. If you write that the CEO of a major business is looking for a new job, the chances are that he or she will deny it even though the story is true.

All sources have points of view, programs to sell, careers to advance, opponents to undercut. It is likely and legitimate that they will try to persuade you of the merit of their viewpoints, try to sell their programs through the columns of your newspaper, try to shape the news to help their careers.

Be wary of sources' efforts to use you. You can lose the critical distance a reporter must maintain from those being covered. When that happens, you start thinking like a participant rather than an observer. You begin writing for your sources rather than your audience. This is a real danger. No one can spend as much time as a reporter on a beat does with sources or devote as much effort to understanding them without becoming sympathetic. When you associate so closely with the insiders, you may forget that you are writing for the outsiders.

ONLINE COVERAGE

Before we apply those principles to specific beats, let's look at the opportunities and challenges that online journalism presents to beat reporters. At the beginning of the chapter, you got a glimpse of those opportunities and challenges at the *Democrat and Chronicle* in Rochester, N.Y. First is the opportunity for instant reporting. With cell phones, digital cameras and laptop computers, reporters can and do file short stories and even photographs for posting on the Web site as the story unfolds. For newspaper reporters, this is a high-tech return to the distant days of multiple editions, when instead of one deadline a day journalists had many. For radio and television reporters, the online opportunities match those of live reporting over the air. Research shows that increasing numbers of online readers rely on Web sites to stay in touch with news as it happens.

Earlier, you met Liz Davis, who added online coverage to her local government beat. What she did—posting to her newspaper's digital edition documents, pictures and sound the newsprint edition couldn't handle—is a good example of the extra work, and the extra storytelling opportunities, for beat reporters with online outlets.

You'll be expected to gather and present to readers more information, more detail and more points of view than either print or broadcast now permits. Readers who care enough to follow an issue online will want and expect to see the source documents you use—and the policy-makers use. They'll want and expect links to other Web sites that will offer related information or further background.

Here's an example, from the *Democrat and Chronicle*. The *D&C* has a weekly award for staffers who seize the opportunities of conver-

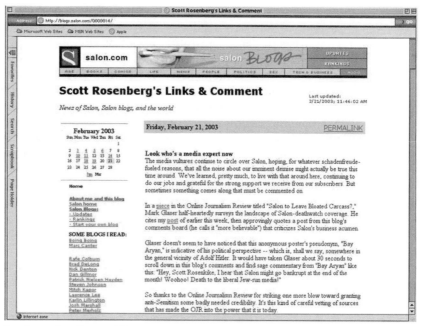

Readers of online publications expect increased detail in the stories they read, and they expect interactivity. Above, Scott Rosenberg of Salon.com, an online magazine, comments daily on news relating to the Web site and responds to critics of the magazine.

gence. Called the Golden Tater Award, it is a humorous way of making a serious point. The news room's daily electronic newsletter announced one award this way:

> The Golden Tater for above-and-beyond service to new media goes this week to Sue McNamara, Paulina Garces-Reid, Matt Leingang, Jamie Germano and Tricia Powers for their outstanding multimedia effort "Matters of the Heart."
>
> This is Sue's second TV-web-print triple play; she oversaw the Guantanamo Bay series and came to the new media department with "Heart" during the reporting phase. Matt recorded audio, told viewers about the reporting process during a strong appearance on Channel 13's morning show and suggested a novel idea—we should host a live online chat with the transplant team and patient. Paulina worked long hours over several weeks to create a multimedia presentation and Tricia reworked her graphics—a case study in how to present something that would be a long print narrative in a web-friendly, interactive piece. . . .

That example shows another important opportunity offered online—interactivity. As you already know, interactivity is what really sets online media apart. It is a term with two practical meanings. First, online journalism permits readers to interact with the information you post. With the proper software, readers can search your Web site's restaurant reviews, lists of dangerous intersections or any other information that can be tailored to individual needs.

The second type of online interactivity is between journalists and readers. Newspapers, magazines and books provide great depth and variety. But they don't provide the opportunity for their readers to converse with either the people between the covers or the authors. Online readers can, and expect to, do just that. So online reporters must be prepared to answer questions, respond to criticisms, elaborate on their written words—and not just to editors or sources but to readers. Many traditional reporters find this prospect terrifying. They're more comfortable in a world of one-way communication, reporter to reader. That world still exists, but anyone preparing to enter the new online world should understand that it demands even more of reporters.

For more on writing online, read the sections in this chapter and see Chapter 13, "Writing Online."

COVERING THE MOST IMPORTANT LOCAL BEATS

Your political science courses will introduce you to the structure of government, but from a reporter's viewpoint, function is usually even more important than structure. You must learn who holds the real power, who has the most influence on the power holders and who are the most likely sources of accurate information. The specifics vary from city to city, but there are some general principles that will help you in covering any state or local institution:

Crucial factors and practical principles for beat reporters

Power: *Information is power.*
Money: *The budget is the blueprint.*
Politics: *Distributing power and money is politics.*

- *Information is power.* The holder of information may be a professional administrator—the city manager, school superintendent, police chief or court clerk—or it may be an elected official: the mayor, chair of the county commission or chair of the school board. The job title is unimportant. Find the person who knows in detail how any organization really works, where the money goes and how decisions are made. Get to know that person because he or she will be the most important person on your beat.
- *The budget is the blueprint.* This principle is a corollary of the first. Just as detailed knowledge of how an organization works is the key to controlling that organization, a budget is the blueprint for the organization's activities. The budget tells where the money comes from and where it goes. It tells how many people are on the payroll and how much they are paid. It tells what programs are planned for the year and how much they will cost. Over several years' time, the

Writing for Readers

What does it mean to write for your readers instead of your sources? It means that you must follow several important guidelines:

Translate. The language of bureaucrats, educators, scientists or lawyers is not the same language most people speak. You need to learn the jargon of your sources, but you also need to learn how to translate it into standard English for your readers. The city planning consultant might say, "Preliminarily, the concept appeared to permit attainment of all our criteria; but, when we cost it out we have to question its economic viability." Your lead could translate that to:

> The proposed plan for downtown redevelopment looks good on paper, but it may cost too much, the city's planning consultant said today.

Make your writing human. In big government and big business, humanity often gets lost in numbers. Your readers want and need to know the impact of those numbers on real people. How many people will be displaced by a new highway? And who are they? Who will be affected by a school closing or a welfare cut? When a police report announced that burglaries were up by 35 percent in the last two months, an enterprising reporter told the story through the eyes of a victim. It began this way:

> Viola Patterson picked her way through the shattered glass from her front door, passed the table where her television used to sit, and stopped before the cabinet that had held her family silver.
>
> She wept.
>
> Mrs. Patterson, 72, is one of the more than 75 people victimized by burglars in the last two months.

Think of the public pocket book. If the tax rate is going up 14 cents, how much will it cost the average homeowner? If employees of a firm are seeking a 10 percent raise, how much will that cost the employer? How much of that increase will be passed on to customers? If garbage collection fees are about to be increased, how do they compare to fees in comparable cities?

The city manager proposed "adjusting" the price of electricity to lower the cost to industrial customers and raise rates to private homes. The city hall reporter did a quick survey of comparable cities around the state. Then she wrote:

> City residents, who already pay more for their electricity than residents of eight similar-sized cities around the state, would be charged an average of $4 per month more under a proposal announced Tuesday by City Manager Barry Kovac.
>
> Industrial users, whose rate now is about average among the nine cities, would enjoy the second-lowest rate under Kovac's proposal.
>
> Kovac defended his plan as "equitable and necessary to ensure continued economic growth for the city."

Get out of the office. City council votes are important, but far more people will have personal contact with government in the form of a police officer, a clerk or a bus driver than with a council member. Go to where government meets its constituents. Ride a bus. Visit a classroom. Patrol with a police officer. Not only will you get a reader's-eye view of your beat, but you may also find some unexpected stories.

(continued)

> **Ask the readers' questions.** "Why?" "How much will it cost me?" "What will I get out of it?" You are the public's ombudsman.
>
> Remember, a good beat reporter has to be prepared, be alert, be persistent and be there. If you keep in mind, too, who you are writing for, you'll keep the customers—and the editors—satisfied.

budget tells where the budget makers' priorities are, what they see as their organization's role in the community.

So, find copies of the last two or three years' budgets for your beat. Try to decipher them. Learn all you can from your predecessor and from newspaper clips. Then find the architect who drew up this blueprint—the budget director or the clerk or the assistant superintendent—and get a translation. Ask all the questions you can think of. Write down the answers.

When budget-making time arrives, follow every step. Attend every public hearing and every private discussion session you can. In those dollar figures are some of the most important stories you will write—stories of how much your readers will be paying for schools and roads and garbage pickup, stories of what they will get for their money. You'll find a guide to understanding budgets in Chapter 5.

▪ *Distributing power and money is politics.* While looking for your beat's power centers and unraveling its budget mysteries, you will be absorbing as well the most interesting part of beat reporting—politics.

At any organizational level in any form, power and money go hand-in-hand with politics. Politics provides the mechanisms through which limited resources are allocated among many competing groups. Neither elections nor political parties are necessary for politics. You will have to learn to spot more subtle forms of political maneuvering.

If you are covering city hall, for example, pay close attention while the city budget is being drafted. You may find the mayor's pet project being written in by the city manager. Nobody elects the city manager, but it is good politics for him or her to keep the mayor happy. Are the builders influential in town? If so, you will probably find plenty of road and sewer projects in the budget. Are the city employees unionized? Look for healthy wage and benefit increases if they are. None of those projects is necessarily bad just because it is political. But you and your readers ought to know who is getting what and why.

Power, money and politics are the crucial factors to watch in any beat reporting. With this in mind, let's take a closer look at the most important local beats.

City and County Government

Most medium-sized cities have council-manager governments. The mayor and council members hire a professional administrator to manage the day-to-day affairs of the city. The manager, in turn, hires the police and fire chiefs, the public works director and other department heads. Under the city charter the council is supposed to make policy and leave its implementation to the manager. Council members usually are forbidden to meddle in the affairs of any department.

Some small towns and a decreasing number of big cities have governments in which the mayor serves as chief administrator. Rudy Giuliani, mayor of New York when the terrorists attacked in 2001, became a national hero for his take-charge approach. Whatever the structure, you will have a range of good sources to draw on:

> *Subordinate administrators.* They know details of budgets, planning and zoning, and personnel matters. They are seldom in the spotlight, so many of them welcome a reporter's attention so long as the reporter does not get them into trouble. Many are bright and ambitious, willing to second-guess their superiors and gossip about politics, again providing you can assure them that the risk is low.
>
> *Council members.* Politicians, as a rule, love to talk. What they say is not always believable, and you have to be wary of their attempts to use you, but they will talk. Like most of us, politicians are more likely to tell someone else's secret or expose the other guy's deal. So ask one council member about the political forces behind another member's pet project while asking the other about the first's mayoral ambitions. That way you probably will learn all there is to know.
>
> *Pressure groups.* You can get an expert view of the city's land-use policies from land developers and a different view from conservationists. The manager or the personnel director will tell one side of the labor-management story. The head of the employees' union tells the other. How about the school board's record in hiring minorities? Get to know the head of the NAACP or Urban League chapter. Public officials respond to pressure. As a reporter you need to understand those pressures and who applies them.
>
> *Public citizens.* Consumer advocate Ralph Nader made the term "public citizens" popular, but every town has people—lawyers, homemakers, business executives, retirees—who serve on charter commissions, head bond campaigns, work in elections and advise behind the scenes. Such people can be sources of sound background information and useful assessments of office holders.
>
> *Opponents.* The best way to find out the weaknesses of any person or program is to talk with an opponent. Seek out the board member who wants to fire the school superintendent. Look up the police captain demoted by the new chief. Chat with the

leader of the opposition to the new hospital. There are at least
two sides to every public question and every public figure. Your
job is to explore them all.

Once you have found the sources, keep looking, listening and
asking for tips, for explanations, for reactions, for stories. The fun is just
starting.

Covering a city is very much like covering a county government.
In both cases you deal with politicians, with administrators, with
budgets, with problems. The similarities may be obscured by differences in structure and style, however.

Cities are more likely to have professional administrators. The
administration of county governments is more likely to be in the hands
of elected commissioners, supervisors or judges. Counties, too, are
more likely to have a multitude of elected officials, from the sheriff to
the recorder of deeds. City governments are more likely to be bureau-
cracies. One way to generalize about the differences is to say that city
governments often are more efficient and county governments are
more responsive.

These differences frequently mean, for a reporter, that county
government is easier to cover. More elected officials means more
politicians. That, in turn, can mean more talkative sources, more open
conflict, more points at which constituents and reporters alike can gain
access to the governmental structure.

The principles and the problems of reporting are the same. The
budget remains the blueprint whether it is drafted by a professional
administrator or an elected officeholder. Knowledge is power whether
it is the city manager or the elected county clerk who knows where the
money goes. Politics is politics.

The Schools

No institution is more important to any community than its schools.
None is worse covered. And none is more demanding of or rewarding
to a reporter. The issues that arise on the school beat are among the
most important in our society. If it is your beat, be prepared to write
about racial tensions, drug abuse, obscenity versus free speech, religious conflict, crime, labor-management disputes, politics, sex—and
yes, education.

You've met Susan Drumheller, who covers the schools in
northern Idaho. "If most beat reporters are like me, they're under a lot
of pressure to produce daily and weekend pieces," she says. Most beat
reporters, in fact, are a lot like Drumheller. For them, and for you, she
has a few tips for keeping up with the issues and the special language
of education.

"One good way is to subscribe to *Education Week* and other trade newsletters or magazines." When outcomes-based education loomed as an issue nationally, Drumheller subscribed to the state's anti-OBE newsletter. "That way I know the lingo and I know what the activists are up to." When AIDS brought sex education to the forefront, she subscribed to Boise's gay and lesbian newspaper for a perspective she wouldn't otherwise get. "And I need to subscribe to *Idaho Family Forum* (related to Focus on the Family and Christian Coalition) newsletter to keep up with them."

She adds, "Oh, yeah—I also get student newspapers for story ideas."

The process of learning and teaching can be obscured by the furor arising from the more dramatic issues. Even when everyone else seems to have forgotten, though, you must not forget that all those are only side issues. The most important part of the school beat is what goes on in the classroom.

Whether those classrooms hold kindergartners or college students, the principles for covering education remain the same. For the most part, so do the issues. When the schools are private rather than public, you have fewer rights of access.

The classroom is not an easy place to cover. You may have trouble getting into one. Administrators frequently turn down such requests on the grounds that a reporter's presence would be disruptive. It would, at first. But a good teacher and an unobtrusive reporter can overcome that drawback easily. Many papers, at the start of the school year, assign a reporter to an elementary school classroom. He or she visits frequently, gets to know the teacher and pupils, becomes part of the furniture. And that reporter captures for readers much of the sight and sound and feeling of education.

There are other ways, too, of letting readers in on how well—or how badly—the schools are doing their job:

- *Examine standardized test scores.* Every school system administers some kind of standard tests designed to measure how well its students compare either with a set standard or with other students. The results of such tests are or ought to be public information. Insist on learning about them. Test scores are an inadequate measure of school quality, but they are good indicators. When you base a story on them, be sure you understand what is really being compared and what factors outside the schools may affect the scores. Find out what decisions are made on the basis of standardized test scores. For example, do schools whose students' average scores are relatively low get additions to their faculty? Do they get special education teachers?
- *Be alert to other indicators of school quality.* You can find out how many graduates of your school system go to college, how many win

scholarships and what colleges they attend. You can find out how your school system measures up to the standards set by the state department of education. Does it hold the highest classification? If not, why not? National organizations of teachers, librarians and administrators also publish standards they think schools should meet. How close do your schools come?

■ *In education, you get what you pay for.* How does the pay of teachers in your district compare with pay in similar-sized districts? How does the tax rate compare? What is the turnover among teachers?

■ *Know as many teachers, administrators and students as possible.* You can learn to pick out the teachers who really care about children and learning. One way to do that is to encourage them to talk about their jobs. A good teacher's warmth will come through.

One reason schools are covered poorly is that the beat often does not produce the obvious, easy stories of politics, personalities and conflict that the city hall or police beats yield. School board meetings usually produce a spark only when a side issue intrudes. Most school board members are more comfortable talking about issues other than education itself, which often is left to the professionals.

The politics and the budgets of schools are very much like those of other institutions. The uniquely important things about the schools are the classrooms and what happens inside them. Your reporting will suffer if you forget that fact. So will your readers.

The Police Beat

The police beat probably produces more good, readable stories per hour of reporter time than any other beat. It also produces some of the worst, laziest reporting and generates many of our most serious legal and ethical problems. It is the beat many cub reporters start on and the beat many veterans stay on until they have become almost part of the force. It offers great frustration and great opportunity. All these contradictions arise from the nature of police work and of reporting.

If you are going to be a police reporter—and nearly every reporter is, at least briefly—the first thing you have to understand is what police officers are and what they do. We hire police officers to protect us from each other. We require them to deal every day with the dregs of society. Abuse and danger are parts of the job, as is boredom. We pay police officers mediocre wages and accord them little status. We ask them to be brave but compassionate, stern but tolerant. What we get very often is less what we ask for than what we should expect. Police work seldom attracts saints. Police officers are frequently cynical, often prejudiced, occasionally dishonest.

When you walk into a police station as a reporter for the first time, expect to be met with some suspicion, even hostility. Young

How to cover the cops

■ *Educate yourself in police lore.*
■ *Try to fit in.*
■ *Lend a sympathetic ear.*
■ *Encourage gossip.*
■ *Talk with other police-watchers.*

reporters often are perceived by police as being radical, unkempt, anti-authority. How closely does that description fit you or your classmates? How many of you are pro-cop?

Police departments are quasi-military organizations, with strict chains of command and strong discipline. Their members are sworn to uphold the status quo. The reasons that police officers and young reporters are mutually suspicious should be clear by now.

Then how do you cover these people? You do so by using the same tricks of the trade you ply at city hall or in the schools. You should:

- *Educate yourself in police lore.* Take a course in law enforcement, if you can, or take a course in constitutional law. You also might read Joseph Wambaugh's novels for a realistic portrait of the police.
- *Try to fit in.* Get a haircut, dress conservatively and learn the language. Remember that police officers, like the rest of us, usually are quicker to trust people who look and act the way they do.
- *Lend a sympathetic ear.* You enjoy talking about yourself to somebody who seems to be interested; so do most police officers. They know they have a tough job, and they like to be appreciated. Open your mind, and try to understand points of view with which you may disagree strongly.
- *Encourage gossip.* Police officers may gossip even more than reporters do. Encourage such talk over a cup of coffee at the station, while tagging along in a patrol car or over a beer after the shift. The stories will be one-sided and exaggerated, but you may learn a lot. Just don't print anything you haven't verified.
- *Talk with other police-watchers.* Lawyers can be good sources, especially the prosecutors and public defenders who associate every day with the police. Other law-enforcement sources are good, too. Sheriff's deputies, for example, may be eager to talk about dishonesty or inefficiency in the city police department, and city police may be eager to reciprocate.

One important reason for all this work is that little of the information you need and want as a police reporter is material you are entitled to under public records laws. By law you are entitled to see only the arrest sheet (also called the arrest log, or the **blotter**). This record tells you only the identity of the person arrested, the charge and when the arrest took place. You are not entitled by law to see the arrest report or to interview the officers involved.

Writing a story depends on securing more than the bare-bones information. Finding out details depends on the goodwill you have generated with the desk sergeant, the shift commander and the officers on the case. The dangers—of being unfair, of damaging your and your paper's or Web site's reputation—are ever-present. Good reporting requires that you know what the dangers are and how to try to avoid them.

The greatest danger arises from the one-sidedness and frequent inaccuracy of arrest reports. At best, they represent the officer's viewpoint. Particularly in cases involving violence, danger, confusion or possible repercussions, there may be plausible viewpoints different from that of the police officer. Conflicting interpretations of the same situation lead many times to the dropping of charges.

To protect yourself, and to be fair to the accused, always be skeptical. Attribute any accusatory statement to the officer who made it. If the room for doubt is great enough, talk to the accused, his or her relatives or lawyer, and any witnesses you can find.

Before Edna Buchanan turned to writing crime novels, she was one of the best-known police reporters in America. She won the Pulitzer Prize for general news reporting. Here are a couple of samples from her work:

> Bad things happen to the husbands of the Widow Elkin.
>
> Someone murdered Husband No. 4, Cecil Elkin, apparently smashing his head with a frying pan as he was watching "Family Feud" on TV.
>
> Husband No. 3, Samuel Smilich, drowned in a weedy South Dade canal.
>
> Husband No. 2, Lawrence Myers, cannot be found, though Metro-Dade homicide detectives, the FBI and the Air Force have searched for him.
>
> Husband No. 1, Wayne Wise, was divorced about 25 years ago. He is alive and well. . . .

And this:

> "My baby was trapped in a dead body," Charles Griffith said Saturday from the Dade County jail where he was stripped naked and charged with first-degree murder.
>
> "I didn't go to the hospital thinking I was going to kill my daughter," said Griffith, 25. "I told the nurse to go call the police, I think, before it happened. It is almost like a dream."
>
> At 10:50 p.m. Friday, Griffith, a projectionist in a porno movie house, fired two bullets into the heart of his comatose 3-year-old daughter, Joy, as she lay in her crib in the special care nursery at Miami Children's Hospital. . . .

In the letter nominating Buchanan, who covered the police beat for *The Miami Herald* for 16 years, her editors made a comment to the Pulitzer Board that sums up the importance and the attraction of the police beat: "In truth, Edna Buchanan doesn't write about cops. She writes about people."

The Courts

One way to begin trying to understand the American judicial system is to think of it as a kind of game. The opposing players in a criminal case are the state, which is the accuser, and the defendant, who is the accused. In a civil case the opponents are the plaintiff and the defendant. Each player is represented by a lawyer, who does everything possible to win for his or her client. The judge referees the contest, insisting that all players abide by the rules. At the end, the judge (sometimes with a jury) decides who won.

Such an irreverent description grossly oversimplifies a system that, because of its independence and usual honesty, stands second only to a free press in protecting the liberty of Americans. But it may help in demystifying a system that also can overawe a beginning reporter.

There is a great deal in courts and the law to inspire awe. Black-robed judges and learned attorneys speak a language full of Latin phrases and highly specialized terms. Written motions, arguments and decisions are laden with convoluted sentences and references unintelligible to the uninitiated. A court can protect your money or your freedom or deprive you of both.

You can hardly cover the courts aggressively while standing awestruck, though, so here are some tips that may help restore your working skepticism:

> **A skeptic's guide to the courts**
>
> - *Never trust a lawyer unless you know him or her very well.*
> - *A judge's word may be law, but it isn't gospel.*
> - *Truth and justice do not always prevail.*

- *Never trust a lawyer unless you know him or her very well.* Although most lawyers are honest, all lawyers are advocates. Consequently, everything they write or say must be interpreted as being designed to help their client and hurt their opponent. That is true whether the lawyer represents the defense or prosecution in a criminal case or represents either side in a civil lawsuit. Bar association codes of ethics forbid it, but many lawyers will try to use reporters to win some advantage. Be suspicious.
- *A judge's word may be law, but it isn't gospel.* Not every judge is a legal scholar. Most judges are, or have been, politicians. All judges are human. They are subject to error, capable of prejudice. Some are even dishonest.
- *Truth and justice do not always prevail.* Prosecutors sometimes conceal evidence favorable to the defense. Defense lawyers sometimes seize on technicalities or rely on witnesses they know to be unreliable in order to win acquittals. Judges sometimes misinterpret the rules or ignore them. Innocent people do go to jail, and guilty ones go free. Courts are no more perfect than are newspapers. The two combined can produce frightening scenes, such as the one in Cleveland in 1954 when the newspapers screamed for blood and a political judge denied Dr. Sam Sheppard the most basic rights before convicting him of murdering his wife. The Supreme Court

decision overturning that conviction became a landmark in spelling out proper trial procedures. In other cases, the press helped correct miscarriages of justice. Reporter Gene Miller won two Pulitzer Prizes for winning freedom for persons wrongfully imprisoned after unjust murder convictions.

The judicial system is not exempt from honest and critical reporting. And the sources of that reporting—just as in city hall or the police station—are records and people. First, a few words about court records, where to find them and how to use them.

Court Records

Whenever a case is filed in court—whether it is a criminal charge or a civil lawsuit—the court clerk assigns it a number. It also has a title. In the case of a criminal charge, the title will be State vs. Joe Doakes, or something similar. (The "vs." is short for "versus," the Latin word meaning "against.") A civil case—a lawsuit seeking damages, for example—could be Joe Doakes vs. John Doe. Doakes would be the plaintiff, the party filing the suit. Doe would be the defendant. In order to secure the records from the court clerk, you must know the case number or case title, which lawyers also call the "style" of the case.

You can follow a case by checking the case file. At least in the more important criminal cases, however, you usually keep track by checking with the prosecutor and defense lawyers.

Once a civil suit has been filed, the defense files a reply. The plaintiff may file a motion seeking information. The defense may file a motion to dismiss the suit, which the plaintiff will answer. The judge rules on each motion. You can follow it all by checking the file regularly. Except in rare cases, all motions and information filed with the court become public records. Often information from lawsuits can provide you with interesting insights into the otherwise private affairs of prominent persons or businesses.

Many lawsuits never go to trial before judge or jury. It is common procedure for lawyers to struggle for advantage over a period of months, filing motions and countermotions to gain the best position or to sound out the other side's strength. Then, after a trial date has been set, one side or the other will propose a settlement, which is negotiated. The case is dropped. One reason for that course of action is that the details of an out-of-court settlement need not be made public, unlike the outcome of a trial.

Human Sources

If a case goes to trial, you cover civil and criminal proceedings in much the same way. You must listen to testimony and, during breaks, corner lawyers for each side to seek explanation and elaboration, while filling

Human sources in court
- Lawyers.
- Judges.
- Other court functionaries.

in the background from court records and your morgue. Your personal contacts are important sources of information during this process.

> *Lawyers.* The best sources on the court beat are likely to be lawyers. Every courthouse reporter needs to win the confidence and goodwill of the prosecutor and his or her staff. Not only can they keep you abreast of developments in criminal prosecution, they often can—because assistant prosecutors generally are young, political and ambitious—keep you tuned in to all sorts of interesting and useful courthouse gossip. They are good sources for tips on who the best and worst judges are, which local officials may be on the take, which defense lawyers are less than upright. Like all gossip, such tips need careful handling and thorough checking.
>
> Lawyers in private practice can be grouped, from a reporter's viewpoint, into two classes—those who will talk and those who won't. The former class usually includes young lawyers, politically ambitious lawyers and criminal defense lawyers, all of whom often find publicity helpful. Cultivate them. Lawyers have egos only slightly smaller than those of reporters. Feed those egos. Encourage them to talk about themselves, their triumphs, their ambitions.
>
> *Judges.* Don't ignore judges as sources, either. Some are so conscious of their dignity and their images that they have no time for reporters. Remember, though, that most judges in most states are elected to their jobs. That makes them politicians, and it is a rare politician who slams the door on a friendly reporter. Even many federal judges, who are appointed by the president, have done a stint in politics and still have their taste for newspaper ink. Judges' egos may be even bigger than reporters'. Treat every judge accordingly.
>
> *Other court functionaries.* Many other court functionaries can be helpful sources. Police officers and sheriff's deputies or U.S. marshals assigned to court duty often are underworked and glad of a chance to talk about whatever they know, which may turn out to be good backstage stuff. The bailiffs who shout for order in court and help the judge on with a robe may be retired police officers or small-time politicians and also talkative. And secretaries, as everywhere, are good to know and even better to have know you.

Religion

If you ever doubted the importance of religion in the world and in the news, just do a quick Google search for the terms "Islamic fundamentalists" and "pedophile priests." Whether your beat is the Pentagon or the police station, you're more likely than ever to find yourself covering stories with a connection to religion. Indeed, the dark side of religion news has become so prominent that it's easy to forget the reality that religion has always been more important to everyday people than it is to journalists.

More Americans attend religious services than attend college football games. More Americans are active in religion than in politics. Overwhelming majorities of Americans say that religion is important in their lives. However, you'd never guess any of those realities from reading or viewing most news reports in print or on television. The typical newspaper offers a weekly Religion page, usually published on Saturday, when circulation and readership are low. The typical television news coverage of religion is even less, often nonexistent.

> **Look for religion stories in**
> - *Social issues.*
> - *Politics.*
> - *Law.*
> - *International affairs.*
> - *Everyday life.*

The impact of such developments as religion-based terrorism and turmoil in the Catholic Church is changing this attitude. Many news organizations have deepened and broadened religion coverage, often moving it to the top of the news. That's not surprising. Just consider the stories:

In social issues, religion plays a role in the continuing debate over sex education, AIDS research and treatment, abortion, the role of women in the church and in secular life, and an almost-endless variety of other policy questions.

In politics, religion has become a key to campaigning and to governing. Presidents from both major political parties proclaim themselves born-again Christians. Candidates at all levels solicit the support of the religious right or, in fewer cases, make the most of their independence from it. In campaigns throughout the country, well-organized and well-financed religious organizations, usually conservative in their theology and their politics, exert influence even beyond their numbers. In major cities, candidates court Jewish and Muslim support.

In law, constitutional questions continue to cloud the relationship of church and state. President George W. Bush made news when he urged federal financial support for the social welfare programs of religious organizations. Many civil libertarians worried that the traditional wall between government and religion was being dismantled. So did some religious conservatives. The hierarchy of the Catholic Church angered many of the faithful when it failed to report to law-enforcement agencies accusations of sexual abuse by priests.

Since Sept. 11, 2001, reporters accustomed to writing about international affairs have found themselves required to explain Islam. While political leaders struggled with unfamiliar names and previously unknown organizations, journalists had to learn the differences between Sunni and Shiite, the role of religion in the politics of Pakistan, and the geography and theology of the world's fastest-growing faith.

In everyday life, religion-based charities assume increasing importance as the American economy leaves behind growing numbers of the unskilled and uneducated. The "Religion Calendar" for just one week in a Midwestern college town includes activities that range from the African Methodist Episcopal women's group to the pagan Wiccan circle to meditation practice at the Zen Center.

So how does a reporter cover such a range of issues, personalities and events?

First, prepare. Read as widely as you can. A good place to start is with a booklet called *Deities & Deadlines*. Its subtitle tells its purpose: *A Primer on Religion News Coverage*. Written for the Freedom Forum by a veteran religion news reporter, John Dart, this little guide is full of specific, helpful advice and information. It includes brief descriptions of the major faiths, summaries of issues and a list of sources, complete with telephone numbers. You can order it from the Freedom Forum First Amendment Center at Vanderbilt University in Nashville, Tenn.

Here are other ways to prepare for religion stories:

- *Read religion magazines.* The best-informed coverage of religion and related issues can be found in such magazines as *Christianity Today*, the *National Catholic Reporter, Christian Century, Cross Currents* and *Worldview*, and in other publications you'll find indexed at your local public or university library.
- *Consult faculty members at the nearest Religious Studies department or seminary.* These people can give you theological expertise and local comment, but beware of their possible biases. Get to know your local religious activists, in the clergy and outside. Who are the rebels and the questioners? Who are the powers behind the pulpit quietly raising money, directing spending and guiding policy?
- *Remember that religion is big business.* Public records and computer databases can help you trace property ownership and finances. Religious organizations often own commercial property, housing, parking lots, educational facilities. Typically, they pay no taxes, but their economic impact can be great. It isn't always positive either. Churches have been found to be slumlords.
- *Check the tax records.* Religious organizations pay no income taxes, but they are required to file federal tax forms (called 990 forms) to maintain their tax-exempt status. These Internal Revenue Service forms are the only income tax forms that are public by law. You'll find readers interested in the finances as well as in the good works of religion.

In addition to ignorance, other obstacles impede effective coverage of religion. Many reporters and editors are reluctant to subject religious leaders and institutions to the same scrutiny as their counterparts in business or politics. Remember that religious leaders are human. They are often good, sometimes devious, occasionally corrupt. Be respectful, but remember that a member of the clergy who demands deferential treatment might be hiding something behind that ecclesiastical smile.

Another special problem in covering religion is the emotional intensity with which many people hold to their beliefs. If you do serious reporting, you will not be able to avoid arousing somebody's wrath. You can avoid arousing it needlessly, however, by doing your homework.

Do not confuse a Southern Baptist with an American Baptist, or a Lutheran of the Missouri Synod with a Lutheran of the Evangelical Lutheran Church of America. You will not get very far interviewing a Jesuit if you ask him what denomination he belongs to. But not every Roman Catholic priest is a Jesuit. Don't attribute the same beliefs to Orthodox, Conservative and Reform Jews. And remember that Jews and Christians, though they dominate American religious life, are only a fraction of the world's religious believers.

Some stories about religion are uplifting. They tell of selfless service to the poor, the sick, the forgotten and abandoned. They illustrate values other than money or power. They describe the courage of people who put lives and property on the line for human rights or in opposition to war. Others are not so uplifting. Parishes run up huge debts. Parochial schools hire badly trained, poorly paid teachers. Blacks are refused admission. Women are refused ordination.

Stained-glass windows are no barrier to politics. Religious issues, such as abortion, homosexuality, child abuse and capital punishment, are often also political issues. Churches, mosques and synagogues may use their economic clout to combat injustice or to support it.

Whatever side of religion it explores, a good story about religion will wind up on the front page along with the best of the city hall or medical stories.

The Environment, Science and Medicine

In surveys, newspaper readers say they want more and better coverage of the environment. That feeling is especially strong among younger readers (and nonreaders, too). Top-quality environment coverage wins important awards and brings prestige to news organizations. For example, a series on threats to the world's fisheries won *The (New Orleans) Times-Picayune* a Pulitzer Prize and an immediate boost in reputation. A report by *The (Spokane, Wash.) Spokesman-Review* on the bungled cleanup of a nuclear-waste site not only won national prizes but led to federal investigations and reforms.

Still, as newspaper editor Greg Favre pointed out to the American Society of Newspaper Editors, "At least 50 percent of our newspapers and 75 percent of our television stations do not have full-time environment reporters, and that's a shame."

From covering the preservation of wetlands and protection of endangered species to investigating abandoned city buildings and polluting sewer systems, reporters working the environment beat find a multitude of challenging and rewarding stories.

For a young reporter with an interest in nature and science, the shame can turn into opportunity. Environment stories are as close as your city parks, the public landfill or the local water supply. Expert sources are as close as the nearest university or state natural resources agency. Well-informed, passionate advocates are as close as the local chapter of the Sierra Club, the Audubon Society or nearly any developer of subdivisions or defender of property rights.

Emilia Askari, president of the Society of Environmental Journalists, prepared some suggestions for editors on responding to reader interest. Her tips offer useful starting points for would-be environment writers. Here are some of them:

- *Define the beat broadly.* The environment includes urban as well as wilderness issues. Think of abandoned buildings, old service stations and sewer systems as well as wetlands and endangered species.
- *Spend time on the beat.* Cultivate sources among experts and activists. Read what they read.
- *Expect pressure and controversy.* Land use, preservation, property rights and economics all can generate emotion as well as interest.

You'll be under critical scrutiny by all sides of every issue you cover.

- *Look beyond purely local issues.* Such broader issues as global warming, deforestation and overfishing have local angles as close as the weather and the grocery store.
- *Educate yourself.* Look for opportunities to attend conferences on topics and techniques. Learn computer-assisted reporting. Take a course or more at the nearest college.
- *Write for kids.* They're interested; they're active; they're the readers and the citizens of tomorrow. Besides, there's no better way to make sure you really understand a complex issue than to explain it successfully to a youngster.
- *Watch for reports of scientific studies and translate them into everyday language.* Many of the best environment stories begin with research reports in scientific journals. Often those reports are picked up first in the specialized publications mentioned below. Make sure you know, and tell readers, the funding sources and any other possible bias in the studies you report.

Askari also offers a good source of information and professional guidance — her society. The SEJ home page can be found at **www.sej.org**. Information from and about the quarterly *SEJournal* can be accessed from this site.

Many of the techniques, the problems and the possibilities of environment reporting are paralleled in reporting on science and medicine. On these beats there will be fewer meetings to attend or offices to visit than on a city hall or school beat. More of the stories here are likely to be generated by your own enterprise or by applying the local touch to a national story. You can find out what a new pesticide ban will mean to local farmers. Or you can determine whether local doctors are using a new arthritis treatment, or what a researcher at the state university is learning about the effects of alcohol on rats.

Where can you look for story ideas? Specialized publications are good places to start. Read the *Journal of the American Medical Association*, the *New England Journal of Medicine* and *Medical World*. New developments and issues in medicine are covered in news stories. *Scientific American* and *Science News* are informed but readable sources of ideas in all the sciences. For environmental issues, read *Natural History* magazine. Your state's conservation department may put out a publication. Get on the mailing lists of the National Wildlife Federation, the Sierra Club, the Audubon Society and Friends of the Earth.

Nearly every community has human sources, too. In medicine, these include members of the local medical association, the administrator of the hospital and public health officials. In the sciences, look for local school or college faculty, employees of government agencies such as extension or research centers, even interested amateurs such as those in astronomy societies. In the area of the environment, there usually is no shortage of advocacy groups or of industries that want to defend their interests. State and federal regulatory and research agencies are helpful, too.

The special problems posed by scientific beats begin with the language your sources use. It is a language full of Latin phrases, technical terms and numbers. You will have to learn enough of it both to ask intelligent questions and to translate the answers for your readers. A good medical dictionary and science dictionary are invaluable. Use them and continue asking for explanations until you are sure you understand.

Another problem may be convincing scientists and physicians to talk to you in any language. Many of them have had little contact with reporters. Much of the contact they have had probably has been unpleasant, either because it arose from some controversy or because the reporter was unprepared. Reluctant sources are much more likely to cooperate if you demonstrate that you have done your homework so you have at least some idea of what they are talking about. Promise to check your story with the sources. Accuracy is as much your goal as theirs.

In medicine a concern for privacy may deter some sources from talking freely. A physician's allegiance is, and should be, to the patient. As a reporter you have no legal right to know a patient's condition or ailment. That is true even if the patient is a public official. In fact, most information about a person's medical history and condition is protected by law from disclosure by government record keepers.

Sources also may be guarded in comments about their work. Most researchers in medicine and science are cautious in making any claims about the significance or certainty of their work. Some are not so cautious. You must be. Before describing any development as "important" or "dramatic" or "frightening," check and double-check with the researcher involved and others knowledgeable in the field.

Sometimes a researcher will be reluctant to discuss his or her work until it has been published in a professional journal or reported at a convention. Such presentation may be more important to the scientist than any newspaper publicity. Funding and fame are high-stakes issues for research scientists. Many, justifiably afraid of having unscrupulous fellow researchers claim credit for their work, maintain secrecy until a study is complete. A researcher's agreement to give you first notice when he or she is ready to go public may be the best you can hope for in this circumstance.

Despite difficulties, the coverage of science, medicine or the environment offers great challenges and rewards. The challenge is to discover and explain developments and issues that are important to your readers. The rewards, as in all other areas of reporting, can be prizes, pay raises or—most important—recognition by your sources and peers of a job well done.

Business

Business reporting is no longer the responsibility of only the specialists. When high-flying entrepreneurs crash, when major accounting firms are discovered doctoring the books, when millions of new investors in the stock market see their pension funds disappear, business news jumps to the top of the newscasts and the front pages. General-assignment reporters suddenly are expected to write clearly and quickly about a world they never knew. Here are some of the secrets of the specialists.

What separates a business story from a soccer story—or, for that matter, a soccer story from a story about atomic particles—is the knowledge and language required to ask the right questions, to recognize the newsworthy answers and to write the story in a way that the reader without specialized knowledge will understand. A reporter who understands the subject can explain what the jargon means.

For example, if banks change their prime rates, the personal finance reporter might be the person to write the story explaining that an increase of one percentage point could result in higher interest rates for car or home loans.

If United Parcel Service workers went on strike, the labor reporter might explore the impact on local workers and the local market. The labor and transportation reporters might work together on a story about an airline strike.

Business reporters must use understandable language. But simplicity can turn readers off. *The Wall Street Journal* avoids both traps by shunning jargon as much as possible and explaining any technical terms essential to the story. In one story, for example, the *Journal* explained the terms "Federal Open Market Committee," "federal funds rate," "M1," "M2" and "free-reserve position." A sophisticated reader might know what those terms mean, but many of the paper's readers would not.

Former presidential economic adviser Gardner Ackley once said he would like to see two things in people covering economics and business news: first, that they had taken a course in economics, and second, that they had passed it.

Yet animosity sometimes exists between journalists and business people. A 1994 study by the First Amendment Center of the Freedom Forum called "The Headline vs. The Bottom Line: Mutual Distrust between Business and the News Media" confirmed what business people and business journalists alike have long suspected: Neither trusts the other.

"Journalists and business executives are not just adversaries," the authors say. "Their relationship is too often characterized by lying and unfair treatment."

The study sheds light on business journalists' biggest challenge: how to get information from someone who does not legally have to tell you anything. It often takes much more clever reporting skills to coax a story out of a business source than it does out of a government official. After all, almost all government information is open to the public. Many business records are not. Such major stories as the collapse of the energy firm Enron require journalists to cultivate within the companies informed sources who have access to those records.

As John Seigenthaler, founder of the First Amendment Center, pointed out, on the one hand, "There is a feeling (among business executives) that the profit motive simply isn't understood as being as American as apple pie by numbers of journalists." But on the other hand, among journalists, "There's a strong sense that business executives malinger, are not responsible and for the most part misrepresent and even more often refuse to communicate."

The mistrust that many business people have of the press can make it difficult to cover stories adequately, even when it would be in the business's interest to see that the story is told. Even if executives are willing to talk, they may become angry if the reporter quotes an opposing point of view or points out a wart on the corporate visage.

The best antidote a reporter can use against this animosity is to report fairly and accurately what a business is doing and saying. By always being fair, you usually can win the trust and confidence of business people.

Because business executives tend to be cautious about talking with reporters, it may help if you dress more like a business manager than, say, a social protester. Appearances count, and business people, like reporters, nurses, generals and linebackers, feel more comfortable with their own kind.

The more you can demonstrate that you understand their business, the more likely you are to generate the trust that will draw out the information you seek. "Understanding" is not synonymous with "sympathy," but ignorance usually means a reporter is likely to misinterpret what is said.

Public-relations people often are helpful in providing background information and directing you to the executives who can provide other comment and information, but you should try to get to know as many company officials as you can. Sometimes you can do this best through a background interview, one not generated by a crisis but intended simply to help you learn about what the company is doing. Perhaps you can arrange to have lunch to see what the officials are thinking

---

Deogun thinks his generalist background, both in liberal arts and in journalism, has prepared him well. Business writers need to understand the social and political context in which their subjects operate.

"I use here the same reporting skills you'd use on any beat," he adds. "If tomorrow I had to go cover fly-fishing, I wouldn't know diddley. But I'd learn. You read a lot and ask people questions."

Too much specialization in a field such as business can even be a handicap. The *Journal* serves an audience more involved in business than the audiences of most daily papers or broadcast outlets, but a reporter's job still includes a great deal of translating from the jargon of the specialist into everyday English.

A business reporter, Deogun understands, must be able to speak the technical language without falling into the trap of also writing it. "Most of your readers don't know that much about business," he observed.

Clear thinking and clear writing remain essential.

about and to give them a chance to see that you are probably not the demon they may have thought you to be.

Always remember that a company, government agency or pressure group may be trying to use you to plant stories that serve some special interest. Companies want a story to make them look promising to investors, in the hope of driving up the price of the company stock, or to make them attractive merger partners. If you are suspicious, do some digging; talk to competitors and analysts and ask detailed questions. Just because a company or some other group is pushing a story does not mean you have to write it.

Conflict-of-interest issues challenge business journalists because they often write stories, some of which are unfavorable, about advertisers. Across the country, business editors have become increasingly concerned as advertisers threaten to pull advertising over unfavorable coverage. A story on how to deal with car salesmen in *The (San Jose, Calif.) Mercury News* inspired area car dealers to stage an advertising boycott that cost the paper $200,000 worth of ads a week.

Real estate agents and grocers, both traditionally large advertisers, have worked together to pressure newspapers. Although newspapers make a show of not caving in to such pressures, advertiser threats can produce a chilling effect in the news room.

It is challenging to cover business. To do so effectively, a business reporter should be all the things any good reporter is—honest, fair, alert to possible new stories and to new angles on old stories. Business writing can be rewarding, both financially (because specialists usually earn premium pay) and intellectually.

Human Sources

Who are the people you should talk to on the business beat? Here are some who are important sources of information:

> *Company officials.* The most valuable information probably will come from the head of a corporation or a divisional head. Chief executive officers are powerful people, either out front or behind the scenes, in your community. They are often interesting, usually well-informed. Not all of them will be glad to see you, though in recent years companies and top executives have started to realize the importance of communicating their point of view to the public.
>
> Don't automatically assume a public relations person is trying to block your path. Many people working in corporate communications are truly professional, and providing information to journalists is part of their job. Remember, though, that they are paid to make the company look good, so they will likely point you in the direction of the company's viewpoint. Assume that

Human sources on the business beat

- *Company officials.*
- *Analysts.*
- *Academic experts.*
- *Associations.*
- *Chamber of commerce officials.*
- *Former employees.*
- *Labor leaders.*

information they give you is being packaged to show the company in its best light.

Analysts. To learn what the experts think about specific companies, many business reporters contact securities analysts. Analysts can be valuable if they are not overused and if you get information on the company from other sources as well. Don't assume that analysts are infallible seers. Remember, too, that a broker is selling stock and is not the same as an analyst. To find the appropriate analyst, consult *Investment Decisions Directory of Wall Street Research*, also called *Nelson's Directory*, which is a must for any business department's library.

Other analysts and researchers, frequently economists, are employed by banks, trade groups, chambers of commerce and local businesses. They often are willing to talk because the exposure is good for their organizations.

Academic experts. Your college or university will have faculty members with training and experience in various areas of business and economics. Often they are good sources of local reaction to national developments or analysis of economic trends. They are usually happy to cooperate. Many university public information offices prepare lists of their nationally or regionally known experts and their phone numbers.

Associations. Although trade associations clearly represent the interests of their members, they can provide expert commentary on current issues or give explanations from the perspective of the industry. When *The New York Times* reported on the revival of the moving industry, the Household Goods Carriers Bureau, a major trade group, proved to be an important source. To find trade associations, look in the *Encyclopedia of Associations* or *National Trade and Professional Associations of the United States.*

Chamber of commerce officials. The bias of chamber officials is clearly pro-business, and they seldom will make an on-the-record negative comment about business, but they usually know who is who and what is what in the business community. The chamber may be involved in such projects as downtown revitalization and industry recruiting.

Former employees. The best business reporters say that frequently their most valuable sources are former employees of the company they're profiling. Writes Chris Welles, who covers business for national publications, "Nobody knows more about a corporation than someone who has actually worked there." He warns, "Many, probably most, have axes to grind, especially if they were fired; indeed, the more willing they are to talk, the more biased they are likely to be."

Labor leaders. For the other side of many business stories and for pieces on working conditions, upcoming contracts and politics, get to know local union officials. The workings, legal and otherwise, of unions make good stories, too.

Others. Don't overlook the value of a company's customers, suppliers and competitors. You also may want to consult with local bankers, legislators, legislative staff members, law-enforcement agencies and regulators, board members, oversight committee members and the like.

Sports

Being Prepared

Before you ever thought about sports reporting, the chances are that you were reading, watching and playing sports. In that sense, at least, preparing to be a sports reporter is easier than preparing to cover city hall. But there is more to preparation than immersing yourself in sports. Competition pushes people to their limits, bringing out their best and worst. So you need to know some psychology. Sports has played a major role in the struggles of blacks and women for equality. So you need to know some sociology and history. Sports, professional and amateur, is big business. So you need a background in economics. Some of our greatest writers have portrayed life through sports. So you need to explore literature.

Being Alert

"It's the writer's responsibility to come up with a different approach," says Peter St. Onge, a reporter and columnist at *The Charlotte (N.C.) Observer*. In his own words, this is how he does it:

> When my editor sent me to a PGA golf tournament, I sat at the most popular spectator hole—one that some pros could drive—and wrote about why the fans loved it. When my editor wanted a Super Bowl preview story, I went around town trying to find someone who truly believed Buffalo would beat Dallas (I didn't find anyone, which made the story even better). When a minor-league baseball player from town got called up to the big leagues, I talked to his high school coach, college coach and best friend and asked them about the moment they got the phone call from the player—and what their thoughts were.

Let's take a quick look at the story that resulted from one of those different approaches. If you read sports, you've read the story of the rookie getting summoned to the big leagues. Often the story is one long cliché, from the obligatory "aw shucks" quote of the athlete to the recitation of statistics. A different approach yields a different and better story. Here's St. Onge's opening:

From the diversity of her experience, she has several pieces of advice for young reporters, in sports or elsewhere:

- Don't specialize too early.
- In beat coverage, you do your readers the most good by reporting on trends.
- Keep track of the documents.
- Don't rely on editors to (a) fill in the blanks for you, (b) save you from error or (c) edit really significant stories "the right way."
- Report on things that you want to read about yourself, even if they don't seem important.

The best friend got the call Wednesday, just before midnight, the phone's jangle jarring him from sleep.

"He called me about two minutes after he got out of his coach's office," Mark Adams remembers. "He said, 'You wanted me to call you when I got called up.'

"Then he said, 'I'm there.'"

The Red Sox. The big leagues. How many times had they talked about this moment? At college, on road trips, on the lake with fishing poles in their hands? They had both been star players, both good enough for a chance at professional baseball. But only one had the opportunity.

Once, Tim VanEgmond had said that he was nervous about being called up. That when he finally stepped on a major-league mound, he might feel more loneliness than anything.

"I told Tim not to worry," the best friend says. "I told him, 'You're not just playing for you. You're also playing for me.'"

After recounting the reactions and recollections of the two coaches, St. Onge summarizes both the story and the relationships:

Today, they will all be thinking of him, for all their own reasons. The best friend, the junior college coach and the college coach will try to find satellite dishes somewhere and lock onto a Boston or Milwaukee station.

But even if they can't, that's OK. The phone will ring again soon, and it will be Tim VanEgmond, the one they saw grow up, the one they grew up with. He'll give them all the real details then. He always does. It's their moment, too.

That story entertains while it informs. It shows readers something of the character of an athlete and the nature of friendship. Here are a few tips to help you be alert to stories that get beyond the cliché:

- *Look for the losers.* Losing may not—as football coaches and other philosophers like to assert—build character, but it certainly bares character. Winners are likely to be full of confidence, champagne and clichés. Losers are likely to be full of self-doubt, second-guessing and surliness. Winners' dressing rooms are magnets for sportswriters, but you usually can tell your readers more about the game and those who play it by seeking out the losers.
- *Look for the bench warmers.* If you follow the reporting crowd, you'll end up in front of your local version of Barry Bonds or Venus Williams every time. Head in the other direction. Talk to the would-be football player who has spent four years practicing but never gets into a game. Talk to the woman who dreams of being a professional golfer but is not yet good enough. Talk to the baseball player who is growing old in the minor leagues. If you do, you may find people who both love their sport more and understand it better than do the stars. You may find less press agentry and more humanity.

Different sports require different approaches. For instance, curling, an Olympic sport, is still relatively unknown. Journalists must learn about the psychology, competitiveness, economics and social role of curling in preparation for their work.

■ *Look beyond the crowds.* Some of the best, and most important, sports stories draw neither crowds of reporters nor crowds of fans. The recent and rapid growth of women's sports is one example. Under the pressure of federal law—the "Title IX" you read and hear about—the traditional male dominance of facilities and money in school and college athletics is slowly giving way to equal treatment for women. From junior high schools to major universities, women's teams now compete in nearly every sport except football. The results of this revolution are likely to be felt far beyond the playing fields, just as the earlier admission of blacks to athletic equality advanced blacks' standing in other areas.

So-called minor sports and participant sports are other largely untapped sources of good stories. More Americans watch birds than play football. More hunt or fish than play basketball. More watch stock-car races than watch track meets.

But those and similar sports are usually covered—if at all—by the newest or least talented reporter on the staff. Get out of the press box. Drop by a bowling alley, a skeet-shooting range, or the local college's Frisbee-throwing tournament.

Being Persistent

It was a big story. A sports agent had told another newspaper that he had given money to and arranged travel for a star college basketball player before and during the player's senior season. The agent saw it as no big deal. He had done the same for players at universities across the country as he tried to win their allegiance for life in the professional leagues. But for the university his allegations, if true, could mean at least embarrassment and at most the forfeiting of NCAA tournament games in which the player had participated.

It was a big problem. The agent had been willing, even eager, to talk to reporters at the metropolitan newspaper that broke the story. He was available to other reporters at other papers with which he was familiar. But he had no time for student reporters at the newspaper of the university most involved. His attitude was discouraging for the reporters, frustrating for their editors and baffling for their readers.

The reporters refused to give up. They got the agent's home phone number, in a city across the continent, from the reporter who had discovered his role. They left message after message. While they waited for the agent's call, they worked at the story from the edges by talking to people less directly involved but more accessible. The player himself, of course, was unavailable to any reporters. Finally, after a week of reading other versions of the story they wanted, the student reporters got a payoff for their persistence. The agent called. Using what they had gleaned from other interviews and previous stories, the students were able to write a story that offered readers a few new tidbits:

> Nate Cebrun on Thursday described prospective agents' year-long courtship of former university basketball player Jevon Crudup as an "out-of-control bidding war."
>
> Cebrun, a self-described middleman, said his dealings with Crudup and his mother, Mary, probably netted them only about $5,000 in cash and other gifts. But sports agents Michael Harrison and Raul Bey must have spent even more money on Crudup, Cebrun said.
>
> "I saw Jevon's mother at Missouri's game against Arizona in tournament action. And I know she wasn't able to afford that with the money she makes," Cebrun said in a phone interview from his Las Vegas home. "But if I were a betting man, I'd almost guarantee Harrison paid for her to go to L.A."

The most important reward of persistence, though, is the loyalty of readers who feel well-served.

Being There and Developing Contacts

Being there is half the fun of sports reporting. You're there at the big games, matches and meets. You're there in the locker rooms, on team buses and planes, with an inside view of athletics and athletes that few fans ever get. If you are to answer your readers' questions, if you are to provide insight and anecdote, you must be there, most of the time.

Sometimes you should try being where the fans are. Plunk down $20 (of the newspaper's money) for an end-zone seat, and write about a football game from the average fan's point of view. Cover a baseball game from the bleachers. Cold hot dogs and warm beer are as much a part of the event as a double play. Watch one of those weekend sports shows on television and compare the way a track meet or a fishing trip is presented with the way it is in person. Join a city league softball team or a bowling league for a different kind of inside view.

A sports reporter must develop and cherish sources just as a city hall reporter must. You look for the same kinds of sources on both beats. Players, coaches and administrators—like city council members and city managers—are obvious sources. Go beyond them. Trainers and equipment managers have insiders' views and sometimes lack the fierce protectiveness that often keeps players, for example, from talking candidly.

Alumni can be excellent sources for high school and college sports stories. If a coach is about to be fired or a new fund drive is being planned, important alumni are sure to be involved. You can find out who they are by checking with the alumni association or by examining the list of major contributors that every college proudly compiles. The business managers and secretaries who handle the money can be invaluable for much-needed but seldom-done stories about the finances of sports at all levels. Former players sometimes will talk more candidly than those who are still involved in a program. As on any beat, look for people who may be disgruntled—a fired assistant coach, a benched star, a big contributor to a losing team. And when you find good sources, cherish them. Keep in contact, flatter them, protect them. They are your lifeline.

Unfortunately, being where a reporter needs to be isn't always easy or pleasant. Just ask Lisa Olson. A young reporter for the *Boston Herald*, Olson was doing her job, interviewing a New England Patriot football player in the locker room, when several other players began harassing her. At least one player made sexually suggestive comments and gestures while he stood nude beside her. After a complaint, and after much national publicity, players and the team owner were fined and reprimanded by the National Football League. Many other women, and some men, have found themselves victims of harassment by athletes, coaches or fans. Sports reporters, especially women, may find their professionalism tested in ways—and in surroundings—seldom encountered by colleagues on beats that usually are considered more serious.

Being Wary and Digging for the Real Story

It is even harder for a sports reporter than it is for a political or police reporter to maintain a critical distance from the beat. The most obvious reason is that most of the people who become sports reporters do so because they are sports fans. To be a fan is precisely the opposite of being a dispassionate, critical observer. In addition, athletics—especially big-time athletics—is glamorous and exciting. The sports reporter associates daily with the stars and the coaches whom others, including cynical city hall reporters and hard-bitten managing editors, pay to admire at a distance. Finally, sports figures ranging from high school coaches to owners of professional baseball teams deliberately and persistently seek to buy the favor of the reporters who cover their sports.

We are taught from childhood that it is disgraceful to bite the hand that feeds you. Professional teams and many college teams routinely feed reporters.

Sports journalism used to be even more parasitic toward the teams it covered than is the case now. At one time, reporters routinely traveled with a team at the team's expense. Good newspapers pay their own way today.

Even today, however, many reporters find it rewarding monetarily as well as psychologically to stay in favor with the teams and athletes they cover. Many teams pay reporters to write promotional pieces for game programs. And writing personality profiles or "inside" accounts for the dozens of sports magazines can be a profitable sideline.

Most sports reporters, and the editors who permit such activities, argue that they are not corrupted by what they are given. Most surely are not. But temptation is there for those who would succumb. Beyond that, any writer who takes more than information from those he or she covers is also likely to receive pressure, however subtle, from the givers.

Anywhere athletics is taken seriously, from the high schools of Texas to the stadiums of the National Football League, athletes and coaches are used to being given special treatment. Many think of themselves as being somehow different from and better than ordinary people. Many fans agree. Good reporters, though, regard sports as a beat, not a love affair.

Sports stories behind the story

- *Money.*
- *The real "why."*
- *The real "who."*

Those sports reporters maintain their distance from the people they cover, just as reporters on other beats do, by keeping their readers in mind. Readers want to know who won and how. But they also want to know about other sides of sports, sides that may require some digging to expose. Readers' questions about sports financing and the story behind the story too often go unanswered.

> *Money.* Accountants have become as essential to sports as athletes and trainers. Readers have a legitimate interest in everything from ticket prices to the impact of money on the actual contests.
> *The real "why."* When a key player is traded, as much as when a city manager is fired, readers want to know why. When athletes leave

school without graduating, find out why. When the public is asked to pay for the expansion of a stadium, tell the public why. One of the attractions of sports is that when the contest is over, the spectators can see who won and how. Often that is not true of struggles in government or business.

The real "who." Sports figures often appear to their fans, and sometimes to reporters, to be larger than life. In fact, athletics is an intensely human activity. Its participants have greater physical skills, and larger bank accounts, than most other people, but they are people.

As Tom Tuley, executive sports editor of *The Cincinnati Post*, observed, sports reporting is much more than covering the contests and perpetuating the myths.

Suggested Readings

Dart, John. *Deities & Deadlines: A Primer on Religion News Coverage*. Nashville, Tenn.: Freedom Forum First Amendment Center, 1995. This booklet is a primer on covering news of religion.

Mitford, Jessica. *Poison Penmanship: The Gentle Art of Muckraking*. New York: Vintage Books, 1957. A classic introduction on sources, especially the trade press. Includes 17 investigative pieces with commentary on the reporting techniques.

Royko, Mike. *Boss*. New York: New American Library, 1971. A classic, brilliantly written study of urban machine politics.

Sports Illustrated. Features the best continuing examples of how sports should be reported.

Weinberg, Steve, et al. *The Investigative Reporter's Handbook*, Fourth Edition. New York: Bedford/St. Martin's, 2002. The first comprehensive guide to using public records and documents, written by members of Investigative Reporters and Editors. A must for serious reporters.

Suggested Web Sites

www.journalismnet.com

A great resource for journalists. You'll find sources for almost any subject.

www.scout.cs.wisc.edu

The *Scout Report* is a weekly publication offering a selection of new and newly discovered Internet sources of interest to researchers and educators.

www.fool.com

The Motley Fool site was chosen by *Brill's Content* magazine as one of the best business and finance sites. Reporters can get the information that investors depend on.

www.opensecrets.org

An invaluable source for reporters covering elections, this site includes searchable campaign donation data from the nonpartisan Center for Responsive Politics.

www.poynter.org

We list this site repeatedly because it is so useful in so many ways. One feature is its links to nearly every professional journalism organization. The home page also includes a regular column of Web tips and sources.

www.ire.org

Investigative Reporters and Editors is the most important source of continuing education for public-affairs reporters. Among other things, IRE maintains an extensive library of some of the best stories done on nearly any topic, both print and broadcast. Also, it is a great place to begin networking with some of the most accomplished professional journalists.

Exercises

1. You've been assigned to cover city government. Do some background reading in your local newspaper and the other sources described in this chapter. Then write a memo describing what you expect to be the most important issues on your new beat and whom you expect to be your most important human resources.

2. Using a computer database, look up three recent national or international stories about a religious issue. Write a memo explaining how you would localize each story for your city. Include possible sources.

3. Examine how two or three major newspapers cover a national beat, such as Congress or a federal agency. What similarities and differences do you see between that work and local coverage? The topics will be different, but what about sources? Do you see any different focus on reader interests?

4. Analyze a local news story about science, medicine or the environment. Identify the sources. If you were reporting this story, what other sources would you consult? What specific questions would you try to get answered?

5. Assume that you've been assigned to cover your school's basketball program. Drawing on sources suggested above and favorites such as **espn.com** and **cnnsi.com,** write a memo describing at least five story ideas. Identify the best sources for each.

6. In your local newspaper find five stories that ran outside of the business section, and explain how they could have been turned into business stories. Identify sources that could be used.

11 Writing News for Radio and Television

When the first and then the second terrorist plane struck the World Trade Center in New York City on Sept. 11, 2001, few people first learned about the attack in the newspapers.

Radio and television did what they do best: They told the world the details of what happened. Moreover, they were able to repeat their reports and update their audience as the news developed. If you tuned in to CNN, you not only saw what happened and listened to commentary, but you were also able to see headlines under the picture and, under that, other news streaming by like a ticker tape. Somewhat like online news, you could pay attention to the news you were most interested in, and you had the feeling that you were up-to-date about what was happening. At times you probably heard the anchor on television say that you should go to the network's or station's Web site for more information.

Of course, radio and television are not always present to record the news while it is happening. Much of the time, these journalists must write and report news after it has occurred. Many, if not most, radio and television stations provide at least some news that is written for them by journalists working for the wire services or employed by the stations themselves.

Selecting and writing news for these media is different from selecting and writing news for print. This chapter explores the differences and discusses news reporting and news writing for television and radio. Even if your primary emphasis is not radio and television news, in this day of converging media in news rooms, you may be called upon to work with radio and television reporters and even to prepare copy for their reports. And if you are writing for radio or television news, almost certainly you will be called upon to contribute to the station's Web site. Radio and television stations have expanded their news operations to give background for stories they have no time for on air. Rather than interrupt programming when new facts arrive on a developing story, they often send listeners and viewers to their Web sites.

Emphases of radio and television news

- *Timeliness.*
- *Information.*
- *Audio or visual impact.*
- *People.*

CRITERIA FOR SELECTING RADIO AND TELEVISION NEWS

All of the news criteria you have learned so far apply to the selection of print and radio and television news. Four criteria distinguish radio and television news selection from print news: these newswriters emphasize timeliness above all other news values, information more than explanation, news with audio or visual impact, and people more than concepts.

Timeliness

The radio and television newswriter emphasizes one criterion of news value—timeliness—more than any other. *When* something happens often determines whether a news item will be used in a newscast. The breaking story receives top priority.

Radio and television news "goes to press" many times a day. If an event is significant enough, regular programming can be interrupted. The sense of immediacy influences everything in radio news, from what is reported to how it is reported. Often this is true of television news. Even when television and radio air documentaries or in-depth segments, they typically try to infuse a sense of urgency, a strong feeling of the present, an emphasis on what's happening now.

Information

Timeliness often determines why a news item is broadcast; time, or lack of it, determines how it is reported. Because air time is so precious, radio and television reporters are generally more concerned with information than with explanation. Most stories must be told in 20 to 30 seconds; rarely does a story run longer than two minutes. A minute of news read aloud is only 15 lines of copy, or about 150 words. After you subtract time for commercials, a half-hour newscast has only 22 minutes of news, which amounts to about one-half of the front page of a newspaper. Although these newswriters may never assume that their audience knows anything about a story, they may often have to assume that listeners or viewers will turn to newspapers, newsmagazines, or the Internet for further background and details.

> "Good television journalism presents news in the most attractive and lucid form yet devised by man."
> —*Bill Small,*
> *Veteran broadcaster,*
> *former president of CBS News*

Of course, because of the long success of *60 Minutes* and because of relatively low production costs, newsmagazine formats such as *20/20, 48 Hours* and *Dateline/NBC* continue to proliferate. *Dateline/NBC* now runs three nights a week, and there's even a *60 Minutes II*. They represent a somewhat different challenge to television newswriters, but even in a newsmagazine format, the writing resembles that done for television news.

Audio or Visual Impact

Another difference between radio and television and print news results from the technologies involved. Some news is selected for radio because a reporter has recorded an on-the-scene audio report. Some news is selected for television because it is visually appealing or exciting. For this reason, news of accidents or of fires that may get attention only in the records column of the newspaper may get important play on a television newscast. If a television crew returns with good pictures of an event, that event often receives prominence in the next newscast.

People

Another important difference between radio and television and print news selection is that radio and television more often attempt to tell the news through people. They follow the "classic writing formula" described by Rudolf Flesch in *The Art of Readable Writing:* Find a problem, find a person who is dealing with the problem, and tell us how he or she is doing. These journalists look for a representative person or family, someone who is affected by the story or who is a chief player. Thus, rather than using abstract concepts with no sound or visuals, television in particular humanizes the story. You can't shoot video of an issue.

WRITING RADIO AND TELEVISION NEWS

Radio and television writing emphasizes certain characteristics that newspaper and online writing do not, and story structure may vary.

Working in a visual medium, television reporters often humanize the news by allowing the people most affected by a story to tell it in their own words. Here, a television news crew interviews a woman at a protest at the Capitol building in Austin, Texas.

Characteristics of Radio and Television Newswriting

Because of the emphasis on timeliness, radio and television news-writers, like online writers, must emphasize immediacy and try to write very tightly and clearly. However, radio and television news-writers must work harder at achieving a conversational style.

> **Radio and television newswriting**
>
> - *Emphasizes immediacy.*
> - *Has a conversational style.*
> - *Is tightly phrased.*
> - *Is clear.*

Immediacy

Radio and television newswriters achieve a sense of immediacy in part by using the present tense as much as possible. Note the use of present-tense verbs (italicized) in this Associated Press story:

> The cost of a college education *is going* up.
>
> A study released today *says* declining tax revenues and the weak economy have led to tuition and fee increases at two- and four-year institutions this school year.
>
> Those increases *average* more than five percent.
>
> The figures were released by the nonprofit College Board, which *owns* the S-A-T college exam.
>
> The board *says* tuition and fees at four-year public institutions now *average* over four-thousand dollars a year. But College Board President Gaston Caperton *says* public colleges and universities *are* "still a remarkable value."
>
> The average yearly cost at a four-year private college also went up more than five percent to about 18-thousand. Financial aid *is* also *growing*. The board *says* a record 90 billion dollars in financial aid—including loans—was handed out during the 2001-2002 school year.

Notice that the verb "is going" in the lead is the progressive form of the present tense. Radio and television writing often uses the progressive form to indicate continuing action. Of course, to be accurate, the past tense is sometimes necessary, as in "The figures *were released* . . ." and "The average yearly cost . . . *went* up. . . ." Try to use the present perfect tense ("have led") more than the past tense because, again, the present perfect indicates past action that is continuing. It's what's happening—now.

Sometimes you stress immediacy by saying "just minutes ago" or, on a morning newscast, "this morning." If there is no danger of inaccuracy or of deceit, though, you can omit references to time. For example, if something happened yesterday, you may report it today like this:

```
The latest rash of fires in southern California is
under control.
```

But if you use the past tense in a lead, include the time element.

```
    The legislature sent a welfare reform bill to the
    governor late last night, finishing just in time
    before the spring recess.
```

The best way to avoid the past tense is to avoid yesterday's story. You can do that by updating yesterday's story. By leading with a new development or a new fact, you may be able to use the present tense.

Remember, radio and television are "live." Your copy must convey that important characteristic.

Conversational Style

"Write the way you talk" is questionable advice for most kinds of writing; however, with some exceptions, it is imperative for radio and television writing. "Read your copy aloud" is good advice for most kinds of writing; for radio and television writing, that's what it's all about.

Write so that your copy sounds good. Use simple, short sentences, written with transitive verbs in the active voice. Transitive verbs do things to things; they demand an object. People rarely use verbs in the passive voice when they talk; it usually sounds cumbersome and awkward. You don't go around saying, "Guess what I was just told by somebody." The verb "was told" is in the passive voice; the subject is acted upon. The preposition "by" also tells you the verb is in the passive voice. "Guess what somebody just told me" is active and more natural, less wordy and stronger. The verb "told" is in the active voice; the subject is doing the acting.

Because casual speech contains contractions, an occasional contraction is OK, too, as long as your pronunciation is clear. The negative "not" is more clearly understood than the contraction "n't." Conversational style also permits the use of occasional fragments. Sentences are sometimes strung together loosely with dashes and sometimes begin with the conjunction "and" or "but," as in the following example from the Associated Press:

> (Spring Lake, N.C.)—Aubrey Cox keeps giving police the slip. But he's had lots of practice— he's been doing it for 41 years.

Writing in conversational style does not mean using slang or colloquialisms or incorrect grammar. Nor does it mean using vulgar or off-color expressions. Remember that your audience includes people of all ages, backgrounds and sensitivities.

Tight Phrasing

You must learn to write in a conversational style without being wordy. That means you must condense. Cut down on adjectives and adverbs. Eliminating the passive voice gets rid of a couple of words. Make each word count.

Keeping it short means selecting facts carefully because often you don't have time for the whole story. Radio and television newscasters want good, tight writing that is easy to follow. Let's look at how a wire story written for newspapers can be condensed for radio and television. Here are the opening paragraphs of a 10-paragraph story from the AP newspaper wire:

DENVER (AP)—Teachers seeking better working conditions and a greater role in school governance struck today for the first time in 25 years, setting up picket lines outside the city's 107 public schools.

Officials worked to keep classes running for the district's 63,000 students with substitute teachers, administrators and regular teachers who declined to strike.

Picket lines went up at daybreak, less than 12 hours after teachers voted to go on strike by a nearly 2-to-1 margin. Talks had broken off Saturday.

Union President Leonard Fox estimated 3,000 of the district's 3,800 teachers stayed away from class. It was not immediately clear to what extent classes were disrupted. There were no reports of violence. School superintendent Irv Moskowitz said all schools were open and administrators were working to bring in more substitutes to staff more classes Tuesday.

"As time goes on, you'll see our programs become more efficient," Moskowitz said.

The story goes on to quote a picketing teacher and a sympathetic high-school student and ends with lots of dollar figures regarding salaries, raises and the pay package.

Here's how the story appeared on the Associated Press broadcast wire in its entirety:

(DENVER)—Denver school officials say all public schools are open today despite a strike by teachers.

Officials say the district's 63-thousand students are being taught by a combination of administrators, substitute teachers and regular teachers crossing the picket lines.

The union estimates three thousand of the district's 38-hundred teachers are on strike.

The teachers voted by nearly a two-to-one margin last night to reject a one-year contract offer.

This is the first teachers' strike in Denver in 25 years.

In the radio version, listeners are given the bare facts. They must turn to their newspapers or online news source for the details. One newspaper story is often two or three broadcast stories and can sometimes be a half dozen online stories.

In radio and television news, tight writing is important even when there is more time. These writers usually strive to waste no words, even in documentaries, which provide in-depth coverage of events.

Clarity

"Short words are best, and old words, when short, are best of all."
—*Winston Churchill*

Unlike newspaper and Internet news readers, television and radio news audiences can't go back over the copy. They see or hear it only once, and their attention waxes and wanes. So you must try hard to be clear and precise. However, all of the emphasis on condensing and writing tightly is useless if the message is not understood.

Clarity demands that you write simply, in short sentences filled with nickel-and-dime words. Don't look for synonyms. Don't be afraid to repeat words or phrases. Oral communication needs reinforcement. Avoid foreign words and phrases. Avoid phrases like "the former" and "the latter." Repeat proper names in the story rather than use pronouns. The listener can easily forget the name of the person to whom the pronoun refers.

When you are tempted to write a dependent clause in a sentence, make it an independent clause instead. Keep the subject close to the verb. Close the gap between the doer and the activity. This version doesn't do that:

```
        A man flagged down a Highway Patrol officer near
    Braden, Tennessee, today and told him a convict was
    hiding in his house. The prisoner, one of five who
    escaped from the Fort Pillow Prison on Saturday, sur-
    rendered peacefully.
```

The second sentence contains 12 words between the subject, "prisoner," and the main verb, "surrendered." By the time the broadcaster reaches the verb, many listeners will have forgotten what the subject was. The story is easier to understand this way:

```
        A man flagged down a Highway Patrol officer near
    Braden, Tennessee, today and told him a convict was
    hiding in his house. The prisoner surrendered peace-
    fully. He's one of five who escaped from the Fort
    Pillow Prison on Saturday.
```

The third sentence is still a complex sentence, but it is easily understood. The complex sentence is often just that—complex—only more so in oral communication.

Clarity also requires that you resist a clever turn of phrase. Viewers and listeners probably are intelligent enough to understand it, but a good figure of speech takes time to savor. If listeners pause to savor it (if they grasped it in the first place), they will not hear what follows. Clever columnists often fail as radio commentators.

Even more dangerous than figures of speech are numerical figures. Don't barrage the listener or viewer with a series of numbers. If you must use statistics, break them down so that they are understandable. For example, it is better to say that one of every six Americans smokes than to say there are 40 million smokers in the United States. You may be tempted to say how many billion dollars a federal program will cost, but you will help listeners understand if you say that it will cost the average wage earner $73 for each of the next five years.

Story Structure

Now that you know the characteristics of radio and television writing, let's examine the story structure. Writers must craft television and radio leads somewhat differently from the way they cast print and online leads. They also must construct special introductions and conclusions to video or audio segments and synchronize their words with taped segments.

Writing the Radio and Television Lead

Like newspaper reporters, television and radio reporters must grab the attention of their audience. Much of what you learned in Chapters 6 and 7 applies to radio and television leads. But be aware that people tend to be doing other things when listening to radio or watching television, so when you write for them, you strive to attract their attention in different ways.

One way is by preparing your audience for what is to come. You cue listeners to make sure they are tuned in. You introduce the story with a general statement, something that will pique the interest of the audience; then you go to the specifics. For example:

General statement	Things are far from settled for Springfield's teacher strike.
Specifics	School officials and union representatives did not agree on a contract yesterday. They will not meet again for at least a week.

ing about the subject or issue at hand. How can they hope to be fair and effective reporters if they are unprepared?

"Young reporters should know that their lack of preparedness is evident to viewers, not to mention being a dis-service to the field of journalism. It takes very little time to search the Internet for informa-tion, or to call a local expert and pre-interview them on the issue."

Lopez strongly recommends that reporters use tape recorders during inter-views. He says that not only will they be able to revisit the interview for writing purposes, but they will also be able to fact-check any quotes. "But do your-self a favor: *listen* to the interview—don't just hear what they are say-ing (and know the dif-ference between the two)."

He also says that reporters should begin writing when they are out in the field while the information is still fresh. "After you com-plete your script, read it aloud. This will help the flow of your report and eliminate wordi-ness.

"Television, and especially radio, re-porters must also be

(continued)

Sometimes the opening sentence will cover a number of news items:

```
There were several accidents in the Springfield
vicinity today.
```

"Cuing in" is only one method of opening a radio or television story. Other leads go immediately into the "what" and the "who," the "where" and the "when." In radio or television news the "what" is most important, followed by who did the "what." The time and place may be included in the lead, but seldom is the "why" or the "how." If time permits, the "why" and the "how" may come later in the story, but often they are omitted.

The first words of the lead are the most important. Don't keep the listener guessing what the story is about. Don't begin with a dependent clause or with prepositional phrases, as in this example:

```
With the strong backing of Governor Minner, a second
state spending-limit bill is scheduled for final
Senate action today.
```

The opening words are meaningless without what comes later. The lis-tener may not know what you are talking about. Here is a better way to introduce this story:

```
The Senate will vote today to make deeper cuts in
state spending—with the strong backing of Governor
Minner.
```

Be sure to "tee up," or identify, an unfamiliar name. By introducing a person, you prepare listeners for the name they otherwise may miss. Do it this way:

```
Veteran Kansas City, Kansas, businessman and civic
leader Ivar Larson died yesterday in a nursing home at
age 83.
```

Don't mislead. The opening words must set the proper tone and mood for the story. Attract attention; tease a little. Answer questions, but don't ask them. Lead the listener into your story.

Writing Lead-Ins and Wrap-Ups

Radio and television journalists must learn how to write a **lead-in** that introduces a taped excerpt from a news source or from another reporter. The functions of a lead-in are to set the scene by briefly telling the "where," the "when" and sometimes the "what," and to identify the source or reporter. The lead-in should contain something substantive. Here's an example:

```
A grand jury has decided not to charge a Springfield
teenager in the killing of his father. Jan Morrow
reports the panel believes the death was an accident.
```

Lead-ins should generate interest. Sometimes several sentences are used to provide background, as in the following:

```
We'll all be getting the official word this morning
on how much less our dollars bought last month. The
consumer price index for March is expected to show
another sharp rise in retail prices. The rate of
inflation was one percent in January and one-point-two
percent in February. Here's more on our inflation woes
from Bill McKinney.
```

Be careful not to include in the lead-in what is in the story. Just as a headline should not steal word for word the lead of a newspaper story, the lead-in should not rob the opening words of the correspondent. The writer must know the contents of the audio report in order to write a proper lead-in.

After the recorded report, you may want to wrap up the story before going on to the next item. The **wrap-up** is especially important in radio copy because there are no visuals to identify the person just heard. If the story reported by Evelyn Turner was about a meeting to settle a strike, you might wrap up Turner's report by adding information:

```
Turner reports negotiations will resume tomorrow.
```

A wrap-up such as this gives your story an ending and clearly separates it from the next story.

Writing for Videotape

Writing for a videotaped report begins with the selection of the subject and deciding how it is to be videotaped. The writing continues through the editing process and is done with the pictures clearly in mind.

Words and pictures must be complementary, never interfering with each other, never ignoring each other. Your first responsibility is to relate the words to the pictures. If you do not, viewers will not get the message because they will be wondering what the pictures are about.

"Writing a silence is as important as writing words. We don't rely on video enough."
—*John Hart, Veteran NBC broadcaster*

You can, however, stick too closely to the pictures by pointing out the obvious in a blow-by-blow account. You need to avoid both extremes and use what Russ Bensley, formerly of CBS News, calls the "hit-and-run" technique. This means that at the beginning of a scene or when a scene changes, you must tell the viewer where you are or what is happening. Once you are into the scene, the script may be more general and less closely tied to the pictures.

Suppose the report concerns the continuation of a hospital workers' strike and the opening scene shows picketers outside the hospital. You can explain the tape by saying:

```
Union members are still picketing Mercy Hospital
today as the hospital workers' strike enters its third
week.
```

Viewers now know two things that are not obvious in the tape: who is picketing and where. If the tape switches to people sitting around a table negotiating, you must again set the scene for viewers:

```
Meanwhile, hospital administrators and union leaders
are continuing their meetings--apparently without suc-
cess.
```

Once you have related the words to the pictures, you may add other details of the strike. You must not only comment on the tape but complete it as well. Part of completing it is giving the report a wrap-up or a strong ending. Don't be cute or obvious, but give the story an ending. Here's one possible ending for the strike story:

```
Strikers, administrators, patients and their fami-
lies agree on one sure effect of the strike--it's a
bad time to be sick.
```

Now that you know some principles of writing radio and television news, let's learn how to prepare the copy.

PREPARING RADIO AND TELEVISION COPY

Preparing copy to be read by a newscaster is different from preparing it for a typesetter. Your goals are to make the copy easy for the newscaster to read and easy for the audience to understand. What follows will help you accomplish these two goals.

Format

Most radio and television news editors want triple-spaced copy. Leave two to three inches on the top of the page and one to two inches on the bottom.

For radio copy, set your computer so that you have 70 characters to a line (see Figure 11.1). Each line will average about 10 words, and the newscaster will average 15 lines per minute. Start each story on a separate piece of paper. That way, the order of the stories can be rearranged, and stories can be added or dropped easily. If a story goes more than one page, write "MORE" in parentheses at the bottom of the page.

Write television copy on the right half of the page in a 40-character line (see Figure 11.2). Each line will average about six words,

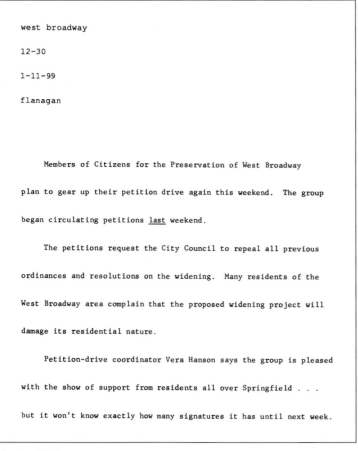

Figure 11.1
Sample of Radio Copy

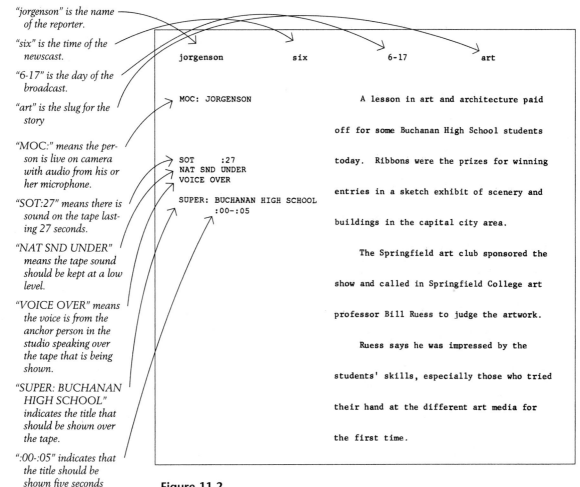

"jorgenson" is the name of the reporter.

"six" is the time of the newscast.

"6-17" is the day of the broadcast.

"art" is the slug for the story

"MOC:" means the person is live on camera with audio from his or her microphone.

"SOT:27" means there is sound on the tape lasting 27 seconds.

"NAT SND UNDER" means the tape sound should be kept at a low level.

"VOICE OVER" means the voice is from the anchor person in the studio speaking over the tape that is being shown.

"SUPER: BUCHANAN HIGH SCHOOL" indicates the title that should be shown over the tape.

":00-:05" indicates that the title should be shown five seconds after the report of this news item begins.

```
jorgenson            six            6-17          art


MOC: JORGENSON                    A lesson in art and architecture paid

                                 off for some Buchanan High School students

SOT      :27                     today.   Ribbons were the prizes for winning
NAT SND UNDER
VOICE OVER                       entries in a sketch exhibit of scenery and

SUPER: BUCHANAN HIGH SCHOOL      buildings in the capital city area.
       :00-:05
                                      The Springfield art club sponsored the

                                 show and called in Springfield College art

                                 professor Bill Ruess to judge the artwork.

                                      Ruess says he was impressed by the

                                 students' skills, especially those who tried

                                 their hand at the different art media for

                                 the first time.
```

Figure 11.2
Sample of Television Copy

and the newscaster will average about 25 lines per minute. Use the left side of the copy for audio or video information. This information, which is not to be read by the newscaster, is usually typed in all caps. The copy that is read generally appears upper- and lowercase. In television copy, number the stories, and start each story on a separate page. If a story goes more than one page, write "MORE" in parentheses at the bottom of the page.

Do not hyphenate words, and be sure to end a page with a complete sentence or, if possible, with a complete paragraph. Then if the next page should be missing in the middle of a newscast, the newscaster could at least end with a complete sentence or paragraph.

At many stations, you prepare copy for a **videoprompter,** an electronic device that projects the copy over the camera lens so the newscaster can read it while appearing to look straight into the lens.

Date the first page of your script, and type your last name in the upper left-hand corner of every page. Stations vary regarding these directions. The newscast producer determines the **slug** for a story and its placement. Some producers insist that the slug contain the time of the broadcast. If a story continues to a second page, write under the slug "first **add**" or "second add," or "page 2," "page 3" and so forth.

Stations with computerized newsrooms may use scripting software that alters these formats somewhat. For information about how a television station works and for tips about writing for television news, take a look at **www.scripps.ohiou.edu/actv-7/manual/**, a guide used by television students at Ohio University's E. W. Scripps School of Journalism's television station.

Names and Titles

In radio and television style, unlike that followed by newspapers, well-known names, even on first reference, are not given in full. You may say Senator Dole of North Carolina or Governor Napolitano of Arizona. Don't use middle initials unless they are a natural part of someone's name (Edward R. Murrow) or unless they are necessary to distinguish two people with the same first and last names, as with George W. Bush.

Titles should always precede names so that listeners are better prepared to hear the name. When you use titles, omit the first name and middle initial. For example, you would say "Federal Reserve Chairman Greenspan" and "Justice Ginsburg."

Pronunciation

You must help the newscaster pronounce the names of people and places correctly. To do this, write out difficult names phonetically in parentheses. MSNBC has its own reference list, and many individual stations have their own handbooks. Look up difficult names in unabridged dictionaries. If you don't find the name there, call the person's office, or the consulate or embassy. If the name is of a U.S. town, try calling someone in that town. There is no rhyme or reason to the way some people pronounce their names or to the way some place-names are pronounced. Never assume. Never try to figure it out. Find out. Here's an example of how you should write out difficult names:

```
(Zamboanga, Philippines-AP)-There's been another
deadly bombing in the Philippines.

A bomb exploded near a Roman Catholic church in the
southern city of Zamboanga (zahm-BWAHNG'-gah), killing
one person and injuring 12.
```

Perhaps most people would know how to pronounce "Lima" (LEE-mah), Peru, but not everyone would correctly pronounce "Lima" (LIE-mah), Ohio. You must note the difference between "NEW-erk," N.J., and "new-ARK," Del., both spelled "Newark." And who would guess that "Pago Pago" is pronounced "PAHNG-oh PAHNG-oh"?

Abbreviations

Generally, you do not use abbreviations in your copy. It is easier to read a word written out than to read its abbreviation. Do not abbreviate the names of states, countries, months, days of the week or military titles.

When you do abbreviate a name or phrase, use hyphens instead of periods to prevent the newscaster from mistaking the final period in the abbreviation for the period at the end of the sentence. You may abbreviate United States when you use it as an adjective—"U-S" would be the correct form. If an abbreviation is well known—"U-N," "G-O-P," "F-B-I"—you may use it. Hyphens are not used in acronyms—abbreviations such as "NATO" and "HUD" that are pronounced as one word.

You may use the abbreviations "Dr.," "Mr.," "Mrs." and "Ms.," and "a.m." and "p.m."

Symbols and Numbers

Do not use symbols in your copy because newscasters can read a word more easily than they can interpret a symbol. Never use such symbols as the dollar sign ($) and the percent sign (%). Don't even use the abbreviation for number ("no.").

Numbers can be a problem for both the announcer and the listener. As in newspaper style, write out numbers one through nine. Also write out eleven, because 11 might not be easily recognized as a number. Use figures for 10 and from 12 to 999. The eye can easily take in a three-digit number, but write out the words "thousand," "million" and "billion"—for example, "3,800,000" becomes "three million, 800 thousand." Write out fractions ("two-and-a-half million dollars") and decimal points ("three-point-two percent").

Some stations have exceptions. Figures often are used to give the time ("3:20 a.m."), sports scores ("ahead 5 to 2") and statistics, market reports ("an increase in the Dow Jones Industrial Average of 2-point-8 points"), and addresses ("30-0-2 Grand Street"; in common speech no one would give an address as "three thousand two").

Ordinarily, you may round off big numbers. Thus "48-point-3 percent" should be written "nearly half." But when dealing with human beings, don't say "more than one hundred" if 104 people died in an earthquake.

Use *"st," "nd," "rd"* and *"th"* after dates: "August 1st," "September 2nd," "October 3rd," "November 4th." Make the year easy to pronounce: "June 9th, 1973."

Quotations and Attributions

Rarely use direct quotations and quotation marks. Because it is difficult and awkward to indicate to listeners which words are being quoted, use indirect quotes or a paraphrase instead.

If it is important for listeners to know the exact words of a quotation (as when the quoted words are startling, uncomplimentary or possibly libelous), introduce the quote by saying "in his words," "with these words," "what she called" or "he put it this way." Most writers prefer to avoid the formal "quote" and "unquote," though "quote" is used more often than "unquote." Here's an example:

```
    In Smith's words, quote, "There is no way to undo
    the harm done."
```

When you must use a direct quotation, the attribution always should precede the quotation. Because listeners cannot see the quotation marks, they will have no way of knowing the words are a direct quote. If by chance they did recognize the words as a quote, they would have no idea who was being quoted. For the same reason, the attribution should precede an indirect quote as well.

If you must use a direct quotation, keep it short. If the quote is long and using it is important, use a tape of the person saying it. If you are compelled to use a quote of more than a sentence in your copy, break it up with phrases such as "Smith went on to say" or "and still quoting the senator." For television, put longer or more complicated quotes on a full-screen graphic display as you read it.

Punctuation

In radio and television copy, less punctuation is good punctuation. The one exception is the comma. Commas help the newscaster pause at appropriate places. Use commas, for example, after introductory phrases referring to time and place, as in the following:

```
    In Paris, three Americans on holiday met their death
today when their car overturned and caught fire.

    Last August, beef prices reached an all-time low.
```

Sometimes three periods are used in place of a comma. Three periods also take the place of parentheses and the semicolon. They signal a pause and are easily visible. The same is true of the dash—typed as two hyphens. Note the dash in the following example:

```
    But the judge grumbled about the news coverage, and
most prospective jurors agreed--saying the news cover-
age has been prone to overstatement, sensationalism
and errors.
```

The only punctuation marks you need are the period, comma, question mark, dash, hyphen and, rarely, quotation marks. To make the copy easier to read, add the hyphen to some words even when the dictionary does not use it: anti-discrimination, co-equal, non-aggression.

Stations vary in writing style and in the preparation of copy. But if you learn what is presented here, you will be well-prepared. Differences will be small, and you will adapt to them easily.

Suggested Readings

Bliss, Edward Jr. and Hoyt, James L. *Writing News for Broadcast*, Third Edition. New York: Columbia University Press, 1994. A classic text that excels in good writing.

Block, Mervin. *Writing Broadcast News—Shorter, Sharper, Stronger*, Second Edition. Chicago: Bonus Books, 1997. An excellent book by a former network newswriter.

Stephens, Mitchell. *Broadcast News*, Fourth Edition. New York: Holt, Rinehart and Winston, 1998. Covers all aspects of broadcast writing and the business of broadcast news.

White, Ted. *Broadcast News Writing, Reporting and Producing*, Third Edition. Boston: Focal Press, 2001. The best book on all aspects of broadcast newswriting.

Suggested Web Sites

www.nab.org

Site of the 75-year-old National Association of Broadcasters. A wonderful resource for all kinds of radio- and TV-related information, including a career center.

www.newscript.com

This site's purpose is to help radio journalists improve their skills as writers and anchors.

www.tvrundown.com

Provides news links to many specialized areas such as medical news. Includes information about television news and job offerings.

www.rtndf.org

The Radio and Television News Directors Foundation promotes excellence in electronic journalism through research, education and professional training. Excellent reports, useful links.

www.newstrench.com

This "Thunder & Lightning News Service" calls itself "the site for TV news gathering . . . and the people who do it." Offers resources for gathering TV news.

Exercises

1. Watch a local evening television newscast. Make a simple list of the news stories. Then try to find those stories in the next morning's local newspaper and compare the coverage.

2. Check to see if the following AP stories written for broadcast follow acceptable broadcast style. Are they technically correct? Do they emphasize immediacy? Change the copy where you think necessary.
   a. (Nice, France-AP) — Positive thinking might make cancer patients feel better, but it won't help their chances of surviving the disease.

      A new study finds that a positive outlook won't improve a person's survival rate.

      The British study looked at whether psychologist-run support groups kept patients alive.

      Researchers analyzed eleven studies that included a total of 15-hundred patients.

      The lead researcher says there was no evidence at all that support groups prolong life in cancer patients.

      However, experts say it's still worthwhile for patients to try to improve their mindsets, perhaps by joining a cancer support group, because it does make them feel better.

      The findings were presented today at a meeting of the European Society of Medical Oncology in Nice, France.
   b. (Atlanta-AP) — Before heading to jail, an Atlanta pastor used his last sermon to encourage his flock to continue whipping disobedient children.

      The Reverend Arthur Allen Junior — convicted of cruelty to children — took off his belt and waved it behind a 14-year-old boy as part of a mock whipping at the House of Prayer.

      Allen and four church members were found guilty Thursday of aggravated assault and cruelty to children for whipping two boys in front of the congregation in February of 2001. The defendants received prison sentences ranging from 20 to 90 days, plus fines and mandatory parenting classes.

      The pretend whipping yesterday mocked a judge's order that Allen and his followers use only an open hand on their own children's buttocks.

3. Rewrite the following AP newspaper briefs in broadcast writing style. Assume that the news is current and that you have time for one paragraph of four or five lines for each story.
   a. ZURICH, Switzerland (AP) — Thieves have stolen seven Picasso paintings worth more than $40 million from an art gallery, police said today.

      Zurich police said the break-in occurred over the weekend through the cellar of a neighboring house.

      A police statement said two works, "Seated Woman," and "Christ of Montmartre," were the most valuable of the paintings stolen. Both paintings were stolen in 1991 from a Zurich gallery and were recovered the following year.
   b. SEAL BEACH, Calif. (AP) — State authorities have disputed a retirement community's rules on keeping its pools and golf courses off-limits to underage users — whom it defines as being under 55.

The State Fair Employment and Housing Department filed a complaint against Leisure World after Alfred and Mary Gray objected last year to a no-access policy for younger spouses at Leisure World's recreational facilities. Mary Gray was 51 at the time.

Operators of Seal Beach Leisure World, whose 9,000 residents comprise one-third of the city's population, have decided to contest the federal Unruh Civil Rights Act cited by state officials, administrator Bill Narans said.

4. Read a copy of a current newspaper; then write a five-minute newscast. Pay special attention to lead-ins and wrap-ups. (Do not include sports material in your broadcast.)

12 Writing for Public Relations

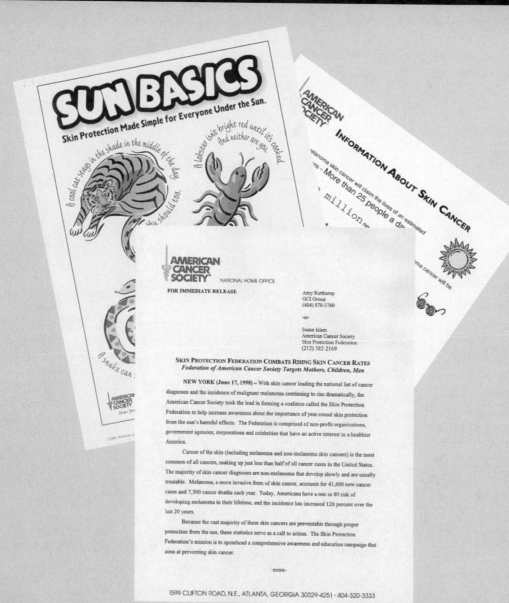

Public Relations: Strategies and Tactics, by Wilcox, Cameron, Ault and Agee, lists these activities as common to those who work in public relations—and all the duties now connected with the Web. Notice how many of them involve writing either directly or indirectly.

> *Advise management on policy*
> *Plan and conduct meetings*
> *Participate in policy decisions*
> *Prepare publicity items*
> *Plan public-relations programs*
> *Talk to editors and reporters*
> *Sell programs to top management*
> *Hold press conferences*
> *Get cooperation of middle management*
> *Write feature articles*
> *Get cooperation from other employees*
> *Research public opinion*
> *Listen to speeches*
> *Plan and manage events*
> *Make speeches*

(continued)

You may not be planning a career in news—you may know already that you are headed toward some area of public relations. Or, as happens to many people, perhaps you will work in news organizations for a while, but at some point you may decide to switch to public relations. Or perhaps you already are writing for public relations.

Few disagree that the skill most required of public-relations people is good writing. Your writing skills should include newswriting, and you should be familiar with the way news operations work. That's why journalism schools traditionally require a course in newswriting for students interested in public relations, and that's why many public-relations professionals like to hire people with some news experience. Only by studying news and how news organizations handle it will you be successful in public relations or in offices of public information. Knowing how reporters are taught to deal with news releases will help you write better releases. Of course, studying news also helps you enormously in the advertising world and in what is now frequently called strategic marketing or strategic communication.

Skilled public-relations or public-information practitioners know how to write news, and they apply all the principles of good newswriting in their news releases. A good news release meets the criteria of a good news story.

These same professionals know that working for an organization and doing internal and external communications demands a different perspective and, in many cases, a different kind of writing. In many ways, of course, good writing is good writing, and what you have learned so far applies to public-relations writing. But you also will be called upon to do writing that is different from the kinds of writing done by those who work for news organizations.

PUBLIC-RELATIONS WRITING: A DIFFERENT APPROACH

Let's begin with a few definitions and distinctions. Rex Harlow, the "father of public-relations research" and perhaps the first full-time public-relations educator, claimed to have found 472 definitions of public relations. The 1978 World Assembly of Public Relations in Mexico came up with this definition: "Public relations is the art and social science of analyzing trends, predicting their consequences, counseling organization leaders and implementing planned programs of action which will serve both the organization's and public interest."

In *Public Relations: Strategies and Tactics,* authors Wilcox, Cameron, Ault and Agee claim these key words are found in all the definitions of public relations:

- *Deliberate:* the "activity is intentional . . . designed to influence, gain understanding, provide feedback, and obtain feedback."
- *Planned:* "organized . . . systematic, requiring research and analysis."
- *Performance:* "based on actual policies."
- *Public interest:* "mutually beneficial to the organization and to the public."
- *Two-way communication:* "equally important to solicit feedback."
- *Management function:* "an integral part of decision-making by top management."

Conduct tours
Write speeches for others
Write letters
Obtain speakers for organizational meetings
Plan and write booklets, leaflets, reports and bulletins
Attend meetings
Design posters
Plan films and video-tapes
Greet visitors
Plan and prepare slide presentations
Screen charity requests
Plan and produce exhibits
Evaluate public-relations programs
Take pictures or super-vise photographers
Conduct fund-raising drives
Make awards

Public relations, then, is not just publicity, which seeks to get the media to respond to an organization's interests. Nor is it advertising, which pays to get the attention of the public, or marketing, which combines a whole host of activities to sell a product, service or idea. Advertising and marketing are concerned with sales.

If you wish to write in the field of public relations, you have many areas to choose to work in. Here are some of the specialties:

- *Media relations:* seeking publicity and answering questions posed by the media.
- *Government affairs:* spending time with legislatures and regulatory agencies and doing some lobbying.
- *Public affairs:* engaging in matters of public policy.
- *Industry relations:* relating to other firms in an industry and with trade associations.
- *Investor or financial or shareholder relations:* working to maintain investor confidence and good relationships with the financial world.

And the list goes on. Whoever said public-relations writing was dull knew nothing of the various worlds these professionals inhabit.

One more term must be introduced before proceeding. More and more today you see the term "**strategic communication**" replacing "public relations." Some say that one simple reason for this change is that the term "public relations" has always suffered a "PR" problem. But, of course, the reasons are much more serious than that.

The demands made of public-relations professionals are greater today than they were a generation ago. As Ronald Smith explains in *Strategic Planning for Public Relations,*

> No longer is it enough merely to know *how* to do things. Now the effective communicator needs to know *what* to do, *why* and how to *evaluate* its effectiveness. Public relations professionals used to be called upon mainly for tasks such as writing news releases, making speeches, producing videos, publishing newsletters, organizing displays and so on. Now the profession demands competency in conducting research, making decisions and solving problems. The call now is for strategic communicators.

In short, the strategic communicator must take a more scientific approach, do some research, make careful choices, and when finished, evaluate the effectiveness of the completed program. Such a communicator would certainly be expected to write clearly and precisely, but differently from reporters.

Journalists will debate forever whether anyone can be truly objective when writing a story. Most settle the argument by saying what is demanded is fairness. Nevertheless, in traditional reporting, writers should strive not to have a point of view. Reporters should not set out to prove something. Certainly they should not be an advocate for a point of view. They should get the facts, and let the facts speak for themselves.

By contrast, columnists have a point of view, and good ones find ways to support it convincingly. Editorial writers use facts to persuade people to change their minds, or to confirm their opinions, or to get people to do something, or to stop doing something.

That's also what public-relations writers do. Though sometimes they wish only to inform their audiences, they most often want to do what the editorial writers do—persuade the audience to a particular position.

However, there's one major difference. Journalists serve the public. Public-relations writers work for an organization or for a client other than a news operation. Their job is to make that organization or client appear in the best possible light. Effective public-relations writers do not ignore facts, even when they are harmful or detrimental to the cause they are promoting. But they are promoting a cause or looking out for the best interests of the people for whom they are working. As a result, they will interpret all news, even bad news, in the most favorable light.

Public-relations writers work much the way attorneys work for clients—as advocates. They don't lie or even distort, but perhaps they play down certain facts and emphasize others. In its "official statement of public relations," the Public Relations Society of America states: "Public relations helps our complex, pluralistic society to reach decisions and function more effectively by contributing to mutual understanding among groups and institutions. It serves to bring private and public policies into harmony. . . . The public-relations practitioner acts as a counselor to management and as a mediator, helping to translate private aims into reasonable, publicly acceptable policy and action."

For a good discussion of what public relations is, check the Web site of the Public Relations Student Society of America at **www.prssa.org.** The Public Relations Society of America has a "Code of Professional Standards for the Practice of Public Relations." The code requires members to "adhere to the highest standard of accuracy and truth, avoiding extravagant claims or unfair comparisons and giving credit for ideas and words borrowed from others." It also requires members not to "knowingly disseminate false or misleading information." See **www.prsa.org/profstd.html** for the rest of the code.

PUBLIC-RELATIONS WRITING: A DIVERSITY OF TASKS

Like all good communicators, public-relations personnel are concerned with three things: the message, the audience and the media to deliver the message.

The Message

Like a good reporter, you must know the message your organization wants to send. That message may be a product, a program or the organization itself. For every message you work on, you must first know what you hope to accomplish, even if your purpose is just to inform.

That's why it is so important for you to be a reporter first, to know how to gather information and to do so quickly. Like any reporter, you may be called upon in an instant to become something of an expert on a topic that you may never have heard of before. The public-relations staff on the Disney Magic of the Disney Cruise Lines may never have heard of the Norwalk virus, but suddenly 104 of the 2,485 passengers and 19 of the 1,003 crew members were suffering from nausea, vomiting, diarrhea, abdominal pain and some fever and headache. All at once, all of the skills of the public-relations professional were called into service.

This incident followed the news of another ship, the Amsterdam, of the Holland America Line, which was being disinfected at Port Everglades in Fort Lauderdale, Fla., after more than 500 passengers and crew members succumbed to the Norwalk virus on its last four cruises.

Perhaps some public-relations effort caused this lead to appear in a *New York Times* story: "Despite recent outbreaks of gastrointestinal illness on cruise ships, federal health officials pronounced the ships safe yesterday and said they would not advise people to delay or avoid taking cruises."

The Audience

Almost as important as knowing all you can about the message is knowing the audience to whom you are directing it. The better you target your audience, the more effective you will be. As in advertising, demographics and psychographics determine the way you write your message, the language you choose, and the simplicity or complexity of the piece you are creating.

Who are those people, what are their attitudes, and what do they do for work and recreation? You will answer these questions somewhat

---

Journalists, especially television journalists, are sometimes accused of creating stories by their very presence, or at least of fanning the flames. Creating news, however, is not in their job description, but a large part of public relations is doing exactly that. Here's a list of how to create news from Wilcox, Cameron, Ault and Agee's Public Relations: Strategies and Tactics:

1. *Tie in with news events of the day.*
2. *Cooperate with another organization on a joint project.*
3. *Tie in with a newspaper or broadcast station on a mutual project.*
4. *Conduct a poll or survey.*
5. *Issue a report.*
6. *Arrange an interview with a celebrity.*
7. *Take part in a controversy.*
8. *Arrange for a testimonial.*
9. *Arrange for a speech.*
10. *Make an analysis or prediction.*
11. *Form and announce names for committees.*
12. *Hold an election.*
13. *Announce an appointment.*
14. *Celebrate an anniversary.*
15. *Issue a summary of facts.*

16. *Tie in with a holiday.*
17. *Make a trip.*
18. *Make an award.*
19. *Hold a contest.*
20. *Pass a resolution.*
21. *Appear before a public body.*
22. *Stage a special event.*
23. *Write a letter.*
24. *Release a letter you received (with permission).*
25. *Adapt national reports and surveys for local use.*
26. *Stage a debate.*
27. *Tie in to a well-known week or day.*
28. *Honor an institution.*
29. *Organize a tour.*
30. *Inspect a project.*
31. *Issue a commendation.*
32. *Issue a protest.*

differently if you write for internal audiences (employees or the managers of those employees) or external audiences (the media, shareholders, constituents, volunteers, consumers or donors).

The first concern of the Disney public-relations staff was the people on the cruise ship Disney Magic. They needed to communicate to the passengers, of course, and they needed to communicate with the captain and crew to tell them how to deal with the situation, how to keep from getting ill themselves, what to say, what not to say. And then there were all of the other media bombarding Disney with questions—not just the news media but travel magazines, Web sites, newsletters and cruise magazines.

In addition, there were moment-to-moment decisions about what to do with the people on board. How do you tell people to be careful (people stopped shaking hands when introducing themselves and touched elbows instead), without making them panic? How many extra perquisites do you offer them? For example, Disney offered to fly sick passengers home, but only one couple accepted. How many people would be demanding their money back or some compensation? How many lawsuits would be filed?

After 14 hours of cleaning at Port Canaveral, the Disney Magic set sail again with 2,400 passengers and 800 crew members. Three days into the cruise, 85 passengers were ill. A Disney Cruise Lines spokesman told the *Orlando Sentinel*, on Nov. 27, 2002, "Federal health inspectors didn't really expect the illness to be completely gone after we cleaned last Saturday. You can't turn this on and off like a faucet."

Did they tell the passengers that before embarking?

On the previous Disney Magic cruise, sick passengers had been charged $90 for a suppository and a shot, so some did not go for treatment. On this cruise, the Center for Disease Control was providing free medical care, although David Forney, a supervisor at the Disease Control Center, said that Disney "was not real proactive in making sure passengers knew that."

The *Sentinel* story concluded: "Jaronski (the Disney spokesman) said late Tuesday that he couldn't immediately comment on the issue of medical care last week."

The cruise ended three days early with 218 ill with the virus. This time, Disney said it was canceling the ship's next cruise and giving it a week for a thorough clean-up.

Nevertheless, on the Disney Web site, nothing was said about the problems the cruise line was having until a couple of weeks later. Then a response to a question in the FAQ (Frequently Asked Questions) assured readers not to be afraid to take a cruise.

Carnival Cruise Lines was similarly silent. On the day the Carnival ship Fascination disembarked 200 sick passengers and crew members, the company Web site—including the "Press Room," "News Releases," "Virtual Press Kit" and "Carnival Facts" sections—made no mention of the Norwalk virus.

The Media

Once you have mastered the message or product and targeted the audience, you then have to choose the best media by which to deliver the message to the audience. For a message that nearly everyone wants or needs to know, television may be your best medium. Procter & Gamble spends millions advertising soap on television because everyone needs soap. Television offers color and motion; television can show rather than tell.

Radio listeners are usually loyal to one radio station. They will listen to your message over and over. The more often they hear it, the more likely they are to retain it.

Print is better for complicated messages and sometimes for delicate messages. Some argue that print still has more credibility than other media and that people can come back again and again to a print message.

More and more people are getting the information and products they need online. And here you have all the media in one medium. Remember, people who are online generally are better educated and more affluent than those who are not. They love the control they have over the messages they find there. They can "click here" on only the information they want, and they can do so in any order they choose.

What is so wonderful (and so frightening) about "new" media is that you are dealing with a mass medium that is highly individualized; you are in the world of what has been called " mass-customization." You must present the message at different levels to different people so that different people feel they have choices, so that everyone feels as if you are writing only to him or her. It's all about individual choices and involving your readers so they interact with you. You will study more about writing online in the next chapter. Just remember, communicating online ideally means that you have all the means of communicating all in one medium.

If you work in internal communications, you may decide to publish a newsletter or magazine. A large number of corporations are now communicating with employees throughout the day by an intranet, an internal online service accessible only to them. As a result, a surprisingly large number of organizations have ceased to publish any regularly published internal print publications.

For messages that need more explanation, such as health-care matters, perhaps a pointed brochure will best do the job. Externally, for matters that may concern the community, you may want to use billboards in addition to paid ads in publications or radio and television. Or you may choose to write news releases and leave it to others to interpret your message.

Sometimes, however, there's no quick fix. What took a long time to build can come tumbling down quickly, and then a long re-building process is necessary.

The cruise industry became incredibly popular in a relatively short time due to a top-rated television program called *The Love Boat*. For years, the industry could not build ships fast enough to fill the demand. Fear of terrorism slowed demand somewhat, and now perhaps the fear of contagious disease will slow it some more. How will public-relations professionals use the media to bring back the industry? Probably, through a long, organized campaign.

The Media Campaign

Research shows that the more media you use, the better chance you have to succeed. That's why effective public-relations people, like those in advertising, think in terms of campaigns and strategies. A campaign assumes that you can't just tell an audience once what you want them to learn, retain and act on. You need a strategy to reach a goal that may take days, weeks, months or even years to attain. Which medium do you use to introduce the subject, which media will you engage for follow-up and details, which aspects of the message are best suited for which media? You accomplish little by sending out the message once and in only one medium. If you send the message in a mix of media in a carefully timed or orchestrated way, the results will be exponentially greater.

Public-relations writers adapt messages to the whole spectrum of media available. To do this, you must learn what each medium does best. Perhaps Marshall McLuhan was exaggerating when he wrote that the medium is the message, but no one doubts there is a great deal of truth to his statement.

You may be hired as a speechwriter or do something as specialized as writing the organization's annual report. Corporations and institutions such as hospitals and universities hire thousands of communicators to get their messages out to the public. Or you may work for a public-relations agency that is hired to do this work for organizations.

Regardless of the means or media you choose to use, your job is to have good relations with the public. You do that best by trying to establish mutually beneficial relationships and by trying to set up win-win situations. All of this is best achieved when you make it possible for two-way communications. You must allow and encourage your

FOR IMMEDIATE RELEASE

Contact: Jim Brown
              Director of Public Affairs
              (520) 529-5317 or jimbrown@mdausa.org

MDA OFFERS NEW VIDEOS ON RESPIRATORY CARE

TUCSON, Ariz., May 12, 2000 — The Muscular Dystrophy Association has produced two new videotapes to help people with neuromuscular diseases and medical professionals better manage breathing problems resulting from the muscle-wasting disorders.

"Breathe Easy: A Respiratory Guide for People with Neuromuscular Diseases" is an authoritative yet easy-to-digest resource to help families understand the importance of monitoring and, when necessary, assisting the respiratory systems of loved ones affected by muscular dystrophy, amyotrophic lateral sclerosis or other neuromuscular diseases. These progressive disorders weaken the diaphragm and other muscles involved in breathing, leading to susceptibility to respiratory infections or acute respiratory failure.

Geared to neuromuscular disease patients and their families, the 28-minute "Breathe Easy" video explains techniques for maintaining respiratory function and equipment options to assist with ventilation. Several physicians and a clinical nurse specialist present the information, which is accompanied by illustrations of each device or technique, and by comments from people with neuromuscular diseases who use them.

"Breathe Easy" is available on loan through any of MDA's 218 offices nationwide. A 45-second preview of the educational video can be viewed by visiting the "What's New" section of MDA's Web site at www.mdausa.org. This site includes a zip code locator for local office information to order the full-length video. "Breathe Easy" can also be ordered through MDA National Headquarters at 1-800-572-1717.

"Almost everyone affected by a neuromuscular disease will experience respiratory distress at some time, and many will ultimately succumb to respiratory failure," said Dr. Leon I. Charash, Chairman of the MDA Medical Advisory Committee.

– More –

People Help MDA...Because MDA Helps People
Muscular Dystrophy Association • 3300 East Sunrise Drive, Tucson, AZ 85718-3208 • (520) 529-2000 • Fax (520) 529-5300
JERRY LEWIS, National Chairman • ROBERT M. BENNETT, President • ROBERT ROSS, Senior Vice President & Executive Director

This is a traditional news release. Note the "For Immediate Release," the date and the contact person. At the bottom of the page, note also the organization's contact information, executive information and Web site address.

various publics to have a voice in what you are trying to achieve. If you involve your audience in what you are trying to achieve, your chances of achieving it increase. Establishing a Web site is an excellent way to get people's ideas and reactions. Of course, you must find ways (notices on bulletin boards, brochures, newsletters, etc.) to make your Web site known.

Corporations and organizations sometimes have newsletters for their employees, such as this prize-winning publication of Merck & Co. edited by Sharyn Bearse. Merck also publishes *The Daily* each working day and has an intranet that is accessible only to employees. Bearse is also in charge of producing the company's annual report.

> *"If you don't understand good journalistic style and format (who, what, when, where and why) for writing a press release, you harm your company and yourself."*
>
> — *G.A. Marken,*
> *President of Marken Communications,*
> *Public Relations Quarterly*

PUBLIC-RELATIONS WRITING: A MATTER OF PERSUASION

Most of the time, your writing will attempt to persuade people. You need to study the techniques of persuasion and to use them carefully. To persuade people, you need to believe three things:

1. *People are essentially good.* You need to be convinced of that and to appeal to people's basic goodness and fairness.
2. *People are intelligent or at least educable.* Don't talk down to people; don't assume that you can trick or fool them.
3. *People are changeable.* You must believe not only that people are changeable but also that you can change them.

First, more than anything else, you need to establish and maintain your credibility and the credibility of the organization you represent. Aristotle wrote that the character of the speaker is the most essential and powerful component of persuasion. Without a doubt, character is the most important thing public-relations people need to have and to develop. A sterling reputation takes a long time to build—and can be lost in an instant.

Second, you must assume goodwill on the part of your audience. You cannot persuade people by beating up on them, by calling them names or by considering them the enemy. This is particularly true regarding your attitude toward the press. Too many public-relations professionals consider the press the enemy, not to be trusted with the truth, to be stonewalled at every opportunity.

If you or your family had turned to the Disney or Carnival Web sites to book a cruise in November or December 2002, you would have seen "business as usual." There was no information about problems of illness and no warnings whatsoever. If you had not been reading the Florida newspapers or paid special attention to the news, you might not have heard of the problems the cruise lines were having—even though the Center for Disease Control said there was some indication that the virus might be brought on to the ships by passengers who were not feeling well before they set sail but were afraid to admit it for fear of not getting their fares returned.

Contrast this with what the University of North Carolina-Chapel Hill did when it learned that People for the Ethical Treatment of Animals had planted a spy in one of its animal-research facilities. The woman had worked there for eight months and secretly videotaped animals and the staff at work. PETA's goal was to defeat the Helms amendment to the 2002 farm bill that would have extended USDA authority for animal welfare to cover laboratory mice, rats and birds. That change, according to those opposed to it, would have meant a great deal more paperwork for the research team and little improvement in animal care. PETA held a press conference and set up a Web site showing lurid photos and making claims of animal cruelty and neglect.

The university's response was rapid, candid and forthright. On the day PETA broke the story, Tony Waldrop, vice chancellor for research, and other university officials held a press conference, promised a thorough investigation and opened the facility in question to reporters. The university did not attempt to deny or discredit the PETA claims. The press had no hint of a cover-up to feed on, and university officials, at least, considered media coverage to be fair and factual, and the story faded from the news in a couple of days. The farm bill passed with the Helms amendment intact.

Meanwhile, the university lived up to its promise to investigate. It spent several thousand hours in internal investigations, and Waldrop commissioned a panel of three outside experts to do an independent review. The university then presented a 40-page report to the federal Office of Laboratory Animal Welfare, and the local press summarized it—again, in a fair, even-handed manner. The report was then published in the university's research magazine: a candid account of what PETA claimed, what the university found in its investigations, and what it did to correct the problem.

That's how public relations can, should and does work.

WRITING NEWS RELEASES THAT GET ATTENTION

Even the smallest newspaper and radio or TV station gets dozens of news releases daily. How do you break through the clutter and get listened to or looked at by the gatekeepers on the news desks? If you send news releases online, your problem is still the same.

> *"Employers want people who can write and communicate ideas—who can pull complex or fragmented ideas together into coherent messages. This requires not only technical skill but also intelligence. It also requires a love of writing."*
>
> —*Thomas H. Bivins,*
> Public Relations Writing

Here are some guidelines to help you get your messages to your intended audiences:

■ *Know what news is and how to write it.* If you are headed toward a career in public relations or public information, you probably are taking this newswriting course to help you understand the principles of news. The news media will not pay attention to copy that is laced with opinion or self-serving quotations. Worse, they will ridicule your work and discard it immediately.

Avoid statements such as this: "Monroe College is recognized as the foremost and most prestigious college of liberal arts in the entire Midwest." Who says? Learn "How to Be Newsworthy" at this Web site: **www.sonic.net/~cuclis/news.html.**

To write for most publications, certainly for newspapers, you need to know Associated Press style. Correct spelling, usage and grammar is essential, of course, but just as important is AP style. Why should news editors take you seriously if you do not bother to write in the style of their publications?

News releases are notoriously inaccurate and inconsistent in style and grammar. How ironic for people so concerned with image to be so careless in how they present themselves to the public.

■ *Know the structure and operations of news rooms.* If you do not get actual experience in a news room in college, find ways to spend some time in one. In Chapter 2, you studied how news rooms are organized. Now use your public-relations skills to get inside one and to experience what goes on there.

The most simple and important thing you can learn about news rooms is that they have deadlines. Learn the deadlines of the media where you work, and respect those deadlines. That means you cannot call in a story to a television news station a half-hour before broadcast time. Not only will the station not use your story, but station employees will resent you and not forget the interruption at a critical time. News organizations will tell you what time you must submit a story to make the news that day.

■ *Know the people in the news media and the jobs they hold.* This is especially true of newspapers. Sending a release addressed simply to a newspaper can be a waste of your time and make you look as if you do not know what you are doing. Sending a release to the business editor or to the features editor makes more sense. Addressing by name the editor of the section in which you wish the release to appear works best.

At a packed meeting of the Publicity Club of New York, Faye Penn, features editor of the *New York Post*, told her audience to stop sending her news releases. First she said she could not possibly read them all; then she said that many of them were about things her section never covered. Later, she admitted that she looked to see who had sent them.

If people in the news media know and trust you, they are more likely to read your releases, and you can sometimes call them with a story and let them write their own stories. There's nothing writers like more than to get wind of good stories. At that same Publicity Club meeting, features editor Barbara Schuler of *Newsday* warned that she never answers her phone but does read all news releases and faxes. She stressed the importance of getting the release into the right hands and handed out a sheet with the names, phone numbers and beat assignments of the reporters on *Newsday*. You need that list for each medium you cover.

Remember, your job is to help reporters write good stories. If you can help them do that and at the same time serve your client's interests, you will be a successful public-relations practitioner.

▪ *Know the style of writing that fits the medium.* Do not make the mistake of sending to the radio or TV station the same news release that you send to the newspaper. Do not expect busy newspeople to translate your newspaper release into broadcast copy. If you can write radio or television copy (see Chapter 11), you have a much better chance of getting the copy read over the air. And if you can supply video, many stations will use it in their newscasts.

Of course, not even the largest newspapers or radio or television networks can reach as many people as online media. Millions of Web sites know practically no limits. First, you must establish your own credible, up-to-date, interactive Web site. Second, you must be thoroughly familiar with Web sites such as **www.online-pr.com, www.prnewswire.com or www.medialink.com,** so that you can distribute your releases online and keep up with what's happening in public relations. Third, you yourself must become expert at using new media (note the plural) in getting across your organization's messages (see Chapter 13).

TYPES OF NEWS RELEASES

News releases generally fall into three categories:

1. *Announcements of coming events or personnel matters—hiring, promoting, retiring and the like.* Newspapers often have a calendar where they place events of interest to their readers. Communities are interested in people's jobs—when they start, when they are promoted and when they retire.
2. *Information about a cause.* Organizations try to be good community members. Often their people do volunteer work such as holding blood drives and raising money for children's hospitals. Organizations such as the American Heart Association find ways to get the community involved in events that raise money for the association.

3. *Information that is meant to build someone's or some organization's image*. Politicians seek to be elected or to be re-elected, so they need to be in the news. Organizations and government agencies often try to burnish their images by promoting some cause or event that demonstrates how they serve the community.

APPROACHES TO WRITING NEWS RELEASES

The Inverted Pyramid

The straight, no-nonsense inverted pyramid news release remains the staple of the public-relations professional. Many believe that any other approach will not be taken seriously by news professionals.

Here's an example. Notice the address and phone number of the organization putting out the release and the name of a contact person. If the news is for immediate release, say so. Otherwise, indicate a release date.

> NEWS
> Missouri Department of Natural Resources
> P.O. Box 176, Jefferson City, Missouri 65102 (573-751-3443)
> For further information contact: Mary Schwartz
> (For immediate release)
> JEFFERSON CITY, MO., FEB. 25, 2003 — The winter solitude of Roaring River, Bennett Spring and Montauk state parks will be shattered by about 8,000 fishing enthusiasts expected to participate in the annual trout opening March 1 in Missouri State Parks.
>
> The start of trout-fishing season in these parks marks the beginning of the vacation season in Missouri state parks, which are administered by the Missouri Department of Natural Resources. The Department also administers 30 other state parks and 22 historic sites, which officially open on April 15.
>
> "Trout opening is definitely a big event for fishermen in Missouri," said John Karel, director of state parks. "But, it's also a big day for state parks since it traditionally marks the beginning of the upcoming vacation season."
>
> Karel notes that park visitors to Montauk, Roaring River and Bennett Spring state parks will be greeted by a number of new construction and major renovation projects. . . .

The release goes on to talk about the projects and about how many trout tags were sold. It's a traditional approach, although the lead attempts to be a bit creative with "winter solitude" being "shattered." The lead jumps to a quote from an authority, John Karel, the director of the state parks, and uses him as the source throughout.

Today's reporters are more likely to receive releases by wire service. Only a grabbing headline or lead will get the reporter to take a second look before hitting the delete key.

Once you get the reader's attention, Johnston says, your job has just begun. Reporters are usually on deadline. "So anything you can do to make the reporter's job easier will increase the odds of getting ink or airtime," she says.

She tries to give technical information in simple language. "First, what's new, and so what, followed by simple descriptions and a complete story that doesn't leave the audience with unanswered questions."

Most of all, she says, "We absolutely refuse to bow to the company's pressure to include 'fluff' in a news release. After all, we're building relationships with reporters, and our reputations are at stake."

Getting beyond the Inverted Pyramid

Let's look now at a different approach; some would call it a feature approach (the information at the top of the release stays the same).

When the siren sounds at 6:30 a.m. March 1 in Bennett Spring State Park near Lebanon, Bill Brooks will be there. He'll be standing knee-deep in icy water as he's done every March 1 since 1970.

Brooks, known in fishing circles as Big Trout, will join an expected 8,000 other Missouri fishing enthusiasts for the opening of trout-fishing season in Missouri State Parks. Missouri's other trout-fishing state parks are Roaring River, near Cassville, and Montauk, near Salem.

Brooks can't imagine anything, short of a death in the family, that would keep him away. "This is just a tradition for me. I'm already making wagers and getting together my equipment."

As an extra measure, Brooks has made a special trip from his Marshfield home to the park just to check stream conditions.

After 32 years of opening days, Brooks has seen some changes. "I guess you could say they've gotten stricter on us. Things used to be a

This photo, provided by the Missouri State Department of Conservation, can accompany press releases promoting trout fishing in Missouri.

lot wilder down there in the old days, until they stopped us from gambling and stopped selling beer. . . ."

The release then introduces fishing expert Jim Rogers, who runs concessions at both Bennett Spring and Roaring River. Rogers tells with specific numbers how he has sold more than double the number of trout tags that he sold just eight years ago.

In this approach, the writer uses a "real person," a long-time fisherman, to introduce the story—rather than a person in authority. By using Brooks and Rogers, the writer tells a story and still gives important information, but in an interesting and appealing way.

Now suppose the writer accompanied this story with a photo from the year before of Big Trout standing knee-deep in icy water. Public-relations professionals know that releases accompanied by photos or art of some kind get more attention and more play.

Some professionals have also begun to place attention-grabbing headlines on top of their releases. Others accompany the head with a summary/contents/benefit blurb. Why should the editor or the intended audience have to read the entire release to find out what it's about?

You might want to go a step further. Why not do some service journalism? Put the parks, their locations and the opening dates in a separate box. How about a map of how to get there? Perhaps you could make a list of the top-10 things to remember on opening day. Maybe you could create an infographic indicating where to get trout tags. Some news organizations will use just one sidebar or graphic of what you send. But the important thing is that if you give them choices, you have a better chance of getting some of your information used.

In the past, some public-relations professionals shied away from what they thought of as gimmicks, for fear that editors would not take them seriously. What they didn't see was the way newspapers were changing, especially some sections.

Why not experiment? Attention is harder and harder to get. Don't be afraid to try a "you" lead or even a question. For example, "Are you ready for opening day at Bennett Springs?" Remember to get to the "so-what" quickly—not the "so-what" of your organization but rather the "so-what" of the audience. What's in it for the reader or listener? Most readers don't care whether AT&T has announced the sale of another company. (Some companies seem never to do anything but "announce" things in news releases.) Readers do care about how this sale might affect them and their phone bills.

Remember, too, that a film clip of Big Trout will more likely be used by a television news producer than will a written release, and a recorded interview might get played on your local radio station.

Tips for writers of news releases

1. Follow an accepted journalistic style of writing. *Use AP style.*
2. Go easy on length. *Hold it to two double-spaced, typewritten pages.*
3. Avoid breaks. *Don't hyphenate words at the ends of lines, and don't split a sentence at the bottom of a page.*
4. Write clearly. *Avoid corporate jargon, legalese or other alien language.*
5. Remember the pyramid. *But don't put all the w's in the lead.*
6. Beware of adjectives. *Especially avoid superlatives.*
7. Make it local.
8. Attribute news to a person. *Not to a company or organization.*
9. Indent the paragraphs.

— Carole Howard and Wilma Mathews, On Deadline: Managing Media Relations

A Day in the Life
of a Public-Relations Professional

Wilma Mathews is the consummate public-relations professional. Her 30-year career includes 15 years with AT&T and 10 years with Arizona State University. Her background includes work with a magazine and newspaper and at a medical center and chamber of commerce. She is a Fellow of the International Association of Business Communicators.

In her position as director of public relations at Arizona State University, her work crosses the borders of legislative affairs, community relations, media relations, events planning, marketing, advertising, employee communication, presidential support and the ever-famous "other duties as assigned."

This particular day points out the variety of problem-solving and opportunity-snatching that comes with a job of this scope. Here she speaks of a typical day.

A Wednesday . . .

Four meetings crowded this day and took precedence over the smaller issues that came up between them.

A colleague at one of our campuses had noticed that the advertising rate issued to us at *The Arizona Republic* newspaper was based on the non-profit status, assuming about $150,000/year in advertising. Since that rate was set, some years ago, many things have changed and it appeared that ASU's cumulative advertising is closer to about $500,000/year, which would qualify the university for a better rate.

I presided at a meeting that included the advertising manager and two representatives from the newspaper, and representatives from the major Arizona State University advertiser organizations: athletics, public events (Broadway and other performances), extended education, College of Business and Public Affairs.

The hour-long meeting confirmed that (a) university units are collectively advertising far more than realized; (b) there is no single representative for the university at the newspaper so individual departments are quoted rates by whatever representative they happen to get; (c) the university had not done a good job of routinely working with the newspaper's advertising department.

Results of the meeting: We agreed to get a three-year look at ASU's advertising, allow the advertising manager and staff to present next month to all ASU public-relations people both the new rate and other advertising opportunities, to have one advertising rep to serve as the coordinator among reps at the newspaper, and to help the paper develop a more accurate list of ASU advertisers.

From that meeting, I went to one of the Sun Devil Advocates, an organization run by the ASU Alumni Association, to help build support for ASU's legislative agenda. The conversation focused on the need to have more face-to-face presentations within the university to departments and leadership, about the serious and critical situation the university will be in for the second half of this fiscal year as well as fiscal '04 and '05. It appears that other channels of communication about the situation have not worked, and only face-to-face is getting people's attention.

I had to leave that meeting early in order to drive to a meeting in downtown Phoenix with Arvizu Advertising and Public Relations, an agency selected just a few days before to help ASU reach the Hispanic and other minority audiences in January and February with face-to-face and print presentations about the state universities' request to increase tuition by 44% while also increasing financial aid significantly. The agency is being asked to turn around an estimate in less than three working days and a draft plan in six working days, in order to get as much accomplished as possible during the year-end holidays. I will be coordinating this program and working with the agency.

> Returning to the office, I e-mailed a summary of the meeting to the provost, vice presidents and directors who are part of the planning group on this issue.
>
> I then left the office for a meeting in Scottsdale with United Blood Services, the organization that conducts blood drives on our campuses. ASU's size is large enough to warrant a single representative from UBS to schedule the drives, find volunteers to help with the drives, develop blood drive "sponsors" from within the university to host drives, and report functionally to me about the program. ASU is one of the largest suppliers of blood in the Valley and has the ability to conduct two-to-three drives each month at various locations. This meeting approved the development plan and goals for the coming year.
>
> In between meetings, I made appropriate notifications within the university and with police regarding two young men soliciting funds in various neighborhoods in the Valley, claiming to be students from our West campus. This required multiple voice mails and explanations and carried over into the next day while I was traveling to Chicago.
>
> I also completed work as a survey participant for a graduate student's paper on crisis communications involving racial disturbances, wrote thank-you notes to two speakers who had presented at the monthly internal public-relations meeting, and wrote and got approved a letter from the president regarding the United Way campaign.
>
> At day's end, I completed my needs for a trip to Chicago and a presentation I was to make there.
>
> A normal day? Yes.

Even if none of these media use your material as you presented it, perhaps you will succeed in grabbing the attention of an editor or reporter. If that person is inspired to pursue the story, you'll still get the information to the public.

Be sure that you make yourself available—by phone, e-mail, fax, Web site, in person—24 hours a day. A reporter on deadline will write the story with or without you. It's better that you talk—it's always better that you talk—to the reporter.

Remember, your job is not just to write news releases. Your job is to get information from your organization to the public. Writing news releases is only one means to that end. As a public-relations writer, you will use your writing skills in myriad ways in all media to serve your clients well.

Suggested Readings

Bivins, Thomas H. *Public Relations Writing*, Fourth Edition. Lincolnwood, Ill.: NTC/Contemporary Publishing Group, 1999. Covers a wide variety of writing expected of public-relations professionals.

Holtz, Shel. *Public Relations on the Net*. New York: Amacom, 1999. Anything Shel Holtz says or writes

about online subjects is worth paying attention to. See also **www.holtz.com**.

Horton, James L. *Online Public Relations*. Westport, Conn.: Quorum Books, 2001. A superb primer and more, beginning by explaining terminology and ending with 85 industry and general information topics to place news and to gather information.

Howard, Carole and Mathews, Wilma. *On Deadline: Managing Media Relations*, Third Edition. Prospect Heights, Ill.: Waveland Press, 2000. A practical book on how organizations should deal with the news media.

Newsom, Doug and Carrel, Bob. *Public Relations Writing, Form and Style*, Sixth Edition. Belmont, Calif.: Wadsworth, 2001. A truly thorough classic. It even has a section on grammar, spelling and punctuation.

Wilcox, Dennis L. *Public Relations Writing and Media Techniques*, Fourth Edition. New York: Longman, 2001. Filled with practical tips in all areas of public-relations writing; handy boxes and sidebars.

Wilcox, Dennis L. and Nolte, Lawrence W. *Public Relations Writing and Media Techniques*, Third Edition. New York: HarperCollins, 1997. Emphasizes writing, producing and distributing a variety of public-relations materials.

Suggested Web Sites

www.online-pr.com

An amazingly helpful site for anyone interested in public relations. A source for numerous useful Web sites.

www.sonic.net/~cuclis/news.html

Site explains "how to be newsworthy" and provides "a checklist to figure out your news angle."

www.prsa.org

Site of the Public Relations Society of America. Has general information about the society; lists its chapters and sections; has publications, membership and accreditation information, recognition and awards, conferences and seminars.

www.prssa.org

Site of the Public Relations Student Society of America. Contains news for members and leaders of the organization, as well as job listings and a calendar of events.

www.silveranvil.org

Site of the Silver Anvil awards—annual awards to public-relations practitioners who "in the judgment of their peers, have successfully addressed a contemporary issue with exemplary professional skill, creativity and resourcefulness."

Exercises

1. Visit the public-relations or public-affairs department of your university or of a major employer in your community. Do a report on what the staff does and what public-relations materials they produce.

2. A classmate was killed in a car accident. A couple of thousand dollars have been raised to set up a scholarship to honor his memory, but much more money is needed to endow the scholarship. Several students in the class have been training to run in the Chicago marathon. A group decides to solicit money for each mile the students complete. Organize a campaign on your campus to get people to pledge or donate money. Answer these questions:
   a. What are your target audiences?
   b. Which media will you use?
   c. What print materials will you develop?

   Then write a news release for the local media.

3. Read the following news release, and note any deviations from AP style. Also note any content that news organizations might object to.

NEWS RELEASE

"Chest Pains", an excellent film in the HEALTHCARE series produced by the American College of Physicians, will be shown from 7:00-8:30 P.M., Wednesday, October 22, at St. Mary's Health Center. Springfield internist, Dr. Harold Kanagawa, will host a question-and-answer period following the film.

Although most people assume that chest pains signify a heart attack, the public is less aware that other conditions—hiatal hernia, ulcers, viral infections of the heart's membranes—can also cause pains that require prompt diagnosis and appropriate medical treatment. Designed to help increase awareness of the symptoms and their possible significance, "Chest Pains" features an internist and actual patients as they work together to resolve underlying medical problems.

Through a warm and engaging human-interest style of presentation, each twenty-five-minute documentary encourages people to take an increased responsibility for their own well-being by establishing healthy habits and assuming a more active role in disease prevention.

The HEALTHCARE series is produced under an educational grant from the Elsworth Company of Midland, Michigan. Other films in this superb, highly acclaimed series cover "Aches, Pains and Arthritis", "Diabetes", and "Abdominal Discomfort".

Doctor Kanagawa, a renowned specialist in internal medicine, is 1 of fifty-thousand members of the American College of Physicians. Founded in 1915, the College is the largest medical specialty society in the U.S. and one of the most prestigious. It represents doctors of internal medicine, related non-surgical specialists, and physicians-in-training.

To register or for more information, contact the Women's Life Center.

4. Interview a student from a small town. Then write a news release about his or her life and activities at the university, and send it to the town's newspaper.

5. Study the Web site of the college or university you attend. Then write a news release for your local paper describing the information and services found on the Web site.

13 Writing Online

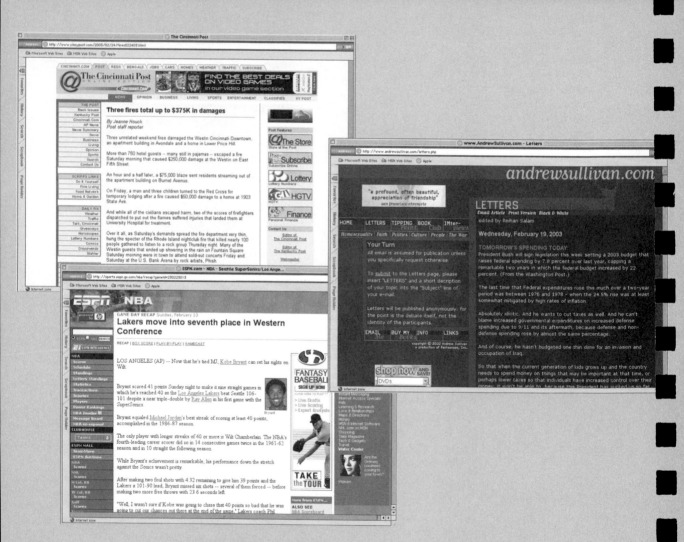

"Computers can:

- *Look things up for us.*
- *Navigate for us ('Please turn to page . . .').*
- *Link words to other words.*
- *Remember where we were and take us back there.*
- *Play audio, video, and animation.*
- *Organize and present information according to a nonlinear structure."*

—*Andrew Bonime and Ken C. Pohlmann,* Writing for New Media

You may have been reading the news online on Feb. 1, 2003, when you learned that the space shuttle Columbia broke into pieces 15 minutes before landing at Cape Kennedy. If you heard the news on the radio or watched it on TV, and if you are like millions of others, you rushed to your PC.

You did that because you wanted to get the most up-to-date news and get it quickly. You didn't want to wait until the radio or television anchors got around to the aspects of the news you wanted to learn. You wanted to be in control. If you went to **www.LATimes.com,** you could read the main story if you wished; you could look at photos; you could view a video of Columbia debris falling over Texas; you could read Texans' account of hearing the explosion and seeing trails in the sky. You might have wanted to be assured that this was not terrorist activity.

If you needed reminding about who was on the Columbia, you could view photos of the crew and read individual biographies. You could witness a video of the liftoff on Jan. 16; you could even digest a well-illustrated history of space-shuttle history.

All of this on your time, under your direction. Television was showing the same pictures over and over and repeating much of the story for those who recently tuned in. But online, you could get what you wanted and spend as little or as much time as you liked, and like print, if you missed something, you could go back and read it again. Unlike print accounts, however, the main story received continual updates, and related stories were added.

Online journalism has changed everything. You already know that without computer skills, your chances of getting a job on a newspaper or a magazine are slim. More than 1,300 North American daily newspapers, as well as 5,000 daily, weekly and other newspapers worldwide, had Web sites as of May 1, 2002. You can link to most of those sites at **www.newspaperlinks.com.** And no longer can anyone say that no one is making money online. According to a 2001 study of newspaper Web sites by the World Association of Newspapers in Paris, 38 percent of newspapers make money, 26 percent break even and 36 percent lose money. As for the future, a Borrell Associates report, based on an analysis of more than 250 dailies, says that newspapers can generate as much as $650 million in annual revenue by 2005 "through reorganization, improved database infrastructure and a Web-focused sales team."

Newspapers have an annual Interactive Newspapers Conference and Trade Show and an annual competition that rewards the best overall U.S. and non-U.S. newspaper online service; best news, sports, business, entertainment, special and classified sections; best design; and best use of interactivity.

As you would expect, all kinds of magazines and newsletters have a presence on the Web. The American Business Press, for example, has become the American Business Media, and its Neal awards include the best Web site. The Newsletter Publishers Association became the Newsletter and Electronic Publishers Association. Radio and television stations and cable outlets, too, have Web sites, some of them, such as **ESPN.com,** among the best online.

A report by Minnesota Opinion Research indicated that 62 percent of 2,000 general Internet users surveyed choose an online newspaper for local news on the Internet. An online survey of 12,429 current online newspaper users found that 86 percent of this group prefer Internet newspapers for local coverage.

All-news television and radio stations have been able to keep people tuned to the latest developments in the news; regular television and radio outlets often interrupt programming to alert us to important news. But online media not only keep readers up-to-the minute with the news; they also keep a record of all that went on before the latest bulletin. They connect us to other sites that give background on breaking news. They include still photographs that the paper has no room to print and that can be studied, and some offer audio and video that can be listened to or viewed over and over. They can fill us in on anything we may have missed while reading or viewing traditional news coverage.

No wonder an increasing number of news consumers turn first to the Internet for news, especially for breaking news. And they are not the only ones. Journalists everywhere have had to learn to find and confirm information on the Internet. A study of 271 political reporters by George Washington University's Graduate School of Political Management revealed that they "read political coverage, research candidates' backgrounds, locate sources and experts, follow poll results, and monitor candidate messages online," reports an October 2002 *Ifra Trend Report*.

You must know how and where to access information on the Internet—and which sources you can trust. The publication you work for may have a list of reliable **URLs** (Uniform Resource Locators). In most cases, you can trust information more if it has a byline you know or a byline that is further identified. Better, you can trust the validity of information on the Web if you know the sponsoring organization that is hosting the information. The publisher of the information, of course, should be neutral and have nothing to sell and no cause to promote. Several books such as Alison Cooke's *Authoritative Guide to Evaluating Information on the Internet* and Web sites such as **thorplus.lib.purdue.edu/vlibary/** help you evaluate the quality and reliability of Web sites.

The 69-year-old Associated Press Managing Editors association amended its bylaws in 2001 to fill one seat of its board of directors with a supervisor of an online news operation, and in 2002, Ken Sands, interactive editor of The Spokesman-Review, *Spokane, Wash., was elected to the board.*

The search engine Google, founded in 1998, now gets 150 million queries a day from more than 100 countries, according to a story in The New York Times.

According to the Newspaper Association of America, the U.S. Internet audience will have 174 million users by 2004. Users in 2002 spent more time online at home than ever before—three and a half hours per month compared with two hours and 45 minutes during 2001. These same people spent less time with other media, notably 23 percent less time with television and 20 percent less time with magazines.

The problem is the material that people "publish" on the Web does not receive the routine copy editing that print-based publications receive. As a result, you find a lot of misspelled names, incorrect titles, wrong dates and so on—even on pages from reliable organizations.

Some Web users argue that there is an evolving ethic on the Web that downplays the importance of accuracy. Some follow personal rules that say never attribute information on the Web unless you have confirmation from a person able to confirm the attribution.

One further caution: You need to be conscious of the massive amount of dated material on the Web. What reads like new information might be years old. Be sure to check the creation date of the material you are citing.

Although you need to remain skeptical about Web reliability, Steve Outing, new-media writer and columnist for *Editor & Publisher* magazine, says more and more content from Internet-originated sources is appearing in reputable newspapers. "Where once print editors distrusted content originating from online content companies, now there is much more acceptance that online content can be every bit as good, if not better, than content acquired from traditional media sources," Outing writes.

You soon may be required to be versatile in using various media when covering a story. You may have to decide whether the online story should be video, audio, print—or all three. Alan Boyles, a writer for MSNBC.com, told columnist Steve Outing, "Seems to me that marriage of sound, text, pictures and interactivity is what the medium's all about."

Or, as John Pavlik writes in *Introduction to Online Journalism* by Roland De Wolk, "In this world of on-demand media, journalism will feature a rich blend of text, audio, video and interactivity to tell virtually any story. To work effectively in this environment, journalists will need to be comfortable with, if not fluent in, the grammar of all media modalities."

HOW TO WRITE ONLINE

Regardless of the media you use, you will need to know how to write online. On a growing number of newspapers, even veteran journalists are being asked to turn in two versions of their stories, one for the newspaper and one for the paper's Web site. At the *St. Paul (Minn.) Pioneer Press*, all print reporters must file a Web story within 30 minutes after witnessing an event or learning about the news. In the old days, newspapers would print several editions a day and occasionally

The Web's Influence on Journalism

A 2000 Pew Research Center biennial survey revealed that one in three Americans goes online for news at least once a week, compared to 20 percent just two years before; 15 percent do so daily, up 6 percent. In the United Kingdom, the Internet leads newspapers and magazines as a source of news, views and entertainment, according to a study conducted for Internet service provider Freeserve. Television is the most popular news source, radio the second and newspapers the fourth. Young people aged 16-34 spend 15 times as much time online as they spend reading newspapers.

Another study of 999 business leaders showed that 90 percent of them say news is the main reason they go online. Of that group, 77 percent said they choose the Internet to find out what's happening in the business world. Another 66 percent said that advertising has the best chance of reaching them on the Web.

And the Web's influence on journalism is just beginning.

"Improved interactive applications will create an entirely new, integrated news experience that will serve to engage consumers in new ways," Merril Brown, senior vice president of RealOne, told the audience in his 2002 keynote address of the Online News Association conference. Later in that address he said, "We've barely scratched the surface in inventing new ways to tell stories. We've only tip-toed down the road of television Internet convergence."

Already we can add streaming audio and video news in real time; reporters can carry the cameras and equipment that provide pictures and sound as the news is happening that arrives into your dorm room or living room; one reporter can do work that used to engage a whole studio of people and equipment.

An interview with Kerry Northrup, executive director of the Ifra Centre for Advanced News Operations, in *EPN World Reporter* addressed this phenomenon:

A lot of people who are journalists today simply cannot be journalists tomorrow. They can't grasp the changes in how people get and use news and information. They won't adapt to thinking in terms of multiple media rather than being concerned only about their personal area of specialization. They are media bigots, for want of a better term, insisting past reason that print is print, broadcast is broadcast, Web is Web, and never will they mesh.

The idea of blending formats to create a story greater than the sum of its parts remains foreign to them. Perhaps the kindest and most effective approach for an editorial organization to deal with this situation is to create new jobs that reflect the new requirements, the new skills, the new compensations, the new realities, and then let those that will evolve into them, and those that won't phase out.

Ifra reports that in the United Kingdom, the BBC and its trade union have a new video-journalist classification with salary increases for journalists "who retrain to report, film and edit their own news stories."

come out with an "extra." Today cyberspace has turned newspapers into 24-hour competitive news machines, and "print reporters" are rapidly becoming a disappearing species.

Good online writing has many of the characteristics of other forms of effective writing. Much of what you have read so far about newswriting applies to online journalism; what you've learned about news-gathering and news-reporting, either in print or broadcast, applies here. The demand for accurate, simple, clear and concise writing is the same for all the media.

Nevertheless, the online journalist must be aware of some fundamental differences. These differences result in stories that look quite different from the stories published on paper or broadcast. One sure way to drive away online readers is to give them **shovelware**—stories as they appeared in print. Hundreds of publications continue to do that—shovel their print stories into a whole new medium, a medium that has its own demands, strengths and even some weaknesses. Most online readers refuse to be buried in shovelware—unless they have a real need for in-depth information.

Admittedly, also, there are readers who want the stories as they appear in the newspaper, not rewritten in some other form. They want shovelware because they want to know what other readers are seeing. Perhaps newspapers will serve this segment of the audience with an online shovelware edition or, as *The New York Times* has done, put out an online version that looks exactly like the newspaper edition.

Writing online is still in an experimental stage. Researchers have yet to establish what works best in this race to capture today's in-a-hurry readers.

This chapter does not attempt to teach you Web coding. That's best learned in a computer class, rather than by reading about it. You may want to check a couple of tutorials such as **www.werbach.com/barebones** or **www.webmonkey.com.** This chapter, however, does show you the best thinking and practice in online writing. You will learn a different way to think about writing and some rules that apply more to online writing than to other forms of writing.

Let's begin with these three principles:

1. The reader rules.
2. The writing is nonlinear.
3. Structure is everything.

The Reader Rules

Unlike print journalists writing for newspapers and magazines, where narrative works fine, newswriters online should keep no secrets from readers; they should not try to withhold information until later in the story. In short, when writing online, you should surrender to readers' control of the story's sequence. Online, authors lose their "position of central author-ity," writes David Weinberger, author/editor of the *Journal of the Hyperlinked Organization*, a newsletter that considers the Web's effect on how business works. Every reader is different; every reader has different needs. Every reader, therefore, not only will pick and choose what to read but also will choose a path that best meets those needs.

Also, readers can come from anywhere in the world, not just from a local audience. And because of the enormous archive retrieval functions of the Internet, readers can come in from any time. As Prof. Phill Brooks of the Missouri School of Journalism tells his students, "Today becomes yesterday tomorrow." In other words, he says, you are writing history to an international audience.

You should think of different ways to present different information for different people at different times. Unlike newspapers and magazines, which must decide how long to make a story, you should layer information in such a way that readers can choose the amount they need at this time. In this chapter we show you ways to do this.

You have learned to write the inverted pyramid story. This much of the traditional news story remains the same. The lead in an online story becomes even more important because, literally, the lead may be all that appears on the screen. Readers may have to click to get more of the story. The lead must nail the "what" or the "so-what" to get the full attention of the reader. In fact, it is similar to the anchor's introduction to a television news story.

The lead is also important because for most search engines, the lead will be the only information provided for the link to the story. You do well to include keywords such as "Maine" and "governor" in the lead about a story concerning the Maine governor.

Sometimes the lead appears like an extended headline, followed by two or three statements that also read as headlines. After the lead, little is the same as in the traditional news story. Readers often can click on the hyperlinked headlines to read the full version of the story on another page within the Web site.

Note again, the reader is active, not passive. Steve Outing writes in Poynter.org:

"If I gave you an assignment to look at the content of 100 news Web sites, you'd probably find that 95 percent of them don't ever go beyond routine presentation of text, images, and the occasional audio or video clip. It's still the rare few that craft content in such ways that go beyond what would be possible in print or broadcast. Rare is the story that uses online interactive techniques that help the user understand the story best by letting him or her interact with and manipulate elements of the story—to experience it, not just read about it." Outing

> *"Hypertext and hypermedia have the following characteristics:*
>
> - *They present ideas nonsequentially.*
> - *They follow the thought process.*
> - *They allow users to choose individual pathways through the information.*
> - *They allow information to transcend individual documents.*
> - *They link text with pictures, audio, and video."*
>
> *—Andrew Bonime and Ken C. Pohlmann,* Writing for New Media

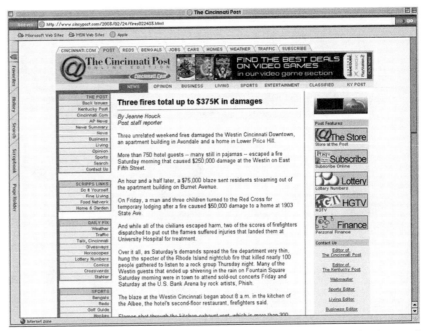

The Cincinnati Post Online Edition (**www.cincypost.com**) uses the inverted pyramid throughout its Web site. In doing so, the site allows readers to find the "what" or the "so-what" without reading the entire story.

writes that good Internet writing says to the reader, "Don't read—do!" It does this because it plays to the essential nature of the Internet—and that is that it is interactive.

The Writing Is Nonlinear

Because most people don't think linearly, writing online is more in line with the way people think. It's even more in line with the way today's readers read. Break the story into short, digestible pieces. Rather than stringing together a long story and trying to get readers to read the whole thing in the order you presented it, keep in mind that many readers don't want to read everything you have to tell them. You must give them choices and let them decide what to read and in what order. Stories that require multiple screens turn off many readers immediately.

Many readers hate to scroll on screen. Some exit even before they get to the bottom of the screen. Few will take the time to read a lot of text in one clump. Note, of course, that this is not true of highly motivated readers who crave your information. At times you may want to send them to reliable databanks where they can read the whole story and get all the facts—preferably, of course, within your own site.

> *"Whether using a mouse or placing a finger on a touch screen, the reader will always choose the information to be accessed, and that information must be organized and presented according to a well-defined structure and syntax that is appropriate for the medium."*
>
> —*Andrew Bonime and Ken C. Pohlmann,* Writing for New Media

The Dallas-Fort Worth-area news site Star-Telegram.com (**www.dfw.com**) lists top stories with a headline accompanied by a brief description.

Structure Is Everything

Some who write online forget entirely about structure. That's a huge mistake. Even though an online story takes on an entirely different structure, it still must be organized in a logical, coherent way. The online reader does not revel in chaos. Even though the story may appear on the screen as a mosaic, the way that mosaic is composed will help attract readers, keep readers and help readers follow what for them is the most logical path.

The online writer must present information in layers. Remember, no two readers are alike. You may present the same information with different degrees of detail and support. The first layer is information that is immediately available to readers—no action or effort is demanded. A second layer, a more substantial read, could be reachable easily by moving the cursor or by scrolling. A third layer may require readers to click on a link that opens up still more information, perhaps audio, video or a source document.

When you write for print, you need to be concerned with continuity, with themes, with working in all aspects of the story while remaining clear and coherent. When you write online, you need to worry not about the structure or flow of the whole piece but rather

to go when I left CNET," he says. "Many online reporters I know—the few of us that are left—have a desire to get back to print. In fact that's the route several of my former News.com colleagues have taken.

"I probably wouldn't turn down *The New York Times* if they came calling, but I really enjoy working online. I love the immediacy of the medium. By the time a newspaper is delivered to a reader's door, many of the stories in it have been online for hours.

"Writing for an online publication brings you closer to your readers. When I wrote for a newspaper, I felt as if my stories were floating out into the ether. I had no idea whether people were reading them. I know how much people are reading my News.com articles by how many e-mail responses I receive.

"The demands can be overwhelming. As I was leaving CNET, the editors there were asking reporters to write at least two headline stories a day and to be working on larger enterprise stories at the same time."

about the relationships of the levels and parts. You need to help readers navigate from place to place to get the information they want. That means you must have clear entrances and exits.

Sometimes you have to give clear directions. For example, if you include a **hyperlink** in your story, more readers will "click here" if you tell them to than if you don't. Sometimes you may take readers down one path that branches into several others. Some call this technique "threading." A plane crash can lead to various threads—the airline and its record of crashes, the plane itself and the record of that type of plane, the place of the accident, the people involved, and so forth.

You need not be concerned about some repetition. Remember, readers choose what parts to read. Besides, a certain amount of repetition or of stating things in different ways, perhaps visually, increases retention. Readers, after all, online or elsewhere, process information differently.

GUIDELINES FOR WRITING ONLINE

Readers online are surfers or scanners, much more so than readers of print—perhaps because it takes 25 percent longer to read online than it does in print. Researchers Jakob Nielsen and John Morkes found that 79 percent of those they tested scanned a new page they came across; only 16 percent read the copy word for word. You can find their study at **www.useit.com/papers/webwriting/index.html**.

Online expert Shel Holtz says you want readers to dive, not to surf. Surfing is what frustrated readers do. Here are 10 ways to make divers of surfers—at least to hold their attention long enough to get your message across.

1. Think Immediacy

Although you must first make sure what you write is accurate, the Internet can deliver news when it is brand new. Writing online is like writing for the wire services. Everyone on the Internet is now like a wire service subscriber. Keeping readers with you means keeping readers up-to-the-minute. You must expect to update breaking stories quickly and to add depth whenever it is available. But just because you can easily correct your mistakes does not mean that you are allowed to make them. Reporter David Broder of *The Washington Post* warned at the annual National Roundtable sponsored by the Scripps Howard Foundation that posting news quickly could sacrifice quality and damage credibility.

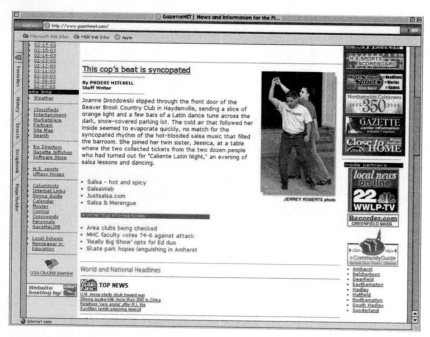

Gazette NET (**www.gazettenet.com**), a Western Mass. news site, links to outside sources on the Web to supplement its coverage.

Nevertheless, newspapers are now using their Web sites to break news. For example, when *The Financial Times* learned that Iranian security forces held a son of Osama bin Laden, it reported the news on its Web site on Saturday because it doesn't publish on Sunday. The Ft. Lauderdale, Fla., *Sun-Sentinel* partners with radio and television, and it may break a story on any of the media. Time usually is the deciding factor.

2. Save Readers' Time

What most readers do not have is time. Whatever you can do to save readers' time is worth your time. It's been said by various people in different ways since philosopher Blaise Pascal first said it: "Excuse me for this long letter; I don't have time to write a short one." For many stories, if not most, perhaps your chief concern should be this: Have I presented this information in such a way as to cost readers the least amount of time?

The best way to save readers' time is to be clear. Choose the simple word; vary the length of sentences but keep them short; write short paragraphs. Help readers. Emphasize keywords by highlighting them or by putting them in color.

Mark Deuze and Christina Dimoudi of the Amsterdam School of Communications Research conclude from their study that online journalism is really a fourth kind of journalism after print, radio and television. Its main characteristic is "empowering audiences as active participants in the daily news." Online journalists have "an interactive relationship with their audience" and a "strong element of audience orientation" and are "more aware of their publics and service function in society than their colleagues elsewhere."

Another reason to write simply, using simple words and simple sentences, is for the auto-translation programs used by some search engines to translate a page. The simpler the words and sentences, the more likely a foreign-language translation of the story will be accurate and understandable.

3. Provide Information That's Quick and Easy to Get

The overall organization of your story must say to the reader that getting this information is going to be quick and easy. Online readers have zero tolerance for confusion and no time at all to be led astray. It's too easy to click on something else.

Don't get carried away by your own eloquence. Be guided by what your readers want or need to know. Make it easy for them. Write short paragraphs with one idea per paragraph.

4. Think Both Verbally and Visually

In the past, writers for print thought little about how their stories were going to appear. Their job was to write the story—period. The designer's job was to make the story fit on the page in some meaningful way. Writers did not worry about headlines, subheads, summary quotes, photos, illustrations or anything else. The story was the thing.

Television newswriters know that they must write to the pictures. Good television has good video; the visual medium tries to show rather than to tell. Words complement pictures; they say what the pictures do not. Many times, of course, the writer does not make the pictures and is not responsible for getting them.

Online journalists may not have to do it all by themselves, but they must think verbally and visually. From the outset, you must be concerned about the most effective and efficient way for the information to appear on the screen. You have to think not only about the organization of the page, but also about ways to use graphics, to be interactive and to use online tools.

No one doubts that photos and graphics grab readers' attention. That's why you see more icons and infographics in magazines and newspapers, and that's why you must think, perhaps with the help of graphic designers, of ways to use graphic elements online.

In short, if you are writing online, you have to be much more than a wordsmith. You must have a pocketful of other skills. Writing online demands a great deal of collaboration and not just with other writers. Working closely with individuals more expert than you in design and photography becomes crucial from the outset.

After a star-studded career in newspapers, television and radio, Karla Vallance, electronic publishing managing editor of The Christian Science Monitor, *now works where she daily does it all. In an interview with* Editor & Publisher, *she discusses her 2002 Online Journalism Award-winning special project on the future of Amtrak. "'All Aboard: Amtrak and the Future of Passenger Rail in America,'" Vallance says, "is a great example of how to take full advantage of the online medium to tell a story."*

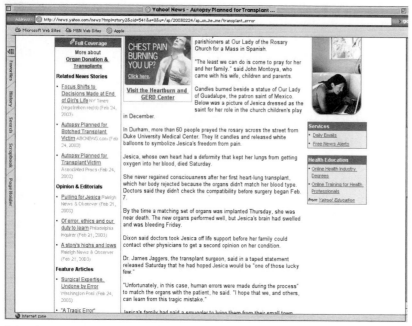

Yahoo! News (**news.yahoo.com**) uses a short, concise story but stuffs a sidebar with links to additional resources.

5. Cut Copy in Half

You probably don't have to be told that writing online must be concise. But you do need to be told to cut your copy in half. Years ago, writing expert William Zinsser recommended that writers take their eight pages and cut them to four. Then comes the difficult part, he wrote—cutting them to three. And that was for print!

Most online readers simply will not read long stories. Even veteran computer users find reading on screen somewhat difficult, even unpleasant, says Jakob Nielsen. Perhaps this will change when larger screens and high-resolution screens become more common by becoming less expensive.

Studies contradict each other about people's aversion to scrolling. In the not-so-distant past, some experts advised getting the whole story on one screen. Because some screens are small, they advised not writing more than 20 lines of text. Now, because of the proliferation of larger and less irritating screens, some readers are finding it easier and less frustrating to scroll for more information. As in newswriting for radio and television, there's little room online to be cute or even literary. Be crisp and clear as in the example from ESPN.

To a greater extent than most sites, ESPN **(espn.go.com)** uses hyperlinks throughout its stories. The hyperlinks lead surfers to related stories, player profiles and audio and video files.

"We have derived three main content-oriented conclusions from our four years of Web usability studies:

■ *users do not read on the Web; instead they scan the pages, trying to pick out a few sentences or even parts of sentences to get the information they want.*

■ *users do not like long, scrolling pages; they prefer the text to be short and to the point.*

■ *users detest anything that seems like marketing fluff or overly hyped language ('marketese') and prefer factual information."*

—*John Morkes and Jakob Nielsen (1997), "Concise, SCANNABLE, and Objective: How to Write for the Web," Useit.com*

6. Use Lots of Lists and Bullets

Often you can cut copy by putting information into lists. As in service journalism, whenever you can make a list, do so. Lists get more attention, better comprehension and more retention than ordinary sentences and paragraphs. Bulleted or numbered lists are scannable. Readers can grasp them immediately. Think of information on the Web as a database. That's how people use their computers, and that's how they use the Web.

Nielsen tested five versions of the same information for usability. Look first at the longest version, what he calls promotional writing, his control condition:

> Nebraska is filled with internationally recognized attractions that draw large crowds of people every year, without fail. In 1996, some of the most popular places were Fort Robinson State Park (355,000 visitors), Scotts Bluff National Monument (132,126 visitors), Arbor Lodge State Historical Park & Museum (100,000), Carhenge (85,598), Stuhr Museum of the Prairie Pioneer (60,002), and Buffalo Bill Ranch State Historical Park (28,446).

Now look at this same material in list form.

The 3-2-2-1 Format

After spending 25 years as a professional newsman, the last four of those as a general manager, Associate Professor Clyde Bentley now teaches classes in online journalism and other courses at the University of Missouri. In one class, students take stories from the newspaper and rewrite them for the online version. Bentley calls the students online "producers" rather than reporters.

"I was surprised at the resistance my students had to changing the copy of reporters," Bentley says. "They preferred the 'shovelware' concept so they would not tamper with the prose of their friends."

In frustration, he instituted what he called a "3-2-2-1" format. "It was a way to force my young journalists to take on a new process."

Here's what the numbers mean:

- *3 subheads.* By inserting three subheads, the producers "chunk" the story into four pieces. "This is easier to read than one long, scrollable piece of text," Bentley says. The subdivisions can be as simple as "who, what, when. . . ."
- *2 external links.* These are directions to further information posted outside the story (to the left of the text in our newspaper (the *Columbia Missourian*) site, often at the bottom in other sites). "For instance, in a story about the local dog pound, we might have external links to the ASPCA and the American Kennel Club."
- *2 internal links.* These are explanatory links tied to text within the story. "In the pound story," Bentley explains, "the word 'Doberman' might be a link that takes one to a breeder's site that explains the Doberman pinscher."
- *1 piece of art not available in the print edition.* Print publications limit art primarily because of space limitations. There are not such limits on the Web. "If a photographer shoots 20 shots, we can run more than one," Bentley says. "More commonly, however, the producers insert mug shots of people mentioned in the story. There is no reason not to run mugs of everyone who is mentioned."

In 1996, six of the most-visited places in Nebraska were:

- Fort Robinson State Park
- Scotts Bluff National Monument
- Arbor Lodge State Historical Park & Museum
- Carhenge
- Stuhr Museum of the Prairie Pioneer
- Buffalo Bill Ranch State Historical Park

The list version of the information scored a 124 percent usability improvement over the first version.

7. Write in Chunks

When you can't put things into lists, you can still organize them into chunks of information. Put information into sidebars or boxes. Readers will read more, not less, if you break up the information into small bites. Research has also shown that putting some information in a sidebar can give readers better comprehension of the subject. But the main objective is to write for diverse readers who want to get only the information they want in the order they want to receive it.

Think of your story as having parts. When writing a story for a newspaper, you need to think of ways to join the various parts of the story, you should craft transitions carefully, and you may even add sub-heads. When writing a story online, instead of writing subheads, make each segment of the story a separate story. Be sure that each part can stand on its own enough to be comprehensible and to make your point. Again, remember the importance of a strong lead in the best inverted pyramid form.

8. Use Hyperlinks

To understand the Web, think of a spider web. The Web, says David Weinberger, is a place of connection; it is a connective place; it is a place where we go to connect. Users of the Internet feel connected. If you want them to read your copy and come back for more, you must satisfy and enhance that sense of being connected.

Being connected means being interactive. Web users want to be actively involved in what they are reading. They are not passive observers. Like video-game players, they want to be in control of where they are going and how they get there. Your copy must be inter-active both internally and externally.

Internal Connections

The most challenging and necessary aspect of online writing is making the copy interactive. You begin that process by streamlining your copy—not including everything. Create hyperlinks, and allow readers to click on information elsewhere on your site.

One of the most perplexing problems writers face is deciding when to include the definition of a word. Will you insult some readers by including the definition? Will you leave others behind if you do not define the term? A similar problem is whether to tell who a person is. Many readers may wonder how stupid you think they are for telling them that actor Fred Thompson is a former Republican senator from Tennessee. Other readers may need or want that information.

The online writer can simply make the word or name a hot spot or a link and hyperlink it to a different "page." Readers need only click on the word to find its meaning or read more about it. No longer do writers have to write, "For more information, see. . . ." Academic writers use footnotes. **Hypertext,** and now hypermedia, linking readers to audio, video and pictures, is much more convenient.

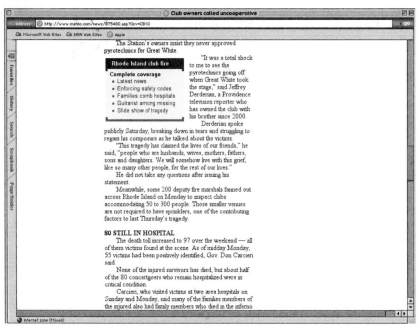

The Station's owners insist they never approved pyrotechnics for Great White.

Rhode Island club fire

Complete coverage
- Latest news
- Enforcing safety codes
- Families comb hospitals
- Guitarist among missing
- Slide show of tragedy

"It was a total shock to me to see the pyrotechnics going off when Great White took the stage," said Jeffrey Derderian, a Providence television reporter who has owned the club with his brother since 2000. Derderian spoke publicly Saturday, breaking down in tears and struggling to regain his composure as he talked about the victims.

"This tragedy has claimed the lives of our friends," he said, "people who are husbands, wives, mothers, fathers, sons and daughters. We will somehow live with this grief, like so many other people, for the rest of our lives."

He did not take any questions after issuing his statement.

Meanwhile, some 200 deputy fire marshals fanned out across Rhode Island on Monday to inspect clubs accommodating 50 to 300 people. Those smaller venues are not required to have sprinklers, one of the contributing factors to last Thursday's tragedy.

80 STILL IN HOSPITAL

The death toll increased to 97 over the weekend — all of them victims found at the scene. As of midday Monday, 55 victims had been positively identified, Gov. Don Carcieri said.

None of the injured survivors has died, but about half of the 80 concertgoers who remain hospitalized were in critical condition.

Carcieri, who visited victims at two area hospitals on Sunday and Monday, said many of the families members of the injured also had family members who died in the inferno

Unlike sidebars in newspapers, sidebars on the Web don't share the same page as the main story. Instead, sites provide boxed links to related stories, as shown in this story on MSNBC.com (**www.msnbc.com**).

Writing concisely has never been easier. Rather than defining words, going into long explanations, giving examples or elaborating on the story itself, you can stick to the essentials and make the rest of the story available to readers who need or want it. A story about a homicide can link to a map where the crime took place, to a chart showing the numbers of homicides this year as compared to last year, to a piece about friends of the victim, to information about violent crimes nationally, and so forth.

Remember, too, that unlike the newspaper that may be short of space, and unlike radio and television where you may be short of time, online you have unlimited space and time to run photos and aspects of stories that could be of real interest to some readers. Sports fans, for example, would probably enjoy seeing a whole gallery of shots from Saturday's championship game. They would read interviews from all of the stars of the victory—or of the defeat.

External Connections

Of course, you can do much more. You can hyperlink to different Web sites. Academic writers include bibliographies. Print journalists often identify sources in their stories. Other writers simply say to readers,

Among other rules for writing online, Ellen Schindler, a senior account executive at Berry Associates, recommends the following:

- *Double-space between paragraphs. Leave two spaces after periods.*
- *Avoid serif type. Serifs get lost on the screen.*
- *Make the text black. It's easier to read.*
- *Simple is best.*

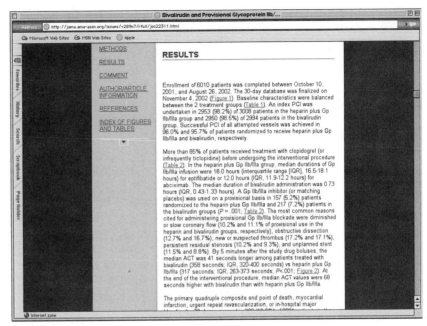

Publications that use technical explanations and examples can stick to the essentials in the text and link to supportive materials. Notice how the Journal of the American Medical Association (**www.jama.com**) uses hyperlinks within the main text to link readers to tables and figures.

that's all I know about the subject, I'm not going to tell you where I obtained my information, and I'm not telling you where you can find more information. Hypertext and hypermedia have changed all that. Not only can you hyperlink online, but readers expect that you will.

Obviously, you are not expected to draw readers away from your site to a competitor, especially on a breaking story. Nevertheless, readers will come to rely on your site to help them find more information about subjects that interest them greatly.

To find appropriate external hyperlinks, you need to know how to use search engines such as Yahoo! (**www.yahoo.com**) and Google (**www.google.com**). Check out "How to Search the Web: A Guide to Search Tools," by Terry A. Gray at Palomar College (**daphne.palomar .edu/TGSEARCH**).

9. Give Readers a Chance to Talk Back

A big part of being interactive is allowing readers to talk back. The Internet has leveled the playing field. Everyone is an owner or a publisher. Everyone feels the right and often the need to write back—if not to the writer of the piece, then to other readers in chat rooms. The

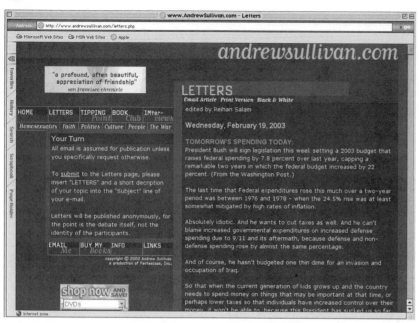

Web logs, or blogs, allow a journalist, pundit or anyone else to post their thoughts as often as they like, be it weekly, daily or hourly. On his blog (**www.andrewsullivan.com**), writer and journalist Andrew Sullivan comments on news items and events throughout the day.

wonderful thing about allowing readers to talk back is that they do. When they do, they will revisit the site again and again. Online readers want to be part of the process. Feedback, yes, instantly! Readers love it when newspapers such as *The Miami Herald* include the reporter's e-mail address in the byline, and many of them respond.

A word of caution: Including e-mail addresses on the Web leaves you open to operations that use a program called an e-mail syphon that scans Web site pages for e-mail addresses that are then used for spam. Depending on your mail-server provider's anti-spamming capabilities, putting your e-mail address in a news story or magazine article can subject you to a deluge of spam. One alternative is, rather than revealing your permanent personal address, include in your stories a different address that you change from time to time.

Never has it been easier to find out what is on the minds of your readers. Print and broadcast have always been mainly one-way communication. Now, not only can you get opinions easily and quickly, but you can incorporate them into your story or at least hyperlink to them. Letters to the editor have always been among the best-read sections in newspapers and magazines. Many readers, especially those reading online, not only want to express their own opinions but love to read the opinions of others. Be sure, however, that you use the same strict standards for publishing others' remarks on your Web site that you use for publishing in your newspaper or magazine. Even e-mail polls can be and have been flooded by advocacy groups. Reporting their results can be meaningless and misleading and certainly unprofessional unless they are monitored carefully.

10. Don't Forget the Human Touch

Veteran correspondent Helen Thomas told the convention of newspaper interactive editors on Feb. 9, 2000: "I do hope the human touch remains in the robotic scheme of things. Human beings still count."

Remember, people make the news. Facts are just facts unless you relate them to people.

LEGAL AND ETHICAL CONCERNS

Online journalists have the same legal and ethical concerns as other journalists (see Chapters 14 and 15). Libel is still libel, and plagiarism is still plagiarism. Just because you are not "in print" doesn't mean that you can destroy someone's reputation or distort the truth. You always must be aware that what is on the Internet is not yours, even though the very design of it allows you to download words and images. If you use someone else's words, put quotation marks around them and cite the source.

Although the Internet makes it easier to find and steal someone else's work, it also makes it easier to get caught doing it. Already there have been several cases where Web readers of local columnists or reviewers have turned in a writer for plagiarism.

Plagiarism is not the only danger. Some areas of ethics are even more touchy and difficult to solve for online journalists:

- *Privacy.* Web sites exist that have files on nearly everyone. Some allow everyone to see what anyone has ever posted on a chat box. What may journalists use? Most everyone agrees that private e-mail is off-limits. But what about material sent to corporate intranets?
- *Advertising.* Newspapers and magazines generally try to label advertising as advertising, and they have rules that require ads to use typefaces different from those the publication uses for news and other articles. There also are rules about the placement of ads.

    Online ads regularly break up the copy of news stories or pop up over news stories. There is no separation of ads from editorial content and no attempt to make any separation.

    Why don't the rules that apply to print apply online? Note what the code of the American Society of Magazine Editors says:

The same ASME principles that mandate distinct treatment of editorial content, advertisements, and special advertisements, and special advertising sections ("advertorials") in print publications also apply to online editorial projects bearing the names of print magazines or offering themselves as electronic magazines. The dynamic technology of electronic pages and hypertext links creates a high potential for reader confusion. Permitting such confusion betrays reader trust and undermines the credibility not only of the offending online publication or editorial product, but also of the publisher itself. It is therefore the responsibility of each online publication to make clear to its readers which online content is editorial and which is advertising, and to prevent any juxtaposition that gives the impression that editorial material was created for—or influenced by—advertisers.

The ASME code then goes on to spell out 10 specific ways to carry out these general guidelines.

The code of the American Society of Business Press Editors says simply: "On all such papers, editors should ensure that a clear distinction is made between advertising and editorial content. This may involve type faces, layout/design, labeling, and juxtaposition of the editorial materials and the advertisement." The ASBPE code adds this important sentence: "Editors should directly supervise and control all links that appear with the editorial portion of the site."

- *Manipulating photos.* Print has not dealt with this problem well either. *New York Times* photographer Fred Ritchin proposed using an icon to flag a digitally altered photo. But how will readers know how much it has been altered? Will readers trust what they see?

- *Concealing your identity.* It's so easy to conceal your identity as a reporter on the Web. At times you may be doing undercover investigative reporting, but usually the time to reveal yourself as a reporter is at the outset of your questioning people online, not after you have gotten to a certain point in your story.

- *Corrections.* Some online news sites act as if they never make mistakes. They simply post new stories with updated information. Surely you owe it to readers to tell them that the story has changed or has been updated with new information and how that was done. Such notice of correction or updating will not be done unless the news site has a clear policy requiring it.

For example, Forbes.com erroneously quoted Disney Chairman Michael Eisner as saying he didn't think his company's network ABC would be operating "in four to five years." In the update to the story, the changed headline read, "Clarification: Eisner Discusses The ABC Brand And Other Brands." In addition to correcting the story, Forbes.com put asterisks next to the changed sentences and included explanations at the bottom of the story, such as: "The original version of this story incorrectly stated that Eisner did not see the third-ranked network being around in four to five years." In his column in *The Washington Post*, Howard Kurtz reported that Forbes.com editor Paul Maidment said his reporter had "extrapolated" without the "broader context."

▪ *Hyperlinks to external sites*. Is raw data journalism? How much and how often may you use raw data, and with what warnings or interpretations?

Also, a new question has arisen about linking to external sites. National Public Radio has banned anyone from linking to its Web pages. What does that mean? Does it have the power to do that? Is it now unethical to do so?

TOMORROW'S READERS

Print has been around for centuries, and we are still figuring out ways to use it effectively. In contrast, writing online is in its infancy. Like all good writers, online journalists must be students of writing. Both writers and readers are still learning the most effective uses of the newest medium, which is a sum of all media that is greater than its parts. The new media are more about showing than telling, about the audience experiencing rather than witnessing, about the audience actively participating rather than being passive, about the audience doing rather than merely reading. Perhaps never have writers been more challenged.

Suggested Readings

Bonime, Andrew and Pohlmann, Ken C. *Writing for New Media*. New York: John Wiley & Sons, 1998. A thorough guide for anyone wanting to learn to write for interactive media, CD-ROMs and the Web.

De Wolk, Roland. *Introduction to Online Journalism: Publishing News and Information*. Boston: Allyn and Bacon, 2001. A short, simple and readable text with a wonderful glossary of terms.

Morkes, John and Nielsen, Jakob. "Concise, SCANN-ABLE, and Objective: How to Write for the Web." Available from **www.useit.com/papers/webwriting/ writing.html**; Internet: Accessed Oct. 7, 1998. A wonderful summary of their research regarding effective online writing.

Nielsen, Jakob. "How Users Read on the Web." Available from **www.useit.com/alertbox/9710a .html**; Internet: Accessed Oct. 7, 1998. Practical advice, including research, on the usability of online copy.

Outing, Steve. "Report Once, Write Twice—for Print and Web." *Editor & Publisher Interactive*. Available from **www.mediainfo.com/ephome/news/ newshtm/news.htm**; Internet. A discussion of how the *Times Record News* in Wichita Falls, Texas, got its writers to supply on its Web site original content that is appropriate online.

Rich, Carole. *Creating Online Media: A Guide to Research, Writing and Design on the Internet*. New York: McGraw-Hill, 1999. A book that is as comprehensive as the title suggests by an author of other well-regarded journalism texts.

Ward, Mike. *Journalism Online*. Oxford: Focal Press, 2002. A non-dogmatic, common-sense approach to all matters regarding online journalism, including good advice for writers.

Suggested Web Sites

www.cincypost.com

Like many daily newspapers, the Cincinnati Post's online edition includes most of the stories from its print edition, along with additional online-only posts.

www.bayarea.com/mld/mercurynews/

The Mercury News, one of the first comprehensive local news Web sites, is a Bay Area, Calif., site that includes area news as well as links to the area's print newspapers.

www.msnbc.com/news/OP_Front.asp?0dm= C---O

This companion site to the cable news channel offers a wealth of news resources. Its opinions section includes, among other things, links to top stories; stories from Slate, another Microsoft Web site; opinion pieces and blogs—online journals written by pundits and journalists.

Exercises

1. Choose a major national story from a recent newspaper or newsmagazine. Then visit two newspaper Web sites and compare the treatment of the story. Write a 300-word critique of the online writing techniques that the Web sites used.

2. Visit your local newspaper or television station and interview individuals who do the news online. Find out how they were trained and what major challenges they face.

3. The professor will assign you a newspaper story. Rewrite it for online use, and indicate any hyperlinks that you might include.

4. Visit five newspaper or magazine Web sites. Then pick the one that does the best job of using online writing techniques, and write a 200-word report on your findings.

14 Law

The First Amendment states:

> Congress shall make no law respecting an establishment of religion, or prohibiting the free exercise thereof; or abridging the freedom of speech, or of the press; or the right of the people peaceably to assemble, and to petition the Government for a redress of grievances.

Read that again: "Congress shall make no law . . . abridging the freedom of . . . the press." No other business in the United States enjoys that specific constitutional protection, unless you count religion as business.

Why should there be such protection for the press? The Supreme Court gave an eloquent answer to that question in a 1957 obscenity decision. The press is protected, the court ruled, to assure the "unfettered interchange of ideas for bringing about the political and social changes desired by the people." The free flow of ideas is necessary in a democracy because people who govern themselves need to know about their government and those who run it, as well as about the social and economic institutions that greatly affect their day-to-day lives. Most people get that information through newspapers, the Internet, radio and television.

In 1966 Congress passed the **Freedom of Information Act** to assist anyone in finding out what is happening in federal agencies. This act, amended in 1996 by the Electronic Freedom of Information Act to improve access to computerized government records, makes it easier for you to know about government business. All 50 states have similar **open-records laws.** The federal government and all the states have **open-meetings laws** requiring that the public's business be conducted in public. However, all of these access laws contain exemptions keeping some meetings private.

The First Amendment and laws on access to information demonstrate America's basic concern for citizen access to information needed for the "unfettered interchange of ideas." Nevertheless, there are laws that reduce the scope of freedom of the press.

In this chapter you will learn:

1. What rights you have as a journalist and the source of those rights.
2. How to spot potentially libelous situations and what to do about them.
3. When you might be invading someone's privacy.
4. What kinds of problems you may face in protecting confidential sources.
5. What rights you have in obtaining access to courtrooms and court documents.
6. What you should know about copyrights and fair use.

"The government's power to censor the press was abolished so the press would remain forever free to censure the government."

*—Hugo Black,
Supreme Court Justice*

LIBEL

Traditionally, most of the laws limiting the absolute freedom of the press have dealt with **libel,** the damage to a person's reputation caused by making the person an object of hatred, contempt or ridicule in the eyes of a substantial and respectable group. These laws result from the desire of legislatures and courts to help individuals protect their reputations. Their importance was explained by U.S. Supreme Court Justice Potter Stewart in a libel case (parentheses added):

> The right of a man (or woman) to the protection of his (or her) own reputation from unjustified invasion and wrongful hurt reflects no more than our basic concept of the essential dignity and worth of every human being—a concept at the root of any decent system of ordered liberty.

"Journalists don't believe . . . the Freedom of Information Act was created to be turned on us as an excuse to hide information."

—Sarah Overstreet,
Columnist

Protection for reputations dates back centuries. In 17th-century England, individuals were imprisoned and even disfigured for making libelous statements. One objective was to prevent criticism of the government. Another was to maintain the peace by avoiding duels. Duels are rare today, and government is freely criticized, but the desire to protect an individual's reputation is just as strong.

A case concerning a general is helpful in understanding libel. The extensively covered trial was held in the winter of 1984-1985 in the federal courthouse in Manhattan. The case was based on a 1983 *Time* magazine cover story, "Verdict on the Massacre," about Israel's 1982 judicial inquiry into the massacre of several hundred civilians in two Palestinian refugee camps in Lebanon.

The *Time* article suggested that Ariel Sharon, then Israel's defense minister and later its prime minister, had ordered the massacre. The general sued *Time*. His attorneys knew they would have to show that their client had suffered hatred, contempt or ridicule because these statements were serious attacks on their client's reputation and not just unpleasant comments.

The jury's decision was in three parts. The first part of the verdict was in answer to this question: Was the paragraph concerning Sharon defamatory? The jury said it was. This meant the *Time* article had damaged Sharon's reputation and brought him into hatred, contempt or ridicule.

The second question for the jury was this: Was the paragraph concerning Sharon and revenge false? Again the jury answered affirmatively. If the answer had been no, the case would have ended there. Truth is a complete defense for libel.

The third question for the jury was this: Was the paragraph published with "actual malice"—with knowledge that it was false or with reckless disregard of whether it was false ("serious doubt" that it was true)? The jury answered no. Thus the trial ended in favor of *Time* magazine, despite the jury ruling that the article was defamatory.

Courts use four categories to help jurors like those in the Sharon case decide if someone's reputation has been damaged because he or she has been brought into hatred, contempt or ridicule. They are:

1. *Accusing someone of a crime.* This may have been the basis in the Sharon case.

2. *Damaging a person in his or her public office, profession or occupation.* If the statements by *Time* against Sharon did not accuse him of crimes, they did damage him in his profession as a military man.
3. *Accusing a person of serious immorality.* The example lawyers often use is accusing a woman of being unchaste. Many states have statutes that make an accusation of unchastity a cause of action in a libel suit.
4. *Accusing someone of having a loathsome (contagious) disease.* This category was fading as an area of defamation; however, the AIDS epidemic helped it reappear.

This does not mean you never can say a person committed a crime, was unethical in business, was adulterous or had a loathsome disease. It does mean you must be certain that what you write is true.

Libel Suit Defenses

There are three traditional defenses against libel: truth, privilege, and fair comment and criticism. Two other constitutional defenses—the actual malice and negligence tests—also help libel defendants.

Truth

Truth is the best defense against libel. In libel cases involving matters of public concern, the burden of proof is on the plaintiff. This placement of the burden, however, does not change the reporter's responsibility to seek the truth in every possible way.

You cannot be certain, for example, whether a person charged with arson actually started the fire. Who told you Joe Jones started the fire? The first source to check is the police or fire report. If a police officer or fire marshal says that Jones started a fire, you can report not that Jones did it but that he has been accused of doing it. Unless you have information you would be willing to present in court, you should go no further. Be sure to report no more than what you know is true.

When a newspaper in Oklahoma reported that a wrestling coach had been accused of requiring a sixth-grader, who wanted to rejoin the team, to submit to a whipping by his fellow students while crawling naked through the legs of team members, the coach sued. He claimed damage to his reputation.

In cases like this, the reporter has to be certain not just that one or more participants told of the incident but also that the statements were true. In court, some participants might testify to an occurrence, and others might testify the incident never took place. A jury would have to decide on the credibility of the participants.

Although you must always strive for absolute truth in all of your stories, the courts will settle for what is known as **substantial truth** in

most cases. This means that you must be able to prove the essential elements of all you write.

Privilege

In addition to truth, the courts traditionally have allowed another defense against libel: **privilege.** This defense applies when you are covering any of the three branches of government. The courts allow legislators, judges and government executives the **absolute privilege** to say anything—true or false—when acting in their official capacities. The rationale is that the public interest is served when an official is allowed to speak freely and fearlessly about making laws, carrying them out or punishing those who do not obey them. Similarly, a participant in a judicial proceeding, such as an attorney, court clerk or judge, is absolutely privileged to make false and even defamatory statements about another person during that proceeding.

In the executive branch it isn't always clear whose statements are privileged and when. The head of state and the major officers of executive departments of the federal and state governments are covered. However, minor officials might not enjoy the protection of absolute privilege.

As a reporter you have a **qualified privilege,** sometimes called *neutral reporting* or *conditional privilege,* to report what public officials say. Your privilege is conditioned on your report's providing full, fair and accurate coverage of the court session, the legislative session or the president's press conference, even if any of the participants made defamatory statements. The privilege is also conditioned on clear attribution to the session or press conference. You can quote anything the president of the United States says without fear of losing a libel suit, even if the president is not acting in an official capacity. Reporters have a qualified privilege to report unofficial presidential statements. But there are many other levels of executives in federal, state and local government. Mayors of small towns, for instance, often hold part-time positions. Although you are conditionally privileged to report on what those officials say when they are acting in their official capacities, a problem can arise when a part-time mayor says something defamatory when not acting in an official capacity. Some jurisdictions might grant a neutral reporting privilege; some might not.

Fair Comment and Criticism

In some writing you may be commenting or criticizing rather than reporting. The courts have protected writers who comment on and criticize the public offerings of anyone in the public eye. Individuals included in this category are actors and actresses, sports figures, public

rooted in professionalism and common sense. Paulson suggests that journalists ask themselves these questions:

- Have I reported fully?
- Have I reported factually?
- Have I reported fairly?
- Have I reported in good faith?

"If you can answer those four questions in the affirmative, the law will take care of itself," he says. Paulson joined the Gannett Company in 1978. He has been executive editor of *Florida Today* in Melbourne, Fla.; editor of the *Green Bay (Wis.) Press-Gazette;* managing editor of the *Bridgewater (N.J.) Courier-News* and executive editor of Gannett Suburban Newspapers in the New York counties of Westchester, Rockland and Putnam.

officials and other newsworthy persons. Most often, such writing occurs in reviews of plays, books or movies, or in commentary on service in hotels and restaurants.

The courts call this **fair comment and criticism.** You are protected as long as you do not misstate any of the facts on which you base your comments or criticism, or as long as you do not wrongly imply that you possess undisclosed, damaging information that forms the basis of your opinion. Merely labeling a fact as an opinion will not result in opinion protection, the U.S. Supreme Court ruled in 1990.

The Actual Malice Test

It was a small but momentous step from fair comment and criticism to the case of *The New York Times* vs. Sullivan. In 1964 the U.S. Supreme Court decided that First Amendment protection was broader than just the traditional defenses of truth and privilege and that the press needed even greater freedom in coverage of public officials.

The case started with an advertisement for funds in *The New York Times* of March 29, 1960, by the Committee to Defend Martin Luther King Jr. and the Struggle for Freedom in the South. The advertisement contained factual errors concerning the police, according to Montgomery, Ala., Commissioner L.B. Sullivan. He thought the errors damaged his reputation, and he won a half-million-dollar judgment against *The New York Times* in an Alabama trial court.

The Supreme Court said it was considering the case "against the background of a profound national commitment to the principle that debate on public issues should be uninhibited, robust and wide open." Thus Justice William Brennan wrote that the Constitution requires a federal rule prohibiting a public official from recovering damages from the press for a defamatory falsehood relating to his or her official conduct, unless the public official can prove the press had knowledge that what was printed was false or that the story was printed with reckless disregard of whether it was false or not.

The justices called this the **actual malice test.**

The decision in the Sharon case discussed earlier in the chapter is an example of the burden of proving **actual malice** against the press. The jury decided that *Time* did not know when the article in question was printed that its statement about Gen. Sharon was false.

In 1991, the Supreme Court decided Masson vs. *The New Yorker,* the so-called "fabricated quotes" case. Masson, a psychotherapist, had sued the magazine and journalist Janet Malcolm, accusing them of making up quotes he never said. Overruling a lower court's decision that journalists could fictionalize quotations by making rational interpretations of speakers' remarks, the Supreme Court protected the sanctity of quotation marks. But the court also made clear that not every deliberate change in a quotation is libelous. Only a "material change in the meaning conveyed by a statement" poses a problem.

Although Masson won the right to try his case, he lost against all defendants. Malcolm won in 1994.

Standards Applicable to Public Figures

The actual malice protection was expanded in two cases in 1967 to include not only public officials but also public figures—persons in the public eye but not in public office.

The first case stemmed from a *Saturday Evening Post* article that accused Coach Wally Butts of conspiring to fix a 1962 football game between Georgia and Alabama. At the time of the article, Butts was the athletic director of the University of Georgia. The article, titled "The Story of a College Football Fix," was prefaced by a note from the editors of the *Post* stating:

> Not since the Chicago White Sox threw the 1919 World Series has there been a sports story as shocking as this one. . . . Before the University of Georgia played the University of Alabama . . . Wally Butts . . . gave (to Alabama's coach) . . . Georgia's plays, defensive patterns, all the significant secrets Georgia's football team possessed.

The *Post* reported that, because of an electronic error about a week before the game, George Burnett, an Atlanta insurance salesman, accidentally had overheard a telephone conversation between Butts and the head coach of Alabama, Paul Bryant.

Coach Butts sued Curtis Publishing, publishers of the *Post*, and won a verdict for $60,000 in general damages and $3 million in punitive damages. Curtis Publishing appealed the case to the Supreme Court and lost. The trial judge reduced the amount of the damages to $460,000.

The second case was decided the same day. Gen. Edwin Walker sued the Associated Press for distributing a news dispatch giving an eyewitness account by an AP staffer on the campus of the University of Mississippi in the fall of 1962. The AP reported that Gen. Walker personally had led a student charge against federal marshals during a riot on the Mississippi campus. The marshals were attempting to enforce a court decree ordering the enrollment of a black student.

Walker was a retired general at the time of the publication. He had won a $2 million libel suit in a trial court. However, the Supreme Court ruled against him.

In both cases the stories were wrong. In both, the actual malice test was applied. What was the difference between the Butts and Walker cases? The justices said the football story was in no sense "hot news." They noted that the person who said he had heard the conversation was on probation in connection with bad-check charges and that *Post* personnel had not viewed his notes before publication. The court also said, as evidence of actual malice on the part of the *Post*, that no one looked at the game films to see if the information was accurate; that a regular staffer, instead of a football expert, was assigned to the story; and that no check was made with someone knowledgeable in the sport. In short, the *Post* had not done an adequate job of reporting.

The evidence in the Walker case was considerably different. The court said the news in the Walker case required immediate dissemination because of the riot on campus. The justices noted that the AP received the information from a correspondent who was present on the campus and gave every indication of being trustworthy and competent.

In the Butts and Walker cases the court used two definitions of a public figure. The first, like Butts, is a person who has assumed a role of special prominence in the affairs of society—someone who has pervasive power and influence in a community. The second, like Walker, is a person who has thrust himself into the forefront of a particular public controversy in order to influence the resolution of the issues involved.

In the 1970s the Supreme Court decided three cases that help journalists determine who is and is not a public figure. The first case involved Mrs. Russell A. Firestone, who sued for libel after *Time* magazine reported that her husband's divorce petition had been granted on grounds of extreme cruelty and adultery. Mrs. Firestone, who had married into the Firestone Tire and Rubber Co. family, claimed that those were not the grounds for the divorce. She also insisted that she was not a public figure with the burden of proving actual malice. The Supreme Court agreed. Even though she had held press conferences and hired a clipping service, the court ruled that she had not thrust herself into the forefront of a public controversy in an attempt to influence the resolution of the issues involved. The court admitted that marital difficulties of extremely wealthy individuals may be of some interest to some portion of the reading public but added that Firestone had not freely chosen to publicize private matters about her married life. The justices said she was compelled to go to court to "obtain legal release from the bonds of matrimony." They said she assumed no "special prominence in the resolution of public questions." The case was sent back to Florida for a finding of fault, and a new trial was ordered. Firestone remarried, and the case was settled out of court.

The second case involved Sen. William Proxmire of Wisconsin, who had started what he called the Golden Fleece Award. Each month he announced a winner who, in his opinion, had wasted government money. One such winner was Ronald Hutchinson, a behavioral scientist who had received federal funding for research designed to determine why animals clench their teeth. Hutchinson had published articles about his research in professional publications. In deciding that Hutchinson was not a public figure, the court ruled that he "did not thrust himself or his views into public controversy to influence others." The court admitted there may have been legitimate concerns about the way public funds were being spent but said this was not enough to make Hutchinson a public figure.

The third case concerned an individual found guilty of contempt of court in 1958 for his failure to appear before a grand jury investigating Soviet espionage in the United States. In a 1974 book published by the Reader's Digest Association, Ilya Wolston's name was included in a list of people indicted for serving as Soviet agents. Wolston, however, had not been indicted, and he sued.

The Supreme Court, in deciding that he was not a public figure, found that Wolston had played only a minor role in whatever public controversy there may have been concerning the investigation of Soviet espionage. The court added that a private individual is not automatically transformed into a public figure merely by becoming involved in or being associated with a matter that attracts public attention.

As a journalist, do you have the same protection from a libel action when you write about a person somewhat connected with a news event as you do when you are certain a person is a public figure or public official? A 1974 Supreme Court decision says the answer usually is no. In the landmark Gertz vs. Welch case, the justices said states may give more protection to private individuals if a newspaper or radio or television station damages their reputations than if the reputations of either public officials or public figures are damaged. Generally, you have protection from a libel action when you write about people who have thrust themselves into the forefront of a controversy or event.

Standards Applicable to Private Citizens

Private citizens who sue for punitive, or punishment, damages must meet the same actual malice test as public officials and public figures. Because of the Gertz case, states have been allowed to set their own standards for libel cases involving private citizens who sue only for actual damages. A majority of states and the District of Columbia have adopted a negligence test, which requires you to use the same care in gathering facts and writing your story as any reasonable reporter would use under the same or similar circumstances. If you made every effort to be fair and answer all the questions a reasonable person might ask, you probably would pass the negligence test.

One state, New York, has adopted a gross irresponsibility test. A few states have established a more stringent standard that requires private citizens to prove actual malice. Some states simply require a jury to find "fault."

Libel Remains a Danger

Despite all the available defenses, libel remains a serious risk to journalists' financial health, as the following example demonstrates: In 1997, a Texas jury awarded a record $222.7 million to a defunct bond-brokerage firm against Dow Jones & Co., which owns *The Wall Street Journal*. The judge threw out $200 million in punitive damages but let stand the $22.7 million in actual damages for a *Journal* story about "bond daddies."

Libel and the Internet

Individuals who libel others over the Internet can be held liable. But the Internet raises the interesting question of whether an online service provider such as America Online or Microsoft Network can be liable for libelous messages of their users.

In 1991, CompuServe successfully defended itself against a libel suit in a New York federal trial court. CompuServe had made a contract with another company to provide an electronic bulletin board in the form of a newsletter about journalism. The second company then used a third company to create the newsletter. Because CompuServe did not try to exercise any editorial control over the newsletter, the court let CompuServe off the hook for libel. The court also reasoned that no library can be held responsible if a book that the librarian has not reviewed contains libel. CompuServe, the court said, was providing an "electronic, for-profit library."

In 1995, however, Prodigy lost a libel case. In order to promote itself as a family-oriented Internet service provider, Prodigy controlled the content of its computer bulletin boards by using screening software to look for forbidden words, and its editorial staff bounced allegedly offensive notes. Unfortunately for Prodigy, no list of software-generated words could screen for libel. A New York trial court said that by holding itself out as exercising editorial control, Prodigy was "expressly differentiating itself from its competition and expressly likening itself to a newspaper." Thus the court treated Prodigy like a newspaper and held it liable for libel posted on one of its bulletin boards.

Congress did not agree with the Prodigy decision, however, and effectively overruled the case in 1996 by passing "protection for 'Good Samaritan' blocking and screening of offensive material." Congress obviously did not support the idea that failure to screen meant protection from libel but any screening meant liability.

INVASION OF PRIVACY

"There are only two occasions when Americans respect privacy. . . . Those are prayer and fishing."
—**Herbert Hoover,**
31st President of the United States

Libel is damage to an individual's reputation. **Invasion of privacy** is a violation of a person's right to be left alone.

As a reporter, you may be risking an invasion-of-privacy suit under any of the following circumstances:

▪ You physically intrude into a private area to get a story or picture—an act closely related to trespass.
▪ You publish a story or photograph about someone that is misleading and thus portray that person in a "false light."
▪ You disclose something about an individual's private affairs that is true but also is highly offensive to individuals of ordinary sensibilities.

Invasion of privacy may also be claimed if someone's name or picture is used in an advertisement or for similar purposes of trade. Called *appropriation*, this does not affect you when you are performing your reporting duties.

Consent is a basic defense in invasion-of-privacy suits. Make sure, however, that your use of the material does not exceed the consent given.

Another basic defense in an invasion-of-privacy suit is that you're a reporter covering a newsworthy situation. The courts usually protect the press against invasion-of-privacy suits when it is reporting matters of legitimate public interest. There are three exceptions, however.

You may be committing invasion of privacy by

▪ *Trespassing on private property.*
▪ *Portraying someone in a "false light."*
▪ *Causing unwanted publicity that is offensive to a person of ordinary sensibilities.*

Trespassing

One exception arises when you invade someone's privacy by entering private property to get a story. You cannot trespass on private property to get a story or take a picture even if it is newsworthy. The courts will not protect you when you are a trespasser. Two *Life* magazine staffers lost an invasion-of-privacy suit because, with one posing as a patient, they went into a man's home to get a story about a faith healer. They lost the case even though they were working with the district attorney and the state board of health. You may enter private property only when you are invited by the owner or renter.

Portraying in a "False Light"

The court also will not protect you if you invade someone's privacy by publishing misleading information about that person. For example, a legal problem arises if a photograph or information from a true story about a careful pedestrian struck by a careless driver is used again in connection with a story, say, about careless pedestrians. The pedestrian who was hit could file a lawsuit charging libel, "false light" invasion of privacy or even both in some states.

Some states do not recognize "false light" invasion of privacy and insist that libel is the appropriate form of suit. But "false light" suits can cover situations where a picture or story is misleading but not defamatory. Even flattering material can place a person in an unwanted, false light.

Causing Unwanted Publicity Offensive to a Person of Ordinary Sensibilities

The third category of invasion of privacy that the courts recognize— unwanted publicity—concerns stories about incidents that, because they are true, cannot be defamatory but can be highly offensive to a person of ordinary sensibilities. An example is a picture published by *Sports Illustrated* in which a football fan's pants zipper was open. The fan sued for invasion of privacy but lost. Also in the area of unwanted publicity, the Supreme Court held in 1975 and again in 1989 that truthfully reporting the name of a rape victim is permitted. In 1976 and in 1979 the justices upheld the right of the press to publish the names of juveniles involved with the law because the information was truthful and of public significance.

The courts say that in order for privacy to be invaded, there must be a morbid and sensational prying into private lives. Merely being the subject of an unflattering and embarrassing article is not enough.

PROTECTION OF SOURCES AND NOTES

Another area you must know about is your ability—or inability—to protect your sources and notes. The problem may arise in various situations. A grand jury that is investigating a murder may ask you to reveal the source of a story you wrote about the murder. You may be asked to testify at a criminal or a civil trial.

The conflict here is between a reporter's need to protect sources of information and the duty of every citizen to testify to help the courts determine justice. Because of the nature of your work as a

> "(The media) seek to maintain a balance on the constantly shifting tightrope of personal privacy, access to information and government accountability."
>
> —*John R. Finnegan Sr.,*
> *Former newspaper editor*

reporter, you will be at the scene of events that are important and newsworthy. Anyone wanting the facts about an event can subpoena you to bring in all the details. Journalists usually resist. They work for their newspaper or radio or television station, not a law-enforcement agency. Their ability to gather information would be compromised if the sources knew that their identities or their information would go to the police.

By 2001 some protection against testifying—**shield laws**—had been adopted by 31 states and the District of Columbia. The states are:

Alabama	Kentucky	New York
Alaska	Louisiana	North Carolina
Arizona	Maryland	North Dakota
Arkansas	Michigan	Ohio
California	Minnesota	Oklahoma
Colorado	Montana	Oregon
Delaware	Nebraska	Pennsylvania
Florida	Nevada	Rhode Island
Georgia	New Jersey	South Carolina
Illinois	New Mexico	Tennessee
Indiana		

Congress had not acted in this area in part because journalists themselves were divided about the desirability of such legislation. However, Congress did pass the **Privacy Protection Act** of 1980. Under that act, federal, state and local enforcement officers generally may not use a search warrant to search news rooms. Instead, they must get a subpoena for documents, which tells the reporters to hand over the material. Officers may use a warrant to search news rooms only if they suspect a reporter of being involved in a crime or if immediate action is needed to prevent bodily harm, loss of life or destruction of the material.

The difference between a *search warrant* and a *subpoena* is great. Officers with a search warrant can knock on the door, enter the news room and search on their own. A subpoena does not permit officers to search the news room. A subpoena for documents requires reporters to turn over the material to authorities at a predetermined time and place. In addition, it gives reporters time to challenge in court the necessity of surrendering the material.

Even in states with shield laws, judges in most criminal cases involving grand juries will not allow you to keep your sources secret. In other criminal cases, courts may allow confidentiality if a three-part test is met. Supreme Court Justice Potter Stewart suggested this test in his dissent in Branzburg vs. Hayes:

> Government officials must, therefore, demonstrate that the information sought is clearly relevant to a precisely defined subject of

government inquiry. . . . They must demonstrate that it is reasonable to think the witness in question has that information. . . . And they must show that there is not any means of obtaining the information less destructive of First Amendment liberties. . . .

In civil litigation you may be permitted to keep sources confidential in most cases unless the court finds that the information sought is unavailable from other sources and highly relevant to the underlying litigation or is of such critical importance to the lawsuit that it goes to the heart of the plaintiff's claim.

If you are sued for libel, you will find it very difficult both to protect your sources and win the lawsuit. The court might very well rule against you on whether a statement is true or false if the statement came from a source you refuse to name.

The best way to avoid such confrontation with the courts is not to promise a source you will keep his or her name confidential. Only for the most compelling reason should you promise confidentiality.

In 1991, the U.S. Supreme Court ruled in Cohen vs. Cowles Media Company that the First Amendment does not prevent a source from suing a news organization if a reporter has promised the source confidentiality but the newspaper publishes the source's name anyway.

ACCESS TO COURTS

The Supreme Court held in 1979 that "members of the public have no constitutional right" under the Sixth Amendment to attend criminal trials. In a reversal exactly one year later, the justices held that the public and the press have a First Amendment right to attend criminal trials. The justices said the right was not absolute but trial judges could close criminal trials only when there was an "overriding interest" to justify such closure. The basic concern of judges when they close trials is to protect the accused person's Sixth Amendment right to an "impartial jury"—often translated by attorneys into "a fair trial."

In addition, the First Amendment prevents the government from conducting business—even trials—in secret. In the Richmond Newspapers case in 1980, Chief Justice Warren Burger traced the unbroken and uncontradicted history of open judicial proceedings in England and the United States. He concluded that there is a "presumption of openness" in criminal trials and pointed out the important role of the news media as representatives of the public.

By 1984 the Supreme Court had decided that openness in criminal trials "enhances both the basic fairness of the criminal trial and the appearance of fairness so essential to public confidence in the system." Public proceedings vindicate the concerns of victims and the community in knowing that offenders are being brought to account for their criminal conduct "by jurors fairly and openly selected." Proceedings of jury selection could be closed, the chief justice said, only when a trial judge finds that closure preserves an "overriding interest" and is narrowly tailored to serve that interest.

Judges are using that option. For instance, when John Gotti was convicted of Mafia activities in New York, the jurors' names were kept secret. Gotti's attorneys unsuccessfully challenged the anonymity. Jurors' names in the Rodney King and Reginald Denny cases in Los Angeles also were withheld.

In 1986 the Supreme Court said only an overriding interest found by a trial judge can overcome the presumption of openness of criminal proceedings. Today, 47 states allow cameras in at least some state courtrooms. Cameras are permitted in some lower federal courts but are excluded from the Supreme Court.

COPYRIGHT AND FAIR USE

The purpose of copyright law is to ensure compensation to authors for contributing to the common good by publishing their works. The Constitution provides for this in Article 1, Section 8, by giving Congress the power to secure "for limited times to authors and inventors the exclusive right to their respective writing and discoveries." The same section indicates that this provision is intended "to promote the progress of science and useful arts" for the benefit of the public. Copyright laws protect your work and prohibit you from using significant amounts of others' writings without permission, and, in some cases, a fee.

Key elements of copyright law include the following:

- Copyrightable works are protected from the moment they are fixed in tangible form, whether published or unpublished.
- Copyright protection begins with a work's "creation and . . . endures for a term consisting of the life of the author and 70 years after the author's death."
- Works for hire and anonymous and pseudonymous works are protected for 95 years from publication or 100 years from creation, whichever is shorter.
- There is a "fair use" limitation on the exclusive rights of copyright owners. In other words, it may be permissible to use small excerpts from a copyrighted work without permission. According to the Supreme Court, these factors govern fair use:
  1. The purpose and character of the use.
  2. The nature of the copyrighted work.

3. The substantiality of the portion used in relationship to the copyrighted work as a whole.
4. The effect on the potential market for or value of the copyrighted work.

Although a work is copyrighted from the moment it is fixed in tangible form, the copyright statute says certain steps are necessary for the work to receive statutory protection. The author or publisher must:

- Publish or reproduce the work with the word "copyright" or the symbol ©, the name of the copyright owner and the year of publication.
- Register the work at the Library of Congress by filling out a form supplied by the Copyright Office and sending the form, a specified number of copies (usually one copy of an unpublished work and two copies of a published work), and a $30 fee to the Copyright Office. The copies and registration fee may be sent together and usually are.

Copyright law has a special provision for broadcasters of live programs. Broadcasters need only make a simultaneous tape of their live broadcasts in order to receive copyright protection. The tape fulfills the requirement that a work be in a "fixed" form for copyright protection. Because a digital form is a "fixed" form, editors of electronic newspapers already meet that copyright requirement.

Some aspects of U.S. copyright law changed in 1989, when the United States finally joined the 100-year-old Berne Convention, an international copyright treaty, primarily to prevent the pirating of American film productions in other countries. The changes include the following:

- *Placing a copyright notice on a work is no longer necessary to preserve a copyright after publication.* This is in line with the Berne Convention principle that the exercise of a copyright should not be subject to formalities. Nevertheless, the copyright notice is still useful because it acts as a bar to an infringer's claim of innocent infringement.
- *Copyright registration is no longer a prerequisite for access to the federal courts for an infringement action.* But registration is required for a copyright owner to recover statutory damages. (Without registration, the copyright owner can recover only the damages he or she can prove, court costs and "reasonable" attorney's fees.) The amount of statutory damages, generally between $750 and $30,000, is determined by the judge. If the infringer was not aware he or she was infringing a copyright, the court may award as little as $200. If the infringement was willful, the court can award up to $150,000. Thus, like the copyright notice, copyright registration remains highly advisable.

Suggested Readings

Carter, T. Barton, Franklin, Marc A. and Wright, Jay B. *The First Amendment and the Fourth Estate*, Sixth Edition. Westbury, N.Y.: Foundation Press, 1994.

Gilmour, Donald M., Barron, Jerome A., Simon, Todd F. and Terry, Herbert A. *Mass Communications Law*, Fifth Edition. New York: West, 1990.

Holsinger, Ralph and Dills, Jon Paul. *Media Law*, Third Edition. New York: McGraw-Hill, 1987.

Middleton, Kent R. and Chamberlin, Bill F. *The Law of Public Communication*, Third Edition. New York: Longman, 1994.

Overbeck, Wayne. *Major Principles of Media Law*. Fort Worth, Texas: Harcourt Brace, 1993.

Pember, Don R. *Mass Media Law*, Sixth Edition. Dubuque, Iowa: McGraw-Hill, 1993.

Teeter, Dwight L. Jr. and Le Duc, Don R. *Law of Mass Communications*, Seventh Edition. Westbury, N.Y.: Foundation Press, 1995.

Zelensky, John D. *Communications Law*. Belmont, Calif.: Wadsworth, 1993.

Suggested Web Sites

www.freedomforum.org/first/timeline97.asp

A wonderful chronology of the "significant historical events, court cases, and ideas that have shaped our current system of constitutional First Amendment jurisprudence," presented by the Freedom Forum. Also, stories, commentaries and round-ups of First Amendment disputes.

www.refp.org

The Reporters Committee for Freedom of the Press maintains online "publications and topical guides on First Amendment and Freedom of Information issues." Current hot stories, plus archives and much more.

www.freedomforum.org/newsstand/reports/sofa/printsofa.asp

The Freedom Forum has online the report *State of the First Amendment* by Donna Demas, also published on paper. Discusses the public's ambivalence about First Amendment issues.

www.ldrc.com

Site of the Libel Defense Resource Center, "a non-profit information clearinghouse organized in 1980 by leading media groups to monitor and promote First Amendment rights, in the libel, privacy, and related fields of law." Includes a 50-state survey of media libel law, 1998-1999.

Exercises

1. Which defense for libel discussed in this chapter would you have used in defending *Time* magazine in the lawsuit filed by Gen. Ariel Sharon? Why?

2. *The New York Times* vs. Sullivan case was significant as a landmark decision in favor of the press. Discuss what the consequences for the press could have been if the decision had been different.

3. You are on an assignment with your photographer, who enters a house without permission and photographs the sale of illegal drugs. Discuss the issues raised by the circumstances, and explain why you would or would not publish the pictures.

4. Using the Lexis database, determine how the U.S. Supreme Court has used Richmond Newspapers vs. Virginia, 448 U.S. 555 (1980), in later cases dealing with openness in criminal proceedings.

15 Ethics

**In this chapter
you will learn:**

1. Philosophical
   approaches that can
   provide answers to
   ethical questions.
2. A means of ethical
   reasoning.
3. Ethical questions of
   special importance to
   journalists.

B ecause of the wide range of the First Amendment and its rela- tively few legal restraints, journalism, perhaps more than any other profession, needs to discuss proper conduct.

Like other professional groups, associations of journalists such as the Society of Professional Journalists have codes of conduct. Of course, journalists do not have to belong to such organizations to prac- tice their profession. A majority of newspapers and television stations now have written codes of ethics. Large news organizations are most likely to have them.

Critics of journalism codes of ethics condemn them either for being hopelessly general and therefore ineffective or for being too restrictive. Some argue that strict codes help improve journalists' credibility, but others say they merely make journalists easy targets for libel suits.

Your organization may or may not have a code of ethics. Either way, you should devise your own ethical values and principles. Your upbringing, and perhaps your religious training and your education, have already helped prepare you to do that.

THREE ETHICAL PHILOSOPHIES

"Ethics is a system of principles, a morality or code of conduct. It is the values and rules of life recognized by an individual, group or culture seeking guide- lines to human con- duct and what is good or bad, right or wrong."

— **Conrad C. Fink,**
Media Ethics professor

Your personal ethics may derive from the way you answer one funda- mental question: Does the end justify the means? Should you ever do something that is not good in itself in order to achieve a goal that you think is good?

If you answer no to that question, you are in some sense at least an *absolutist* or a legalist, and you would most likely subscribe to *deon- tological ethics*. If you answer yes to that question, you are more of a *relativist* and would subscribe to *teleological ethics*. If you answer maybe or sometimes, you would subscribe to a form of *situation ethics*.

Don't be put off by the jargon of philosophers. To understand ethical thinking, to be able to discuss ethics and to solve ethical prob- lems that arise on the job, you need to learn the vocabulary of ethicists (**www2.hawaii.edu/~tbrislin/jethics.html/**).

Deontological Ethics

Deontological ethics is the ethics of duty. According to this philoso- phy, you have a duty to do what is right. Deontologists believe that some actions are always right, some always wrong; that there exists in nature (or, for those with religious faith, in divine revelation) a fixed set of principles or laws from which there should be no deviation. For a deontologist, the end never justifies the means. That belief is why some refer to this ethical philosophy as **absolutism** or legalism.

An absolutist or legalist sees one clear duty—to discover the rules and to follow them. For example, if it is wrong to lie, it always is wrong to lie. Suppose a murderer comes to your door and asks where your roommates are so that he or she can murder them. If you were an absolutist, you would not lie to save their lives.

One such absolutist was Immanuel Kant (1724-1804). Kant proposed the "categorical imperative," a moral law that obliges you to do only those things that you would be willing to have everyone do as a matter of universal law. Once you make that decision, you must regard your decision as "categorical" and without exception, and you must do what you decide.

Many people draw support for their absolutism or legalism from their religious beliefs. They cite the Bible, the Koran or another religious source. If they themselves cannot resolve an ethical dilemma, they may turn to a minister, priest, rabbi or guru for the answer. The absolutist is concerned only with doing what is right and needs only to discover what that is.

The absolutist journalist is concerned only with whether an event is newsworthy. If an event is interesting, timely, significant or important, it is to be reported, regardless of the consequences. The duty of the journalist is to report the news. Period. Walter Cronkite once said that if journalists worried about what all the possible consequences could be for reporting something, they would never report anything.

> "I tell the honest truth in my paper, and I leave the consequences to God."
> —*James Gordon Bennett,*
> *Newspaper publisher, 1836*

People rely on the news media to keep them informed. That is why journalists enjoy First Amendment privileges. Charles A. Dana, who in 1868 began a 29-year career as editor of the *New York Sun*, said, "Whatever God in his infinite wisdom has allowed to happen, I am not too proud to print."

Absolutists discount any criticism of the press for printing or broadcasting certain stories. Stop blaming the messenger, they say. We don't make events happen; we just report them.

Teleological Ethics

Teleological ethics is the ethics of final ends. According to this philosophy, what makes an act ethical is not the act itself but the consequences of the act. Teleologists believe that the end can and often does justify the means. In this philosophy, ethics are more relativistic than absolutist.

From a teleological perspective, stealing, for example, may not always be wrong: A mother who steals food for her starving child would be performing a virtuous act. Similarly, a teleologist would say, a person who lies to save someone's life would be acting ethically, and a person who kills to protect his or her own life would be acting morally.

An important consideration in teleological ethics is the intention of the person performing the act. What one person would declare unethical, another person would do for a good purpose or a good reason. For example, police often work undercover, concealing their identity in order to apprehend criminals. In the course of that work, if they must lie or even get involved in criminal activity, the teleological response would be: So be it. Their purpose is to protect the public; their intention is to work for the good of society. The end justifies the means.

Some journalists would not hesitate to do the same. Some would require some conditions to be in place before they would steal or use deceit, but then they would proceed. They believe their purpose is to be the watchdog of government, to protect the common good, to keep the public fully informed. Whatever they must do to accomplish these goals, they argue, is clearly ethical.

Situation Ethics

Situation ethics is the ethics of specific acts. When asked whether the end justifies the means, a person subscribing to situation ethics would reply, "It all depends." Here are six philosophies that make use of some form of situation ethics.

Antinomianism

Antinomianism is the belief that there are no moral absolutes and that there is only one operative principle: Every person and every situation is unique, and to resolve an ethical dilemma by applying principles held by others or principles that apply in other cases is unethical. An antinomian believes that because each situation is unique, each ethical problem must be judged entirely on its own merits.

John Merrill's Deontelics

Other proponents of situation ethics are not as extreme as the antinomians. Some ethicists shy away from absolutism and advocate considering both the act and the consequences of the act. Journalism scholar and ethicist John Merrill calls such ethics **deontelics**—a word he coined combining deontological and teleological ethics. To act responsibly, Merrill says, journalists must consider more than just the ethics of the act, though they dare not ignore that some acts are by their very nature unethical in most cases.

For a journalist, telling the truth is paramount and lying is unethical—in most cases. According to deontelic theory, there may be a rare time when lying is justifiable for a good purpose. For example, an investigative reporter might justify lying about his or her identity as a journalist if that is the only way to get information for an important story.

Love of Neighbor

A third type of situation ethics has been described by Joseph Fletcher. Fletcher bases his philosophy on love of neighbor as articulated in the Golden Rule and the maxim "You shall love your neighbor as yourself." He presents his ethic from a Christian perspective with roots in Judaic teaching, but one need not profess Christianity to share the conviction that all principles are relative to one absolute—love of neighbor. Indeed, most religions, as well as secular humanism, hold human values as the highest good.

Although persons who subscribe to this belief understand and accept other ethical maxims and weigh them carefully when facing an ethical decision, they must be prepared to set them aside completely if love of neighbor demands it. In the broad sense, followers of Fletcher's form of situation ethics always place people first. In every ethical dilemma, they always do what is best for people. Sometimes they must choose between love for one person and love for a larger community of people.

Utilitarianism

The thinking that Fletcher advocates leads to another form of situation ethics: utilitarianism. From the utilitarian perspective, your choices are ethical if you always choose the action that is likely to bring the most happiness to the greatest number of people. This theory, formulated by John Stuart Mill (1806-1873) and Jeremy Bentham (1748-1832), was later modified to emphasize the greatest good rather than the greatest happiness. Some utilitarians also add the words "over a long period of time," because some actions may seem wrong if one looks merely at the present situation.

Most journalists probably subscribe to a utilitarian philosophy. They know, for example, that publishing a story about the infidelities of a public official may destroy the person's reputation, hurt his or her family and perhaps even lead to suicide, but, taking a utilitarian view, they decide that for the greater good, the public should have this information. The decision to publish would seem even more justifiable if the public official were involved in embezzlement or bribery.

John Rawls' Veil of Ignorance

Political theorist John Rawls would have you treat all people the same, as if all differences in social or economic status were concealed behind a "veil of ignorance." Behind the veil, all people would be equal, regardless of their race, gender, age and looks. If there were any unequal treatment, it would benefit the least advantaged person or persons.

first world news editor of MSNBC Interactive. He is now production support manager for global information technology at Microsoft Consulting Services.

From early experiences, particularly from one "bloody fable with a messy lesson," Callan developed his first principles of ethics as a news room manager:

1. Every decision you make has ethical and causal implications in the life, the work and the ethics of reporters.
2. You cannot ensure that reporters will act professionally and ethically in all situations, but you can choose reporters who will act professionally and ethically in most situations.
3. If you do not create a culture and an environment in which reporters can act ethically, you can't hope that they will, and you are responsible for their ethical lapses if they do not.

Rawls argues that these considerations would make people act more in tune with their rational self-interest. People would be more likely to look out for themselves if they placed themselves in the position of others.

In our society, research indicates that wealthy white men and poor African-American men who commit the same crimes seldom receive the same sentences. The "veil of ignorance" would help judges and juries to disregard racial and other differences.

Journalists often treat famous people, especially politicians, more harshly than they treat average citizens. If journalists placed themselves with politicians behind the veil, perhaps their adversarial attitude would dissipate somewhat.

Aristotle's Golden Mean

Another form of situation ethics derives from Aristotle's notion of the **Golden Mean,** a moderate moral position that avoids either of two extremes. Aristotle states that after considering the extremes, a person is likely to find a rational and moral position somewhere in between—and not necessarily in the middle.

Journalists make choices ranging from running no photographs of a crime to running the most graphic display of a violent death. A person who subscribes to the ethics of the Golden Mean would try to run a photo that indicates the horror of the tragedy without offending the sensibilities of the audience or of the family involved.

SOLVING ETHICAL DILEMMAS

Unless you are an absolutist, ethical reasoning can take many forms. You may adopt one or more ethical stances, and they will guide your day-to-day ethical decision making. What is paramount is that you engage in **principled reasoning.** You must deliberate by reflecting on ethical principles—principles that will help you decide on proper or moral ways to act.

Principled reasoning assumes that you are not acting ethically if you do something simply because you have been told to do it or because that's what everyone else does. You are not ethical if you report a story just to beat the competition.

To help journalists and others make ethical decisions, ethicists Clifford Christians, Kim Rotzoll and Mark Fackler have adapted a model of moral reasoning devised by Dr. Ralph Potter of the Harvard Divinity School. Called the Potter Box (see Figure 15.1), the model has four elements:

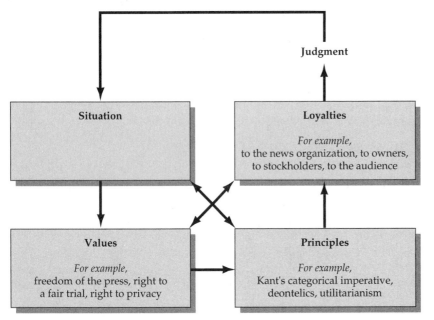

Figure 15.1
The Potter Box can help journalists analyze and resolve ethical problems.

1. *Appraising the situation.* Making a good ethical decision begins with good reporting. You need all the facts from a variety of sources. Reaching a decision without trying to know all the facts makes any ethical decision impossible.
2. *Identifying values.* What are your personal values, your news organization's values, your community's values, the nation's values? For example, you may place high value on your personal credibility and that of your news organization. Certainly, freedom of the press is a value prized by this nation.
3. *Appealing to ethical principles.* You need to look at the various ethical principles discussed previously. The principles are not meant to be a shopping list from which you pick and choose items that serve your personal interest. To be ethical, you may have to choose a principle or principles that are far from expedient.
4. *Choosing loyalties.* You owe a certain loyalty to your news organization, yes, but you must also be loyal to your readers, listeners or viewers. And what about loyalty to your sources and to the people about whom you are reporting?

Usually there is not one clear answer to an ethical dilemma. Seldom do the most reasonable and experienced news veterans agree completely. But principled reasoning at least makes an ethical decision possible.

The four elements in the box need not be considered in any particular order. Also, don't stop reasoning after you have touched upon

"Journalists demean themselves and damage their credibility when they misrepresent themselves and their work to news sources and, in turn, to the public at large."
—*Everette E. Dennis,*
Executive Director,
Freedom Forum Media
Studies Center

the four elements. Principled reasoning should continue, even to another discussion of another ethical dilemma.

This continuing ethical dialectic or dialogue helps create ethical journalism and ethical journalists. Journalists should not just reflect society. They should present a reasoned reflection. Journalism should be done by people who make informed, intelligent and prudent choices.

The main objection to the Potter Box is that using it takes too much time and is impractical in the deadline business of journalism. However, as you become better acquainted with ethical principles and more practiced at principled reasoning, you will be able to make ethical decisions much more quickly and reasonably.

Although each case is different and you always must know the situation, you need not always start from the beginning. After a while you will know what your values are, where your loyalties lie and which principles will most likely apply.

ETHICAL PROBLEMS

Because of the First Amendment, society has relatively few "rules" for journalists in spite of the special problems they face. In the following sections, we discuss some of those problems.

Deceit

Ethical problems faced by journalists

- *Deceit.*
- *Conflicts of interest.*
- *Friendship.*
- *Payola.*
- *Freebies.*
- *Checkbook journalism.*
- *Participation in the news.*
- *Advertising pressure.*
- *Invasion of privacy.*
- *Withholding information.*
- *Plagiarism.*

Perhaps the most bothersome ethical problem facing journalists involves using deceit to get a story. Deceit covers a wide range of practices. When may you lie, misrepresent yourself, use a hidden tape recorder or camera? When may you steal documents? For absolutists, the answer is simple: Never! For others, the answer is not easy.

A group of journalists in an ethical decision-making seminar at The Poynter Institute for Media Studies devised a list of criteria to justify the use of deceit. The sidebar on page 337 synthesizes their conclusions. All of the criteria listed there must be present.

Conflicts of Interest

Reporting generally assumes that the reporter starts out with no point of view, that the reporter is not out to get someone or to get something out of the story. This basic assumption is the foundation of any and all credibility.

Most news-media codes of ethics devote the bulk of their substance to determining what constitutes a conflict of interest. And well they should.

Friendship

Perhaps the most obvious, the most frequent yet the most overlooked conflict of interest confronting journalists is friendship. Friendship may be the greatest obstacle to the flow of information.

No one knows whether friendship causes more stories to be reported or more stories to be killed. Either way, it sets up a powerful conflict of interest.

If you ever find yourself covering a story that involves a personal acquaintance, ask your supervisor to assign the story to someone else.

Payola

Journalists may not accept payment for a story other than from their employer. Also, news organizations frown upon reporters doing promotional work for people they cover. For example, when Lou Dobbs was managing editor of Cable News Network business news, he was reprimanded by CNN for making promotional videos for Wall Street firms.

Other conflicts of interest are not so obvious. *The (San Jose, Calif.) Mercury News* prohibits its business news reporters and editors from owning stock in local companies.

Will news agencies prohibit journalists from accepting speakers' fees? Will Congress attempt to legislate full disclosure of journalists' income and associations?

Freebies

When journalists accept free gifts from people they cover, the gifts always come with a price:

- Can reporters remain objective?
- Do reporters write stories they otherwise would not write?
- Does the public perceive the reporter who accepted or is suspected of accepting freebies as objective?

The perception of conflict of interest is what bothers most news organizations. Some argue that the least reporters must do is disclose prominently in their stories any freebies they accepted. As in any case of deceit, reporters must disclose how they were able to get the story and why accepting freebies was necessary.

For example, travel writers are offered free trips, free cruises, free hotel accommodations and other freebies by companies that expect them to write about what they experience. Many small news outlets cannot afford to send their travel writers on expensive tours. Travel

Conditions Justifying the Use of Deceit by Journalists

- An issue of profound public importance:
  - —of vital public interest, revealing system failure at high levels.
  - —a preventive measure against profound harm to individuals.
- All other alternatives exhausted.
- Eventual full disclosure of the deception and the reason for it.
- Full commitment to the story by everyone involved.
- The harm prevented outweighs any harm caused.
- A meaningful, collaborative and deliberative decision-making process that takes into account:
  - short- and long-term consequences of the deception.
  - the impact on credibility.
  - motivations for actions.
  - congruence between the deceptive act and the organization's editorial mission.
  - legal implications.
  - consistency of reasoning and action.

writers who accept freebies should mention doing so in their stories and let readers decide whether to trust the reporting.

Most news organizations have rules against accepting freebies. The Scripps-Howard newspaper group says, "When the gifts exceed the limits of propriety, they should be returned." The Society of Professional Journalists says, "Nothing of value shall be accepted." Is a cup of coffee something of value? The Associated Press expects its staff members to return gifts of "nominal value." Is a baseball cap of nominal value?

You must learn the ethics code of your news organization. Sometimes, your personal code may be more stringent than the code of your organization. In that case, follow your own code. Remember, you may not think a freebie will influence your reporting. But does your audience think it might?

If you choose a career in public relations, remember that the code of the Public Relations Society of America states that you are to do nothing that tempts news professionals to violate their codes.

"But I don't believe that paying sources is unethical, as long as it's disclosed to the reader; in some cases I think it makes for better journalism. It gives a fair share of the profits to sources who spend time and take risks."

—*John Tierney,*
from "Newsworthy,"
reprinted from
The New York Times Company

Checkbook Journalism

Will the audience believe your story if you paid your source for it? Should you always report that you had a paid source? Is it ethical to pay a source for an exclusive story? Should newspeople be in the business of keeping other newspeople from getting a story? Are paid sources likely to have an ax to grind? Do they come forward only for financial gain?

The terrible consequence of checkbook journalism is that even legitimate news professionals may be cut off from sources who want and expect pay. Some sources have begun asking for a fee even for good news. The increase in tabloid journalism, both in print and in broadcast, has brought the opportunists out in droves. The networks say that they do not pay for interviews, but the tabloids say payments are disguised as consultant fees, writes Richard Zoglin in *Time* magazine. Shouldn't sources be paid for contributing to a commercial product?

Surely, good reporting demands that you pay sources only when necessary and only if you can get other sources to corroborate your findings. You'd also better be sure that your bosses know that you're doing it.

Participation in the News

You'd also better let your bosses know which organizations you belong to. *The Washington Post* issued a memo to staffers that barred any reporters who had participated in a pro-abortion rights march in Washington "from any future participation in coverage of the abortion issue." Don Kowet reported in *The Washington Times* that the same memo prohibited any "news room professional" from participating in such a protest.

But what about participating in a political campaign? And must a religion reporter be an atheist?

According to Kowet, Richard Harwood, *Washington Post* ombudsman at the time, told a conference of journalists: "You have every right in the world to run for office, or participate in a political activity or lobbying activity. You don't have the 'right' to work for *The Washington Post*."

Nevertheless, some worry that uninvolved journalists will be uninformed journalists, an unconnected group of elitists. The problem is compounded when editors and even news organizations are involved in community projects. May the editor join the yacht club? May the station support the United Way? Is *New York Times* coverage of the Metropolitan Museum of Art influenced by its generous support of that institution? May an HIV-positive journalist report on AIDS?

Finally, should journalists demand of themselves what they demand of politicians—full disclosure of their financial investments and memberships, as well as public knowledge of their personal tastes, preferences and lifestyles?

> "If you're not involved in the community at all and you're totally neutralized, you end up not knowing enough about the community, not being able to get enough leads and so on in order to do your job."
>
> —*Tony Case,*
> *quoting ethicist*
> *Louis W. Hodges*
> *in* Editor & Publisher

Advertising Pressure

It's quite possible that you won't work long at a news organization before you realize some subjects are taboo to write about and others are highly encouraged. If you are lucky, you will work for a paper, station or magazine with a solid wall of separation between editorial and advertising, sometimes referred to as the separation of "church" and "state."

However, in some places, advertising salespeople are allowed to peek over that wall and see what stories the publication or station is planning to run. That information might help sell some advertising. Some say, what could be wrong with that?

The next step is for the advertising department to climb over the wall and suggest that editorial do a story on some subject so that advertising can be sold.

And then the next step isn't too far away. Advertising begins to suggest or even to dictate what must and must not be printed or broadcast. In print media, advertising may want the layout, design and type of their ads or sections to look like the publication's normal layout, design and typefaces.

Although some newspaper companies have allowed advertising and news personnel to become a bit chummier, some magazines have gone much further. The Southern Progress Corp., for example, a big moneymaker for AOL Time Warner and publisher of *Southern Living*, *Southern Accents*, *Progressive Farmer*, *Cooking Light* and other successful magazines, has stopped worrying about the separation of advertising and editorial. In a *Wall Street Journal* story by Matthew Rose, former Southern Progress editor Michael Carlton said, "There is no church and state. They all sit in the same church, maybe in different pews." In the same story, another former chief executive of the Southern Progress unit is quoted as saying, "For me, the acid test was: Am I serving the reader well?"

Not only does Southern Progress tip off advertisers as to what editorial is going to do, but they also sometimes allow advertisers into planning sessions and to make suggestions.

With Southern Progress boasting high renewal rates and high profits, is this the future? Currently the Meredith and Hearst magazine corporations have not followed suit.

The question of advertisements online is dealt with in Chapter 13. Radio newscasters generally separate themselves from the commercials. Yet popular long-time commentator Paul Harvey and, more recently, Rush Limbaugh and Charles Osgood have not refrained from reading the commercials with the same gusto with which they say everything else. What has it done to their credibility? Television suffers the same advertising pressures as print with the added problem that there are only so many minutes in a newscast. How ethical is it to cut a complicated international story to 90 seconds just to make time for one more commercial?

Invasion of Privacy

Most journalists would cry out against an invasion of their own privacy. Yet many of them argue for a vague "right to know" when they report on others, especially if those others are public officials or public figures. The head-on collision of the right to know and the right to privacy will confront you every day of your reporting life. The Constitution mentions neither "right."

The most obvious and talked-about issue dealing with the right to privacy is naming crime survivors, especially rape and abuse survivors. The state of Florida legislated against publishing rape survivors' names, only to have the law struck down by a Florida District Court. The Supreme Court has held that news agencies cannot be punished for publishing lawfully obtained information or information from a public record. Meanwhile, legislators in many states are looking for ways to close the records on rape and to punish police, hospitals, court clerks and other officials for releasing survivors' names.

So it comes down to a matter of ethics, and, as usual, there is no complete agreement. Not publishing the name continues the stigma that somehow the rape was the survivor's fault. Publishing the survivor's name is heaping more suffering upon that person. Do we name the accused? What if it is a false accusation? Few news outlets would publish a rape survivor's name without the survivor's approval.

A similar problem arises with publishing the names of juvenile offenders. News agencies, traditionally, have not published them because they have held that juveniles are juveniles and are entitled to make juvenile mistakes, even if those mistakes are crimes. Juvenile court records are, after all, sealed. Again, the courts have upheld the right to publish juvenile offenders' names that are on the public record.

Some media critics, such as *The Fresno Bee*'s former editor and ombudsman Lynne Enders Glaser, have applauded the publication of the names of juvenile offenders. Glaser wrote: "It doesn't take a rocket scientist to figure out that more and more violent crimes are being committed by young people. And in increasing numbers, *Bee* readers have challenged the law and the media to stop protecting the identity of criminals because of their age."

However, in addition to the stigma forever attached to the juvenile offender's name and the embarrassment of his or her parents and family, some worry that in some groups a youth's notoriety will encourage other young people to violate the law. Others argue that shame will stop other juveniles from committing crimes.

Reporting on crime victims and reporting on juvenile crimes are just two of the myriad privacy issues you will face. Journalists are still protected when writing about public officials and public figures—most of the time. But what about the children of politicians or celebrities? Noelle Bush was in the national news when she used a fake prescription to buy the anti-anxiety drug Xanax and again when she was found with a piece of crack cocaine in her shoe while in an Orlando treatment center. Why? Because she is the daughter of Florida Gov. Jeb Bush, the brother of President George W. Bush.

Photographers and videographers must be especially concerned with privacy. How often and under what circumstances do we stick cameras into people's grieving and anxious faces?

Withholding Information

May you ever withhold information from the news organization for which you work? If you are writing what you hope to be a best-selling book, may you save some "news" until after the book is published?

If you work as a journalist, are you ever off-duty? A doctor isn't. Doctors take an oath to treat the sick. If you witness something at a friend's house or at a party, do you tell your news director about it?

One reporter was fired when his boss discovered that he attended a post-concert party of a rock band where lines of cocaine were openly available. The reporter did not include this information in his coverage of the band. His defense was that if he reported the drug abuse, he would never get interviews or get close to other rock groups, and he would be finished as a music critic. His defense didn't work.

If you learn that a political candidate is "sleeping around," would you withhold that information? Would you do so even if you knew that if the public had that information, the candidate would not be elected? Suppose after the election it became clear that you had had the information before the election but did not publish it? *The (Portland) Oregonian* apologized to its readers for not publishing reports about Sen. Bob Packwood's alleged sexual harassment charges until after he was re-elected.

Plagiarism

No one wants you to use his or her work as your own. No one condones plagiarism. The problem is defining exactly what constitutes plagiarism. Most of the time you know when you plagiarize even if no one else does **(cjr.org/year/95/4/plagiarize.asp)**.

Beware of Plagiarism!

Taking material verbatim from the newspaper library. Even when the material is from your own newspaper, it is still someone else's work. Put it in your own words or attribute it.

Using material verbatim from the wire services. Sometimes writers take Associated Press material, add a few paragraphs to give some local flavor, and publish it as their own work. Even though it is a common practice, it is not right.

Using material from other publications. Some blame electronic databases for a whole new explosion of plagiarism. Sometimes writers steal the research of others without attribution. And sometimes they use others' work without realizing it.

Using news releases verbatim. The publicists are delighted, but you should be ashamed—especially if you put your name on an article. Rewrite it, except perhaps for the direct quotations, and use them sparingly. If you use a whole release, cite its source.

Using the work of fellow reporters. If more than one reporter works on a story, if you use a byline on top, put the other names at the end of the story.

Using old stories over again. Columnists, beware! Your readers have a right to know when you are recycling your material. Some of them might catch you at it, and there goes your credibility.

—Roy Peter Clark

In the daily practice of journalism, reporters, consciously or unconsciously, deal with many situations that could involve plagiarism. Roy Peter Clark of The Poynter Institute has listed them (see above). Sometimes writers plagiarize and have absolutely no idea that they are doing so. Apparently, sometimes something one has read becomes so familiar to the reader that the reader later considers it his or her own. Sometimes it might be a matter of sloppy note taking. Of course, many reporters say that nothing whatsoever excuses plagiarism.

Nevertheless, you must fight every impulse, question and check any doubts, and avoid any hint of plagiarism. And just as certainly you must resist temptations to make up people, to fabricate events and to invent quotations from fictional people. A reporter on *The Sacramento Bee* did that, and he was fired. An AP Washington reporter did that, and he was fired.

A student at Northwestern University made a habit of fabrication. The Medill News Service sent out a notice that it could not verify information in two stories written by the student, and three papers where he had interned found that they could not verify that 30 sources in 17 stories he had written ever existed.

Three final guidelines

- *Be free of obligations to anyone or to any interest except the truth. As scholar John Merrill has written, the primary obligation of the journalist is to be free.*
- *Be fair. Even children know when you treat them unfairly or when they are being unfair. So do you.*
- *Remember good taste. Some actions and stories may be ethical, but they may be in bad taste.*

Should his actions have caused him to forfeit his journalism degree? Northwestern tossed him from the graduate program but awarded him an undergraduate degree. Medill also began asking its students to sign a statement indicating that they understood the school's code of ethics. Should every journalism program do the same?

It's hard to say what's worse—making up material or stealing it. Don't do either. Ever.

Suggested Readings

Christians, Clifford G., Fackler, Mark, Rotzoll, Kim B. and McKee, Kathy Brittain. *Media Ethics: Cases and Moral Reasoning*, Sixth Edition. New York: Longman, 2001. Applies the Potter Box method of principled reasoning to dozens of journalism, advertising and public-relations cases.

Day, Louis Alvin. *Ethics in Media Communications*, Fourth Edition. Belmont, Calif.: Wadsworth, 2003. Begins with a superb discussion of ethics and moral development, ethics and society, and ethics and moral reasoning and goes on to discuss nearly every problem facing journalists, accompanied by actual cases.

Fletcher, Joseph. *Situation Ethics: The New Morality*. Philadelphia: Westminster Press, 1966. A classic work on Christian situation ethics.

Lambeth, Edmund B. *Committed Journalism*, Second Edition. Bloomington: Indiana University Press, 1992. Creates an ethics code specific to the practice of journalism.

Merrill, John. *The Imperative of Freedom: A Philosophy of Journalistic Autonomy*. New York: Hastings House, 1974; Lanham, Md.: University Press of America, 1990. Establishes freedom as the primary imperative of the journalist.

Merrill, John. *Journalism Ethics: Philosophical Foundations for News Media*. New York: St. Martin's Press, 1997. Provides in-depth understanding of the philosophical and theoretical underpinnings of journalism morality.

Wilkins, Lee and Patterson, Philip. *Media Ethics, Issues and Cases*, Fourth Edition. Dubuque, Iowa: McGraw-Hill, 2002. An excellent discussion of journalism ethics with up-to-date cases.

Suggested Web Sites

www.ijnet.org/code.html

Site of the International Journalists' Network. Here you can find the codes of ethics of nearly every country or press association that has one. It also reports on the state of media around the world and contains media directories.

www.spj.org/ethics/asp

Ethics site of the Society of Professional Journalists. It provides the SPJ code of ethics, ethics news, an ethics hotline, an SPJ ethics listserv and other ethics sources.

www.journalism.indiana.edu/ethics/

This site of the School of Journalism of Indiana University-Bloomington contains a large set of cases to help you explore ethical issues in journalism. The initial cases were published in *FineLine*, a newsletter of Barry Bingham Jr.

www.ojr.org/ethics/

A Web-based journal produced at the Annenberg School for Communication at the University of Southern California. The section on ethics provides articles dealing with specific cases.

www.silha.umn.edu/resources.htm

Site of the Silha Center for the study of media ethics and law at the University of Minnesota. You can find lists of Web sites and publications about ethics and law from this site.

Exercises

1. You learn that the daughter of a local bank president has been kidnapped. The kidnappers have not contacted the family, and police officials ask you to keep the matter secret for fear the abductors might panic and injure the child. Describe how a deontologist, a teleologist and a situation ethicist would make their decisions about how to handle the situation.

2. Is a travel writer ever justified in accepting a free trip? Explain your answer by using various theories of situation ethics.

3. For at least a year, on four or five occasions, reporters on your paper have heard rumors that a retirement home is negligent in its care of the elderly. Your editor asks you to get a job there as a janitor and report what you find. What would be your response?

4. Do a computer search of articles written in the past three years on whether journalists should publish the names of rape victims. Then write a brief summary of your findings.

APPENDIX 1: Copy Editing and Proofreading Symbols

Writing and editing for today's media are done almost exclusively on computers. Only in the book industry are most manuscripts still prepared on paper. Nevertheless, at some small newspapers and magazines, editors prefer to edit on paper. For that reason, failure to learn the copy editing symbols used in manuscript preparation is a mistake. There is a good chance you will need to use those symbols at some point in your career, if only to satisfy the occasional editor who prefers doing things the old-fashioned way.

You are even more likely to use proofreading symbols, which are used on galley proofs and page proofs to correct typeset copy. There are some similarities in the two sets of symbols, but there also are differences. The chart on page 346 shows the most common copy editing symbols (used in manuscript preparation), and the following chart illustrates the most common proofreading symbols (used to correct typeset copy).

Symbol	Meaning	Symbol	Meaning
∧	Insert at this point.	✓✓	Space evenly.
⊥	Push down space.	⊂	Close up entirely.
ℯ	Take out letter, letters or words.	⊏	Move to left.
ɘ	Turn inverted letter.	⊐	Move to right.
(lc)	Set lowercase.	⊔	Lower letter or word.
(wf)	Wrong font letter.	⊓	Raise letter or word.
(ital)	Reset in italic type.	(out, see copy)	Words are left out.
(rom)	Reset in roman (regular) type.	//	Straighten lines.
(bf)	Reset in boldface type.	(¶)	Start new paragraph.
⊙	Insert period.	(no ¶)	No paragraph. Run together.
⸴	Insert comma.	(tr)	Transpose letters or words.
;	Insert semicolon.	(?)	Query; is copy right?
=/	Insert hyphen.	⊢⊣	Insert dash.
∨	Insert apostrophe.	□	Indent 1 em.
∨ ∨	Enclose in quotation marks.	□□	Indent 2 ems.
≡	Replace with a capital letter.	□□□	Indent 3 ems.
#	Insert space.	(stet)	Let it stand.

Proofreading Symbols

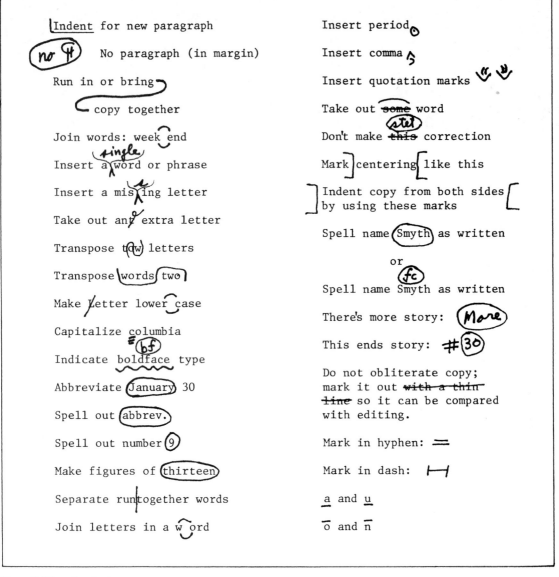

Copy Editing Symbols

Style Summary

Most publications adhere to rules of style to avoid annoying inconsistencies. Without a stylebook to provide guidance in such matters, writers would not know whether *president* should be capitalized when preceding or following a name, whether the correct spelling is *employee* or *employe* (dictionaries list both), or whether a street name should appear as *Twelfth* or *12th*.

Newspapers use the wire service stylebooks to provide such guidance. The Associated Press and United Press International collaborated to establish a consistent style, although AP and UPI styles still differ in minor ways. Most newspapers follow the Associated Press style.

This appendix is a brief summary of the primary rules of wire service style. We include the rules used most frequently, arranged by topic to make them easy to learn. About 10 percent of the rules in a stylebook account for 90 percent of the wire service style you will use regularly; the rest of the rules you will use about 10 percent of the time. Thus, learning the rules you will use most often makes sense. This summary should be helpful even if you do not have a stylebook, but we assume that most users of this book have one.

ABBREVIATIONS AND ACRONYMS

Punctuation of Abbreviations

- Generally speaking, abbreviations of two letters or fewer have periods:

  600 B.C., A.D. 1066
  8 a.m., 7 p.m.
  U.N., U.S., R.I., N.Y.
  8151 Yosemite St.
  EXCEPTIONS: AM radio, FM radio, 35 mm camera, the AP Stylebook, "LA smog," D-Mass., R-Kan., IQ, TV.

- Generally speaking, abbreviations of three letters or more do not have periods:

  CIA, FBI, NATO
  mpg, mph
  EXCEPTION: c.o.d.

Symbols

- Always write out % as *percent* in a story, but you may use the symbol in a headline.
- Always write out & as *and* unless it is part of a company's formal name.
- Always write out ¢ as *cent* or *cents: 7 cents.*
- Always use the symbol $ rather than the word *dollar* with any actual figure, and put the symbol before the figure: *$5.* Write out *dollar* only if you are speaking of, say, the value of the dollar on the world market.

Dates

- Never abbreviate days of the week.
- Don't abbreviate a month unless it has a date of the month with it: December 2003; Dec. 17; Dec. 17, 2003.
- Never abbreviate the five months spelled with five letters or fewer: *March; April 20; May 13, 2003; June 1956; July of that year.*
- Never abbreviate *Christmas* as *Xmas,* even in a headline.
- Always write out *Fourth of July.*

People and Titles

- Some publications still use courtesy titles (*Mr., Mrs., Ms., Miss*) on second reference in stories, although most seem to have moved away from them as sexist. Many publications use them only in quotations from sources. Others use them only in obituaries and editorials or on second reference in stories mentioning a husband and wife. In the last case, other newspapers prefer to repeat the person's whole name or, especially in features, use the person's first name. The Associated Press suggests using a courtesy title when someone requests it, but most journalists don't bother to ask.
- Use the abbreviations *Gov., Lt. Gov., Rep., Sen.* and *the Rev.,* as well as abbreviations of military titles, on first reference; then drop the title on subsequent references. Some titles you might expect to see abbreviated before a name are not abbreviated in AP style: *Attorney General, District Attorney, President, Professor, Superintendent.*
- Use the abbreviations *Jr.* and *Sr.* after a name on first reference if appropriate, but do not set them off by commas as you learned to do in English class.

Organizations

- Write out the first reference to most organizations in full rather than using an acronym: *National Organization for Women.* For *CIA, FBI* and *GOP,* however, the acronym may be used on the first reference.
- You may use well-known abbreviations such as *FCC* and *NOW* in a headline even though they would not be acceptable on first reference in the story.
- Do not put the abbreviation of an organization's name in parentheses after the full name on first reference. If an abbreviation seems likely to be con-

fusing, don't use it at all; instead, refer to the organization as, for example, "the gay rights group" or "the bureau" on second reference.

▪ Use the abbreviations *Co.*, *Cos.*, *Corp.*, *Inc.* and *Ltd.* at the end of a company's name even if the company spells out the word; do not abbreviate these words if followed by words, such as "of America." The abbreviations *Co.*, *Cos.* and *Corp.* are abbreviated, however, if followed by *Inc.* or *Ltd.* (and, by the way, *Inc.* and *Ltd.* are not set off by commas even if the company uses them).

▪ Abbreviate political affiliations after a name in the following way:

Sen. Christopher Bond, R-Mo., said . . .

Note the use of a single letter without a period for the party and the use of commas around the party and state.

▪ Never abbreviate the word *association*, even as part of a name.

Places

▪ Don't abbreviate a state name unless it follows the name of a city in that state:

Nevada; Brown City, Mich.

▪ Never abbreviate the six states spelled with five or fewer letters or the two noncontiguous states:

Alaska, Hawaii, Idaho, Iowa, Maine, Ohio, Texas, Utah

▪ Use the two-letter postal abbreviations only when a full address is given that includes a ZIP code.

▪ Use the traditional state abbreviations in normal copy:

Ala.	Md.	N.D.
Ariz.	Mass.	Okla.
Ark.	Mich.	Ore.
Calif.	Minn.	Pa.
Colo.	Miss.	R.I.
Conn.	Mo.	S.C.
Del.	Mont.	S.D.
Fla.	Neb.	Tenn.
Ga.	Nev.	Vt.
Ill.	N.H.	Va.
Ind.	N.J.	Wash.
Kan.	N.M.	W.Va.
Ky.	N.Y.	Wis.
La.	N.C.	Wyo.

▪ Use state abbreviations with domestic towns and cities unless they appear in the wire service dateline list of cities that stand alone. Many publications add to the wire service list their own list of towns well-known in the state or region.

▪ Use nations' full names with foreign towns and cities unless the towns and cities appear in the wire service dateline list of cities that stand alone. Once a state or nation has been identified in a story, it is unnecessary to repeat it unless clarity demands it.

- The lists of cities in the United States and the rest of the world that the wire services say may stand alone without a state abbreviation or nation are too lengthy to include here. Consult the appropriate stylebook. A handy rule of thumb is that if it's an American city and has a major sports franchise, it probably stands alone. Likewise, if it's a foreign city that most people have heard of, it probably stands alone.
- Don't abbreviate the names of thoroughfares if there is no street address with them:

Main Street, Century Boulevard West

- If a thoroughfare's name includes the word *avenue, boulevard, street* or any of the directions on a map, such as *north* or *southeast*, abbreviate those words in a street address:

1044 W. Maple St.; 1424 Lee Blvd. S.; 999 Jackson Ave.

- In a highway's name, always abbreviate *U.S.* but never abbreviate a state's name. In the case of an interstate highway, the name is written in full on first reference, abbreviated on subsequent ones:

U.S. 63 or U.S. Highway 63; Massachusetts 2
Interstate 70 (first reference); I-70 (second reference)

- Never abbreviate *Fort* or *Mount*.
- Use the abbreviation *St.* for *Saint* in place-names.
EXCEPTIONS: *Saint John* in New Brunswick, *Ste. Genevieve* in Missouri, *Sault Ste. Marie* in Michigan and Ontario.
- Abbreviate *United States* and *United Nations* as *U.S.* and *U.N.* when used as adjectives, but spell them out as nouns.

Miscellaneous

- Use the abbreviation *IQ* (no periods) in all references to *intelligence quotient*.
- Abbreviate and capitalize the word *number* when followed by a numeral: *No. 1*.
- Use the abbreviation *TV* (no periods) only in headlines, as an adjective and in constructions such as *cable TV*. Otherwise, write out *television*.
- Use the abbreviation *UFO* in all references to an *unidentified flying object*.
- Use the abbreviation *vs.*, not *v.*, for *versus*.

CAPITALIZATION

- Proper nouns are capitalized; common nouns are not. Unfortunately, this rule is not always easy to apply when the noun is the name of an animal, food or plant or when it is a trademark that has become so well-known that people mistakenly use it generically.
- Regions are capitalized; directions are not:

We drove east two miles to catch the interstate out West.

- Adjectives and nouns pertaining to a region are capitalized: *Southern accent, Western movie, a Southerner, the Midwestern drought.*
  - A region combined with a country's name is not capitalized unless the region is part of the name of a politically divided country: *eastern United States, North Korea.*
  - A region combined with a state name is capitalized only if it is famous: *Southern California, southern Colorado.*
- When two or more proper nouns share a plural common noun, the shared plural is lowercased:

  Missouri and Mississippi rivers
  Chrisman and Truman high schools

- Government and college terms are not always as consistent as you might think:
  - *College departments* follow the animal, food and plant rule. Capitalize only words that are already proper nouns: *Spanish department, sociology department.*
  - Always capitalize a specific government department, even without the city, state or federal designator, and even if the department's name is turned around with *of* deleted: *Police Department, Fire Department, State Department, Department of Commerce.*
  - Capitalize college and government committees if the formal name is given; lowercase any shorter, descriptive designation: *Special Senate Select Committee to Investigate Improper Labor-Management Practices; rackets committee.*
  - Spell out and lowercase the names of academic degrees: *bachelor of arts degree, master's degree.* Avoid the abbreviations *Ph.D., M.A., B.A.,* etc., except in lists.
  - Always capitalize (unless plural or generic) *City Council* and *County Commission* (but alone, *council* and *commission* are lowercased). Capitalize *Cabinet* when referring to advisers. Capitalize *Legislature* if the state's legislative body is formally named that. *Capitol,* meaning the building, is capitalized; *capital,* meaning the city, is not.
  - Never capitalize *board of directors* or *board of trustees* (but capitalize *Board of Curators* and *Board of Education*). Do not capitalize *federal, government* and *administration.*
  - Capitalize *president* and *vice president* before a name; otherwise, lowercase.
  - Capitalize military titles *(Sgt., Maj., Gen.,* etc.) before a name. Capitalize *Air Force, Army, Marines* and *Navy* if referring to U.S. forces.
  - Capitalize political parties, including the word *party: Democratic Party, Socialist Party.* Capitalize words such as *communist, democratic, fascist* and *socialist* only if they refer to a formal party rather than to a philosophy.
- Religious terms are variously capitalized and lowercased:
  - *Pope* is lowercased except before a name: *the pope, Pope Gregory.*
  - *Mass* is always capitalized.
  - Pronouns for *God* and *Jesus* are lowercased.
  - *Bible* is capitalized when meaning the Holy Scriptures and lowercased when referring to another book: *a hunter's bible.*

- Sacraments are capitalized if they commemorate events in the life of Jesus or signify his presence: *Baptism, Communion.*

- Actual race names are capitalized, but color descriptions are not:

  Caucasian, Mongoloid, Negro
  white, red, black

- Formal titles of people are capitalized before a name, but occupational titles are not:

  President George W. Bush, Mayor Dennis Archer, Coach Mike Martz, Dean Fred Wilson
  astronaut Mary Gardner, journalist Anita Black, plumber Phil Sanders, pharmacist Roger Wheaton

  When in doubt about whether a title is formal or occupational, put the title after the name, set off with commas, and use lowercase.

- Formal titles that are capitalized before a name are lowercased after a name:

  George W. Bush, president of the United States
  Dennis Archer, mayor of Detroit
  Mike Martz, coach of the St. Louis Rams
  Fred Wilson, dean of students

- Formal titles that are abbreviated before a name are written out and lower-cased if they follow a name:

  Gov. Gray Davis; Gray Davis, governor of California
  Rep. Lindsey Graham of South Carolina; Lindsey Graham, representative from South Carolina

- The first word in a direct quotation is capitalized only if the quote meets these three criteria:

  - It is a complete sentence. Don't capitalize a partial quote.
  - It stands alone as a separate sentence or paragraph, or it is set off from its source by a comma or colon.
  - It is a direct quotation (It appears in quotation marks).

- A question within a sentence is capitalized: *My only question is, When do we start?*

NUMBERS

- Cardinal numbers (numerals) are used in:
  - Addresses: Use numerals for street addresses: *1322 N. 10th St.*
  - Ages: Use numerals, even for days or months: *3 days old; John Burnside, 56.*
  - Aircraft and spacecraft: *F-4, DC-10, Apollo 11.* EXCEPTION: *Air Force One.*
  - Clothes sizes: *size 6.*
  - Dates: Use the numeral alone—no *nd, rd, st* or *th* after it: March 20.

- Decades: *the '80s.*
- Dimensions: *5-foot-6-inch guard* (but no hyphen when the word modified is associated with size: *3 feet tall, 10 feet long*).
- Highways: *U.S. 63.*
- Millions, billions, trillions: *1.2 billion, 6 million, 4 trillion.*
- Money: Use numerals: *18 pesos, 10 francs.* Write millions, billions and trillions like this: *$1.4 million, £10.7 billion.*
- Numbers: *No. 1, No. 2.*
- Percentages: Use numerals except at the beginning of a sentence: *4 percent.*
- Recipes: Use numerals for ingredient amounts: *2 teaspoons, 3 cups.*
- Speeds: *55 mph, 4 knots.*
- Sports: Use numerals for just about everything: *8-6 score, 2 yards, 3-under-par, 2 strokes.*
- Temperatures: Use numerals for all except *zero.* Below zero, spell out *minus: minus 6,* not *-6* (except in tabular data).
- Times: *4 a.m., 6:32 p.m., noon, midnight, five minutes, three hours.*
- Weights: *7 pounds, 11 ounces.*
- Years: Use numerals without commas. A year is the only numeral that can start a sentence: *1988 was a good year.*

- Numerals ending with *nd, rd, st* and *th* are used for:
  - Amendments to the Constitution after the *Ninth.* For *First* through *Ninth,* use words: *First Amendment, 16th Amendment.*
  - Courts: *2nd District Court, 10th Circuit Court of Appeals.*
  - Military sequences: *1st Lt., 2nd Division, 7th Fleet.*
  - Political divisions (precincts, wards, districts): *3rd Congressional District.*
  - Streets after *Ninth.* For *First* through *Ninth,* use words: *Fifth Avenue, 13th Street.*

- Words are used for:
  - Any number at the start of a sentence except for a year: *Sixteen years ago. . . .*
  - Casual numbers: *about a hundred or so.*
  - Fractions less than one: *one-half.*
  - Numbers less than 10, with the exceptions noted above: *five people, four rules.*

- Numerals are used for fractions greater than one: *1 1/2*
- Roman numerals are used for a man who is the third or later in his family to bear a name and for a king, queen, pope or world war: *John D. Rockefeller III, Queen Elizabeth II, Pope John Paul II, World War I*

INTERNET WEB SITES FOR JOURNALISTS

The Associated Press provides wire news through sites of its member newspapers. To access the AP wire online, follow this link and select a newspaper: **wire.ap.org.**

APPENDIX 3: Twenty Common Errors of Grammar and Punctuation

Grammar provides our language's rules of the road. When you see a green light, you proceed on faith that the other driver will not go through the red light. Drivers have a shared understanding of the rules of the road. Writers have a shared understanding of the grammar rules that ensure we understand what we are reading. Occasionally, as on the road, there is a wreck. We dangle participles, misplace modifiers and omit commas. If we write "Running down the street, his pants fell off," we are saying a pair of pants ran down a street. If we write "He hit Harry and John stopped him," the missing comma changes the meaning to "He hit Harry and John."

To say what you mean—to avoid syntactical wrecks—you must know the rules of grammar. We have compiled a list of 20 common errors that we find in our students' stories and in the stories of many professionals. Avoid them, and you'll write safely.

1. Incorrect comma in a series in Associated Press style

Use commas to separate the items in a series, but do not put a comma before *and* or *or* at the end of the series unless the meaning would be unclear without a comma.

INCORRECT
COMMA BEFORE
"AND"
The film was fast-paced, sophisticated, and funny.

CLEAR
WITHOUT COMMA
The film was fast-paced, sophisticated and funny.

UNCLEAR
WITHOUT COMMA
He demanded cheese, salsa with jalapeños and onions on his taco.

A comma before *and* would prevent readers from wondering if he demanded salsa containing both jalapeños and onions or if he wanted the salsa and the onions as two separate toppings.

COMMA
NEEDED BEFORE
"AND"
He demanded cheese, salsa with jalapeños, and onions on his taco.

2. Run-on sentence

An independent clause contains a subject and a predicate and makes sense by itself. A run-on sentence—also known as a *comma splice*—occurs when two or more independent clauses are joined incorrectly with a comma.

RUN-ON   **John Rogers left the family law practice, he decided to become a teacher.**

You can correct a run-on sentence in several ways. Join the clauses with a comma and one of the coordinating conjunctions—*and, but, for, nor, or, yet* or *so*—or join the clauses with a semicolon if they are closely related. Use a subordinating conjunction such as *after, because, if* or *when* to turn one of the clauses into a dependent clause. Or rewrite the run-on as two separate sentences.

CORRECTING A RUN-ON WITH A COMMA AND A COORDINATING CONJUNCTION

John Rogers left the family law practice, for he decided to become a teacher.

CORRECTING A RUN-ON WITH A SEMICOLON

John Rogers left the family law practice; he decided to become a teacher.

CORRECTING A RUN-ON BY MAKING ONE INDEPENDENT
CLAUSE A DEPENDENT CLAUSE

John Rogers left the family law practice when he decided to become a teacher.

CORRECTING A RUN-ON BY WRITING TWO SEPARATE SENTENCES

John Rogers left the family law practice. He decided to become a teacher.

3. Fragment

A fragment is a word group that lacks a subject, a verb or both yet is punctuated as though it were a complete sentence. Another type of fragment is a word group that begins with a subordinating conjunction such as *because* or *when*, yet is punctuated as though it were a complete sentence.

FRAGMENTS   **After she had placed her watch and an extra pencil on the table.**

                  Without feeling especially sorry about it.

Correct a fragment by joining it to the sentence before or after it or by adding the missing elements so that the fragment contains a subject and a verb and can stand alone.

CORRECTING A FRAGMENT BY JOINING IT TO ANOTHER SENTENCE

After she had placed her watch and an extra pencil on the table, the student opened the exam booklet.

CORRECTING A FRAGMENT BY TURNING IT INTO A SENTENCE

She apologized to her boss for the outburst without feeling especially sorry about it.

4. Missing comma(s) with a nonrestrictive element

A nonrestrictive element is a word, phrase or clause that gives information about the preceding part of the sentence but does not restrict or limit the meaning of that part. A nonrestrictive element is not essential to the meaning of the sentence; you can delete it and still understand clearly what the sentence is saying. Place commas before and (if necessary) after a nonrestrictive element.

UNCLEAR	The mayor asked to meet Alva Johnson a highly decorated police officer.
CLEAR	The mayor asked to meet Alva Johnson, a highly decorated police officer.
UNCLEAR	His wife Mary was there.
CLEAR	His wife, Mary, was there.

5. Confusion of *that* and *which*

The pronoun *that* always introduces restrictive information, which is essential to the meaning of the sentence; do not set off a *that* clause with commas. The pronoun *which* introduces nonrestrictive, or nonessential, information; set off a nonrestrictive *which* clause with commas.

INCORRECT	The oldest store in town, Miller and Company, <u>that</u> has been on Main Street for almost a century, will close this summer.
CORRECT	The oldest store in town, Miller and Company, <u>which</u> has been on Main Street for almost a century, will close this summer.
INCORRECT	The creature, <u>which</u> has been frightening residents of North First Street for the past week, has turned out to be a screech owl.
CORRECT	The creature <u>that</u> has been frightening residents of North First Street for the past week has turned out to be a screech owl.

6. Missing comma after an introductory element

A sentence may begin with a dependent clause (a word group that contains a subject and a verb and begins with a subordinating conjunction such as *because* or *when*), a prepositional phrase (a word group that begins with a preposition such as *in* or *on* and ends with a noun or pronoun), an adverb such as *next* that modifies the whole sentence, or a participial phrase (a word group that contains a past or present participle, such as *determined* or *hoping*, that acts as an adjective). Use a comma to separate these introductory elements from the main clause of the sentence.

DEPENDENT CLAUSE	<u>After the applause had died down,</u> the conductor raised his baton again.
PREPOSITIONAL PHRASE	<u>Without a second thought,</u> the chicken crossed the road.
ADVERB	<u>Furthermore,</u> the unemployment rate continues to rise.
PARTICIPIAL PHRASES	<u>Waiting in the bar,</u> Jose grew restless. <u>Saddened by the news from home,</u> she stopped reading the letter.

Although it is always correct to use a comma after an introductory element, the comma may be omitted after some adverbs and short prepositional phrases if the meaning is clear:

Suddenly it's spring.

In Chicago it rained yesterday.

Always place a comma after two or more introductory prepositional phrases.

In May of last year in Toronto, Tom attended three conventions.

Here are more examples:

INCORRECT	Shaking her head at the latest budget information the library administrator wondered where to find the money for new books.
CORRECT	Shaking her head at the latest budget information, the library administrator wondered where to find the money for new books.
INCORRECT	After a week of foggy, rainy mornings had passed he left Seattle.
CORRECT	After a week of foggy, rainy mornings had passed, he left Seattle.

7. Missing comma(s) between coordinate adjectives

Adjectives are coordinate if they make sense when you insert *and* between them or place them in reverse order.

| COORDINATE ADJECTIVES | The frightened, angry citizens protested the new policy.
 The frightened and angry citizens protested the new policy. |

The adjectives make sense with *and* between them, so they are coordinate.

The angry, frightened citizens protested the new policy.

The adjectives make sense in reverse order, so they are coordinate. Separate coordinate adjectives with commas.

INCORRECT	**The gaunt lonely creature was also afraid.**
CORRECT	**The gaunt, lonely creature was also afraid.**

8. Missing comma(s) in a compound sentence

Two or more independent clauses—word groups containing a subject and a verb and expressing a complete thought—joined with a coordinating conjunction (*and, but, for, nor, or, yet* or *so*) form a compound sentence. Place a comma before the conjunction in a compound sentence to avoid confusion.

UNCLEAR	**She works as a pharmacist now and later she plans to go to medical school.**
CLEAR	**She works as a pharmacist now, and later she plans to go to medical school.**

9. Missing semicolon(s) between items in a series with internal commas

When commas appear within the items in a series, separate the items in the series with semicolons for clarity.

UNCLEAR	**The injured include Barney Corrigan, 31, of 445 Main St., Sheila Okafur, 28, of 333 Elm St., and Shawna Taylor, 35, of 71 Edgewood Ave.**
CLEAR	**The injured include Barney Corrigan, 31, of 445 Main St.; Sheila Okafur, 28, of 333 Elm St.; and Shawna Taylor, 35, of 71 Edgewood Ave.**

10. Misplaced or dangling modifier

Modifiers are words or phrases that change or clarify the meaning of another word or word group in a sentence. Place modifiers immediately before or directly after the word or words they modify. A *misplaced* modifier appears too far from the word or words it is supposed to modify in the sentence. A *dangling* modifier appears in a sentence that does not contain the word or words it is supposed to modify. A modifier at the beginning of a sentence should refer to the grammatical subject of the sentence.

MISPLACED MODIFIER	*subject* **Having predicted a sunny morning, the downpour surprised the meteorologist.**
CORRECT	*subject* **Having predicted a sunny morning, the meteorologist did not expect the downpour.**

	subject
DANGLING MODIFIER	<u>Working in the yard,</u> the sun burned her badly.
	subject
CORRECT	Working in the yard, <u>she</u> became badly sunburned.

11. Missing or misused hyphen(s) in a compound modifier

A compound modifier consists of two or more adjectives or an adjective-adverb combination used to modify a single noun. When a compound modifier precedes a noun, you should hyphenate the parts of the compound unless the compound consists of an adverb ending in *-ly* followed by an adjective.

INCORRECT	His over the top performance made the whole film unbelievable.
	The freshly-printed counterfeit bills felt like genuine dollars.
	The local chapter of Parents without Partners will sponsor an open-toga party on Saturday.
CORRECT	His over-the-top performance made the whole film unbelievable.
	The freshly printed counterfeit bills felt like genuine dollars.
	The local chapter of Parents without Partners will sponsor an open toga party on Saturday.

12. Missing or misused apostrophe

Do not confuse the pronoun *its*, meaning "belonging to it," with the contraction *it's*, meaning "it is" or "it has." The possessive form of a noun uses an apostrophe; possessive pronouns never take apostrophes.

INCORRECT	The car is lying on it's side in the ditch.
	Its a blue 1999 Ford Taurus.
	That new car of her's rides very smoothly.
CORRECT	The car is lying on its side in the ditch.
	It's a blue 1999 Ford Taurus.
	That new car of hers rides very smoothly.

For clarity, avoid using the contraction ending in *-'s* to mean "has" instead of "is."

UNCLEAR	She's held many offices in student government.
CLEAR	She has held many offices in student government.

13. Incorrect pronoun case

A pronoun that is the subject of a sentence or clause must be in the subjective case (*I, he, she we, they*). A pronoun that is the direct object of a verb, the indirect object of a verb, or the object of a preposition must be in the objective case (*me, him, her, us, them*). To decide whether a pronoun in a compound construction—two or more nouns or pronouns joined with *and* or *or*—should be subjective or objective, omit everything in the compound except the pronoun and see whether the subjective or objective case sounds correct.

INCORRECT   **He took my wife and I to dinner.**

(Try that sentence without the first part of the compound, *my wife and.*)

CORRECT   **He took my wife and me to dinner.**

INCORRECT   **Her and her family donated the prize money.**

(Try that sentence without the second part of the compound, *and her family.*)

CORRECT   **She and her family donated the prize money.**

The pronouns *who* and *whom* often cause confusion. *Who* (or *whoever*) is subjective; *whom* (or *whomever*) is objective. If the pronoun appears in a question, answer the question using a pronoun (such as *I* or *me*) to determine whether to use the subjective or objective form.

INCORRECT   **Who does Howard want to see?**

Answering the question—*Howard wants to see me*—reveals that the pronoun should be objective.

CORRECT   **Whom does Howard want to see?**

When *who* or *whom* is not part of a question, it introduces a dependent clause. Determine the case of the pronoun in the clause by removing the clause from the sentence and replacing *who* or *whom* with *I* and *me* to see which form is correct.

INCORRECT   **She welcomed whomever knocked on her door.**

The clause is *whomever knocked on her door.* Replacing *whomever* with *I* and *me*— *I knocked on her door; me knocked on her door*—reveals that the subjective form *whoever* is correct.

CORRECT   **She welcomed whoever knocked on her door.**

14. Lack of agreement between pronoun and antecedent

Pronouns must agree in number (singular or plural) and person (first, second or third) with their *antecedents*—the nouns or pronouns to which they refer. Do not shift, for example, from a singular antecedent to a plural pronoun, or from a third-person antecedent to a first- or second-person pronoun.

INCORRECT   **The class must check their work.**

CORRECT   **The class must check its work.**

                 Class members must check their work.

15. Biased language

Avoid stereotypes and biased language. Take special care to avoid gender-specific pronouns.

BIASED A reporter must always check his work.

ACCEPTABLE Reporters must always check their work.

If you are a reporter, you must always check your work.

BIASED Local politicians and their wives attended a dinner in honor of the visiting diplomat.

ACCEPTABLE Local politicians and their spouses attended a dinner in honor of the visiting diplomat.

16. Lack of agreement between subject and verb

Subject and verb must agree in number. Use the form of the verb that agrees with a singular or plural subject. Be especially careful to identify the subject correctly when words separate subject from verb.

INCORRECT The bag with the green stripes <u>belong</u> to her.

CORRECT The bag with the green stripes <u>belongs</u> to her.

A compound subject with parts joined by *and* is always plural. When parts of a compound subject are joined by *or*, make the verb agree with the part of the compound closest to the verb.

INCORRECT A mystery writer and her daughter <u>lives</u> in the house by the river.

CORRECT A mystery writer and her daughter <u>live</u> in the house by the river.

INCORRECT Either Mike or his sisters <u>has</u> the spare key.

CORRECT Either Mike or his sisters <u>have</u> the spare key.

17. Incorrect complement with linking verb

A linking verb such as *be, appear, feel* or *become* links a subject with a word or words that identify or describe the subject. When the identifying word—called a *subject complement*—is a pronoun, use the subjective case for the pronoun.

INCORRECT That was <u>him</u> on the telephone five minutes ago.

CORRECT That was <u>he</u> on the telephone five minutes ago.

When a word or words describing the subject follow a linking verb, the word or words must be adjectives.

INCORRECT   She feels <u>terribly</u> about the things she said.

CORRECT   She feels <u>terrible</u> about the things she said.

18. Incorrect use of subjunctive mood

Conditions contrary to fact require a verb to be in the subjunctive mood. Apply this rule in stories about all pending legislation at all levels of government. Use the subjunctive mood in "that" clauses after verbs of wishing, suggesting and requiring; in other words, use the subjunctive in clauses, dependent or independent, that do not state a fact.

INCORRECT   The bylaws require that he <u>declares</u> his candidacy by
                   April 10.

CORRECT   The bylaws require that he <u>declare</u> his candidacy by
                   April 10.

INCORRECT   The bill <u>will</u> require everyone to register for the draft at
                   age 18.

CORRECT   The bill <u>would</u> require everyone to register for the draft at
                   age 18.

19. Wrong word

Wrong-word errors include using a word that sounds similar to, or the same as, the word you need but means something different (such as writing *affect* when you mean *effect*) and using a word that has a shade of meaning that is not what you intend (such as writing *slender* when you want to suggest *scrawny*). Check the dictionary if you are not sure whether you are using a word correctly.

INCORRECT   Merchants who appear <u>disinterested</u> in their customers
                   may lose business.

CORRECT   Merchants who appear <u>uninterested</u> in their customers
                   may lose business.

INCORRECT   The guests gasped and applauded when they saw the
                   <u>excessive</u> display of food.

CORRECT   The guests gasped and applauded when they saw the
                   <u>lavish</u> display of food.

20. Incorrect verb form

Every verb has five forms: a base form, a present-tense form, a past-tense form, a present-participle form used for forming the progressive tenses, and a past-participle form used for forming the passive voice or one of the perfect tenses.

   Dropping the ending from present-tense forms and regular past-tense forms is a common error.

INCORRECT	The police are <u>suppose</u> to protect the public.
CORRECT	The police are <u>supposed</u> to protect the public.

Regular verbs end in *-ed* in the past tense and past participle, but irregular verbs do not follow a set pattern for forming the past tense and past participle, so those forms of irregular verbs are frequently used incorrectly. Look up irregular verbs if you are uncertain of the correct form.

INCORRECT	The manager was not in the restaurant when it was robbed because he had <u>went</u> home early.
CORRECT	The manager was not in the restaurant when it was robbed because he had <u>gone</u> home early.
INCORRECT	The thieves <u>taked</u> everything in the safe.
CORRECT	The thieves <u>took</u> everything in the safe.

As mentioned in Chapter 9, crime and accidents, fires, and disasters are staples of news reporting. Almost every journalist working on a newspaper will write these types of stories, and many cover such stories very frequently. Unfortunately, gaining real-world experience with this reporting is nearly impossible in an introductory newswriting class. Robberies, house fires and car accidents do not fit neatly into a syllabus, nor do listening to a police scanner and driving to such events fit neatly into a student schedule.

The exercises in Chapter 9 of the *Workbook for* TELLING THE STORY provide a good starting point for learning the fundamentals of crime and accident, fire, and disaster reporting, but they can't simulate the news-gathering process. To help prepare you for the crime and the accident/fire/disaster genres, we provide a CD-ROM simulation of an actual tragedy, the shooting of a police officer and four bystanders in St. Joseph, Mo.

TIPS FOR USING THE PROGRAM

The simulation program puts you in the news room the night of the shooting. After a brief introduction and opening segment, you begin your news-gathering at your desk in the news room. Your job is to get information from paper, human and electronic sources as the night progresses and then to write up a story as more information becomes available (see the section "Types of Articles and Assignments" for possible stories/assignments). The simulation progresses from approximately 5 p.m. until deadline, at 11 p.m.

The main interface is the news room cubicle. On and around your desk are items to click on to get information, as the accompanying screen capture illustrates.

Clicking on the Desk Items

Just as in real-world reporting, sources develop over the course of the story, and some will not be immediately available to you. For example, when the scenario first begins, the reporters dispatched to the scene (under Map of Area) will not be ready to talk to you, nor will a phone call to the police station or hospital give you

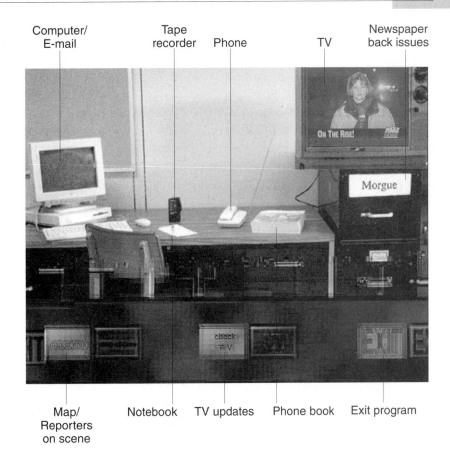

Computer/E-mail · Tape recorder · Phone · TV · Newspaper back issues · Morgue · Map/Reporters on scene · Notebook · TV updates · Phone book · Exit program

any information. Be sure to check back on these sources multiple times as the night progresses and as more bits of news become available. The sources include the following:

- *Television.* You will watch actual news broadcasts from the night of the shooting.
- *Phone book.* Good reporters make good use of the phone. You will call some of your sources, and they will give you quotes and information.
- *Phone.* Sources will call you with updated information throughout the night.
- *Morgue.* Background research is crucial to quality reporting, and you will want to check to see if there are any related articles from back issues of the newspaper.
- *Map/Reporters.* Three reporters will be on the scene, and they will give you updates and quotes from eyewitnesses.
- *Notebook.* Reporters will bring back their notebooks with interview notes for you to use in your story.

- *Tape recorder.* One reporter will bring back a tape-recorded interview from the scene.
- *Computer/E-mail.* There will be e-mail and Web sources for you to use. In addition to the information provided on the CD-ROM, you may wish to do additional Web research.

Because these sources will be available at different times, be sure to click on all of the buttons in the time periods between the TV clips.

Pacing Yourself

The simulation covers a period of approximately six hours, but it will likely only take you between 30 and 60 minutes to run through the scenario. If you are running the program during a 75-minute or longer class, you should not have much difficulty in finishing the simulation during a full class period. If you are trying to complete the program within a 50-minute class period, be sure to be in class on-time or early, take notes quickly and make good decisions about what information you will likely not need to copy down. Remember the principles of newsworthiness and definitions of "news" outlined in Chapter 1, and consider what information your readers will be interested in knowing.

Taking Notes

We pointed out in Chapter 1 that accuracy is a cornerstone of good journalism. Accuracy is especially important—and difficult—in breaking news stories about tragedies, stories that often are at the top of Page One and are read by nearly all of your audience. So be sure to take careful notes. This is not like a book exercise for which you can easily copy down notes and double-check them at a later time. Just as in real-world reporting, for many of these sources you will have only one opportunity to get the information right and to decide what information and quotes to include in your notes. If you're using the TV sources, you won't be able to replay those segments, so take good shorthand and reconstruct your notes after each segment, as we suggested in Chapter 3.

For your notes, you may wish to use a legal pad or a reporter's notebook. Depending on your writing and typing skills, you may prefer to take notes on the computer because you can later cut/copy/paste segments from your computer notes into your final draft. In order to take the computer notes, you'll want to open up a word processing program before starting the simulation and move the program's window to the side of the screen so you can click back and forth between the simulation program and the word processing window when taking notes. Be sure to save your computer notes often, in case your computer crashes.

Using the TV

Good news reporters watch their broadcast colleagues—and competitors—all the time, especially during tragedies. You'll be watching several clips from the local TV station, which include selections from the local 6 p.m. and 10 p.m. newscasts and cut-ins with breaking news before and after those newscasts. In all, there are

10 video clips, some of which play automatically and some that play when you click on the Check TV button. *Be sure to try all of your other sources before you click on the Check TV button,* because the TV segment will jump you to a later part in the scenario.

Typically, a print journalist will not use quotes from radio or TV broadcasts. Before you begin the simulation, be sure to check with your instructor about using quotes from the television in your story. Your instructor may forbid you from using any TV quotes or allow you to cite such quotes sparingly (example: "In an interview with KQ2 TV last night, witness James Smith said, . . ."). He or she may allow you to quote the sources (not the reporters or anchors) as if you were interviewing them yourself. You need to know your instructor's wishes *before* you start the simulation so you know how carefully to take notes during the TV segments. You won't have a chance to hear and see those segments again.

Adjusting Sound and Using Headphones

Before you begin the scenario, you'll want to test the sound levels of your computer and make sure the sound is working, because you'll need to hear all the audio and video clips in order to write up your story. In addition, you may want to bring headphones that fit your computer port, to keep sound levels in the room down and to muffle the sound coming from nearby computers. Then again, the wide array of sounds and voices coming from a dozen or more computers does help mimic the bedlam found in a news room near deadline!

Quitting/Restarting the Program

Because the program replicates the timing and flow of information in a tragedy, you will not be able to jump around in the program or quit and later restart the program where you left off. If you have to restart the program, you will be placed back at the very beginning of the scenario. So be absolutely sure you want to quit before you click on the red EXIT button. Likewise, to prevent the program from crashing and thus prevent you from needing to start over, make sure you are working on a reliable computer with sufficient RAM available.

For this assignment, your instructor may want you to run through the program only once, because you would get only one shot at gathering information under deadline in any crime or accident, fire, or disaster story. Or your instructor may allow you to run through the program multiple times to make sure you find all of the sources.

TIPS FOR WRITING YOUR ARTICLE

Keep in mind one key tip in newswriting: Listen carefully to your editor—in this case, your instructor—about what type of article he or she wants you to write. For a spot news story like this, neither you nor your editor would have time to do a rewrite.

In addition, make sure you understand the nature of the publication and your audience. If you are wishing to replicate the actual situation, assume you are writing for the *St. Joseph News-Press*, an independently owned daily that has a circulation of approximately 40,000 and serves the 70,000 residents of St. Joseph, as well as people in the surrounding counties in northwest Missouri. Your instructor may prefer you to write the story for a larger paper, such as the *Kansas City Star*, or for a small, nearby weekly or for the Associated Press or another wire service. Which publication you write for will help determine how you write your story and what information you include.

Because most people will be writing an inverted pyramid account of the main story, the majority of the other tips in this section are geared toward that type of story. If you are writing a different type of story, you may want to refer to the sections of the book that address that type of story in more detail.

Rank Your Information in Order of Importance

You will have a lot of information to deal with and try to fit into your story. To write an inverted pyramid story, you may want to rank or mark each fact or quote to help you decide what material will go near the beginning, the middle and the end of the story and what information you probably won't need to use.

Prepare Information for a Summary Lead

You may not end up using a summary lead in your final draft, but drafting up such a lead will help you write the rest of the story. Using the ranking mentioned above, write down the key answers to these questions:

Who?
What?
Where?
When?
Why?
How?

Decide which of these items need to be in the lead (the "why," for example, might not be necessary or may be unknown). Put the most important of the 5Ws and H at the beginning of the lead. As mentioned in Chapter 6, try to keep the lead to 25 or 30 words and preferably to one sentence.

Write Several Alternate Leads

Even if you think you are going to use a straight summary lead, you should try other types of leads as well; you may discover one of those other leads works much better. Given the complexity of the situation, you may decide to use a multiple-element lead. Maybe the best choice will be a delayed identification, as shown in the I-70 accident examples in Chapter 9. If you are writing for the St. Joseph community, you may realize an immediate-identification lead is most appropriate.

After trying several lead types, you may find that a flair lead that contains elements of description or narration would work best.

Draw a Map

Drawing a map of the scene or the area on a piece of paper can help you organize your thoughts and understand what happened, especially if you are a visually oriented person.

Make a Chronology

Even if you don't use a chronological format for your article, a timeline of the events will help you understand the events and write your article.

TYPES OF ARTICLES AND ASSIGNMENTS

In a situation such as this tragedy, the entire reporting and editing staff is mobilized. Those who were off for the day or who had already put in their hours are called back, and the whole staff works together to produce the in-depth coverage that readers will want and expect. Some reporters go to the scene and collect information. Others are stationed at the police department, city hall or hospital, while still other staffers may research information in the morgue or online. Using all of these resources, the staff produces not only one main article but also three, four or more sidebars to accompany it.

The simulation program lends itself well to writing a variety of different stories and sidebars. Before you begin the simulation, you'll need to be clear about exactly what type of article or articles your instructor wants you to write, because the article's focus will affect what notes to take and what sources to pay especially close attention to.

The most typical assignment is covering the main story and using the inverted pyramid, the organizational format most often used for hard news stories like crime and accidents, fires, and disasters. Before you write such a story, be sure to reread Chapter 6 to review the principles for writing inverted pyramid stories. Carefully consider what information is most important, and put that information early in the story. Don't bury key information that may end up getting cut or not getting read.

Using the inverted pyramid is not the only way to tell the story. In Chapter 9 the example of the Kansas man who was killed by a police marksman illustrates how a chronological approach sometimes works better. Your instructor may choose to have you write a chronological story instead of—or in addition to—an inverted pyramid account. To do this, you probably will want to reconstruct a timeline and reorganize your notes to represent the order in which events happened, instead of the order in which the information became available to you. Your instructor may also assign you or give you the freedom to use one of the other alternatives to the inverted pyramid outlined in Chapter 7.

Regardless of which story type you are assigned, remember to include the key information and sources for crime and accident, fire, and disaster stories:

- Eyewitnesses.
- Police or other officials in charge of handling the situation.
- Victims and friends and relatives of the victims (when possible and appropriate).

Chapter 9 also stresses the importance of obtaining official documents for these types of stories, such as an accident report, a fire marshal's casualty report or a police report. For this simulation, however, an official document is not available before your deadline.

Your instructor may give you a word limit for your article, in the same way a managing editor, news editor or copy editor might tell a reporter in this situation, "Make it x inches, no more, no less," because the number of column inches allotted to the story might already be set by the time the writer finishes the story. The editors and layout personnel would likely have been scrambling to assemble all of the new shooting-related articles, photos and informational graphics. The main story might have been held until the very last minute so that the most current information would appear in the next day's paper. Consequently, there might have been precious little leeway given for the length of the article.

A word or inches limit is a restriction for print newspapers only, of course. Chapter 1 illustrates how the space limitations of the physical newspaper don't apply in an online environment. The print newspaper might have space for only a 700-word article and two photos, but the online edition could have 1,000-plus words and nearly unlimited photos and graphics.

Your instructor may choose one of the following articles or exercises or may choose some other possible assignment.

Main Story

Inverted Pyramid

Write a main news story that contains all of the important facets of the story. This is the story that would run under the headline at the top of Page One if you were writing for the local newspaper (see notes in the previous section about what publication you are writing for).

Alternative Organization

Consulting Chapter 7, use a different organizational method for writing the story, such as narration (chronological), vivid scenes, a focus structure or anecdotes.

Early Online Edition

Readers in the community and across the state or country who heard about the shooting are not going to be content to wait until the next morning to find out more. As suggested on the first page of Chapter 1, the reporter will need to create text—and perhaps prepare multimedia—for the newspaper's Web site so readers can access that information very soon after the incident. Readers may return several times in the next 24 hours, expecting updates.

There are two places in the CD-ROM simulation where you will be able to stop and write a story and an update for the online edition.

Wire Story

Assume that you are responsible for writing a story that will go out on the Associated Press wire and will likely be picked up by many of the daily newspapers across the state. Write a 750-word story.

Sidebar Stories

Shooting injuries   Write a sidebar about the people injured. As detailed in Chapter 9, be sure to include the names, ages, addresses and conditions of the victims.

Neighbor/witness accounts   Write a sidebar that focuses on the eyewitnesses and includes quotes and anecdotes about the shooting and the shooter.

Killing the shooter   Write a sidebar about the killing of the shooter, making sure to include details about the event, eyewitness quotes and information about police procedures and policy during and after a shooting.

Historical/contextual piece   This type of sidebar could take one of several different paths. It could look at the history of officers killed in the line of duty in the area. It could look at other mass shootings in the area. Or it could look at police officer deaths from a national perspective, requiring you to go online and research statistics.

Practice and Follow-Up

Writing leads   Write a variety of leads for a main story, following the advice in Chapter 6 when composing an immediate-identification lead, a delayed- identification lead, a multiple-element lead and one or more flair leads.

Interviewing   Pick two sources mentioned in the simulation that you would like to be able to interview in greater depth, and write up 10 questions for each person. As you learned in Chapter 3, you'll want to phrase and order those questions carefully because this situation is so sensitive. Because you will be wanting detailed quotes, make sure that at least seven of the questions are open-ended.

Ethics

After reading Chapter 15 and the section in Chapter 9 about victims/witnesses in the accidents, fires and disasters section, write a pro or con essay about calling to interview the wife of the slain police officer. If you would call the wife, explain why and describe the approach you would take. If you would not call the wife, explain why and cite examples from the ethical codes to support your decision.

Glossary

absolute privilege   The right of legislators, judges and government executives to speak without threat of libel when acting in their official capacities.

absolutism   The ethical philosophy that there is a fixed set of principles or laws from which there is no deviation. To the absolutist journalist, the end never justifies the means.

actual malice   Reckless disregard of the truth. It is a condition in libel cases.

actual malice test   Protection for reporters to write anything about an officeholder or candidate unless they know that the material is false or they recklessly disregard the truth.

add   A printed page of copy following the first page. "First add" would be the second page of printed copy.

advance   A report dealing with the subjects and issues to be dealt with in an upcoming meeting or event.

advertising department   The newspaper department responsible for advertisements. Most advertising departments have classified and display ad sections.

anchor   A person in a television studio who ties together a newscast by reading the news and providing transitions from one story to the next.

anecdote   An informative and entertaining story within a story.

angle   The focus of, or approach to, a story. The latest development in a continuing controversy, the key play in a football game or the tragedy of a particular death in a mass disaster may serve as an angle.

antinomianism   The ethical philosophy that recognizes no rules. An antinomian journalist judges every ethical situation on its own merits. Unlike the situation ethicist, the antinomian does not use love of neighbor as an absolute.

AP   The Associated Press, a worldwide news-gathering cooperative owned by its subscribers.

APME   Associated Press Managing Editors, an organization of managing editors and editors whose papers are members of the Associated Press.

arithmetic mean   See *average*.

assessed value   The amount that a government appraiser determines a property is worth.

assistant news director   The second in command in a television station news room.

average   A term used to describe typical or representative members of a group. In mathematics, it refers to the result obtained when a set of numbers is added together, then divided by the number of items in the set.

background   Information that may be attributed to a source by title but not by name; for example, "a White House aide said."

backgrounder   A story that explains and updates the news.

beat   A reporter's assigned area of responsibility. A beat may be an institution, such as the courthouse; a geographical area, such as a small town; or a subject, such as science. The term also refers to an exclusive story.

blotter   An old-fashioned term for the arrest sheet that summarizes the bare facts of an arrest. Today this information is almost always stored in a computer.

books   Assembled sheets of paper, usually newsprint, and carbon paper on which reporters prepare stories. Books are not used with modern computerized processes.

bureau   A news-gathering office maintained by a newspaper at other than its central location. Papers may have bureaus in the next county; in the state capital; in Washington, D.C.; or in foreign countries.

byline   A line identifying the author of a story.

calendar year   The 12-month period from January through December.

change of venue   An order moving a court proceeding to another jurisdiction for prosecution. This transfer often occurs when a party in a case claims that local media coverage has prejudiced prospective jurors.

circulation department   The department responsible for distribution of the newspaper.

city editor   The individual (also known as the *metropolitan*, or *metro, editor*) in charge of the city desk, which coordinates local news-gathering operations. At some papers the desk also handles regional and state news done by its own reporters.

clips   Stories clipped from newspapers.

closed-ended question   A direct question designed to draw a specific response; for example, "Will you be a candidate?"

community portals   Web sites designed as general entry points for users in a city and its nearby suburbs.

compound interest   Interest paid on the total of the principal (the amount borrowed) and the interest that has already accrued.

conditional privilege   See *qualified privilege*.

constant dollars   Money numbers adjusted for inflation.

Consumer Price Index   A tool used by the government to measure the rate of inflation. CPI figures, reported monthly by the Bureau of Labor Statistics of the U.S. Department of Labor, compare the net change in prices between the current period and a specified base period. Reporters should use this data to accurately reflect the actual costs of goods and services.

contributing editor   A magazine columnist who works under contract and not as an employee of the magazine.

convergence A term defined in different ways by different people in the media industry but generally used to describe the coordination of print, broadcast and online reporting in a news operation in some way.

copy What reporters write. A story is a piece of copy.

copy desk The desk at which final editing of stories is done, headlines are written and pages are designed.

copy editor A person who checks, polishes and corrects stories written by reporters. Usually copy editors write headlines for those stories, and sometimes they decide how to arrange stories and pictures on a page.

cover To keep abreast of significant developments on a beat or to report on a specific event. The reporter covering the police beat may be assigned to cover a murder.

cutline The caption that accompanies a newspaper or magazine photograph. The term dates from the days when photos were reproduced with etched zinc plates called *cuts*.

deadline The time by which a reporter, editor or desk must have completed scheduled work.

deep background Information that may be used but that cannot be attributed to either a person or a position.

delayed-identification lead The opening paragraph of a story in which the "who" is identified by occupation, city, office or any means other than by name.

deontelics Ethical thinking that considers both duties and ends.

deontological ethics The ethics of duty.

desk A term used by reporters to refer to the city editor's or copy editor's position, as in "The desk wants this story by noon."

desk assistant An entry-level position in television news rooms. Desk assistants handle routine news assignments such as monitoring wire services and listening to police scanners.

developing story A story in which newsworthy events occur over several days or weeks.

dialogue A conversation between two or more people, neither of whom normally is the reporter.

documentary In-depth coverage of an issue or event, especially in broadcasting.

editor The top-ranking individual in the news department of a newspaper, also known as the *editor in chief*. The term may refer as well to those at any level who edit copy.

editorial department The news department of a newspaper, responsible for all content of the newspaper except advertising. At some papers this term refers to the department responsible for the editorial page only.

editorialize To inject the reporter's or the newspaper's opinion into a news story or headline. Most newspapers restrict opinion to analysis stories, columns and editorials.

editorial page editor The individual in charge of the editorial page and, at larger newspapers, the op-ed page. See also *op-ed page*.

executive producer   The television executive with overall responsibility for the look of the television newscast.

fair comment and criticism   Opinion delivered on the performance of anyone in the public eye. Such opinion is legally protected if reporters do not misstate any of the facts on which they base their comments or criticism, and it is not malicious.

field producer   A behind-the-scenes television reporter who often does much of the field work for a network's on-camera correspondents.

fiscal year   Any 12-month period used to calculate annual revenues and expenditures.

flat-file database   A simple database program that allows users to keep track of data of almost any type.   A simple address book is an example.

follow   A story supplying further information about an item that has already been published; *folo* is an alternate spelling.

foreshadowing   A technique of teasing readers with material coming later in the story as a way of encouraging them to keep reading.

Freedom of Information Act   A law passed in 1966 to make it easier to obtain information from federal agencies. The law was amended in 1974 to improve access to government records.

free-form database   A database that is not limited in structure and allows almost any type of content to be included.

free press-fair trial controversy   The conflict between a defendant's right to an impartial jury and a reporter's responsibility to inform the public.

full-text database   A database that permits searches of any text in an article.

futures file   A collection—filed according to date—of newspaper stories, letters, notes and other information to remind editors of stories to assign. See also *tickler.*

gatekeepers   Editors who determine what readers or viewers read, hear and see.

Golden Mean   A moral position, derived from Aristotle, that avoids extremes.

graf   A shortened form of *paragraph*, as in "Give me two grafs on that fire."

graphics editor   Usually, the editor responsible for all non-photographic illustrations in a newspaper, including information graphics, maps and illustrations.

handout   See *news release.*

hard lead   A lead that reports a new development or newly discovered fact. See also *soft lead.*

hard news   Coverage of the actions of government or business; or the reporting of an event, such as a crime, an accident or a speech. The time element often is important. See also *soft news.*

HTML   Abbreviation for hypertext markup language, the coding language used to create texts on the Web.

hyperlink   A connection among two places on the Web.

hypermedia   Web links among audio, video and pictures.

hypertext   A Web document coded in HTML.

immediate-identification lead The opening paragraph of a story in which the "who" is reported by name.

inflation A term that describes the rising cost of living as time goes by. See also *Consumer Price Index*.

infomedium Short for information medium, a term coined to represent the merger of the Internet, television, wireless and other technologies as the medium of the future.

information graphic A visual representation of data.

interest A measurement of the cumulative effect of all the news values. The more elements of each of the six news values that appear in the story, the more interesting that story will be to readers.

Internet The vast network that links computers around the world.

interviewing Having conversations with sources.

invasion of privacy Violation of a person's right to be left alone.

inverted pyramid The organization of a news story in which information is arranged in descending order of importance.

investigative piece A story intended to reveal material not generally known.

investigative reporting The pursuit of information that has been concealed, such as evidence of wrongdoing.

IRE Investigative Reporters and Editors, a group created to exchange information and investigative reporting techniques. IRE has its headquarters at the University of Missouri School of Journalism.

lay out (v.) The process of preparing page drawings to indicate where stories and pictures are to be placed in the newspaper.

layout (n.) The completed page drawing, or page dummy.

lead (1) The first paragraph or first several paragraphs of a newspaper story (sometimes spelled *lede*); (2) the story given the best display on Page One; (3) a tip.

lead-in An introduction to a filmed or recorded excerpt from a news source or from another reporter.

libel Damage to a person's reputation caused by a false written statement that brings the person into hatred, contempt or ridicule or injures his or her business or occupational pursuit.

line-item budget A budget showing each expenditure on a separate line.

maestro The leader of a news-gathering team. Reporters, copy editors, editors and graphic designers work with a maestro to create special reports.

managing editor The individual with primary responsibility for day-to-day operation of the news department.

median The middle number in a series arranged in order of size; it is often used when an average would be misleading. (If the series has an even number of items, the median consists of the average of the two "middle" numbers.) See also *average*.

millage rate The tax rate on property, determined by the government.

mobile telephones   Cellular and digital telephone instruments.

more   A designation used at the end of a page of copy to indicate one or more pages follow.

morgue   The newspaper library, where published stories, photographs and resource material are stored for reference.

multimedia assignment desk   The news desk in a converged news room where the efforts of print, broadcast and online reporters are coordinated. See also *convergence.*

multimedia editor   An editor responsible for coordinating or producing news content for various media.

multimedia journalist   Journalist capable of producing content in more than one medium such as radio and newspapers.

multiple-element lead   The opening paragraph of a story that reports two or more newsworthy elements.

narration   The telling of a story, usually in chronological order.

negligence test   The legal standard that requires reporters gathering facts and writing a story to use the same degree of care that any reasonable individual would use in similar circumstances.

network correspondent   A television reporter who delivers the news on-camera. Network correspondents do not necessarily do the actual news-gathering for their stories.

new media   Emerging forms of computer-delivered news.

news conference   An interview session, also called a *press conference*, in which someone submits to questions from reporters.

news director   The top news executive of a local television station.

news editor   The supervisor of the copy desk. At some newspapers, this title is used for the person in charge of local news-gathering operations.

news release   An item, also called a *handout* or *press release*, that is sent out by a group or individual seeking publicity.

news story   A story, often written in inverted pyramid style, that emphasizes the facts.

news value   How important or interesting a story is.

nominal dollars   Money numbers not adjusted for inflation.

not for attribution   An expression indicating that information may not be ascribed to its source.

nut paragraph   A paragraph that summarizes the key element or elements of a story. Usually found in a story not written in inverted pyramid form. Also called a *nut graf.*

off-camera reporter   A reporter who gathers news for television but does not report on the air.

off the record   An expression that usually means "Don't quote me." Some sources and reporters use it to mean "Don't print this." Phrases with similar, and equally ambiguous, meanings are "not for attribution" and "for background only."

online editor   The editor of a Web site for a newspaper or television station.

online media   See *new media*.

op-ed page   The page opposite the editorial page, frequently reserved for columns, letters to the editor and personality profiles.

open-ended question   A question that permits the respondent some latitude in the answer; for example, "How did you get involved in politics?"

open-meetings laws   State and federal laws, often called *sunshine laws*, guaranteeing public access to meetings of public officials.

open-records laws   State and federal laws guaranteeing public access to many—but not all—kinds of government records.

payola   Money or gifts given in the expectation of favors from journalists.

percentage   Mathematical way to express the portion of a whole. Literally means a given part of every hundred. Determined by taking the number of the portion, dividing by the number of the whole and moving the decimal point right two places.

percentage change   A number that explains how much something goes up or down.

personal digital assistant (PDA)   A hand-carried device that allows the user to keep track of contacts, appointments, electronic mail and the like.

photo editor   The individual who advises editors on the use of photographs in the newspaper. The photo editor also may supervise the photography department.

piece   See *story*.

plagiarism   The use of any part of another person's writing and passing it off as your own.

play   A shortened form of *display*. A good story may be played at the top of Page One; a weak one may be played inside.

population   In scientific language, the whole group being studied. Depending on the study, the population may be, for example, voters in St. Louis, physicians in California or all residents of the United States.

press   The machine that prints the newspaper. Also a synonym for *journalism*, as in the phrase "freedom of the press." Sometimes used to denote print journalism, as distinguished from broadcast journalism.

press box   The section of a stadium or arena set aside for reporters.

press conference   See *news conference*.

press release   See *news release*.

principal   The amount borrowed.

principled reasoning   Reasoning that reflects ethical principles.

Privacy Protection Act   A law passed in 1980 that requires federal, state and local enforcement officers to get a subpoena to obtain documents from reporters and news rooms, rather than a search warrant—unless the reporter is involved in a crime or immediate action is needed to prevent bodily harm, loss of life or destruction of the material.

privilege   A defense against libel that claims the right to repeat what government officials say or do in their official capacities.

production department   The department of the newspaper that transforms the work of the news and advertising departments into the finished product. The composing room and press room are key sections of this department.

profile   A story intended to reveal the personality or character of an institution or person.

program budget   A budget that clearly shows what each agency's activities cost.

proportion   An explanation that relates one specific number to another or to the quantity or magnitude of a whole; for example, "The Tigers finished fifth among 20 teams."

public figure   A person who has assumed a role of prominence in the affairs of society and who has persuasive power and influence in a community or who has thrust himself or herself to the forefront of a public controversy. Courts have given journalists more latitude in reporting on public figures.

public information utilities   Commercial online services such as CompuServe.

public journalism   The new (or rediscovered) approach to journalism that emphasizes connections with the community rather than separation from it. Among the newspapers best known for practicing public journalism are *The Wichita (Kan.) Eagle* and *The Charlotte (N.C.) Observer.*

publisher   The top-ranking executive of a newspaper. This title often is assumed by the owner, although chains sometimes designate as publisher the top local executive.

Pulitzer Prize   The most prestigious of journalism awards. It was established by Joseph Pulitzer and is administered by Columbia University.

qualified privilege   The right to report what government officials say or do in their official capacities if the report is full, fair and accurate. Also called *conditional privilege.*

quote   As a noun, the term refers to a source's exact words, as in "I have a great quote here." As a verb, it means to report those words inside quotation marks.

rate   The amount or degree of something measured in relation to a unit of something else or to a specified scale. In statistics, rate often expresses the incidence of a condition per 100,000 people, such as a murder or suicide rate. Rate also can reflect the speed at which something is changing, such as inflation or the percentage increase in a budget each year.

records column   The part of the newspaper featured regularly that contains such information as routine police and fire news, births, obituaries, marriages and divorces.

relational database program   A database program that permits users to determine relationships between two or more dissimilar databases. For example, a relational database program would enable a reporter to compare one database of people convicted of drunken driving with another database of school-bus drivers. The result would show how many bus drivers had drunken-driving convictions.

relevance   The impact of a story as measured by the number of readers it affects and how seriously it affects them.

reporter   A person whose job is to gather and write the news for a publication or a broadcast outlet.

roundup   A story including a number of related events. After a storm, for example, a reporter might do a roundup of accidents, power outages and other consequences of the storm.

sample   A portion of a group, or population, chosen for study as representative of the entire group.

second-cycle story   A second version of a story already published, also called a *second-day story*. It usually has new information or a new angle.

senior editor   A person who edits sections of major magazines.

senior writer   A title reserved for a magazine's best and most experienced reporters.

series   Two or more stories on the same or related subjects, published on a predetermined schedule.

service journalism   An aspect or type of journalism that recognizes usefulness as one of the criteria of news. Taking into consideration content and presentation, service journalism presents useful information in a usable way—for instance, by placing key information in a list or graphic box.

set-up   In broadcasting, an introductory statement to pique the interest of listeners or viewers. In written accounts, the material between the opening of a narrative story and the body. It generally consists of the transition to the theme paragraph, the theme paragraph, and, when appropriate, the "so-what" and "to-be-sure" statements and foreshadowing.

shield laws   Legislation giving journalists the right to protect the identity of sources.

shovelware   Stories posted on the Web exactly as they appeared in print.

show producer   A television news specialist who produces individual newscasts and who reports to the executive producer.

sidebar   A secondary story intended to be run with a major story on the same topic. A story about a disaster, for example, may have a sidebar that tells what happened to a single victim.

simple interest   Interest paid on the *principal*, or amount borrowed.

situation ethics   The philosophy that recognizes that a set of rules can be broken if circumstances indicate that the community would be served better by breaking them. For example, a journalist who generally believes that deceiving a news source is unethical may be willing to conceal his or her identity to infiltrate a group operating illegally.

slug   A word that identifies a story as it is processed through the newspaper plant or on broadcast news. A slug is usually placed in the upper left-hand corner of each take of a newspaper story. See also *take*.

sniff   The preliminary phase of an investigation.

soft lead   A lead that uses a quote, anecdote or other literary device to attract the reader. See also *hard lead*.

soft news   Stories about trends, personalities or lifestyles. The time element usually is not important. See also *hard news*.

sources   People or records from which a reporter gets information. The term often is used to describe persons, as opposed to documents.

spot news   A timely report of an event that is unfolding at the moment.

spreadsheet   A computer program adept at analyzing numbers. It is often used in tracking changes in budgets and expenditures.

story   The term most journalists use for a newspaper article. Another synonym is *piece*, as in "I saw your piece on the mayor." A long story may be called a takeout or a blockbuster.

strategic communication   A "new" name for public relations (sometimes including advertising) that emphasizes a stronger role of professionals in these fields in areas of conducting research, problem solving and decision making.

stylebook   A book of rules on grammar, punctuation, capitalization and abbreviation in newspaper text. The AP and UPI publish similar stylebooks that are used by most papers.

substantial truth   The correctness of the essential elements of a story.

summary lead   The first paragraph of a news story in which the writer presents a synopsis of two or more actions rather than focusing on any one of them.

sunshine laws   See *open-meetings laws*.

take   A page of printed copy for newspaper use.

teleological ethics   The ethics of final ends.

30   A designation used to mark the end of a newspaper story. The symbol # is an alternate designation.

tickler   A file of upcoming events kept on paper or stored electronically at the assignment desks of most news organizations. See also *futures file*.

tie-back   The sentence or sentences relating a story to events covered in a previous story. Used in follow-up or continuing stories or in parts of a series of stories. Also, the technique of referring to the opening in the ending of the story.

truth   Actuality or reality. Truth is the best defense against libel.

universal desk   A copy desk that edits material for all editorial departments of a newspaper.

update   A type of follow that reports on a development related to an earlier story. See also *follow*.

UPI   United Press International, a worldwide news-gathering organization that is privately owned.

URL   Uniform Resource Locator, the address of an Internet site.

usefulness   A quality of news that increases the impact of the story. The story has information that readers can use to act on, such as notification of a meeting before it occurs.

videographer   A television camera operator.

videoprompter   A mechanical or electronic device that projects broadcast copy next to the television camera lens so that a newscaster can read it while appearing to look straight into the lens.

Web site   A location on the World Wide Web, the Internet service that connects hypertext data.

wrap-up   The completion of commentary that comes at the end of a taped segment in broadcasting; a strong ending to a report.

Acknowledgments

American Medical Association. Screen shot of "Results" from A. Michael Lincoff et al., "Bivalirudin and Provisional Glycoprotein IIb/IIIa Blockade Compared with Heparin and Planned Glycoprotein IIb/IIIa Blockade during Percutaneous Coronary Intervention REPLACE-2 Randomized Trial" from *Journal of the American Medical Association*, Vol. 289, no.7 (2003). Copyright © 2003 by The American Medical Association. Reprinted with permission.

AP bylines. Excerpts from several *Associated Press* bylines. Reprinted with the permission of *The Associated Press*.

The Cincinnati Post Online Edition and screen shot of Jeanne Houck. "Three fires total up to $375K in damages" (February 24, 2003). **www.cincypost.com/2003/02/24/fires022403.html**. Reprinted by permission.

CNN. Screen shot of home page (February 11, 2003). **www.cnn.com**. Reprinted by permission.

Tom Diana and Kristen Burrier. Story about hospital surgeons at Ohio Valley Medical Center and Wheeling Hospital taking leaves of absences in January 2003. Published in the *Wheeling News-Register*, Wheeling, West Virginia. Reprinted by permission.

ESPN. Screen shot of "Lakers move into seventh place in Western Conference" (February 23, 2003). **http://sports.espn.go.com/nba/recap?gameid =230223013**. Reprinted by permission.

Ken Fuson. "Top Ten Hints" list for improving the writing skills of reporters. Reprinted by permission.

GazetteNET. Screen shot of Phoebe Mitchell. "This cop's beat is syncopated" (February 2003). **www.gazettenet.com**. Reprinted by permission.

Fred Kaplan. Story about the World Trade Center and Pentagon attacks, September 11, 2001. From the *Boston Globe*, September 12, 2001. Republished by permission of The Boston Globe, in the format Textbook via Copyright Clearance Center.

Stan Ketterer. "Guidelines for Evaluating Information on the Web." Reprinted by permission.

Susan Kinzie. Excerpt from story about a family taking generic tests to investigate a shared cancer DNA. Published in *The News & Observer*, Raleigh, North Carolina. Reprinted by permission.

Jane Meinhardt. Story about an unusual burglary ring. Published in the *St. Petersburg Times*. Reprinted by permission.

TheMercuryNews. Screen shot of home page (February 11, 2003). **www.bayarea.com/mld/mercurynews/**. Reprinted by permission of the San Jose Mercury News.

MSNBC. Screen shot of "Club owners called uncooperative." Reprinted by permission.

Salon.com. Screen shot of Scott Rosenberg. "Look who's a media expert now" (February 23, 2003). **www.blogs.salon.com/0000014/**. Reprinted with permission.

Star-Telegram.com. Screen shot of home page (February 24, 2003). **www.dfw.com/mld/dfw/**. Reprinted by permission.

AndrewSullivan.com. Screen shot of "Letters" (February 19, 2003). **www.andrewsullivan.com/letters.php**. Reprinted by permission.

Bartholomew Sullivan. Excerpt from award-winning story about trial of former klansman who testified against the former Imperial Wizard. From *The Commercial Appeal*, August 22, 1999. Copyright The Commercial Appeal, Memphis, Tennessee. Reprinted by permission.

Tampa Bay Online. Screen shot of home page (February 2003). **www.tbo.com**. Reprinted by permission.

Kelly Whiteside. "Dunk Rocks Women's Hoops." From *USA TODAY*. Copyright 2000, USA TODAY. Reprinted with permission.

Yahoo! News. Screen shot of Jessica Santillan article (February 24, 2003). **http://news.yahoo.com**. Copyright 2003 by Yahoo! Inc. YAHOO! And the YAHOO! Logo are trademarks of Yahoo! Inc.

Fig. 2.1. "Media Share of Advertising Dollars (2001)." Courtesy of the Newspaper Association of America, Reston, Virginia.

Photo Credits

xi © Joel Gordon; **xii** © Joel Gordon; **xiii** © Johnny Crawford/The Image Works; **xiv** © Reuters NewsMedia Inc./CORBIS; **xv** © Erik Lesser/Getty Images; **1** © Joel Gordon; **14** © Tom Carter/Photo Edit; **31** © Joel Gordon; **37** © Joel Gordon; **45** © Robert Kalman/The Image Works; **49** © AFP/CORBIS; **58** © AFC/CORBIS; **63** © Spencer Grant/Photo Edit; **82** © Joel Gordon; **89** From "Dying Young" series, by Shoshana Hoose and Kay Lazar; Reprinted with permission of Portland Press Herald/Maine Sunday Telegram. Reproduction does not imply endorsement.; **109** © Robin Weiner/WirePix/The Image Works; **126** © AP Photo/The St. Augustine Record, Peter Willott; 134 © Johnny Crawford/The Image Works; **154** © AP/Wide World; **160** © PA/Topham/The Image Works; **162** © AP/Wide World; **172** © Reuters NewsMedia Inc./CORBIS; **190** © AP/Wide World/Mark Foley; **193** © AP/Wide World; **202** © James Leynse/CORBIS SABA; **202** © AP/Wide World; **212** © Peter Morgan/CORBIS; **233** unknown; **242** © Reuters NewsMedia Inc./CORBIS; **248** © Erik Lesser/Getty Images; **251** © Bob Daemmrich/The Image Works; **268** Reprinted by the Permission of the American Cancer Society, Inc.; **276** Courtesy of the Muscular Dystrophy Association, Tucson, AZ; **277** Courtesy of Merck & Co., Inc; **282** Courtesy of the Missouri Department of Conservation; **311** © AP/Wide World ; **328** © AP/Wide World.

Index